Also by John McCain and Mark Salter

FAITH OF MY FATHERS

WORTH THE FIGHTING FOR

WHY COURAGE MATTERS

CHARACTER *Is* DESTINY

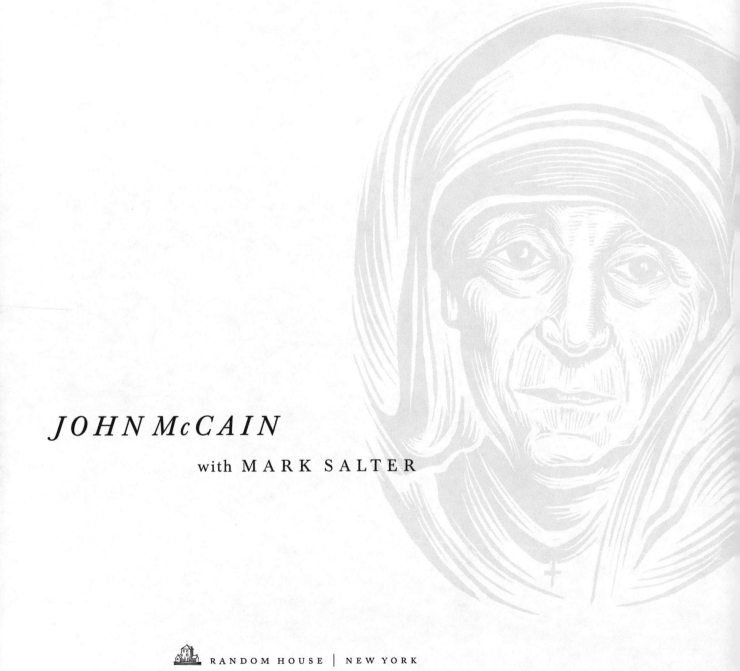

JOHN McCAIN

with MARK SALTER

RANDOM HOUSE | NEW YORK

Inspiring Stories Every

Young Person Should Know and

Every Adult Should Remember

CHARACTER *Is* DESTINY

Published in the United States by Random House,
an imprint of The Random House Publishing Group,
a division of Random House, Inc., New York.

RANDOM HOUSE and colophon are registered
trademarks of Random House, Inc.

Grateful acknowledgment is made to Writers House,
LLC, for excerpts from "Letter from Birmingham Jail"
by Martin Luther King, Jr. Copyright © 1963
Martin Luther King, Jr., copyright renewed 1991
by Coretta Scott King. Reprinted by permission of
the Heirs to the Estate of Martin Luther King, Jr.,
c/o Writers House, LLC, as agent for the proprietor.

ISBN 1-4000-6412-0

Printed in the United States of America on acid-free paper

www.atrandom.com

9 8 7 6 5 4 3 2 1

FIRST EDITION

Book design by Barbara M. Bachman

FOR SHEPP AND CAROLINE McCAIN,

ANDREW AND MARGARET McCAIN,

AND MOLLY AND ELIZABETH SALTER,

with love

CONTENTS

INTRODUCTION

I DON'T BELIEVE IN DESTINY. WE ARE NOT BORN TO BECOME ONE THING OR ANother, left to follow helplessly a course that was charted for us by some unseen hand, a mysterious alignment of the stars that pulls us in a certain direction, bestowing happiness on some and misfortune on others. The only fate we cannot escape is our mortality. Even a long life is a brief experience, hard as that is to believe when we are young. God has given us that life, shown us how to use it, but left it to us to dispose of as we choose. Our character will determine how well or how poorly we choose.

It is your character, and your character alone, that will make your life happy or unhappy. That is all that really passes for destiny. And you choose it. No one else can give it to you or deny it to you. No rival can steal it from you. And no friend can give it to you. Others can encourage you to make the right choices or discourage you. But you choose.

Your happiness is at stake in every difficult decision you must make about what kind of person you will be: honest or deceitful; responsible or unreliable; brave or cowardly; kind or cruel. Your talents have little to do with it. Your looks don't matter at all. You don't need to be good at sports. You don't need to be popular with other kids. You need not be smarter than others. Those things are nice and useful and pleasing. But they won't by themselves make you happy. Looks change. People for no good reason can sometimes treat us unfairly, and friends come and go as our lives take us to new schools, different jobs, and faraway places. Our strength and speed and agility grow for a few years, and then, for most of our lives, we get weaker, slower, and clumsier. However smart we are, there are always other people who know more than us.

The stories in this book, those that are well known and those that are not, are the stories of remarkable people who chose well. Most are people of exceptionally good character. All, no doubt, had flaws. Everyone does. But they all exemplify one or more essential attributes of good character.

I would be proud to be among their number. But were I to use my own character as an example of how to build yours, I would lack one of the most important qualities of good character—honesty. My own children, who have suffered, as they often remind me, considerable embarrassment already from their father's public and unconvincing attempts at proving himself a role model for the young, have taught me just enough humility to avoid that conceit. Rather than cause them any further discomfort, I have relied instead on the example of people who have no need to prove themselves worthy of admiration. They have earned much more than public acclaim.

The best I can claim for my own character is that it is still, even at this late date, a work in progress. The most important thing I have learned, from my parents, from teachers, from my faith, from many good people I have been blessed to know, and from the lives of people whose stories we have included in this book, is to *want* what they had, integrity, and to feel the sting of my conscience when I have chosen a course that has risked it for some selfish reason. As I am blessed with a naturally optimistic disposition, I'm still working on my character, although I am sixty-eight years old as we write this.

Thus, I can profit as much as any reader from the examples of character we celebrate in the following pages. We have intended this work to be of interest not only to young readers but to parents and readers of any age. However numerous our achievements and experiences, most of us can still stand a little improvement. Even the most crowded, accomplished life can still suffer a sense of incompleteness. Our character is a lifelong project, and perhaps the older we are, and the more fixed our shortcomings are, the more we can use inspiration to encourage our escape from the restraints of our deficiencies.

The greatest writer in the English language, William Shakespeare, wrote plays and poems that taught such important lessons about human nature and the qualities of good and bad people, few things written before or after have explained them better. His plays, written more than four hundred years ago, were a little hard for me to understand when I was young. But I had a teacher who loved them, and he taught me to love them. Thanks to him, those plays are for me more moving than anything we have for entertainment today.

I imagine you know some of his plays and remember some of their most famous lines. *We few, we happy few, we band of brothers. For he today that sheds his blood for me shall be my brother.* Those two lines are from my favorite play, *Henry V.* They are spoken by a king as encouragement to his soldiers who are about to fight a battle in which they are greatly outnumbered. It is a soldier's play, and I have never tired of it.

One of the most often quoted passages in English literature and the theme for countless graduation speeches and self-help essays comes from *Hamlet.* A character named Polonius tells his son, Laertes: "This above all: to thine ownself be true, and it must follow, as the night the day, thou cannot then be false to any man."

Many people remember only the first part of the line, *to thine ownself be true,* and they interpret it to mean we should do whatever we want to do, whatever feels good to us. But I've always interpreted it to mean we must be true to our conscience, and to do that, *you cannot be false to any man.* In other words, being true to our conscience, being honest with ourselves, will determine the character of our relations with others. That is a concise definition of integrity.

The individuals whose stories we tell were chosen because they had a special quality, a particular strength of character that made their lives and their world better. They chose to live their lives in ways that we admire because they believed their principles were their most important possessions. Not their looks or their abilities, not their comfort or pleasure, not their job or house or car or toys or how many friends they had or how much money they made. They were true to themselves, and were not false to anyone.

I hope their stories will, in some small way, help you prepare for the important choices in your own life. Not because you will face the same choices they faced. Few of us will. But they began their lives as we began ours, creatures of their appetites and entirely dependent on others, some with more advantages than you have, many with considerably fewer. We are born with one nature. We want what we want, and we want it now. But as we grow, we develop our second nature, our character. These stories are about that second nature. And if the character of these heroes, what they sacrificed for it, and what they accomplished with it, inspire you as much as they inspire me, you will find their lives to be excellent teachers.

Your best teachers, of course, are your parents. From their example, even more than their instruction, you will first learn to love virtue. Their responsibility to you is much more than to feed, clothe, and house you. You are or should be the great work of their lives. Parents are not the all-knowing, ideal people we would like you to think we are. We've made wrong choices before, and will again, like everyone else. But our mistakes are not the measure of our love for you. You are that measure, and how well you are prepared to make better choices than we have made.

Sometimes we forget how important we are to you, even more important than we often pretend to be, though it is rarely an intentional failure. I have sometimes forgotten it. The work I have chosen for my life has too often kept me apart from my family. Once, it kept me away for a very long time. That was not as I wished it to be, but the choice of professions was mine nonetheless. I have earned its rewards and the regrets that disturb my conscience. During my absence, I took comfort in the knowledge that their mother offered a better example to them than I did.

My mother, Roberta McCain, remains a great influence in my life. She is the daughter of an Oklahoma oil wildcatter who made a fortune and retired early to devote himself to his children. She and her identical twin sister, Rowena, were renowned for their beauty, which has hardly faded over the years that have passed since heads first turned in their direction. But their personalities have always been their most attractive feature. My mother was raised to be a strong, determined woman who thoroughly enjoyed life, and always tried to make the most of her opportunities. She was encouraged to accept, graciously and with good humor, the responsibilities and sacrifices her choices have required of her. I am grateful to her for the strengths she taught me by example, even if I have not possessed them as well and as comfortably as she does.

Among her greatest qualities is her endless curiosity about the world, about natural history and, even more so, human history. She is unusually well traveled and has had more adventures in her life than most people have. Yet she has never lost one bit of her interest in and enthusiasm for the work, the ideas, the passions, and the accomplishments of the world's civilizations. The joy of her life is learning about people and places, and coming to know them as well as she can; she never loses the desire to know them better. She has a remarkable capacity for delight. Life, all its adventures and many interests, thrills her as much in her late years as it did in her childhood. It is the main source of her charm, which anyone who knows her—and many, many people claim the pleasure of her friendship—can assure you she has in abundance. Her delight is infectious, and becomes in her company, yours. She has a great gift, and it is all the greater for the ease and happiness with which she shares it.

We moved often because of my father's work. And it was my mother's job to move us, quite often very great distances. Every couple of years, she would pack our belongings, ship them ahead to our destination, crowd her three children into the car, and drive us, sometimes across the entire country, to our new home. En route, and for days on end, she would endure the nearly constant arguing and whining of my sister, brother, and me, along with the other discomforts and boredom of traveling by car. Yet she never seemed bored. And to ensure that she wasn't and that her children would not have good reason to complain (although that seldom prevented us from doing so), she would take time and considerable trouble to make sure we saw and learned interesting things along the way.

She took us to dozens of famous art galleries, museums, and historical sites. Our jaws dropped in awe at the Grand Canyon, the Carlsbad Caverns, and many other natural phenomena. She once drove us hundreds of miles out of our way through Texas, and to the city of Juárez, across the Mexican border, to see a beautiful cathedral that her father had once taken her to see. After we reached the city, which was much changed since her last visit, we got lost. We looked for hours for the church that had so impressed her as a girl, but could not find it. Eventually, we found ourselves in a pretty tough neighborhood, crowded with people who did not seem to want us to enjoy our visit and gave us the impression that they thought they could make better use of our car and belongings than we could. Still, my mother persisted in her search, trying not to let the sensation of danger, which by now her children were experiencing, interfere with the enjoyment of our adventure. Eventually, as our circumstances became undeniably menacing, she abandoned our exploration, and we sped off for the relative safety of El Paso, Texas. We were disappointed, of course, but much relieved. And, after all, we had managed to see a few things we had not seen before, and to learn a lesson or two about human nature we had not known before.

My mother is a stickler for courtesy and good manners. She once read a story about a time in my life when I was physically mistreated by bad men who, for a while, kept me in prison. The story quoted me calling my captors some very bad names. The words I had used were not appropriate for polite company, and I wouldn't like to hear my children use such language. But I thought my behavior, if not all that it should have been, was understandable in the awful circumstances I found myself in. My mother was less forgiving. She immediately called me to tell me she had read the article, which included vivid descriptions of the mistreatment I had suffered, and had been deeply offended by the language I had chosen to express my resentment of the abuse. "But, Mother," I argued, "they were very bad men." "That doesn't matter," she replied, "I never taught you to use that kind of language, and I have half a mind to wash your mouth out with soap." I was over sixty years old when I received this rebuke from my mother, a fact that only added to my embarrassment. And, I'm further embarrassed to admit, she has felt it necessary many times since to rebuke me for forgetting the good manners she had taught me never to discard.

She always stressed the importance of humility in developing good character, a quality that, to her great regret, she worries I do not fully appreciate. As a member of Congress, and because I suffer from a hard-to-control impulse to express my views to as many listeners as I can reach, I am often on television and my name is frequently in the newspapers. Even though some people, not to mention myself, occasionally feel that I have something to say worth hearing, my mother finds the habit a little too unbecoming for people who value their dignity. She is full of aphorisms, short, wise little observations that are meant to educate the person with whom she shares them. When a reporter once asked her if she was proud to see her son become such a prominent person, she replied, "Fools' names and fools' faces are often seen in public places." This is the lesson she derives from my public appearances, which is to her far more important than whatever observation or opinion I had tried to express.

She is an excellent teacher, as I have learned and relearned many times in my life. As we began this book, she was ninety-two years old, and is at this moment driving around India with her identical twin sister and best friend, Rowena, taking another look at fascinating places she has seen before, but learning, always learning something new and well worth her time.

My father was an admiral in the navy, as was his father before him. He was often at sea, and absent from our home. But his children felt his influence as strongly as if he had been in our company every day of our lives. He was honest, hardworking, loyal, and one of the bravest men I've ever known. He had his flaws. Neither I nor he would ever pretend otherwise. But I don't believe he ever told a lie or refused to do his duty or acted in any way that he considered dishonorable.

He had a lion's courage. In his first war, he commanded a submarine. After a long battle, and many hours beneath the sea, with little air left to breathe in the sub, he told his men they could either surrender or surface and fight, although their chances of success were very poor. They were outgunned. They were exhausted. Some of the men were delirious from the lack of oxygen in the submarine. They were all afraid, including my father. But they were good men, and they knew their skipper, my father, believed fighting was the right thing to do. So they chose to fight, every one of them.

He believed dishonesty was a personal disgrace, and the very thought of being deceitful, even in small, inconsequential matters, upset him. Once, my mother jokingly accused him of cheating at cards. He shot up from the table, in great distress, and begged her never, ever to doubt or even pretend to doubt his honesty. That was an excessive and unnecessary response to what was, after all, just a little harmless teasing by his wife. She knew he was an honest man, and he knew she knew it. But it gives you an idea of how extraordinarily important his honesty was to him. He simply couldn't bear the idea of being deceitful or being accused, wrongly, of deceiving anyone.

At times like that, perhaps, his virtues, as admirable as they were, made him too proud. He lived a code of honor that he had learned from his father, the man whom he admired above all others. The memory of his father, and his father's honesty and courage and sense of duty, was so important to him that he believed that he must behave at all times in ways that honored his father's name. Sometimes, I think he forgot that the only person who must believe in your integrity is yourself. That is an easy mistake to make even for people with great integrity. Many good people mistake their reputation for their character. It is a mistake I have made many, many times. Of course, our reputation should be a reflection of our character. But sometimes, through no fault of our own, it is not. And although it hurts when people think less well of us than we deserve, our integrity, our self-respect, and our happiness do not ultimately depend upon the opinion of others. They depend upon our own conscience. We must be true to ourselves. And we must be true to others, whether they believe we are or not.

My father was true to himself. Whatever his faults, whatever mistakes his pride might have caused, he tried hard all his life to keep his integrity, and to accept and faithfully fulfill the demands of his conscience. He faced many difficult choices in his life. His choices were harder to make than most of ours will be. But he had the character for them.

He fought in three wars, and in his last war, Vietnam, he commanded all our country's forces in the Pacific, including those who fought in Vietnam. I am his oldest son and namesake, and I fought under his command. For several years I was held as a prisoner of war in the enemy's capital, the city of Hanoi. When the president of the United States and his advisors decided to try to shorten the war by bombing Hanoi, it was my father's duty to order it done.

The planes that flew to Hanoi on his orders were B-52s. They were the largest bombers in the air force. They could carry the largest and the most bombs. They flew at high altitudes, but unlike those aircraft used by our air force today, they did not have the technology to be very accurate in their targeting. The pilots knew Americans were being held captive near their targets. So did the man who commanded them, my father. He knew where I was, and he loved me. He prayed on his knees every day for my safe return. Whenever he visited his soldiers in Vietnam, he would end his day by walking to the northern end of the base and standing quietly alone, looking toward the place where his son was held. But his conscience required him to do his duty, and his duty required him to risk his son's life. And so he did.

That is a very hard decision for a father to make. Few of us will ever have to face such a difficult choice. Even fewer of us would have the character to make the right decision. But he did. The memory of him and the example he set for me helped to form my own conscience, and shame me when I disobey it. I don't think there is anything greater a parent can do for you.

Your parents, and all those who love you, are trying to the best of their ability to give that gift to you, an example of character that you cannot forget, when you follow it and when you don't. The stories in this book are intended to help reinforce the lessons they are teaching you. Some of these stories were first brought to my attention by my parents. Some I learned in school or happened upon by chance. Many of them you know. A few you won't. I hope you find some of them to be exciting stories of heroism. I hope they are all interesting to you. They might entertain you. I hope they inspire you as well.

Some of them, because their heroes sacrifice so much to keep their integrity, will make you sad. That's not their purpose, but it can't be helped. Many good people have suffered for their principles. Some have died for them. But however cruel their end, they were surely comforted by the knowledge that they had made the right choice, and they had had the character to live a good life. Whether anyone knew how great their courage had been would not matter as much to them as the knowledge that they had chosen well, that their cause had been just, and their character worthy of its demands. They did not submit to an inevitable destiny. They believed their values were the power that directs our lives, and lights the world in which we burn our little candle, before our work is done and we take our rest.

I don't believe in destiny. I believe in character. So I leave you with thirty-four stories of character, with the hope that they will entertain and inspire you as much as they have me.

PART ONE

Honor

Greatness knows itself.

—HENRY IV

HONESTY

Thomas More

He surrendered everything for the truth as he saw it,
and shamed a king with the courage of his conscience.

SUCH A SCENE IT MUST HAVE BEEN, THAT IT BROKE THE HARDEST HEART that witnessed it. Margaret More Roper, beloved oldest daughter of Sir Thomas More, pushed through the crowd and past the armed guards to embrace and cover her father with kisses as he was escorted to his place of imprisonment, from where, in six days, he would be executed for the crime of being honest.

Thomas More blessed his daughter and tenderly consoled her before she reluctantly let go of him, and the somber party resumed its progress to the Tower of London. But her distress was too great to be restrained, and she again rushed to his side, to hold and kiss him. Her husband, William Roper, remembered that most of the large crowd that had gathered in curiosity to see the famous prisoner, who had been one of the most powerful men in England, wept at the sight of this sad parting of a loving father and daughter.

Thomas More was born in 1478 into a prosperous London family, but not part of the nobility that ruled England in the fifteenth century. The Mores had no inherited titles to ease their way in the world. They succeeded by their own industry, intelligence, and character. Thomas's father, John, was a successful and influential lawyer, who could afford to send his oldest son to a good school, St. Anthony's, where young Thomas impressed his tutors as a gifted, hardworking, and good-humored boy.

At the recommendation of St. Anthony's headmaster, Thomas was sent to serve as a page to the second-most-powerful man in England, Cardinal John Morton, the archbishop of Canterbury, at the archbishop's court, Lambeth Palace. It must have been a dazzling experience for a young boy, for only in the royal court was there greater splendor or more important activity; the old archbishop managed, on the king's behalf, and his own, to restrain the power of the feudal lords, who had made England in the past nearly impossible to govern. Morton was a wise and great statesman as well as a faithful prince of the Church. Thomas closely observed, admired, and learned from his master's genius for politics, which in those times was a dangerous profession, and his sincere priestly devotion. For his part, the archbishop felt great affection for his cheerful and precocious page, who he proclaimed would someday "prove to be a marvelous man."

He was so impressed by young Thomas's talents and character that he sponsored his education at Oxford University, where Thomas was a brilliant student. He loved learning, and would for the rest of his life prefer the less prestigious but more satisfying rewards of a scholar to the riches and power of the king's court. He began his studies at Oxford in the same year Columbus discovered the New World, and the Renaissance was flowering in Southern Europe. In England, the era of feudalism, when nobles ruled their lands with the power of life and death over the serfs who slaved for them, was approaching its end, and the influence of merchants, lawyers, and other prosperous commoners was on the rise.

More's father gave him only a small allowance while he was at Oxford so that he wouldn't have money to tempt him toward "dangerous and idle pastimes." Despite his poverty, Thomas couldn't have been happier. He thrived among his fellow scholars, who were making their presence felt in this period of historic change, as the dark and brutal Middle Ages began to give way to a more hopeful age of learning and reason.

He was part of a movement called humanism, whose followers were faithful to the Church but hoped to encourage a better understanding of the Gospels and their more honest application to the workings of society. They studied the great Greek and Roman philosophers, whose views on morality and just societies they believed complemented their Christian principles. They were passionate in pursuit of the truth as revealed by God, and by discovery through study and scholarly debate and discussion. They thought the world could be made gentler with Christian love and greater learning—love and learning that served not only the nobility of court and Church, but all mankind.

Thomas's father didn't approve of this new thinking, and after two years ordered him to leave Oxford and study law in his offices. Thomas obeyed his father's command, for he was an obedient man all his life, not without regret, but without complaint. He became a successful lawyer, even more so than his father. But he remained a dedicated scholar and a humanist also, and that calling would bring him more lasting and widespread fame than the high offices he would gain as an honest and admired man of law.

Thomas was a devout Christian, and for a time lived in a monastery with the intention of entering the priesthood. The monastic life was one of isolation and self-denial. And though he took his religious devotion seriously, he loved the comforts of family life, and the rewards of learning and earthly pleasures as well: music and art, reading and writing, friendship and conversation and jests. He loved his city, London, then the greatest capital of Northern Europe. He loved life. So he left the cloister for a wife and family, and returned to the worldly affairs of men.

His first wife, Jane, bore him three daughters and a son. It was a happy marriage, but brief. Jane died at the age of twenty-two. He knew his children needed a mother, and he a mistress to manage his household, so he quickly married again to a widow seven years his senior, Alice Middleton. It, too, was a happy marriage, marked by mutual affection and deep friendship. In an age when a man could legally beat his wife, with a "stick no wider than his thumb," he was a tender and respectful husband. Their large and comfortable home on the banks of the River Thames, in a part of London called Chelsea, then still countryside, was a warm, loving environment where his children thrived and he sought refuge from the increasing demands of his growing public life. It had a beautiful garden that opened to the river, and was filled with many different kinds of birds and animals, which fascinated him. There he supervised his children's education, although it was unusual for women of that time even to learn to read, and when they had grown, his home served as a school for his grandchildren. His love of learning and truth was second only to his love of God, and he encouraged his children, for the sake of their happiness, to seek truth through learning as well as scripture. Margaret, his oldest and favorite child, would become a woman of great learning, perhaps the most celebrated female scholar in all of Europe.

He was devoted to his children, and prized their company above all others. He engaged their minds with his great wit and skill in conversation, and by the example of his own serious scholarship. He wrote a book, *Utopia*, about an imaginary and idealized civilization that won him wide praise and international fame. He cultivated friendships, and exchanged letters with some of the greatest minds in Europe, including with the Dutch priest and famous humanist philosopher Erasmus, who became More's greatest admirer outside his family, and whose description of More became the title by which he is still remembered to this day: "a man for all seasons."

The Mores' house was often filled with guests, who were as often his poorer neighbors as the rich and powerful, and were attracted by the family's well-known hospitality, high spirits, and witty conversation. The young king himself, Henry VIII, who, although temperamental and selfish, admired learning and wit, visited often. Henry took great pleasure in the company of his honest, loyal, and amusing host, and valued not only his opinion and his service to the crown but his friendship.

Thomas More would have preferred never to leave his home if he could have secured the means to support his family without venturing outside it, and if he could have been spared the attentions and the needs of his king. But that was not to be.

His scholarly reputation and his reputation as a skillful and, more remarkable for those times, scrupulously honest lawyer first gained the attention of the king's most powerful counselor, the lord chancellor of England, Cardinal Thomas Wolsey. An ambitious and shrewd politician, Wolsey recognized the younger man's talents, and pressed him into the king's service.

Serving first as a diplomat, then in a series of increasingly powerful offices at court, knighted, and given lands and wealth, More became a favorite of Wolsey's and Henry's. And while he might have preferred the life of a philosopher, husband, and father to the rigors of public life, he no doubt took pride in the king's confidence and favor. All the more so because the king and he, for much of that time, shared the same philosophical and religious views.

When Wolsey's downfall came, from the same source that would lead in time to Thomas's death, Henry made his friend lord chancellor. It was the highest office at court, and Thomas More was the first layman to hold it. His appointment was greeted favorably by the court and public alike, for Thomas was known by one and all as an honest man, who would conscientiously discharge the duties of his office.

As it turned out, he was too honest for his king.

The protests of a devoted and tempestuous priest in Germany by the name of Martin Luther against the corrupt practices of the Catholic Church had set in motion a conflict that would rip apart Europe for centuries. The Protestant Reformation that Luther began was the lasting tear in the unity of the Catholic Church, and the beginning of the end for the old order in Europe. In time, it would set kings against kings, families against families, and cause wars that would last for generations.

Thomas More waged an intellectual and judicial war against the followers of Luther that was at times surprisingly aggressive and even cruel for such a reasonable and just man. In the beginning, he had the king's full support in his persecution and prosecution of "heretics." More defended the Church out of religious principle, and because he and the king feared the uncontrollable social disorder that a permanent split among the faithful would surely cause. But his hatred, if it could be called that in such a mild man, was for the heresy and not the heretics. Death was the judgment for heretics in the courts that Thomas More governed, but he went to great lengths to encourage the accused to recant their views and escape their sentence. In fact, in the many cases he prosecuted, all the accused except for four poor souls, who went to their deaths rather than recant, escaped the headman's ax. More was diligent in his duty, but a much more powerful threat than Luther's protests had encouraged was growing to the Catholic Church in England.

Henry's queen, Catherine of Aragon, had failed to produce a surviving male heir. Only their daughter, Mary, lived to adulthood. Henry was determined to have a new wife who could give him a healthy son. Other kings and nobles had received from the pope annulments of their marriage. But the most powerful king in Europe, the Holy Roman Emperor Charles V, was Catherine's nephew, and he had great influence with Pope Clement VII. He persuaded Clement not to grant an annulment that would remove the crown from his aunt's head.

Once Henry fell in love with Anne Boleyn, the fifteen-year-old daughter of a scheming courtier, he would no longer accept papal opposition to his desire to remarry. In this dangerous and growing conflict, Thomas More became a central figure, and he would struggle with all his intellect, lawyer's skills, and courage to obey his king without forsaking his church. It would prove impossible.

Initially More dutifully served the king's wishes, arguing in Parliament that there were grounds to consider the marriage to Catherine unlawful. But when the king declared himself, and not the pope, to be the supreme head of the Church in England, More offered the king his resignation. Henry refused it, and promised his friend that he would never be forced to take any action that his conscience would not permit. But the king's assurance was hollow, and soon both he and More realized that the king's desires and More's conscience could not be reconciled. More again asked the king to accept his resignation, and this time, Henry agreed. Thomas More, no longer a public man, was content to return to his home and loving family, his friendship with his king at an end.

For many months, he was careful not to speak against the king's wishes, in public or in private. But he declined to attend the king's wedding to Anne Boleyn. When Parliament passed a law requiring the king's subjects to sign an oath recognizing Anne as queen, and any children she might bear Henry as legitimate heirs to the throne, he refused to sign it because it denied the pope's authority over the Church in England. When shown the long list of those who had already signed it, he responded, "I myself cannot swear, but I do not blame any man who has sworn." He gave his conscience as the reason for refusing, but he would not say what he thought of the king's actions. On that he kept silent. And for this modest act of conscience, a mere "scruple of faith," as it was remembered, Thomas More was prepared to face the king's anger in an age when, he was reminded, "the King's wrath is death."

He was arrested and imprisoned in the Tower of London. He remained there until his trial fifteen months later. He was allowed to attend Mass daily, to keep and read books, and to write. For a time he was allowed regular visits by his family and to exchange letters with them. They begged him to sign the oath, and by so doing, return to their home. Margaret expressed her fear that his health was being ruined by imprisonment. He responded by reminding her that but for his love of his family, he would have chosen to live in even worse circumstances as a monk. When Alice criticized him for preferring to live among filth and rats than among his loving family, he gently countered that this home was as near to heaven as his own.

Eventually, his books and writing material were confiscated, and most of his visitors refused. His health declined in the damp and cold of the Tower. His hair and beard grew long and unkempt, and he became thin and aged.

He prayed, contemplated the suffering of Christ, and prepared himself to die. But he did nothing that would hasten his fate except continue to refuse the oath. Henry sent emissaries to persuade him to sign. They did not succeed, but neither did they hear him speak against the oath. And when Thomas was brought to trial for treason and repeatedly asked his opinion about the legitimacy of the king's claims, he remained silent. He was too weak to stand and was allowed to remain seated, but he argued his case with great skill, claiming it a matter of conscience, but he did not say what his conscience held.

Only one man, the king's solicitor general, Richard Rich, claimed he had witnessed Thomas denounce the law. More replied that he had known his accuser since Rich had been a boy, and had always known him to be dishonest, and therefore, it was hard to believe that he would say to Rich what he had declined to say to any other man. When Rich asked two men who had witnessed the interview in which he claimed More had spoken treason to confirm his testimony, they said they could not. It mattered little. The jury, which included Anne Boleyn's father, brother, and uncle, found him guilty and sentenced him to be hanged, and drawn and quartered. Then More spoke his conscience, and said he could not in his own heart accept the king as head of the English Church.

The captain of the guard who escorted More back to the Tower after his trial wept as he discharged his sad duty. More comforted him. Then he saw his children. His son John asked for his blessing, and Margaret, the daughter he loved so tenderly, and whose character and intelligence so pleased him, embraced and kissed him for the last time.

The death to which he was first sentenced would have been a far slower and more painful death than he was made to suffer in the end. Henry, mercifully, permitted his old friend and counselor to die by beheading.

Back in his cell, More prepared for death, prayerfully, bravely, and cheerfully, by all accounts. When a barber came to trim his hair and beard, he refused the service, noting that the king intended to have his head, and "I shall spend no further cost upon it." He wrote a last prayer, in which he confessed his sins. Alice visited him for the final time. He comforted his grieving wife, and gave her a letter for Margaret, in which he thanked God for his family, blessed them, and asked for their prayers.

On the day of his execution, he had some difficulty climbing the scaffold steps. He thanked the guard who helped him, but joked that he should be allowed to "shift for myself" when he came back down. He recited a prayer of repentance. The hooded executioner, as was the custom, begged the condemned man's forgiveness. More gave him a coin, kissed him, and thanked him for giving him a "greater benefit than ever any mortal man can be able to give me." And then the man who had all his life loved to jest, made one last joke. As he knelt to place his head upon the block, he asked for a moment to arrange his long beard so that it wouldn't be severed by the ax, observing that as far as he knew his beard had not offended the king.

In his last address, spoken moments earlier, he had asked the crowd of witnesses to pray for his soul and for the king, for he died "the King's good servant, but God's first."

One swift stroke and the king's will was done. The life on earth of honest Thomas More was ended. His glory had just begun.

RESPECT

Gandhi

*He could not harm a soul, but his heart would not
yield to power, and would triumph over the empire that opposed him.*

H E WAS A SHY, AWKWARD CHILD, THE YOUNGEST OF FOUR CHILDREN in a middle-class Indian family. It would have been hard to see any greatness in him as a boy or even later as an English-educated lawyer, practicing a profession without the necessary skills to impress anyone as an advocate or, for that matter, to make any impression at all. His first appearance in court was a disaster. His shyness was so extreme that he couldn't open his mouth to argue his case. Yet he would find his voice, a voice like no other, a voice so compelling—not for its resonance or eloquence, but for the decent convictions it expressed—that he would become one of the most important figures of the twentieth century, and an inspiration to countless crusades for justice on all the continents of the earth.

The life of Mohandas K. Gandhi was too consequential and involved in the important world events of his times to be described in detail in this one brief chapter. The significant episodes of his life were many, each offering a testament to the virtues essential to good character, certainly to the most essential virtue of all—love. Any one of them will do as an example of the principal character attributes recommended in this book. I can't offer you an informed explanation of Gandhian philosophy; it is too rooted in his religious devotion, derived mostly from Hindu beliefs, for me to fully comprehend, much less explain, even though his beliefs were influenced by the traditions of all major religions, including mine. I cannot even claim to share all of his convictions, even those I do understand.

I will only share my admiration for one quality of Gandhi's character that has impressed me as indispensable to a sense of honor: respect for all human life, which begins with self-respect.

Long before he became the Mahatma (Great Soul), before he became Bapu, the father of his country in its struggle for independence from British rule, Mohandas Gandhi was a young, unknown lawyer, with poor prospects for success, on his way from India to British-ruled South Africa in 1893. Educated in the law in London, where he dressed the part of an English gentleman in top hat and tailored suit, a gold chain fastened to a watch in his vest pocket, he looked like any other aspiring young colonial subject who had embraced the style and manners of his foreign rulers. Having made little progress in his practice in Bombay, he eagerly accepted an offer of a year's employment by an Indian company operating in South Africa. He left his wife, whom he had married at thirteen, and young son behind.

From the moment he reached Durban, South Africa, he realized that although in his own country he was a subject of the British crown, Indians, at least in the upper and middle classes, were accorded some respect. It was their country, after all, despite the conceit that the British had come to civilize a backward culture. In South Africa, Indians were politely referred to as "coloreds"; less politely, and more often, they were "coolies" or "Sami." The majority of Indians in South Africa were laborers and servants. Many were successful merchants and businessmen, teachers, and even a few doctors and lawyers. But in Durban, to the British and Dutch settlers, Gandhi wasn't a London-trained, English-speaking lawyer, he was a coolie lawyer, and entitled to little more respect than the coolie who worked in the mines or waited on tables or swept the floors of their houses.

At his first appearance in a Durban court, dressed in an English suit but now wearing an Indian turban rather than a top hat, Gandhi was instructed to remove his headgear, for Indians were forbidden to wear turbans in court. Gandhi refused and angrily left the court, feeling humiliated. Afterward, he discussed the incident with his client, a Muslim Indian merchant, Abdullah Seth. Gandhi was inclined to stop wearing a turban rather than suffer any further insults, but Seth argued that were he to submit to this prejudice, he would discourage other Indians who insisted on wearing their turbans. Gandhi accepted the advice, and wrote to a Durban newspaper, defending his right to dress in the custom of his countrymen. "The question was very much discussed in the papers," he recalled, "which described me as an 'unwelcome visitor.' " The shy, awkward Gandhi had begun to find his voice, and his calling: a lifelong campaign for justice based, as all true justice must be, on respect for the natural rights and dignity of all human beings.

Several days later, Seth sent Gandhi to Pretoria with a first-class train ticket. A white passenger who entered the first-class compartment was displeased to discover a coolie in English clothes comfortably sharing the ride with Europeans. He complained to the conductor, who promptly ordered Gandhi to move to the third-class car. Gandhi refused. Moments later he was shoved off the train, his luggage confiscated, and left to shiver through a cold winter night in the station's waiting room.

The next day he boarded another train without incident. But he suffered a worse insult on the part of his journey that required travel by stagecoach. The conductor ordered Gandhi to ride on top of the coach next to the driver, while the conductor sat inside the coach with the white passengers. Gandhi did not argue, and did as he was instructed, not wishing to be again refused transportation. But when the conductor ordered Gandhi to move to the coach's footboard, so that he could smoke a cigar in Gandhi's seat, Gandhi refused. The infuriated conductor began to beat him severely, and would have seriously injured him had not the other passengers intervened, and insisted that he be allowed to sit with them.

Gandhi suffered other insults on his travels, as he would throughout his time in South Africa. He had in his few weeks there discovered that Europeans in the nineteenth century perceived a natural hierarchy in the human race, with they on top, and the coloreds, who were their colonial subjects, on the bottom. His experiences on the way to Pretoria worked an extraordinary change in him. Gone was his timidity. Gone was his indifference. Gone was his naivete about how the world worked. Gone were his simple personal ambitions to make a decent living for his family in an honorable profession. Gone was the pride in his own vanity, replaced by a firm sense of self-respect and—this is what truly made him Mahatma—by a respect for the dignity of every human being, friend and foe alike, no more but no less great than his respect for his own dignity. He would look back with a kind of gratitude for the petty indignities he had been forced to suffer, for they were a great revelation to him. He always regarded them as the turning point of his life.

He quickly educated himself in the plight of his fellow Indians in South Africa, and took a leadership role in a movement to assert and demand respect for their rights. Within days he had called a meeting of Indians in Pretoria, and made his first public address to great applause. He urged them to stand together in their demands for justice, and to forget the prejudices of their own traditions. Most in the community were Muslims. In India, which itself maintained an unjust division among people based on economic, ethnic, and religious differences, Muslims and Hindus, if not always openly hostile to one another, preferred to keep as separate socially as they were in religious practice. This was a separation that the new, enlightened Gandhi would no longer observe, and which he would struggle to overcome in his native country all the days and at the cost of his life.

While he worked on his client's case in Pretoria, he formed a political association to protect the interests of Indians there, volunteering his legal services to its members without a fee. He became a respected leader of the community during the year he remained in the city. But when the case he was working on concluded, he returned to Durban and prepared to sail home to India. On the night before he left, at a farewell party held in his honor, a friend showed him a newspaper report about a bill pending in the legislature that would deny Indians the right to vote. He urged his friends to stick together to fight the measure, but they seemed resigned to it. "If you think we should fight it," they argued, "then why won't you stay to help us?" He agreed to stay for a month. He was just twenty-five years old. It would be twenty years before he would return to India for good, as Mahatma Gandhi.

"Thus God laid the foundations of my life in South Africa," he wrote, "and sowed the seed of the fight for national self-respect."

Almost overnight he became the political leader of Indian South Africans, organizing them into one large movement, the Natal Indian Congress. He wrote a petition to the legislature and another to a senior British official protesting the legislation, and collected thousands of signatures. His efforts failed to prevent the bill from becoming law, and Indians from losing their right to vote. But he attracted international attention to their cause. And he ceaselessly continued to press Indian grievances before the legislature, courts, and government ministries. Although he devoted most of his time to the cause, he never accepted a fee for his services. He had to practice law in whatever spare time he had to earn a modest income.

He went home to India for several months in 1896, to collect his family and bring them to South Africa. While he was in India he spoke to the public and press about South Africa's treatment of its Indian minority. When he and his family arrived back in Durban, he found waiting for him a large mob of white settlers who were enraged by reports of Gandhi's comments in India. As he disembarked from the ship, they fell on him, beat and stoned him. They would have lynched him if the brave wife of the local police chief hadn't grabbed Gandhi and escorted him through the mob until police arrived.

When the British government learned of the assault, it ordered local authorities to arrest and prosecute the ringleaders. But Gandhi refused to press charges. He made a vow that he would never seek legal redress for an injury done only to him. His commitment was to his community, and he would sacrifice whatever he must on their behalf. "We must be the change we wish to see in the world," he said.

Nor would he permit retaliation in kind for the physical mistreatment Indians suffered. He used only nonviolent resistance to protest mistreatment and injustice. To Gandhi, nonviolence was more than a tactic of passive resistance to oppression. It was an ideal, or more accurately, a means to achieve an ideal—truth, the truth in which, Gandhi believed, God resided. He didn't hate his enemies. He sought to change them. He saw the good in them—even if for most of us, there would have been little good to see—and he intended by his example of nonviolence and kinship with all human beings to rouse the moral conscience of his oppressors.

During the Boer War, in which Dutch settlers rebelled against British authority in South Africa, Gandhi organized over a thousand Indians to serve as stretcher bearers. Under his leadership, the volunteers of the Indian Ambulance Corps distinguished themselves repeatedly under fire as they rescued and treated the wounded, British and Boer soldiers alike, earning the admiration of both sides. They would do the same a few years later, during a war between European settlers and the native Zulu population, nursing wounded Zulus whom white doctors would not treat.

More impressive still, and a source of great satisfaction to Gandhi, was the way in which Indians of all classes and religions served in the corps together, forgetting their prejudices to brave danger as brothers in the same cause. That they sacrificed on behalf of people who had not forgotten their prejudices and refused to respect the rights of the Indians who risked their lives for them, was more than an act of uncommon decency. It was an awe-inspiring example of respect and love for their fellow man. Pitiably, the white rulers of South Africa were not so inspired that they felt obliged to reciprocate in kind.

In 1907, in a part of South Africa called the Transvaal, the Dutch settlers who governed there (known as Boers, or Afrikaners) passed the Black Law, which required Indians to register with the government and be fingerprinted. Gandhi refused, and peacefully accepted imprisonment rather than obey an unjust law.

General Jan Smuts, the leader of the government of the Transvaal, promised Gandhi that he would abolish the Black Law if Gandhi agreed to register. Gandhi complied and was released from prison, but Smuts broke his promise and the law remained in place. So Gandhi resumed the protest, and returned to prison. Thousands of Indians followed his example, and over the next several years their protests grew to include virtually all of the Indian community. Indian workers went on strike, and went to jail. Women went to jail. Many Indians lost the means to support their families. Many were beaten and whipped. Many were killed. But they would not relent. They turned the other cheek to the violence done to them, as the Mahatma wished them to, and suffered terribly for it. But they refused to obey a law that refused to respect their rights.

When the South African supreme court ordered that only Christian marriages would be recognized as lawful, thereby making illegal the marriages of thousands of Hindu and Muslim couples, their protests grew in strength, crippling the South African economy and forcing General Smuts to negotiate with Gandhi and, finally, to agree to his demands that the offending laws be repealed.

A great victory had been achieved, although for nearly a century longer, Indians and the majority black population of South Africa were denied their full rights as equal citizens under the law, until an admirer of Gandhi's, Nelson Mandela, led them to freedom. But, with an end to the laws that had sparked their nationwide protests, Gandhi felt it was time for him to return to his native country.

Like many of Gandhi's future adversaries, General Smuts felt both animosity for his opponent's unyielding resistance and admiration for the Great Soul who confronted him with respect and extraordinary generosity. During one stretch of imprisonment, Gandhi, who had by now stopped practicing law and had renounced worldly possessions, taught himself the simple craft of making sandals. He made a pair for General Smuts, and presented it to his adversary shortly before he departed for India. In later years, Smuts remembered thinking on the day Gandhi left, "I hope [he has left] forever." And then he recalled Gandhi's last act of generosity to him. "I have worn these sandals for many a summer since then even though I may feel that I am not worthy to stand in the shoes of so great a man."

When he returned to India he began the struggle to liberate his country from British rule, a struggle that would last for over thirty years. He would die shortly after his dream was realized, murdered by a Hindu who resented the respect Gandhi showed Muslim Indians. During his years in India, he lived in a community he founded with Indians of all ethnic, religious, and economic backgrounds. Among them were Indians from the lowest caste, an oppressed and humiliated minority called untouchables by other Indians. When neighbors of the community objected to the presence of untouchables, Gandhi moved his followers to a city neighborhood that was populated almost entirely by these poor outcasts of Indian society.

As he lived and as he died, he was the change he wished to see in the world.

AUTHENTICITY

Joan of Arc

At the command of voices that only she could hear,
she rode to battle and saved her country.

S HE COULD NOT READ OR WRITE, BUT SAINTS AND ANGELS SPOKE TO HER. Michael the Archangel, and Catherine and Margaret, the patron saints of France, commanded the thirteen-year-old peasant girl to pray vigilantly and attend Mass regularly. She listened and obeyed, as she would for all but a single moment of her life.

Joan of Arc was born in 1412 in the French village of Domrémy, during a war between England and France that lasted more than a hundred years. English armies and their French allies, the forces of the duke of Burgundy, had conquered most of France for their king, Henry VI. The rightful heir to the throne of France, the Dauphin Charles, controlled only the Loire Valley, where he kept his court, surrounded on nearly every side by the English and Burgundians. Charles and his counselors lacked the determination and courage to drive the English from his country and claim the crown his father had worn. Reims, the city where French kings were crowned, was held by his enemies, who now prepared to attack Orléans, the city that would gain them access to the last of Charles's territory. The dauphin's situation was nearly hopeless.

Joan's saints appeared to her with the message that God had chosen her to lead an army against the English at Orléans and save Charles and France. At their command, she cut her hair short like a boy's, and went to ask Lord Robert de Baudricourt, who was loyal to the dauphin, for a military escort to take her to Charles. He refused and ordered her to return home. It is said that before she departed, Joan predicted that the French would soon suffer a defeat at Rouvray. When Baudricourt received the news that the disaster Joan had foretold had occurred, he sent for her. He gave her a horse, and six men to escort her safely to Charles.

After eleven days, she reached Chinon, where Charles held court. She was brought into a room where Charles stood disguised among his courtiers. But Joan knew him instantly, walked directly to him, and kneeling before him declared, "Noble Dauphin, I have come and am sent in the name of God to bring aid to you and the kingdom." To convince Charles of her sincerity, she repeated to him a private prayer he had offered some months before asking God's help in his campaign to take the throne. Witnesses said Charles became "radiant" upon hearing from Joan that God recognized him as the legitimate king of France.

She asked him for an army to lead to Orléans. Charles, instead, sent her to be interviewed by priests whom he charged with determining the sincerity of her claims to be God's messenger. They questioned her for many days, trying the patience of the simple, pious girl who stood before them. Yet her replies greatly impressed her examiners. When one of them asked her for some sign to prove that God was working through her before they could recommend that the king trust her with his soldiers, she responded, "Send me to Orléans, and I will show you the signs for which I was sent."

Charles gave her an army. She wore boy's clothing, and a suit of armor Charles had made for her, and carried a war banner of her own invention, a picture of God holding the world in His hands, angels at His side, on a white background with gold lilies, the symbol of France. Her sword had been brought to her from the Church of St. Catherine. A voice had told her that a sword with five crosses was hidden behind the church's altar, and that she should retrieve it and carry it into battle. She wrote the priests there and asked them to bring it to her. Thus attired, she led an army of three thousand men toward Orléans, with priests marching in front of them, singing hymns.

She is remembered as very beautiful, a slight seventeen-year-old girl with black hair who could ride for long hours in heavy armor without any sign of discomfort. She kept silent for long periods, but could be roused to great anger at men swearing or behaving in some other sinful manner. She prayed and fasted often, and seemed most comfortable in the company of poor priests. Before they embarked, she had dictated to a priest a letter for the English commanders in

Orléans, warning them to "go away back to England . . . or I will drive you out of France." This is the first the English had ever heard of Joan of Arc. To the French, and their dauphin, who now placed their trust in her, she was becoming a saint.

As they marched to Orléans, she saw to the spiritual needs of her soldiers, ordering them to abandon their vices, to refrain from looting and harming civilians, to confess their sins and attend Mass regularly, which they did. Men who had refused to serve Charles in what they believed was a losing cause now rushed to her standard, and prepared for battle.

They marched for three days along the south bank of the Loire River. Orléans and the English were on the other side. On the third day, she led a small advance party across the Loire without being detected by the English, and entered Orléans, where she was welcomed by the joyful inhabitants as their savior. The city was surrounded by a series of English forts, and Joan was eager to force an engagement. But the French generals who accompanied her, as well as the brother of the duke of Orléans, who had been charged with defending the city, argued that the English were too many to attack before the rest of her army arrived. So she sent a herald to the English with another message for them to leave France. They refused to heed her demand, and threatened to burn the herald at the stake for following the orders of a woman they denounced as a witch. She mounted a horse and rode out of Orléans toward the nearest English fort. When she was close enough for her enemies to hear her, she shouted at them to surrender. They cursed and threatened her in reply.

A few days later, the rest of her army began to arrive with much needed supplies, just as word was received that another English army was marching to the aid of her enemies. She went to sleep that night happy in the knowledge that the moment was at hand when she would accomplish what her saints had commanded her to do.

She awoke in the middle of the night, and stirred her generals with the news that they must attack immediately. In fact, a battle had already begun at the nearest English fortification. Joan commanded her page to bring her horse, as she dressed in her armor, and then raced to join the fight carrying her banner. When she reached her soldiers, she saw that they were losing the battle, but her presence inspired them, and they rallied to take the fort. After the battle Joan wept for the fallen, French and English alike.

On the next day they took another English fort, and the day after one more. But the fighting during the third battle had been ferocious. Joan was wounded by an arrow through her shoulder as she attempted to scale one of the fort's walls, and was carried to safety. Seeing her hurt and carried from the field, her troops lost courage, and the assault was suspended. Some witnesses say she removed the arrow herself. Others remembered her soldiers treating the wound. Whatever the case, legend has it that she responded to her soldiers' fears by telling them to rally to her when they saw her banner strike the fort's wall. And when they did see it, they recovered their courage and took the fort.

The next day the English abandoned the siege. Orléans was saved. Both English and French generals gave the credit to Joan. She gave it to God. Then she rode to meet Charles. When they met, she bowed to him, and urged him to hasten to Reims, where his crown awaited him. But Charles hesitated. His will was weak, for he was not a man of great courage, and his advisors at court, some of whom resented Joan's interference, cautioned him to proceed slowly, for there were still many powerful English armies in France that had to be destroyed.

So Joan and her comrade-in-arms, the duke of Alençon, led her army in a series of battles along the Loire. Each one ended in triumph. The last one was fought at Patay, where both the English and French had assembled huge armies and the fighting was fierce. Joan, as always, rode in the front, carrying her banner, urging her soldiers to victory. Inspired by her courage, and by the obvious favor of God that protected her, they carried the day, routing the English and opening the road to Reims. The English and all the French, those loyal to the dauphin and those who fought for Henry, recognized that this strange young girl, now known as the Maid of Orléans, must be in the service of a sovereign more powerful than any earthly king.

She returned to Charles, and overcoming the continued opposition of his counselors, persuaded him to march to Reims. She rode by his side, as they fought two battles on the way, and as the gates of the city were opened to them, and Reims prepared to meet its king. And she stood near him in the great cathedral, holding her banner in front of her as the archbishop placed the crown upon Charles's head.

After his coronation, Joan encouraged him to march on Paris. But King Charles VII, who had gained no stronger heart with his crown, wished to return instead to the safety of the Loire Valley. An English army blocked his way. So he and Joan rode together through Île-de-France, the heartland of the country, where much of France's history was made, expecting and receiving promises of loyalty from the inhabitants of the towns they visited. They fought a few skirmishes with the English before retiring to the city of Compiègne.

Charles's emissaries sought to negotiate a truce with the duke of Burgundy, which they concluded on August 21, 1429. For reasons that are difficult to understand, although probably attributable to the indecision and weakness of the French king and his counselors, the four-month truce granted many concessions to Burgundy and effectively halted the progress of the French army even though Joan had led them to the brink of sweeping victory.

Two days later, Joan and Alençon, trusting neither Burgundy, the English, nor their timid king, left Compiègne without Charles's permission and led their army to Paris. They reached the French capital on September 8, but on the first day of the siege, Joan was again wounded as she stood before her army demanding the city's surrender, and, against her will, was carried from the field. Charles ordered the army to retreat, and when he learned that Alençon intended to resume the siege, he ordered a bridge destroyed to prevent him from reaching the city. Alençon, in disgust, abandoned the fight, and returned to his estate. The king returned to the Loire.

Joan, with only a few men, captured another town from the English. She was laying siege to another when her supplies ran out, and no one came to her relief. She was forced to withdraw and rejoin the king.

She remained with him for several months, forbidden to take part in more fighting. When Alençon wrote the king to ask that Joan be allowed to join him on a campaign in Normandy, Charles refused. But when Burgundy and the duke of Bedford, England's regent in France, began a new campaign against the king, Charles realized he had been deceived by the enemy's assurances of peace, and allowed Joan to go to the aid of Compiègne, where the people were desperately resisting Burgundy's attack.

She left with only a few men, among them her brother, and a few weeks later entered the city with her small army, to the people's great relief. While she prayed in one of the city's churches, her saints appeared to inform her she would soon be captured and that she should not lose heart but resign herself to her fate. A witness recounted that she had left the church saddened, and remarking that she had been betrayed. That same day she led her soldiers outside the city to repel an attack by one of Burgundy's armies, led by John of Luxembourg. Twice she pushed her foes from the field, but English soldiers ambushed her as she made her way back to the city. She remained with her army's rear guard, fighting the enemy until most of her soldiers safely reached the city. She was probably betrayed by someone, though that is not known with certainty. But when she had finally fought her way back to the gates of Compiègne, she found them closed. She, her brother, and a few of her soldiers were trapped, and quickly seized by enemy soldiers. She would not surrender, though, until one of Burgundy's men pulled her from the saddle.

Luxembourg took her to his castle, where, distraught over the fate of the people of Compiègne, she twice tried to escape, once by jumping from a castle tower into the moat below. Attempts to ransom her were refused, as were French attempts to liberate her by force. After several months, Luxembourg handed Joan over to the English, and she was taken to the city of Rouen, where a corrupt bishop, Pierre Cauchon, was instructed to put her on trial for heresy. The rules of war did not permit the English to condemn Joan for opposing them in battle. So they sought her death by falsely accusing her of witchcraft.

Cauchon tried for weeks to compel her to confess, but despite threats of torture and execution, she steadfastly refused to divulge her conversations with Charles or to concede that the saints who spoke to her were demons or merely inventions of her own blasphemy. She was denied permission to attend Mass and receive the sacraments. She was often kept in chains and became very ill. Yet she stayed true to herself, and to her saints.

Her trial was a farce, and its outcome a forgone conclusion. She was accused of various crimes, none of which she conceded. Many of the charges were eventually dropped because Joan effectively refuted them. She was convicted of the crime of wearing men's clothing, which was considered profane and proof of her heresy. But this she had done for both modesty's sake and because it was appropriate attire for a soldier.

She wore a dress when they brought her to a church cemetery to hear her sentence read, condemning her to be burned at the stake. She asked that her conviction be appealed to the pope. Her persecutors refused her. And then, Joan of Arc, for the first and only time in her brief life, tried to be someone she was not.

Fearing the flames, she confessed to being a heretic, recanted her claim to have heard and obeyed her saints, and begged her enemies for mercy. Mercy they had little of, but having taken from her what their armies could not, they no longer thought her life such a great thing that it could not be spared. She was now nothing more than a confessed imposter. They had wanted to destroy her truth, that she was God's messenger. Having done so, it mattered little whether she died or suffered long imprisonment. Their work done, they left her in her cell, to the taunts and abuses of the guards, and commanded her to dress only in women's clothes.

When they next saw her, a few days later, she was attired in the clothes of a boy. She had recovered her courage and her truth. Her saints had reproached her for denying them, and she had begged their forgiveness. She had become her true self again. She was the Maid of Orléans, a pretty, pious nineteen-year-old girl who had left her father's house and taken up arms for more than a year, as heaven had commanded her. And with heaven's encouragement she had defeated France's enemies in battle after battle, frightened and awed the bravest English heart, rallied a nation to her banner, and made a weak, defeated man a king.

God's messenger went bravely to her death, forgiving her accusers and asking only that a priest hold high a crucifix for her to see it above the flames. She raised her voice to heaven, calling out to her saints and her Savior. Even her enemies wept at the sight. Her executioner was shaken with remorse, and an anguished English soldier who witnessed the crime feared for his soul. "God forgive us," he cried, "we have burned a saint."

LOYALTY

Sir Ernest Shackleton

He was a driven man, and a tough, demanding boss,
and he would triumph over impossible odds to keep faith
with the men who trusted him.

THEY RACED FOR THEIR LIVES OVER A DAUNTING, BROKEN WHITE landscape, through blinding blizzards, down icy mountains and past deadly, hidden crevasses where a man could plunge to his death, as they nearly had on several occasions. They had crossed the Ross Barrier and the treacherous Beardmore Glacier. On January 9, 1909, they had come within less than a hundred miles of their goal, to be the first men to reach the South Pole. But blizzards, illness, and starvation had forced them to turn back. Still they had reached the point farthest south any human being had ever attained after enduring one of the most astonishing journeys in the history of exploration. Three exhausted, starving men, urged on by their relentless, determined "boss," Ernest Shackleton, who had abandoned his chance for glory for the sake of his men's survival, heroically persevered through the worst conditions on earth. They were desperately making for McMurdo Sound, where they had begun their seventeen-hundred-mile journey, and where, with any luck, their ship would be waiting in the harbor to take them back to New Zealand, and from there, home to England. If they were too late, the ship would have left without them, presuming them dead.

One of the party, John Robert Francis "Frank" Wild, a short, quiet, capable British sailor from Yorkshire, had, like Shackleton, previously failed to reach the South Pole as a member of Captain Robert Falcon Scott's 1902 expedition. He hadn't particularly liked Shackleton then, an opinion he had not yet completely revised on their present journey. But he soon thought better of the boss, and felt such loyalty to the man that he would, five years later, follow him again to the ends of the earth.

Wild recorded in his diary an evening meal on the hard march back to McMurdo Sound, when they were still nearly a month out from their destination. They had few provisions left, and were subsisting on a little pony meat and four dry biscuits a day. They were slowly starving to death, as all of them knew but, for the sake of their flagging morale, would not admit to one another. That evening, Shackleton offered one of his biscuits to Wild, who refused it. Shackleton insisted that the smaller man, who appeared to be in worse shape than he, take his portion. Finally, Wild accepted the offer gratefully. He wrote in his diary: "I don't suppose anyone in the world can thoroughly realize how much generosity was shown by this. I do by God [and] I shall never forget it."

Ernest Shackleton had many qualities that make someone a successful leader of others in desperate circumstances. His optimism, determination, reliability, judgment, and composure inspired confidence in his men. But the quality that most inspired confidence in his leadership was his loyalty to his men. They knew he would always put their welfare before his own ambitions, and they trusted him almost as faithfully as small children trust their father. His loyalty, and theirs to him, would, on their next journey, save their lives again, in an epic of heroic survival that has not been equaled since.

Ernest Shackleton was born on February 15, 1874, in County Kildare, Ireland, to an English doctor and an Irish mother, the second of eight children. The family moved to England when Shackleton was nine. By all accounts, he was a confident, charming boy, showing early signs of the winning personality that would attract the patronage of his expeditions' wealthy sponsors, and the trust of the men who followed him. Charming though he was, he proved to be an uninspired student at school, attributing his indifferent scholarship to the effects of constant boredom. He dreamed of going to sea, and at the age of sixteen he finally secured his father's permission. In 1890, as an apprentice merchant seaman, he boarded the sailing ship *Hoghton Tower*, bound for Valparaiso, Chile, around Cape Horn, where the most treacherous waters in the world threatened many a ship and sailor with grave harm.

It took the *Hoghton* two months to round the Horn, ceaselessly fighting winter storms and the huge, boiling black seas that mercilessly battered and tossed the wooden ship. It cannot have been a pleasant introduction to the life of a sailor, but it was surely a good education for a boy who dreamed of dangerous adventures. Evidently, the voyage didn't cause Shackleton much distress or encourage him to consider some other, more tranquil line of work. Whatever it was in his personality that derived such deep satisfaction from life-risking adventures must have been in some way delighted by his arduous maiden voyage. In fact, it was this voyage that Shackleton would later recall as the inspiration for his desire to explore the unknown, frozen world of Antarctica. "I felt strangely drawn towards the mysterious south [as] we rounded Cape Horn in the depth of winter. It was one continuous blizzard all the way. . . . Yet, even in the midst of all this discomfort, my thoughts would go southward." Discomfort, it seems, had an appeal for him, or at least, it did not discourage him from the hard, dangerous life he chose for himself.

Neither did his rough passage round the Horn impede his progress as a professional sailor. He continued sailing on merchant vessels, mostly between England and Asia, for several years, excelling in the profession as he never had at school. His nautical education taught him more than good seamanship. It taught him a great deal about friendship, and the unique bonds of trust and affection between men engaged in difficult, dangerous occupations.

On merchant ships, officers and crew mixed more easily than the rank and class consciousness that prevailed on British Navy ships allowed. Camaraderie among men under stress, which Shackleton attributed to personalities that were naturally lighthearted and optimistic regardless of how serious or dire their circumstances, was essential to succeeding in difficult enterprises. He learned that lesson as a merchant sailor, and never forgot it. "There are lots of good things in the world," he said, "but I'm not sure comradeship isn't the best of them all." Nor did he forget how loyalty engendered loyalty in return, encouraged a crew's trust and discipline, and thus was the most indispensable quality of a leader. These lessons must have aided his impressive rise in the ranks of the merchant marine. He made first mate by the age of twenty-two and master two years later.

By 1900, however, Shackleton longed to fulfill the destiny he had perceived on that first storm-tossed voyage round the Horn. He learned that Robert Falcon Scott, a British naval captain, was planning an expedition to the South Pole, and he set about pestering various influential sponsors of the expedition until they prevailed on Scott to take him along. He set sail with Scott in the summer of 1901, bound first for New Zealand, and then on to McMurdo Sound to begin the trek to the Pole.

The expedition was a near disaster. Neither Scott nor his crew had adequate experience on skis or with dogsleds—the most effective and quickest means of travel in an ice wilderness—over an expanse of seventeen hundred miles. Instead, Scott and the two men from his crew he chose to accompany him to the Pole, Edward Wilson, a doctor of medicine, and Shackleton, would eventually haul their sleds themselves, their skis stored with the gear, and their uncooperative sled dogs trotting along next to them.

Their supplies were inadequate, and they lived on short rations for most of the trek. Their poor diet resulted in scurvy, a disease caused by a lack of vitamin-C-rich fruits and vegetables. Shackleton was afflicted the worst, and for long stretches had to be carried in the sled. The terrain was even more foreboding than imagined, and the worst calamity was always one wrong footstep away. It was an impossible journey from the start, but if Shackleton was less than thrilled to be a part of it, he gave little indication of his disappointment. As with every endeavor, he was learning, always learning, to be a leader of men.

Shackleton and Scott did not like each other. Whether hard feelings were present at the beginning of the adventure or developed sometime on their failed race to the Pole is not known. But at some point, Scott's imperious naval-officer personality struck Shackleton as insufferable arrogance, and Scott considered Shackleton's more familiar, casual attitude toward his superior intolerable insolence. They fought often, which must have made the grueling journey all the more punishing.

Their provisions nearly depleted, their dogs dead or dying, ill health and wicked weather crippling their advance, Scott ordered his team to turn back more than seven hundred miles short of the Pole. They reached McMurdo Sound, exhausted, three months after they had begun. Scott sent Shackleton, still suffering from scurvy, back to England ahead of the rest of the expedition, further straining relations between Scott and his disappointed subordinate. But, to Shackleton's great surprise, he arrived in England to discover that he and the rest of the expedition were national heroes for the courage they had shown in the face of such daunting odds. And Shackleton, never a man much at ease when resting, conceived another try for the Pole. Only this time he would choose a better leader. Himself.

He spent the next several years using his newfound celebrity to attract sponsors for his expedition. With typical confidence and enthusiasm, which proved infectious to the subjects of his persuasion, he threw himself into planning and recruiting a crew, and finding a ship. During a brief lull in his efforts, he married and began a family. Among the first of the crew chosen was Frank Wild, whom he had met on Scott's expedition. He paid particular attention to finding those he thought were the right kind of men for the adventure. They must be capable, self-reliant individualists, who, somewhat paradoxically, "could live together in harmony for a long period of time without outside communication." He chose six officers for the three-masted ship he acquired, the *Nimrod,* and ten men for the overland journey. Three would travel with him to the Pole, and the others would journey north to the South Magnetic Pole. He also decided to bring fewer dogs than Scott did, substituting Manchurian ponies, bred to endure harsh winters, to haul the sleds.

They set off in July 1907, and arrived in New Zealand four months later. After difficult encounters with mammoth bergs and pack ice, they reached McMurdo Sound during the southern summer and, after further struggles with the ice and elements, reached the shore several days later. Once they made landfall they constructed the hut in which they would live and work and plan through the summer and coming winter, waiting for the southern spring before they would begin the march to the Pole.

Shackleton, Wild, and two other men, along with four ponies, set out on October 29, 1908, for a second try at the Pole. The four companions returned to base camp four months later having turned back just short of their goal, and after surviving the deadly journey described at the beginning of this chapter. Shackleton remarked of his second failure, "better a live donkey than a dead lion." His optimism, so remarkably durable considering his terrifying experiences, was rooted in his unyielding confidence that he would always have another chance. Nor was his second venture considered a failure by Shackleton, his men, or the nation that had sent him. They arrived home heroes, who had ventured farther south than any men had ever reached. Shackleton was knighted. More important, he had learned more valuable lessons. Ponies didn't work. They had shot and eaten most of theirs, and lost the rest in crevasses. Dogsleds and skis were the only transportation that could take a team to the Pole in the time necessary to reach it. Also, Shackleton discovered that Frank Wild was a good man to risk your life with. He would put the lessons to good use as he planned yet another expedition to the Pole.

Captain Scott would beat him there. And a Norwegian explorer, Roald Amundsen, using skis and a team of well-trained dogs to pull his sleds, would beat Scott by just days. Scott and his party of five men would never return alive. They died on the ice of hunger only a few miles from a supply depot that would have replenished them. Whatever aspects of Scott's personality that had angered Shackleton, the heroic explorer's courage in the face of doom inspired the world, and, no doubt, Shackleton. He meticulously recorded the last, grim days of their misadventure in his diary and offered detailed accounts in letters that would be found when their bodies were discovered. "Had we lived," he wrote, "I should have had a tale to tell of hardihood, endurance, and courage of my companions, which would have stirred the heart of every Englishmen. These rough notes and our dead bodies must tell the tale."

Not long after England received word of the gallant Scott's death, Shackleton began promoting and planning his next adventure. Since Amundsen and Scott had already reached the Pole, Shackleton would do them one better. He would cross the continent from Weddell Sea in the northeast, eighteen hundred miles to the Ross Sea in the west. As always, he planned carefully. He bought from a Norwegian shipbuilder a ship that had never sailed but had been built especially to withstand damage from the pack ice that flowed in the unpredictable currents and weather of the most inhospitable place on earth, and could crush wooden ships, as if in a vise, to splinters. He named it the *Endurance,* after his family motto, "By endurance we conquer."

Of course, he exercised the greatest care in selecting the men on whom he would rely to accomplish his great task, and to whom he would be bound by true loyalty. He had a large pool of applicants from which to choose. Five thousand men answered an ad he placed in London newspapers.

MEN WANTED: FOR HAZARDOUS JOURNEY. SMALL WAGES, BITTER COLD, LONG MONTHS OF COMPLETE DARKNESS, CONSTANT DANGER, SAFE RETURN DOUBTFUL. HONOR AND RECOGNITION IN CASE OF SUCCESS. SIR ERNEST SHACKLETON.

What an invitation. It's hard to imagine such a dire summons to adventure and valor attracting many favorable responses today. But Shackleton had more than he could use, and from five thousand volunteers, he selected twenty-seven hardy souls, several of them with previous Antarctic experience. The first among them was his friend Frank Wild, who would serve as Shackleton's loyal second-in-command. Also chosen was an Australian photographer, Frank Hurley, a veteran Antarctic explorer whose courage and fortitude would leave a moving and astonishing visual record of the expedition.

The expedition embarked on August 1, 1914, at the outset of World War One. None of the men aboard the *Endurance* would set foot on the continent of Antarctica. But in the expedition's failure, Ernest Shackleton and his men would write a record of endurance, courage, loyalty, and leadership that may never be equaled again.

They picked up the last members of the crew in Buenos Aires in October, and left for a remote, desolate, sparsely inhabited whaling station on South Georgia Island. When they left

South Georgia on December 5, no one could have imagined that he would not touch land again for sixteen months or return to civilization for twenty-two months.

Even for that famously hostile place, the weather and ice were exceptionally awful as the *Endurance* left South Georgia for Weddell Bay. Six weeks' rough voyage after leaving the South Georgia whaling station, and one day's sail from the continent, the *Endurance* was trapped by gale winds in pack ice it would never escape. For ten months the expedition struggled to free the ship from the ice, hoping they might drift on the floes close enough to open water to get her afloat again. On November 21, 1915, several days after the boss had given the order to abandon ship, the *Endurance* was crushed by the pressing ice, and sank.

For five more months, with meager provisions, the men lived in five small tents on the ice floes, trekking for days to find open water where they might make for land in three open lifeboats they had rescued from their lost ship. For a month they marched west on the dangerous ice, with cracks in the floe constantly threatening them, until Shackleton realized that further effort was only likely to deplete their supplies and energy more rapidly than if they made camp and waited for the ice floes to drift to within sight of open water. Several times, the floe on which they drifted cracked and split up, forcing the men into the boats to paddle for another floe. Finally, on April 16, 1916, fifteen months after they had first become trapped on the ice, the expedition went to sea in their lifeboats, having spotted a small spit of land a few days earlier.

They sailed through a gale in the open boats for a week before they reached the small, rocky, and utterly desolate Elephant Island. The men renamed it Hell of an Island. Most of them would live there, subsisting on fish and penguin, for nearly five months.

Once the *Endurance* had been destroyed, Shackleton had taken personal command of the desperate expedition, no longer communicating with his men through his subordinate officers. Throughout their ordeal, he had been a source of unflagging encouragement to them. He personally saw to their needs, shared their sacrifices, conferred with them, joked with them, sang with them. He tried to give each man work that he was best suited for. He seldom lost patience with them, even those who complained the most, "the pessimistic ones," he would call them—the most derogatory term in his vocabulary. He was careful never to embarrass a man by publicly criticizing his effort. Thomas Orde-Lees, a captain in the Royal Marines who was chosen to teach the others how to use skis, remarked, "What sacrifices would I not make for such a leader as this." He was an extraordinary inspiration to men who had no realistic expectation of survival. They would almost certainly perish in that strange, violent world of ice. But Shackleton didn't believe it or at least he would never become resigned or let his men become resigned to their ultimate doom. He would see them through, no matter what.

Realizing how dire were their circumstances did not make Shackleton forlorn. It spurred him to even greater heroics. So, one week after they had landed on Hell of an Island, he and five others, including the captain of the *Endurance,* Frank Worsley, set out in one of the lifeboats, the twenty-two-foot *James Caird,* for South Georgia over eight hundred miles of the worst water in the world. It was, even more than the one they had already survived, an impossible journey. He left Frank Wild in command of the twenty-two men who remained on the island, the best of his many wise decisions.

For more than four months on that bleak island, Wild kept the men organized, usefully employed, fed, and sheltered as best he could. He was determined not to break faith with them or Shackleton, and he did all that he could to keep their spirits up as well as the boss had, long past the point when strong men would have been forgiven for abandoning all hope.

Shackleton's accomplishment was even more impressive. The small crew of the tiny *James Caird* sailed for seventeen days through a hurricane and raging seas, before, soaked to the bone and dead weary, they made landfall on South Georgia Island. All along, the boss had insisted on regular mealtimes and good order, knowing that lacking comfort of any kind, a disciplined routine would keep up his men's hope and determination.

Glad as they all were to reach South Georgia, their hopes were soon dashed when they realized they had reached the wrong shore. The whaling station was on the other side of the island, and between them and salvation stood glacier-covered mountains many thousands of feet high. After a week's rest, Shackleton and two others began the climb and long march toward the whaling station, leaving behind three comrades who were too weak to make the crossing to wait for their return. After thirty-six hours of the most indescribably daunting climb over one mountain after another, Shackleton and his men reached the whaling station. On the afternoon of May 20, 1916, their wet clothes (near the end of the journey they had to pass through a waterfall) in rags, bearded, their long hair matted, filthy, frozen, beyond exhaustion, gallant, and relieved, they walked into Stromness whaling station, trying to hold their shoulders back and their heads high, and asked for help.

They cleaned up, ate, and sent Worsley on a whaler to rescue the three men they had left behind on the other side of the island. The next day Shackleton, Worsley, and Tom Crean, the expedition's second officer, a big, tough Irishman, left on a whaler for Elephant Island. Sixty miles from their destination, pack ice forced them to the Falkland Islands. There, Shackleton persuaded the Uruguayan government to lend him a fishing trawler and sailed for his men on June 10. Again, the ice forced him back. He borrowed money to rent a schooner and tried again to rescue his men on July 12. One hundred miles out the engine quit and he was forced back again. On his fourth try, on August 30, with the steamer *Yelcho,* borrowed from the Chilean government, he reached them. "I felt jolly near bubbling for a bit," remembered Frank Wild, "and could not speak for several minutes," when he glimpsed his friend and boss coming ashore in a lifeboat. "Are you all well," Shackleton shouted over the water as he approached. "All well," they shouted back. "Thank God," came the reply. Not a single man lost. Sir Ernest Shackleton had remained loyal to the end, and his men would never forget it. "Behind his every calculated word and gesture," Worsley remembered, "lay the single-minded determination to do what was best for his men."

Shackleton dedicated *South,* the book he wrote about their extraordinary exploits, "To My Comrades." In one especially moving passage he observed: "In memories we were rich. We had pierced the veneer of outside things. We had suffered, starved and triumphed, groveled down yet grasped at glory, grown bigger in the bigness of the whole. We had seen God in His splendors, heard the text that nature renders. We had reached the naked soul of man."

Sixty years after they had been rescued, the expedition's first officer, Lionel Greenstreet, was asked how they had done it, how had they survived such a deadly misadventure. Greenstreet gave a one-word response: "Shackleton."

DIGNITY

Viktor Frankl

*When he had lost everything he loved, suffered the worst
of human cruelty, and stood on the threshold of death,
he gave his life purpose and value.*

THEY HAD TAKEN FROM HIM ALL THEY COULD. THEY HAD TAKEN his freedom, his vocation, his family. They had starved him, beaten him, cursed him, and worked him almost beyond endurance. They had set his life upon a precipice, from which, at any moment they chose, they could push him as they had pushed so many thousands. Yet that cold winter morning as they drove him into the fields like an animal, striking him in the back with the butts of their rifles, Viktor Frankl's mind rose above his torment and his tormentors, taking leave of their cruelty for a few moments to contemplate the image of his wife. He did not know if she was alive or dead, but in his heart he heard the words of the eighth Song of Solomon: *Set me like a seal upon thy heart, love is as strong as death*.

"My mind clung to my wife's image, imagining it with uncanny acuteness. . . . Real or not, her look was more luminous than the sun which was beginning to rise. . . . Then I grasped the meaning of the greatest secret that human poetry and human thought and belief have to impart: the salvation of man is through love and in love," Frankl relates in *Man's Search for Meaning*.

Though he suffered a captivity so utterly degrading that it will stand for all time as a black monument to human cruelty, he held on to his love for his wife, and with his love he kept from his enemies the thing they thought they had destroyed, the one thing that no human being can take from another, for it can only be surrendered. He kept his dignity.

Viktor Frankl had been something of a prodigy. He was the second child of a self-made, stern, and principled man and a kind, loving mother. At the age of four, he decided to become a doctor. He grew up in Vienna, the birthplace of modern psychiatry and the home of Sigmund Freud, its most famous practitioner, and as a very young man decided on a career in that field of medicine that sought to heal the human mind. He was a brilliant student. When he was sixteen he wrote an essay on the teachings of Freud, and sent it to him. Freud wrote in response that he had been impressed by the work, and had taken the liberty of recommending it to a journal for publication. Politely, he hoped his young correspondent wouldn't object to his work being published.

He began practicing psychiatry after graduating Doctor of Medicine from the University of Vienna in 1930. Though he revered Freud, he came to conclusions about mental illness that differed significantly from the great man's theories. Freud believed mental illness was caused by conflicts between a person's unconscious drives and instincts and the customs and values of society. Frankl believed that a person's emotional well-being depended upon his or her ability to find meaning in their lives greater than the satisfaction of their instincts. The search for meaning in our lives, he believed, allows us to rise above not only our selfish desires, but also to transcend great misfortune and cruelty inflicted on us by others. His views were as informed by the study of philosophy as they were by clinical analyses. And it was Frankl's fate that they would soon be tested by the cruelest personal experience.

The Frankls were Jewish, and when German storm troopers marched into Austria in 1938, they, like all Austrian Jewish families, were subjected to violent persecution by the Nazis' monstrous bigotry. At first, Viktor was allowed to work in the only hospital in Vienna the Nazis permitted to treat Jews, and he spent much of his time trying to save his patients from Nazi policies that removed them to concentration camps or executed them because they were mentally ill. He also began work on a manuscript explaining his theories that he titled *The Doctor and the Soul.*

He had applied to immigrate to America to pursue his professional ambitions free of the racist restrictions that constrained his work in Vienna, and after a long wait he received a visa. But the visa was for him alone. He would have had to leave his family behind to suffer without him whatever cruelty the Nazis had in store for them. As he walked home from the U.S. consulate, he asked God for a sign to help him decide what to do. When he entered his house he found his father had retrieved a piece of marble from the rubble of a synagogue the Nazis had destroyed, on which was chiseled a letter from the Fifth Commandment, *Honor thy father and thy mother.*

Viktor let his visa expire. He decided to remain with his father, mother, and brother (his sister had immigrated to Australia) to face the coming Holocaust together.

He fell deeply in love with a pretty nurse, Mathilde "Tilly" Grosser, and they married in December 1941, the last Jewish couple in Vienna to be allowed to wed. Nine months later, the entire Frankl family, Viktor and Tilly, his father, mother, and brother, were arrested and deported to the concentration camp Theresienstadt, near Prague.

There were worse camps than Theresienstadt. It had no gas chambers and crematoriums, and the conditions weren't as wretched as they were in most other camps. Yet his father died there, in Viktor's arms, and the rest of the family would not long remain at the camp. They would all be transferred to the most infamous of the camps, Auschwitz. Viktor was the first to be ordered to leave. Tilly, because she worked in a nearby munitions factory, had received a two-year exemption from deportation to another camp. But against Viktor's wishes and without his knowledge, she volunteered to be transferred with her husband. Viktor's mother and brother would soon follow. His mother was murdered upon her arrival there. His brother would die later in a coal mine at one of the smaller camps at Auschwitz.

Upon their arrival, he and Tilly were quickly separated into camps for men and women. He would never see her again. Only when the war had ended would he learn she had died at another camp, Bergen-Belsen, shortly after British troops liberated it from the Nazis.

All the time he had been at Theresienstadt, he had managed to hold on to *The Doctor and the Soul,* which had been the most important work of his career. Right before they were transferred to Auschwitz, Tilly had sown it into the lining of Viktor's coat. As the guards were mustering prisoners into separate lines, Viktor's thoughts were focused on keeping possession of his manuscript. What he did not realize at the time was that he had been ordered into a line for prisoners who would be sent directly to the gas chambers. The infamous Dr. Mengele, known by his victims as the "Angel of Death," had pointed him to the line for execution. But Viktor, who didn't recognize anyone in the line, slipped without Mengele's notice into the other line, where he had seen a few of his friends standing.

Such a slender chance of fate separated the living from the doomed at Auschwitz. But those who were given even this small chance for survival would need something else, a hard thing to keep in such a place. They would need hope, and in their hope find a meaning for their suffering. Viktor would lose his manuscript only moments after he had unwittingly saved his own life when the guards ordered them to surrender all their possessions. A man to whom he tried to explain how important it was to him only laughed at him with contempt. In this new life, Viktor now knew that he could not rely on others for justice or for simple human compassion. He accepted that he was fortunate just to be alive. He did what was required of him. "I struck out my whole former life." And then he began to build a new one.

At night, on small scraps of paper, he worked on reconstructing his manuscript. And he thought of his wife, imagining the day when they would be reunited. He accepted the wisdom of the philosopher Nietzsche, who wrote that a man "who has a *why* to live for can bear with almost any *how*." For three years he suffered every cruelty, every degradation, every inhumanity imaginable. Yet he kept his hope, even as his body failed him. He contracted typhus, but survived. He was beaten, threatened, and many times narrowly escaped death. He was forced to do hard labor with only a crust of bread and a bowl of thin soup to sustain him. But he kept his hope, and his will to live. Those who abandoned hope, even those who were in better physical shape than others, perished. Their mistake, he observed, was that they expected something from life, and when life gave them nothing but cruelty they gave up on it. Survival depended on understanding and accepting what life expects of us, and, by so doing, finding a meaning for our life even in the worst human suffering, and taking comfort in the few treasures that remained to us: the unexpected kindness of another, the beauty of a sunrise, the glory of a blossoming tree in spring.

Though he lived at the whim of his tormentors, his fate was still his to determine. To live or die, that was largely beyond his control. But whether to remain a decent man or become, as other inmates had, an indecent man who acted with cruelty and injustice.

This was dignity's secret, which Viktor understood better than many. Dignity was not kept with pride or power. Everything could be denied you but your dignity. Dignity was a moral decision that no one could prevent you from making. Your whole life could be at the mercy of another. You could be reduced to an utterly powerless, degraded, dirty, pitiful physical presence, but one freedom, one choice remained to you, the decision to be good or bad. We are more than animals with needs and wants and appetites. And though our enemies might believe they have the power to reduce us to animals, they do not. That is something only we can do to ourselves. We have a conscience. No matter what. And how well we obey it, even in the worst conditions, will determine whether we live and die with dignity.

"We who lived in concentration camps can remember the men who walked through the huts comforting others, giving away their last piece of bread," said Frankl in *Man's Search for Meaning*. ". . . everything can be taken from a man but one thing: the last of human freedoms—to choose one's attitude in any given set of circumstances, to choose one's own way."

It is my good fortune to have had experiences in my life that allow me to attest with some authority to the truth of Viktor Frankl's understanding of dignity. I have not suffered as he suffered. But I lost my liberty for a time, and, in one instance, when I was forced to do something I thought dishonored me and my family, I feared I had lost everything of value to me, and that my life had lost its purpose. Then, by the example of other, better men, I realized that I still had a choice. I could choose to accept my misfortune and make it count for something. I could choose to acknowledge my weaknesses, and to try again to transcend them, and reclaim my dignity. Nothing in my life, before or after, has ever had more meaning, and I count myself privileged for the experience.

Viktor Frankl taught that meaning in life could be achieved in three ways: "by creating a work or doing a deed, by experiencing someone . . . and by the attitude we take toward unavoidable suffering." He worked at reconstructing his manuscript and counseling other prisoners. He experienced his wife's love by thinking of her hourly, and imagining their reunion. And he bore his suffering with dignity by acting decently, justly.

He would later describe an especially moving scene in the last year of his imprisonment. He and the other prisoners, crowded into the small hut they lived in, had been denied food that day because they would not identify to the guards a prisoner who had stolen a few potatoes. They were all feeling very low, and though the end of their suffering was not far off, many prisoners were on the verge of losing hope. That evening, the senior prisoner asked Viktor to speak to the other men, and encourage them not to give up.

I told my comrades . . . that human life, under any circumstances, never ceases to have a meaning, and that this infinite meaning of life includes suffering and dying, privation and death. . . .

And . . . I told them of a comrade who on his arrival in camp had tried to make a pact with Heaven that his suffering and death should save the human being he loved from a painful end. For this man, suffering and death were meaningful; his was a sacrifice of the deepest significance. He did not want to die for nothing. None of us wanted that. (from *Man's Search for Meaning*)

Eventually, the end came. American soldiers liberated his camp, and the surviving prisoners walked into freedom. But many were not yet free of suffering. For those, like Viktor, who would learn that their loved ones had perished in other camps, as Tilly had, they must suffer the end of the hope that had sustained them through their misery, the hope of reunion with their beloved. A few days after the Americans had arrived, Viktor took a walk in the country, where he chanced upon a man who was carrying a pendant. The pendant was identical to one he had purchased for Tilly on her first birthday after they had married, a golden globe with the oceans painted blue. It bore an inscription: *The whole world turns on love.* The man had acquired it from a nearby warehouse where the Nazis had stored valuables taken from concentration camp inmates. Viktor believed it had been taken from Tilly. "I bought the pendant from the man. It was dented slightly, but the whole world still turned on love." And so it did.

When he at last returned home to Vienna, he discovered Tilly had died, along with the rest of his family. It was a hard blow for a man who had already suffered so much. But he accepted it, and lived. He lived a hopeful, purposeful life with dignity.

He was given a position at a hospital where he returned to the practice of psychiatry, more certain now in his convictions than before his terrible crucible. He counseled his patients, as he had once counseled his fellow prisoners, that anything could be borne with dignity if a person had hope and meaning. Happiness, he said, cannot be pursued. Happiness ensues from a meaningful life, from making the right moral decisions, from loving someone.

He lived to love another, Elly, with whom he had a daughter and remained devotedly married for fifty years. He finished and published his manuscript, and would write twenty-two other books. In one of them, *Man's Search for Meaning,* he interprets his and others' experiences in the camps through the principles of his philosophy and therapeutic theories. He wrote it in nine days. It has sold ten million copies, and is considered by many to be one of the most important books of our time. He climbed mountains, and at sixty-seven learned to fly. He lived well into his nineties. He never retired.

PART TWO

Purpose

There is a tide in the affairs of men.
Which, taken at the flood, leads on to fortune;
Omitted, all the voyage of their life
Is bound in shallows and in miseries.

—JULIUS CAESAR

IDEALISM

Sojourner Truth

The slave who helped teach America the meaning of freedom

IN THAT THRILLING YEAR WHEN THE CITIZENS OF THE SOVIET UNION AND its Eastern European empire approached the dawn of their liberation, I felt privileged to watch, as millions of others did, so many inspiring scenes of people claiming for themselves the rights Americans believe are God-given. It inspired in me, as I'm sure it did in others, a feeling very close to patriotism. For in America, our patriotism is or should be an allegiance not just to a physical place or people but to the very same ideals that these long-oppressed millions were now demanding for themselves. To see our own idealism in action in foreign places where cynics had argued it would never thrive reaffirmed the convictions of our own Founding Fathers, convictions that we, in our own nation's often troubled history, still struggle to achieve in full. One scene in particular moved me.

In 1989, a Czech student stood before a million of his countrymen, in Prague's St. Wenceslas Square, while a hundred thousand Soviet troops still occupied his country, and declared a new day for the people of Eastern Europe. But he began the new day with borrowed words as he read: "We hold these truths to be self-evident; that all men are created equal and endowed by their Creator with certain unalienable rights; that among these are life, liberty and the pursuit of happiness."

All Americans should have felt then a kinship with the courageous men and women—the students, the workers, the professionals, the clergy, the artists, the intellectuals—who with their words and deeds and sacrifices tore down the Berlin Wall, restored self-determination to their captive nations, and, in Russia itself, brought an end to the tyranny that had misruled that vast nation for most of the twentieth century. It was an extraordinary time to be alive, and to feel so much a part of one of history's great turning points.

I had in the years before the final collapse of the Soviet Union come to admire greatly some of the more celebrated heroes of that struggle: the Czech playwright and future president, Václav Havel, an artist who never wavered in his demands for freedom and justice, although he suffered long years of imprisonment for his convictions; Lech Wałesa, the unemployed Polish electrician who climbed over the wall of a Gdańsk shipyard and took charge of an independent labor movement that endured martial law and wholesale arrests to liberate the Polish people; Andrei Sakharov, the brilliant Soviet nuclear physicist who gave up the privileges of a famous son of the Soviet state for exile and the gulag, because his conscience demanded his opposition to the government that had once favored him; Natan Sharansky, a man who truly believes in the justice and power of democracy, and who suffered greatly for the right of Soviet Jews to emigrate.

These brave souls are among the greatest heroes of the twentieth century. They are revered as some of the most determined, imaginative, and eloquent of freedom's champions. But their eventual triumph was not theirs alone, as they would be the first to acknowledge, but was achieved by the sacrifices and courage of thousands. Many of those thousands lacked the education and opportunities of their movement's leaders. Many could not claim a commanding presence or the eloquence of a Havel or the borrowed words uttered by that Czech student. But they were as indispensable to the triumph of liberty as were the greatest orators who ever silenced a crowd in Rome or Philadelphia or Paris.

In our country we, too, revere the memory of our Founding Fathers, as well we should. But America's struggle for freedom was not their achievement alone. Many thousands deserve that tribute, and our gratitude for struggling to extend the promises of freedom to all Americans for many years beyond the lives of our founders.

In 1850, an aged former slave dictated her memoirs to a young white woman, Olive Gilbert, an abolitionist. *The Narrative of Sojourner Truth: A Northern Slave,* from which much of what follows is taken, describes the life of one American who would make, in her own unique way, as stirring a claim to liberty and justice as ever flowed from the pen of Thomas Jefferson.

Isabella Baumfree was born in 1797, not long after the birth of her nation, to the slaves James and Betsy Baumfree in Ulster County, New York. Slavery had been abolished in most of the Northern states but still persisted in New Jersey and New York. It might have disappeared from the South but for Eli Whitney's invention of the cotton gin, which made the institution of slavery more lucrative in the era when cotton picked by slaves was king.

James and Betsy, and now the infant Isabella, were the property of Colonel Ardinburgh, a Dutch American landowner. He died not long after Isabella was born. His son Charles inherited his father's estate, including the slaves, and Isabella remembered her parents describing him as a comparatively kind master. She couldn't recall how many brothers and sisters she had, perhaps as many as twelve. She was the second youngest, and all but one of her siblings, her younger brother Peter, had been sold to other slaveholders by Colonel Ardinburgh before she was born.

Among the many comforting myths that slave owners who thought themselves to be kind masters used to excuse the inherent cruelty of keeping other human beings in bondage was that their slaves, being less than fully human, did not share the same strong bonds of devotion to their offspring that white people felt for their children. Slave owners had to deny what their own eyes witnessed when slave families were separated, or else begin to doubt their own humanity.

When Charles Ardinburgh built a new house, the estate's slaves were given quarters in the cellar, all of them crowded together in the dark and dank room. There Isabella would eat and sleep until the age of nine, when she was torn from her family and sold along with some sheep to a new master, who lived not far from the Ardinburghs, a master no slave could consider kind. "Now the war begun," Isabella remembered, when she passed into the possession of John Nealy.

She had until then only spoken Dutch, which Nealy could speak a little, and his wife not at all. The young slave's inability to understand the commands of her English-speaking master and mistress caused her a great deal of trouble. Rather than accept that the child's failure to obey was not intentional, they would become angry with her, and often whip her. Each time she failed to respond correctly to a shouted order, they became more enraged, and exacted harsher punishment. Finally, one Sunday morning, Nealy took Isabella to the barn, tied her hands together, took rods that he had heated in a fire, and beat her unmercifully, "till the flesh was deeply lacerated, and the blood streamed from her wounds, and the scars remain to the present day." All this because a little girl couldn't speak English.

She could not read or write in any language. But her mother had, in their few years together, impressed her daughter with the concept of a loving God, and urged her to appeal to a Father who lived in the sky when her troubles became too much to bear. Isabella appealed to Him now, telling Him her troubles, begging his protection, talking aloud, for she didn't know that God heard silent prayers or knew our thoughts, and asking Him if He thought this was any way to treat a human being.

She prayed for her father to come to see her. Her prayer was answered not long after when James Baumfree got leave from his master to visit his little daughter. When she saw him, she told him how cruelly the Nealys treated her, and begged him to find her a kinder master. He managed to find her one, possibly through the intervention of one of the Ardinburghs, though no one knows for sure how he did it. But soon enough Isabella was sold to a fisherman named Scriver, who also ran a tavern. The Scrivers, and their tavern's clients, were a rough class of people, but they treated Isabella much better than had the Nealys and she was happier there. A year later, when Isabella was thirteen, the Scrivers sold her to John Dumont for less than they had paid for her, and she remained the Dumonts' property for seventeen years.

John Dumont was also a kinder master than John Nealy. For an illiterate young slave who knew no other life, a master who "whipped me soundly, but never cruelly" appeared to be a benevolent man. He was not exceptionally cruel. He offered moral instruction to his slaves, encouraging them not to lie or steal, although it's hard today not to marvel at the hypocrisy of a man who thought himself virtuous enough to see to the character education of people he held in bondage. His wife wasn't a particularly kind mistress, and would treat Isabella with less patience and civility than Dumont did. Isabella recalled several instances when he protected her from his wife's wrath. Isabella responded to Dumont's relative kindness by working hard for him, and striving to impress him with her honesty and industry. By her own account, at this point in her life she regarded the institution of slavery as part of the natural order of life. Good fortune to her was a kind master.

As she grew older she attracted the attention of a slave, Robert, from a nearby estate who, it seems, wished to marry Isabella. Robert's master did not want his slaves to marry slaves from other estates. He wanted the offspring of his slaves to remain his property. So he ordered Robert not to see Isabella again. But when Isabella became ill, Robert defied his master and left to visit her. When his master discovered him missing, he and his son went to the Dumonts to find him. Once there, in front of Isabella, they viciously thrashed him with their canes until John Dumont intervened to stop them. Isabella remembered her gratitude to her master for finally stopping the beating, and for following the brutal men home to make sure they did no more harm to Robert.

Robert never paid another visit to Isabella, and a few years later she was married to an older slave, Thomas, with whom she had five children. She continued her tireless efforts to retain the goodwill of her master, although she must have greatly feared that the day would come when her children would be taken from her and sold off as she had been taken from her loving parents. Nevertheless, she remained an honest, hardworking slave, who would let her own children go hungry rather than steal food from the Dumonts. Dumont, in kind, showed a greater sympathy for her children and her need to tend to them than his less patient wife did.

For most of her time with the Dumonts, Isabella seemed as satisfied with her lot as it was possible for a slave to feel. But eventually, fearing the separation of her family that was the slave's frequent misfortune, she came to desire her freedom. The New York legislature promised the emancipation of slaves in that state in 1828. Dumont promised to let Isabella go and make her own way in the world a year earlier if she agreed to work hard and honestly until then. She kept her end of the bargain, but when the agreed date for her emancipation arrived, Dumont broke his vow. Isabella had grown into a determined and resourceful woman, and she would not accept her owner's bad faith. One morning, before dawn, she simply ran off, not knowing where to go, or how she might recover her children. She had talked it over with God and it seemed the right and necessary thing to do.

By some stroke of good fortune she came upon the home of a kindly Dutch family, the Van Wageners, who hated slavery. They took her in, gave her a home, and when John Dumont arrived one day to take her back, Mr. Van Wagener arranged to pay him twenty dollars to rent Isabella for the year remaining before the law would free her. The Van Wageners paid her for her labor, and tried to provide her a rudimentary education to prepare for life as a free woman, although she would never learn to read or write.

Her life, as it turned out, was not yet free of sorrow. The Dumonts sold one of her children, her son Peter, to a Dr. Gedney, who took him to New York City. Not much later, Gedney sold the boy to his brother, who in turn sold him to his brother-in-law, a terribly cruel Alabama plantation owner. The law forbade the interstate sale of slaves at that time, but the Gedneys didn't care about legal formalities. They didn't bargain on how determined the boy's mother would be.

When Isabella discovered what had happened, she resolved to get her son back, no matter how daunting a task that would prove. She had the law on her side, of course, but those who enforced the laws were seldom disposed to see them work on behalf of a black woman. At the Van Wageners' suggestion, she sought the advice of antislavery Quakers, who helped her sue the Gedneys for illegally selling her son. After many months, she succeeded in getting him back. She was the first known black woman in America to win a legal suit against a white man. Sadly, when her son was brought before her in the presence of the judge, he would not acknowledge Isabella as his mother. He had been badly beaten by the cruel plantation owner, who had ordered him to deny her. But the judge determined that the boy was her son, and returned custody of him to Isabella.

She returned to the Van Wageners with Peter and her youngest daughter (her other children remained with their father). She stayed there until she had a vision that changed her life forever. She was frightened by visible signs of an angry God, who might strike her dead for failing to keep her promises to live a devout life after He had helped her win her freedom and recover her son. Then, suddenly, she observed the presence of another heavenly figure. He revealed Himself to her as Jesus Christ, and promised to intercede with the Father on her behalf. Not long after this revelation, she packed up her children, thanked and bid good-bye to the Van Wageners, and left for New York City.

There, she worked as a servant, making a meager living, and spent her free time seeking spiritual growth through various religious associations. She undertook to learn the Bible, but since she couldn't read, she would ask others to read passages to her. She would often ask that a passage be reread a second and third time so she could better understand its meaning, and she became annoyed when adults who read to her, rather than simply repeating the passage as she had requested, offered their own explanations to her about its meaning. She wanted to interpret its meaning for herself. So, she decided in future to ask children to read to her because they would do as she asked without offering their own opinions.

In 1843, at the age of forty-six, her children now grown and on their own, Isabella had another revelation. She was inspired to become an itinerant evangelist, wandering the country preaching the good news of Christ's salvation. God told her, she claimed, to take a new name, Sojourner (or traveler) Truth. And so, Sojourner Truth was born, and left New York to begin her wandering ministry.

She was an unusually tall woman for that time, nearly six feet, and towered over most women and men. She was a compelling presence, but not a handsome one. She looked many years older than her age, which is certainly understandable considering the harshness of her life. She had a deep bass voice that caused some people to suspect she was a man. But she used her voice and her newly acquired knowledge of scripture to become a powerful speaker, and a compelling hymn singer. She traveled the eastern United States preaching at religious revivals, on each occasion attracting more and more listeners, who were held spellbound by this strange old black woman who spoke coarsely but passionately and provocatively, and sang with such force and beauty that her audiences wouldn't let her leave.

She eventually came to the attention of leading abolitionists, and joined the Northampton

Association, an antislavery community in Massachusetts, where she gained the respect of such celebrated members as Frederick Douglass and William Lloyd Garrison. It was Garrison who persuaded her to dictate her memoirs, and their publication won her a national audience. Soon, she was traveling throughout the East and Midwest, preaching the gospel and the abolition of slavery. She also began an association with the women's suffrage movement, seeing in both slavery and the unequal status of women an injustice that her faith in Jesus Christ demanded she oppose.

So it was that Sojourner Truth was invited to attend a women's rights convention in Akron, Ohio, in 1851, where she would offer one of the simplest but most stirring testaments to the common humanity of all God's children, the faith that lies at the heart of American ideals of liberty and equal justice for all.

The convention was a raucous affair. Many men in the audience, including a good number of clergy, were not sympathetic to the cause of women's suffrage. Accounts record that some of them didn't support the abolition of slavery either. One female speaker after another was subjected to taunts and jeers from the audience, and lectures from some of the haughtier ministers of God, who dismissed the movement as an affront to the divinely inspired order of relations between the sexes.

One man accused the suffragists of ignoring that Eve had induced Adam to eat the forbidden fruit, introducing original sin into the world. Another suggested that women's inferior intelligence accounted for the necessary differences in the status of men and women. Yet another dismissed women as weaker beings in need of men's protection and incapable of exercising the responsibilities of freedom.

Associates of the convention's president, Mrs. Frances Gage, who had invited Sojourner, begged her not to permit the former slave to speak, fearing that mixing the causes of abolition and women's suffrage would further enflame their opponents. But Mrs. Gage dismissed their concerns, confident in Sojourner's ability to overcome discord in the hall and quiet the angriest critic with her powerful testimony.

For most of the convention, Sojourner had sat quietly, betraying little reaction to the contentious debate or the racial slurs that some of the cruder hecklers directed at her. On the second day of the convention, she slowly rose to make her way to the podium. Dressed in the Quaker style in simple black clothes and white bonnet, stretched to her full height, her "head erect, and eyes piercing the upper air like one in a dream," she drew the attention of every person in the hall. While jeers and shouts of "nigger" echoed in the hall, she began in her deep, forceful voice to subdue the clamor.

"Well, well, children, what is this racket. There must be something out of kilter. I think between the Negroes in the South and the women in the North—all talking about rights—the white men will be in a fix pretty soon. But what's all this talking about?"

Addressing one of the offended ministers, she declared, "That man over there says women need to be helped into carriages, and lifted over ditches, and to have the best place everywhere. Nobody helps me to any best place. And ain't I a woman?

"Look at me. Look at my arm," she commanded as she rolled up her sleeve to expose the sinews of her arm muscled by decades of hard toil. "I have plowed, planted and I have gathered into barns. And no man could head me. And ain't I a woman?

"I could work as much, and eat as much as a man—when I could get it—and bear the lash as well. And ain't I a woman?

"I have borne children and seen most of them sold into slavery, and when I cried out with a mother's grief, none but Jesus heard me. And ain't I a woman?"

By the time Sojourner Truth finished, to wild cheers and applause, she had shamed into silence the most arrogant and outspoken critics in the audience.

IN SEVERAL SPEECHES I gave at the end of the Soviet Union and the Cold War, I often quoted a passage I much admired from the address the great American writer William Faulkner gave when he accepted the Nobel Prize for Literature. "I decline to accept the end of man," he declared. "I believe that man will not merely endure: he will prevail. He is immortal, not because he alone among creatures has an inexhaustible voice, but because he has a soul, a spirit capable of compassion and sacrifice and endurance."

Faulkner, a Southerner whose wisdom about the awful legacy of slavery gave his work its powerful majesty, could have had no greater proof of his prophecy's accuracy than the life of Sojourner Truth. And the eloquence of his prose, like the eloquence that attires the idealism of our Declaration of Independence, gives no more powerful expression to our ideals than her four repeated words—"ain't I a woman." Hers was the inexhaustible voice and the unvanquished spirit of an illiterate former slave who taught us how to be Americans.

RIGHTEOUSNESS

Romeo Dallaire

*When the rest of the world looked away, he stayed behind
in a manmade evil for the sake of duty and justice.*

I T WAS MY FAULT, TOO. LIKE MOST OF MY COLLEAGUES IN CONGRESS, LIKE the president of the United States, like most Americans, and, tragically, like most of the world, I thought the problems of one small African country were not my responsibility. I had no objection if something could be done to prevent bloodshed without risking the lives of my countrymen. Many officials in the countries of what we proudly identify as the civilized world felt the same way. Let the diplomats do what diplomats do, and try to talk these remote and very foreign people into not butchering one another. But let's not make the mistake of sending our soldiers into another troubled country's civil war where we couldn't tell who was fighting who and why.

And, thus, not so long ago, in a faraway place that most Americans had never heard of, in the short span of a hundred days, 800,000 Rwandans of the Tutsi tribe were murdered by their fellow Rwandans of the Hutu tribe, while the civilized world watched and did nothing.

The United States and the rest of the world weren't indifferent to their suffering, of course. We had, after all, agreed to send 2,500 lightly armed, poorly supplied United Nations peacekeeping soldiers to Rwanda after the two tribes had agreed to share power in 1993. But in April 1994, Hutus accused Tutsi rebels of murdering the Hutu president, and the Hutu government, army, and militia began the mass slaughter of the Tutsi minority that had been planned for months, first in the capital, Kigali, and then throughout the countryside.

In the opening hours of the genocide, Hutu soldiers killed ten Belgian peacekeepers who were protecting Rwandan prime minister Madame Agathe Uwilingiyimana, a Tutsi. She was killed with them. Within a few days, troops from several European countries arrived in Rwanda, not to stop the murders, but to evacuate Europeans who were working there. The United States evacuated its personnel as well. The government of Belgium ordered the withdrawal of the rest of its almost five hundred soldiers in Rwanda, the largest, best-trained and -equipped unit in the UN peacekeeping force. As they departed, the Belgian soldiers threw their blue UN berets on the tarmac of the Kigali airport, indicating their disgust with their government and the futility of their mission. The United Nations, at the behest of the United States government, soon ordered the withdrawal of all but a few hundred of the remaining peacekeepers. Rwanda was abandoned.

Left behind with the small and utterly overwhelmed, mostly African peacekeeping force was the man who refused to leave, their commander, a French Canadian major general, Romeo Dallaire.

Romeo Dallaire still looks like a Hollywood version of a dashing military officer, even today, eleven years after the genocide, grief-stricken, heartsick, discharged from the Canadian Army, and still suffering from the trauma of having witnessed one of the greatest crimes against humanity in the twentieth century. He bears himself like a model officer, his shoulders back, his head erect, as if in defiance of the terrible memory that assails him. His manner, his broad shoulders, wide chest, square jaw, and bristling mustache are a portrait of military elegance, and the piercing blue eyes that reflect his quiet anguish give him dignity denied to the subject of Gilbert and Sullivan's comic opera mocking the manners of the "very model of a modern major general."

He had always wanted to be a soldier. He loved the army. But soldiers are trained to fight, and Canada fought its last war many years before he put on the uniform. So Romeo Dallaire became a peacekeeper, assigned by the Canadian Army to UN peacekeeping missions in Cambodia and Bosnia. He jumped at the chance to command the mission in Rwanda, the biggest opportunity of his career, never imagining that a professional opportunity would become, as he described it, an encounter with the devil. By his own reckoning he failed his mission, and he is ashamed.

In those savage one hundred days, amid the carnage and terror, the complete hopelessness, the failure of mankind's conscience, the apathy and deceitfulness of the governments of the civilized world, there remained in Rwanda men and women of courage and decency. They were the few righteous among the wicked, in a time of terrible but preventable suffering and inexcusable moral failure. Romeo Dallaire was one of them. He deserves no share of the blame that rightfully belongs to those of us who could have helped him, and the Rwandans he so desperately wished to save, and did not.

Before the killings began, an informant in the Hutu government told Dallaire that genocide was imminent, that Hutu militia units could kill a thousand Tutsi every twenty minutes. He told Dallaire where the Hutus had hidden weapons. Dallaire faxed the information to his superiors at the United Nations in New York, and asked for permission to raid the weapons caches. He ended his message with an appeal: "Where there's a will, there's a way. Let's go." The UN official to whom he communicated his concerns and plans dismissed the information, and ordered Dallaire not to act on it, warning him not to intervene militarily in a civil war, not to let another Somalia happen. Dallaire was authorized to use force only to defend his own troops. He was not there to prevent Rwandans from killing Rwandans. In exchange for the alarming information he provided, Dallaire's informant had asked that his wife and children be protected. The UN official who ignored the warning instructed Dallaire to let the Hutu president know there was an informant in his government.

After the genocide began, Dallaire begged the UN for more troops, arguing that he could put an end to the killings with just five thousand men. He could gather the Tutsis into Rwandan soccer stadiums and protect them there with just a small force. His request was denied, and his aide remembers the arrogance of UN officials who treated the general as an inexperienced and naive do-gooder, telling him to "shut up. You're a soldier. Let the experts handle this."

His request for more troops was refused. Worse, the United States government, worried that attacks on UN peacekeepers would compel us to intervene militarily, urged the other countries on the UN Security Council to withdraw all peacekeepers from Rwanda. They were only targets, we thought, and withdrawing them from harm's way would remove the only potential cause that might compel the United States to act. At our urging, Dallaire's forces were reduced to a pitifully small number; Europe and the United States evacuated their people from Rwanda. It was shameful enough that we wouldn't help, but that we actually discouraged others from helping was and always will be unforgivable.

This was exactly what the murderers had hoped would happen, that the world would simply look the other way while they went about the business of mass killing. And they responded to our moral blindness by enthusiastically escalating the slaughter. Romeo Dallaire would not look the other way. He would not go home. He was left to witness the result of our indifference. But he did more than witness it. His listened to his conscience, and did all that he could to obey it. He and the few soldiers who remained under his command saved as many as they could.

In 1948 the United States along with most of the other countries of the world signed an international treaty preventing genocide. Genocide is the attempt to destroy an entire ethnic population. That is what Nazi Germany had committed when it murdered six million Jews. And that is what the Hutus were attempting to do to the Tutsis in Rwanda. The Genocide Convention, as it was called, required the United States and the other signatories to intervene in any place where one ethnic group was trying to eliminate another. Dallaire, the Tutsis, the press, and many concerned observers called the murders by their name—genocide. The U.S. government, our allies, and the United Nations went to extraordinary and ridiculous lengths to avoid using the term, aware that once genocide was acknowledged, they would have to act. To most of America's elected leaders, Democrats and Republicans, myself included, Rwanda was just another Third World civil war in which we couldn't tell the good guys from the bad guys. We should have listened to Romeo Dallaire. God knows he was trying to be heard.

Some credit him with saving as many as 25,000 Rwandans, a large number, to be sure, but tragically few when compared with the scale of the killing. Eight hundred thousand dead is the most conservative estimate. Many people believe the total exceeded one million. But General Dallaire persisted in believing that something could be done. He would use his troops to protect as many Tutsis as he could. He would leave a few men to guard shelters here and there that contained as few as a couple dozen Tutsis and as many as a thousand, while thousands of gun- and machete-carrying Hutus waited for the opportunity to strike. Day after day, long night after long night, for over three months, more men, women, and children were added to the rolls of the victims by their hate-crazed persecutors. Romeo Dallaire soldiered on, saving those he could and agonizing over those he couldn't, all the while begging the UN, and the world, to send more troops, to do something, anything, to help.

There were other brave people in Rwanda who did what they could to save lives. Paul Rusesabagina, the manager of the Hotel Mille Collines in Kigali, a Hutu married to a Tutsi, and the hero of the recent, deservedly acclaimed motion picture *Hotel Rwanda,* courageously sheltered as many as a thousand Tutsis in his hotel, risking again and again his own life, as he kept the killers from turning the Mille Collines into another Rwandan slaughterhouse. Thousands of Hutus prowled the neighborhood surrounding the hotel. A few of Dallaire's peacekeepers stood, unarmed, in front of the hotel, risking their lives by pretending to protect its inhabitants.

It was too much a burden for any one man, no matter how righteous he was, to accept without experiencing soul-crushing anguish over the horrors he could not prevent. Dallaire is the first to claim a share of the blame for what happened in Rwanda, although he is the least to deserve it. In his telling, his mission was to keep peace; peace was destroyed by unimaginable violence, and many thousands died. He failed. He tried to convince his superiors to send him more men. He failed. He tried to get the United States and other powerful countries to listen to their consciences and help. He failed. He tried to persuade the world to stop genocide. He failed. And while many, many people who had a responsibility to stop the killings looked the other way and never had a moment of doubt or a night of troubled sleep, Romeo Dallaire took his failures very, very seriously. A righteous person, no matter how blameless, will always take humanity's failures personally.

In the last weeks of the genocide, he often rode through the streets of Kigali unarmed and exposed. He thought death might give him an honorable exit from the failures that he accepted as his own. And his sleep has been troubled for many nights since, as he hears, sees, and smells in his dreams the sad, avoidable devastation, the unspeakable inhumanity it was his lonely responsibility to witness, and his brave determination to help prevent.

The United States and its allies finally, after most of the killing was done, decided to intervene in Rwanda. But the genocide ended only because Tutsi rebels, far smaller in number than the Hutu army and militia, fought and defeated the killers, and took control of most of Rwanda. The Hutus who had instigated the reign of terror weren't even particularly brave or capable soldiers. They had the skill and courage to destroy only the unarmed innocent. When the civilized world finally sent soldiers to Rwanda, the Hutus responsible for the killing were already on the run, making a final mockery of our pride and the sense of moral responsibility we claim, often deservedly, as our country's most important virtue. The genocide was over, stopped by the Tutsi rebels; those Hutus with a conscience; courageous people from other countries, like those who worked for the Red Cross in Rwanda; a few dedicated journalists; five hundred peacekeepers; and their fine and noble commander, Romeo Dallaire. The rest of us had done nothing.

The genocide was over. The world had awakened. And Romeo Dallaire went home.

He had a hard time of it. He could not forget what he had been powerless to stop. He was made to retire from his beloved army because he would not forget how the world had failed Rwanda. He testified in the trials of those Hutus who were brought to justice. In one trial, he described in honest but certainly not exaggerated terms how wrong those countries had been to abandon Rwanda when the killings began, leaving him and his small force to remain as our only response to genocide. When a defense attorney asked him if he regretted it, he replied, "You cannot even imagine." He couldn't sleep. He took medication for the psychological injuries he had suffered. He drank too much. One night, many years after he had come home, he was found unconscious on a park bench in Hull, Quebec.

He wrote a book, and made a return trip to Rwanda, the place where he feels he belongs. He is doing much better now than he did in those first years back from the killing fields. And the world now recognizes how badly we failed in Rwanda, and again, the governments of the civilized world have solemnly promised never to permit genocide to occur, anywhere, even in Africa. Time will tell if we have the conscience to be true to our pledge. For now, whatever shame we feel over our indifference to a small, poor African country's terrible suffering is acknowledged but manageable. We are a little ashamed, but I'm not sure we've lost a lot of sleep about it. In a better world, of course, we would have the nightmares, and Romeo Dallaire would sleep the sleep of the righteous, and rest comfortably through the night.

CITIZENSHIP

Pat Tillman

*He gave away the fortune and fame of a celebrity to serve his country
in its time of need and leave us with a lesson of real heroism.*

H E WAS QUITE A MAN, TOUGH, HONEST, OVERACHIEVING, INTENSE, colorful, daring. A California kid who wore his blond hair long when short hair was in fashion and short when long hair was in fashion, and dressed routinely in shorts, T-shirt, and flip-flops. He came from a good family, who were as close as a family could be. His parents were strict, but fun and encouraging. He was raised to be brave, work hard, not to brag but to believe in himself. He married his high school sweetheart. He is remembered as the first one to help a friend in trouble, to stand up to a bully, to try to do the right thing. He thought for himself, and had, without doubt, the courage of his convictions.

He had played for the football team many of its fans argued was the best they had ever seen, San Jose's Leland High School Chargers. At the start of the second half of a game that had become a Leland rout, the Chargers' coach benched his starters and sent his subs in to finish off their overmatched opponents. Pat snuck back onto the field and returned a kickoff for a touchdown. That's one of the stories you always heard when someone was describing the larger-than-life legend that Pat Tillman has become.

I'm a sports nut, and I was a Pat Tillman fan when he played for the Arizona State Sun Devils and the Arizona Cardinals. But I never met him. I wish I had. I wish I had known him all his life.

No one in Arizona expected much from him. At two hundred pounds, and under six feet, he was thought to be too small to play linebacker. He was offered Arizona State's last football scholarship in 1994, and the coach, although he was impressed by the young man's confidence and determination, never thought he would start a game, probably wouldn't even play at all unless the Sun Devils were ahead in a rout. He suggested to Pat that he red-shirt his freshman year. He thought that Pat should take the extra year to develop physically into a player who might have a shot at winning some playing time. Pat told him to forget it. He wasn't going to stay in college for five years, even if he sat on the bench his entire college career. He had other plans, and he was in a hurry. He completed the courses required for graduation in three and a half years, with a grade point average just a little short of perfect, and, to everyone's astonishment except his, was named the Pac-10 Conference Defensive Player of the Year. Thanks in large part to Pat Tillman's tough, smart, aggressive play, Arizona State had an 11–1 season his senior year and came within a whisker of being the national champions.

Still, everyone knew he was too small and too slow to play professional football. Everyone except Pat, and those who knew him well. He was chosen by the Arizona Cardinals in the seventh round of the 1998 NFL draft, the 226th player picked. Everyone thought he would sit on the bench, have some fun in the league as a kid who had no business in professional sports but would get to bask in the reflected glory and high living of marquee athletes for a couple of years, and would then, with his marketing degree from Arizona State, go do something else for a living. Two years later, as a strong safety for the Cardinals, hard-hitting Pat Tillman broke the team record for tackles, 224, each one of them bone-rattling. The next year, the Super Bowl champions, the St. Louis Rams, offered Pat a nine-million-dollar contract. He turned them down. The Cardinals, who had given him a chance when others wouldn't, could afford to pay him less than half that generous sum. But they had his loyalty. And loyalty is something Pat Tillman took very seriously.

His agent, Frank Bauer, didn't have many clients whose first priority was something other than making the biggest salary he could negotiate for them. But that was Pat Tillman, a different kind of man altogether from your typical professional athlete. He always had other priorities. He never charged a kid for his autograph. He never slowed down or tried to avoid fatigue or injury by giving less than a 100 percent effort on the field or in the rest of his life. He didn't hog the spotlight, but he wasn't shy. He just didn't believe he needed publicity to be a better football player or to feel better about himself. He loved challenges, and when he had accomplished something unexpected, he wanted a bigger challenge. He wanted to be the best football player he could, but much more important to him was becoming the best man he could.

He expressed his opinions on just about any subject, with the self-assuredness that marked him as an overachieving athlete. But he was smart enough, wise enough to keep an open mind, and let new experiences teach him, and information or a better argument persuade him. Honesty, like loyalty, was important to him.

In his senior year in high school, he got into trouble. When a friend of his was beaten up outside a local pizza parlor, Pat jumped in and beat the other kid to a pulp. He was arrested and sentenced to thirty days at a work farm for juvenile offenders. He thought his dreams of playing college football were over. But they weren't. Because he was a juvenile, the incident was erased from his record. No one outside his family and Leland High School need ever have found out about it. But he didn't hide it from anyone. He regretted the mistake. "I learned more from that one bad decision than all the good decisions I've ever made," he said. "It made me realize that stuff you do has repercussions. You can lose everything."

That's a good lesson to learn, and the earlier you learn it the better. But he didn't lose everything. He lost thirty days, and gained a little wisdom in exchange. When a reporter who knew nothing of the incident asked him if he had ever been arrested, he admitted that he had, and then, not because he had to, but because he felt he should, he described the offense and its repercussions in full.

I suppose September 11, 2001, is the day that young Americans will remember as I remember Pearl Harbor, a dividing line between the past and the present, unforgettable, and the day my father left for war to return years later a different man. Pat Tillman took the attacks on our country personally. Every American should have. He had been loyal to his football team, an honorable thing, but not the most important thing in someone's life. He knew Americans had much more important allegiances that we must live up to, and he intended to live up to his. He told a reporter the day after the attacks that he had relatives who had fought in America's previous wars, and he worried that, "I really haven't done a damn thing as far as laying myself on the line like that. . . . I have a lot of respect for those who have and what the flag stands for."

Our country's security doesn't depend on the heroism of every citizen. Nor does our individual happiness depend upon proving ourselves heroic. But we all have to be worthy of the sacrifices made on our behalf. We have to love our freedom, not just for the ease or material benefits it provides, not just for the autonomy it guarantees us, but for the goodness it makes possible. We have to love it so much we won't let it be constrained by fear or selfishness. We have to love it as much, even if not as heroically, as Pat Tillman loved it.

A few months after September 11, Pat Tillman told his agent he should concentrate on negotiating new contracts for his other clients, because he might have different plans. He married Marie Ugenti, the only girl he had ever loved, and spent a two-week honeymoon in Bora-Bora. I once saw a picture of them taken at their wedding reception. Pat was laying his head on his beautiful wife's lap, as happy as any man can be. It almost hurt to look at it. So young, so beautiful, so happy, at the beginning of what would surely have been a long and happy marriage. Not many people will ever have all the blessings Pat Tillman enjoyed on that fine May day when he married his one true love. Wealthy, famous, loved, and happy. It was a lot to put at risk. But he did risk it, all of it, because he knew he had obligations that could not be ignored without feeling ashamed of himself.

He and his brother, Kevin, a minor league baseball player who played his sport with as much courage and fierce determination as Pat played football, had been talking about their responsibilities to their country after we had been attacked. They decided that they should enlist in the military, and help defend the rest of us from the bin Ladens of the world. They decided they would become Army Rangers, an elite, special force reserved for some of the toughest, hardest combat assignments.

Pat walked into his coach's office just after he returned from his honeymoon, and told him that he was going to leave football, and his $3.9 million salary, and join the army. His coach, knowing that his star defensive player was an exceptional man, wasn't particularly surprised by the decision. He was proud of him, and thankful for the privilege of having coached the best man he had ever met in football. Then Pat and Kevin drove to Denver, Colorado, where they hoped no one would notice them as they walked into a recruiter's office, and enlisted in the United States Army.

They intentionally refused to talk about their decision. They shunned all publicity. They refused all requests for interviews. They didn't believe their decision was any more patriotic than the decisions of the less famous, less fortunate Americans who loved our country enough to volunteer to defend us in a time of peril. They didn't think they were better than any other soldier. And they were right. They were special, but no more special than the Americans they served with. But their modesty, as much as their sacrifice, taught us the first lesson of patriotism. Patriotism is a lot more than flag waving or singing the anthem at ball games. Patriotism is the recognition that each of us is just one small part of a cause that is greater than ourselves, one small part, but a part we are honor bound to play. America is dedicated to the proposition that all men are created equal, and have an equal right to freedom and justice. That is our cause: to prove the truth of that proposition. And that cause is far more important than the ambitions and desires of any individual. To understand that truth is to be a true citizen of a great republic, a true citizen like Pat and Kevin Tillman.

Pat and Kevin were as close as brothers could be, "tighter than you could ever possibly know," a family friend observed. They cared about the same things, each other, their family, their honor, their country, and their responsibilities. They cared about being good men. So they left for Ft. Benning, Georgia, and the hard training of Army Rangers, stood out in their new profession as they had stood out in every other endeavor they had undertaken, and then they went to war.

They served in the same platoon, first in Iraq, where they distinguished themselves, and then in Afghanistan, where they joined the hunt for Osama bin Laden. In between tours they came home to rest and train.

Their Ranger battalion's home base was Ft. Lewis in Washington State. The Cardinals' coach, Dave McGinnis, got in touch with Pat and asked him to come see the team when they played the Seattle Seahawks shortly before the Tillmans would leave for Afghanistan. Pat agreed, but insisted that he greet his teammates just as a friend, and not as somebody special who had come to lecture them on their duty to God and country. Pat walked into the locker room that Sunday and the Cardinals crowded around him, showing him their respect and thanking him. The undersize strong safety was, as he had often been in the past, the biggest man in the room.

He was happy to be in their company again but wouldn't talk about why he had given up the rewarding life of a professional football player for the $18,000 salary of an Army Ranger. Nor would he regale his teammates with combat stories or accept any tribute for his sacrifice. He had his reasons for serving, but he kept them to himself. He wished them luck, thanked his coach for the invitation, and left by a side door so no one would notice that Corporal Pat Tillman had come back to football, if just for a moment.

Combat veterans often refer to the "fog of war," because warfare, even today in this high-tech, precision-guided age, is inherently confusing. In Afghanistan it can be especially confusing. Dry and dusty, mountainous, where ambushes are easy to conceal and difficult to escape, where civilians can be hard to distinguish from enemies, it is an ancient killing ground where invading armies for centuries have been brought to grief by Afghans bred from birth to fight. Bad things can happen in the fog that make the losses incurred in war all the harder to bear, harder to forget, harder to forgive.

Something terrible happened in the early evening of April 29, 2004, on a mountain road near an Afghan village called Sperah, twenty-five miles from the nearest American base. As dusk dissolved into night, it was even harder to see what a soldier needed to see than it had been in the sun-blazed afternoon. The army got the story wrong at first. I don't know if they withheld the facts intentionally, but they surely waited inexcusably long before they informed Pat Tillman's family of how he had lost his life on that mountainside. Most of the facts are known now, and yet it still confuses those of us who did not see what happened with our own eyes. In truth, even some who witnessed the event are confused about how it occurred and why.

Suffice it to say that Pat Tillman died as he had lived, bravely, in the service of his country. His unit was looking for Taliban and al Qaeda fighters. They were divided, and separated at a distance that made it hard for the Rangers in each squad to see one another. The sound of gunfire, real or mistaken, caused the Rangers to believe they were under attack. Someone in the squad behind Pat Tillman mistook Pat and his squad for the enemy, and began to fire at them. Pat was killed.

That is an abrupt and colorless account of a good man's death. The details are easy enough to find if you're interested, but the fog of war, and this tragic, terrible mistake are hard things to comprehend even if you have all the facts. But the precise manner in which he lost his life makes him no less heroic. Soldiers go to war knowing they might lose everything. Pat Tillman knew he might lose everything. That he risked it anyway when no one expected him to made him a great man.

Kevin brought his brother's body home to California and his heartbroken family. His family, his friends, and his country wish they could have him back. We can only remember him as someone to admire, someone to emulate if we have his courage and decency and patriotism. I have used his life as an example of patriotism that I admire and encourage others to admire. I doubt he would approve. He didn't brag or, I suppose, like to hear others brag about him. So how should we remember him?

When he played for Arizona State, Pat used to like to climb one of the two-hundred-foot light towers at the stadium, and stay up there for some time contemplating what his future would be, what kind of man he would become. I think I'll remember him climbing down from the tower with the right answers to his questions.

DILIGENCE

Winston Churchill

He persevered through every trial and misfortune to alert his countrymen to the approaching danger, and to save them when they ignored his warning.

H E HAD RETURNED AGAIN TO HARROW, HIS OLD SCHOOL, A PLACE that evoked memories of long-ago loneliness and disappointment. But he liked to come back now, during what he called "the sterner days," to hear the boys sing the old patriotic songs that stirred his heart and brought tears to his eyes. It was the school's annual speech day, and as the most famous orator and leading statesman in England, his address was the most anticipated event of the occasion.

On October 29, 1941, the day he rose to speak to Harrow's students, Winston Churchill had been Britain's prime minister for just seventeen months. He had assumed the office just days before France had fallen to Hitler's invading armies, and the defeated and demoralized British Army was miraculously rescued on the beaches of Dunkirk. He had led Britain through a grave and terrifying year, when his country alone had stood against the seemingly unstoppable armies of the Third Reich, until Hitler's invasion of the Soviet Union added another ally to the cause.

The Battle of Britain had begun and ended in victory for the beleaguered British, who had resolved to fight to the death the German invaders who awaited Hitler's order to cross the English Channel and conquer their last remaining foe. The German Air Force, the Luftwaffe, had swarmed in the English sky, day after day, in a merciless bombing campaign of British airfields, ports, and military bases intended to bring the nation to its knees. But England, its Royal Air Force (RAF), and their inspirational leader would not yield. The heavily outnumbered RAF had mounted a heroic defense of the nation, greater than Hitler had believed possible, and had saved the country from invasion. Hitler canceled his planned invasion of England in September 1940.

In North Africa, the British Army had scored important victories against Germany's Italian allies, and against Hitler's best general, Erwin Rommel. And in June 1940, Hitler had foolishly opened another front in the war by ordering the invasion of the vast and ultimately unconquerable Soviet Union.

Still, almost four more years of war remained, and while Britain's defeat was no longer inevitable, its success was far from certain. German bombs still rained down on English cities, wreaking extraordinary devastation. The brilliant Rommel wasn't finished yet, and would soon command a great if short-lived victory against the British at Tobruk in Libya. Germany had invaded and conquered Yugoslavia and Greece. German divisions had surrounded Moscow and subjected the Soviet capital to a horrific siege. The United States was providing Britain with armaments and supplies, but Pearl Harbor, and America's entry into the war, was still six weeks away. England had not reached the end nor even the beginning of the end, as Churchill acknowledged, but had perhaps reached "the end of the beginning."

Harrow had expected a stirring speech, but did not know what inspiration the former student had planned for them. It was a short address. Legend has it that Churchill spoke only a few words, but reports of the speech transformed its most memorable passage into the entirety of his address. He spoke more than those few words, but it's appropriate that they should be so exalted in memory, for they offered a deeply moving summary of Churchill's life and a fitting testament to his extraordinary character.

He removed his top hat and set it on the podium, gathered his thoughts for a moment, wiped from his eye the last tear he had shed when he had joined the boys in song, and then spoke briefly and generally about the difficulties the country had suffered and overcome, and of the hard road ahead. As he neared the end, he uttered the words that would soon become legend: "Never give in. Never give in. Never, never, never, never—in nothing great or small, large or petty—never give in, except to convictions of honor and good sense."

He was approaching his sixty-seventh birthday, past the age of retirement for most people. He had lived a life of extraordinary accomplishments and humiliating defeats long before he had become prime minister. He had suffered a lonely and oppressive childhood. He had been an unhappy and unsuccessful student. He had, by conspicuous courage and daring, become a famous war hero. He had entered politics and risen as fast as anyone ever had to the heights of his profession and crashed, went back to war, and then reentered politics, only to rise and crash again. He was a bestselling and prolific author. He had made, spent, and lost several fortunes. He had been celebrated for his genius and disparaged for his lack of judgment. He had married Clementine Hozier, who would be the only truly close friend of his adult life. He had suffered so terribly from bouts of depression that he feared he might take his own life. And before the start of World War Two, he had been, if not forgotten, regarded with either annoyance or amusement as an eccentric relic of the past. Throughout it all, he had never given in.

He was born, two months prematurely, in 1874, into a famous aristocratic family, during the reign of Queen Victoria, at the height of the British Empire. His parents were celebrities, his mother a famous American beauty, Jennie Jerome Churchill, and his father, Lord Randolph Churchill, a renowned if erratic politician. They were a glamorous, scandal-plagued couple who, for all their talents, utterly failed Winston as parents. Young Winston was a small, sickly, accident-prone boy who had nearly died of pneumonia when he was eleven, and at seventeen had lain unconscious with a fractured leg for three days after jumping off a bridge during a game of tag. These were hardly the only instances of ill health and calamity he would suffer. His childhood is a lengthy chronicle of sickness and misfortune. He seems to have always been recovering from one or another ailment or accident. He always had to struggle to improve a naturally weak physique. What success he had as an athlete and, later, as a cavalry officer was hard-won for a boy who was slightly built and inclined to flabbiness.

More discouraging was the apparent indifference of his parents to his suffering, which they regarded as little more than a nuisance. They were busy people, and selfish, and in any case, the customs of the British aristocracy at the time permitted little attention to children, who were given to nurses, nannies, and boarding schools to raise. When he was ten, and away at school, a fellow student stabbed him in the chest with a penknife. In a letter describing the incident, his mother suggested that Winston had probably provoked the attack, which she hoped "would be a lesson to him."

He was sent away to school when he was eight. He hated it. St. George's was a miserable place, where he was frequently and cruelly bullied by other boys, and where the masters routinely whipped students with birch branches for various infractions of the rules or for shirking their studies. Winston, who was a defiant, uncooperative, and desperately homesick student, received quite a lot of punishment, and worse, the increasing disapproval of his parents, who received a constant flow of letters from school officials complaining about his inadequacies as a student.

He often wrote his parents loving letters begging them to let him come home or to visit him. They were rarely successful. His mother, who, Winston would later recall, "shone for me like the Evening Star. I loved her dearly—but at a distance," was consumed with the gossip, parties, balls, weekends at country estates, and other preoccupations of high society, as well as the demands of her husband's political career.

Lord Randolph had a brilliant career as a politician, rising to the second-highest office in the land, chancellor of the exchequer (the treasury ministry). But he was beginning a steep decline, owing to rashness, scandal, and a disease that affected his body and mind and would claim his life at the age of forty-five. He was an even more distant parent than his wife, who seldom had time for his son, and never had patience for the normal ups and downs of a boy's life. A Churchill cousin recalled an occasion when he and Winston had wanted to put on a play for Lord Randolph, who warned that he would watch the production with a "stony and acid silence."

He could be a terribly cruel father, quick to condemn his son's failures, and slow to praise any success or acknowledge the depth of his son's love for him. And his son did love him deeply. He idolized both his parents, and would strive for much of his life to defend his father's reputation and emulate his political successes. But his mother would become interested in his life only when he was older and embarking on his own career. His father never saw much promise in the boy at all, and the irritation he felt when Winston disappointed him at St. George's and later at Harrow would eventually become what appears to be contempt for his own son.

The only unqualified parental love he ever received was from his nanny, Elizabeth Anne Everest, "Wooms," as he affectionately called her. He loved her and revered her memory all his life. It was Wooms, he later wrote, "who looked after me and tended all my wants. It was to her I poured out my many troubles."

Early in his life, his "many troubles," besides his unfilled longing for his parents' attention, were school related. After St. George's he was sent to Harrow, where, now that he had become accustomed to life at boarding school, he was better adjusted, but still often unhappy, always begging his parents for recognition of his small accomplishments or to visit him or let him come home. He was not a successful student, certainly when it came to the core curricula of Latin and Greek and mathematics. But early on he showed a flair for history and the English language, the foundations of his extraordinary intelligence and his greatest attributes as a statesman. These talents were, on the whole, ignored or dismissed by most of his teachers and his parents. But he persisted, in his own way, to become a person of merit to the disinterested parents he idolized. He became the school's fencing champion, read books that were far advanced for his age, and, while quite young, showed a prodigious talent for memorizing thousands of lines of English verse, preferably the poems of heroic endeavors that appealed to him, which he could recall with almost complete accuracy seventy years later.

Lord Randolph, who despaired that his son hadn't the talent for success in his profession, decided that Winston should not go to a university after Harrow but to the British military academy, Sandhurst. He wanted him to join the infantry, the most prestigious service, where he hoped Winston would prove to be less of a disappointment than he had been at Harrow. Winston tried to honor his father's wishes but failed twice to pass Sandhurst's entrance exams. On the third try, he managed to pass them, but barely, and his marks weren't good enough for the infantry. He would be trained for the cavalry. Nevertheless, he excitedly wrote his father to share with him the good news that he would enter Sandhurst after all. His father's reply was typically disapproving:

> With all the advantages you had, with all the abilities which you foolishly think yourself to possess . . . this is the grand result that you come up among the 2nd rate and 3rd rate class who are only good for commissions in a cavalry regiment.
>
> Now it is a good thing to put this business very plainly before you. Do not think I am going to take the trouble of writing you long letters after every folly and failure you commit and undergo. I shall not write again on these matters and you need not trouble to write any answer to this part of my letter, because I no longer attach the slightest weight to anything you may say about your own achievements and exploits.

His father closed his awful rebuke by warning Winston that if he continued his slothful ways he would "become a mere social wastrel, one of the hundreds of public school failures, and you will degenerate into a shabby unhappy and futile existence. If that is so you will have to bear all the blame for such misfortunes yourself."

It would not be so. His life would be neither shabby nor futile. He would lead one of the greatest lives in the twentieth century, perhaps the greatest. The cause of the unhappiness he experienced, and it was considerable, could probably be laid at the doorstep of his cruel father. He called them his "black dogs," the recurring bouts of serious depression he suffered all his life, and which he could only chase away with ceaseless activity.

But he would chase the black dogs away, with accomplishments so numerous and great that they cannot be described in detail in this brief account of his life. That many of his accomplishments would be the product of his lifelong effort to win a dead father's approval made them all the more touching and remarkable. He could have turned out, as many children of emotionally abusive parents do, to be the failure his father had predicted.

His father died shortly after Winston was commissioned a second lieutenant in the British cavalry, and with his death, Churchill remembered, "all my hopes for comradeship ended." He distinguished himself as a daring officer in heavy fighting in India and the Sudan, where he participated in the last British cavalry charge in history, in the great British victory at Omdurman. He managed while serving on active duty to write newspaper accounts of the battles he had participated in, beginning a lifelong occupation as a writer that would be his primary source of income. He resigned his commission in 1899, and ran unsuccessfully for Parliament.

After he lost the election, he traveled to South Africa to cover the Boer War as a newspaper correspondent, and was captured and held prisoner by Boer guerrillas. He managed a spectacular escape, over hundreds of miles of hostile country, rejoined the army, fought bravely in combat, and was recommended for the Victoria Cross. His exploits won him considerable fame in England, and on his next try for Parliament he succeeded.

The story of his life accelerates at this point. Only a few years after first winning a seat in Parliament in 1900, as a member of the Conservative Party, he changed allegiances to the Liberals, and was asked to join the cabinet of a newly elected Liberal government in 1908, the same year he married Clementine. Three years later, he was made first lord of the admiralty, the head of the navy, a position of great honor and importance.

He was first lord when World War One began, and was regarded as among the most brilliant, industrious, and controversial (he was always controversial) men in government. He conceived one of the most strategically brilliant attempts to overcome the trench-war stalemate on the western front by using the navy to force the Dardanelles strait in Turkey, knock Turkey out of the war, and flank the Germans in the east. It was brilliantly conceived but terribly executed, and it failed, leaving exposed many thousands of soldiers, mostly Australian, to be slaughtered on the beaches at Gallipoli. The devastating defeat forced him to resign his office, and rather than return to Parliament, he accepted a commission in the army, and led a regiment in the trenches in France.

Cleared of blame in 1917 for the Dardanelles disaster, he rejoined the cabinet and served at the end of World War One as secretary for war and air, and later as colonial secretary, in charge of the still-vast expanses of the British Empire. But he soon suffered a great personal tragedy, the death of his three-year-old daughter, Marigold, which nearly destroyed him.

In each office he held, he was a daring innovator, sometimes reckless, always astonishingly hardworking, and not always successful. In 1922 he lost reelection to his seat in Parliament, and lost two successive elections. He again switched parties, back to the Conservatives, and was elected. In 1924, he became chancellor of the exchequer, the highest post his father had held. But within a few years, his mistake in returning the British economy to the gold standard and his opposition to the government's India policy would again force him from the cabinet, and back to the back benches. He was believed by many observers to have begun the last years of his political career, destined to rise no further than his erratic father had, never again to command the public stage as he once had. He was fifty-seven years old.

He was about to begin what would become known as his "wilderness years," perhaps the bravest and the loneliest time in his public life. It began inauspiciously with the loss of almost all his wealth in the Wall Street crash of 1929, and a near fatal accident when he was struck by an automobile in New York City. But it was his early warnings about the ambitions of Adolf Hitler and Germany's rearmament that would expose him to ridicule and contempt.

World War One had destroyed an entire British generation, and few Britons, and even fewer British politicians, wanted to contemplate another war with Germany. So the nation and its leaders, under a succession of prime ministers—Ramsey McDonald, Stanley Baldwin, and Neville Chamberlain—looked the other way as Hitler took power in Germany, began to rearm the country in violation of the Versailles Treaty, and marched into the Rhineland and Austria. Through out this sad history of appeasement, as a preventable war approached closer and closer, Churchill, almost alone among political leaders, remained steadfast in opposition to the government's policy of accommodating Hitler, and warned in ever-increasingly apocalyptic terms about the "gathering storm."

He developed his own intelligence network within government ministries, which provided him with critical information about German rearmament and the lack of a British response that the government was hiding from the public, and which he broadcast in his public speeches. He had a few loyal associates who shared his concerns, but most of Britain's leaders despised him. Conservative leaders tried to turn his constituents against him, and almost succeeded in defeating him at the polls. Baldwin and Chamberlain hated him. Much of the country believed he had lost his mind. Even the king seemed to dislike him. One notable British figure of the day, a Conservative member of Parliament whom Winston often sparred with, Lady Nancy Astor, led a British delegation to Moscow. They met with Stalin, who, like Churchill, viewed the rise of Hitler's Germany with alarm. He asked her about Churchill's political future. "Churchill," she responded with surprise. "Oh, he's finished."

She was not the first nor the last to underestimate him. For almost eight years in the wilderness, he kept up his campaign, beseeching the government to recognize what was plain for all to see—that Germany was preparing for war while England was disarming. In 1938, as Germany appeared poised to invade Czechoslovakia, Prime Minister Chamberlain traveled to Moscow to meet with Hitler, from where he returned waving an agreement that abandoned the Czechs, but which, he claimed, promised "peace in our time." Churchill denounced the Munich agreement in some of the most devastatingly effective speeches of his career. He said Chamberlain had been "given the choice between war and dishonor. You chose dishonor and you will have war."

After three days of parliamentary debate on the agreement, he rose to offer further denunciation. As his critics in the House of Commons taunted and jeered him, Churchill picked to pieces the agreement, and the foolish sentimentality that produced it, condemning the betrayal of the Czechs, the lack of any worthwhile commitment from Hitler, and the certainty of Germany's bad faith, and predicting the ultimate coming of war. All that Chamberlain's accommodation in Munich had accomplished was that Hitler, "instead of snatching his victuals from the table, has been content to have them served to him course by course."

"This is only the beginning of the reckoning," he warned. "This is only the first sip—the first foretaste of a bitter cup which will be proffered to us year by year. Unless—by a supreme recovery of our moral health and martial vigor—we arise again and take our stand for freedom."

After Hitler invaded Czechoslovakia, the British public began to turn on Chamberlain, and pay renewed respect to the man they had dismissed as "finished." When Germany invaded Poland in 1939, violating the Munich agreement, as Churchill warned it would, Chamberlain had no choice but to offer Winston a government office. He returned as first lord of the admiralty. Overjoyed, all British ships at sea flashed one another the signal, "WINSTON IS BACK." And as German panzers swept through Belgium and into France, Chamberlain submitted his resignation to the king, and advised His Majesty that he would have to turn to the man who had predicted the disaster that had come to pass, and was now the only Briton who could lead the nation through the terrible storm. The king didn't want to do it. But he had no choice.

Winston Churchill—the abandoned child, the failed student, the war hero, the controversial statesman, the failed, scorned, reviled, and forgotten politician, who stood alone as Britain's Horatio at the Bridge, and wanted to fight an enemy when they were still weak enough to be defeated—whose life's accomplishments were greater than a hundred men could produce, became the king's first minister on May 10, 1940. "It is a short walk from the Admiralty to Buckingham Palace," he remembered. "Yet I felt I had been walking with destiny and that all my life had been preparation for this trial and this hour."

This extraordinarily diligent man, who would not give in to many bitter trials that would have forced most of us to surrender to a cruel and unrelenting fate, who had fought, been beaten, and risen again so many times to take his place among the great democratic leaders of world history, would, by the power of his speech and the unyielding courage of his example and convictions, lead his country through the most dangerous experience of its long history. He stood alone first, and then as Britain's leader as she stood alone, letting no defeat, no danger, no impossibly overwhelming odds destroy his courage or his will. He would not give in. Never, never, never, never. And, due in great part to the courage he inspired in others, neither would his country.

RESPONSIBILITY

Lord Nelson and
His Lieutenants

The bold and brave admiral who taught men how to fight
and made the British Navy the most powerful in the world

NEAR CAPE ST. VINCENT, OFF THE COAST OF PORTUGAL, ON THE FOURteenth of February, 1797, fifteen British ships of the line under the command of Sir John Jervis, commander-in-chief of Great Britain's Mediterranean fleet, attempted to bring to battle the much larger Spanish fleet of twenty-seven battleships and twelve frigates. Though outnumbered, the British fleet was superior to their foe in experience and training. The Spanish commander thought it better to outrun the danger, and ordered his ships to steer north and away from British guns.

Jervis had given command of the twelfth ship in the line, the *Captain*, to a favored young officer whom he had recently promoted to commodore, an officer who had long before determined to become a great and famous man.

When Jervis observed the Spanish sailing north in the opposite direction from his ships, making battle impossible, he ordered his ships to tack, turn into the wind, one at a time, and chase the departing enemy. Pacing on the quarterdeck of the *Captain*, the impatient young commodore worried that Jervis's order would take too long to execute and the Spanish would escape battle long before the British ships had completed the maneuver. So he disobeyed his orders. He ordered his ship's captain to turn away from the wind and sail headlong into the enemy line. Within minutes his insubordination would bring him into battle with seven enemy ships. But Commodore Horatio Nelson, arguably the greatest fighting naval commander of all time, trusted that his officers and crew, some of whom he had served with before, were superior to the dangerous challenge he had given them. And so they were.

As Spanish cannon blasted away at the English attacker, Captain Ralph Miller, who had served with Nelson in earlier engagements, and who respected and trusted him, rammed his ship, at Nelson's order, into one of the Spanish ships, the *San Nicholas.* Nelson ordered his men to draw their swords and board the *San Nicholas,* which was itself entangled with another Spanish ship of the line, the *San Josef.* Nelson led his crew onto the first Spanish ship, waving a cutlass that had belonged to his great-uncle, and laid into the enemy crying, "Death or glory!" When the officers and crew of the *Captain* had subdued the crew of the *San Nicholas* and struck her colors, they scrambled over the deck to board the second Spanish ship, and quickly subdued her.

Many admirals would have reacted to seeing a subordinate leave the line of battle and sail into the enemy's line—a violation of the fighting orders that astonished other officers of the fleet and outraged more than a few of them—by flying into a rage, cursing his insubordinate officer, and clapping him in irons if he survived the reckless assault. Jervis reacted quite differently. He immediately grasped the sense of Nelson's charge and ordered his other captains to follow Nelson into battle. When the smoke cleared, the British had won the day, taking as prizes four Spanish ships, two of which belonged to Nelson, along with their treasure. While some of his officers sharply criticized Nelson's action, Jervis praised his daring subordinate's "creative disobedience," and embraced him.

The Battle of Cape St. Vincent won Nelson fame and fortune. He was knighted, and quickly promoted to rear admiral, although he had not yet reached his fortieth birthday. Most important, it reaffirmed Nelson's supreme confidence in the innovations he intended to bring to the traditions and tactics of the British Navy, innovations that would influence generations of British officers, and would, in the relatively brief but spectacular rise of Lord Nelson, bring a glory to its author greater than that earned by any other naval hero. From his death to this very day, two hundred years after his greatest victory, naval officers in Great Britain and elsewhere rise when the toast is given to "the immortal memory." No name is ever given to the memory's subject. It is always to Nelson, and Nelson alone.

He had been a small, unhealthy, and motherless twelve-year-old when he joined the navy as a midshipman on his uncle's ship. But with no wars to fight at the time, Nelson's uncle had him transferred to a merchant ship bound for the Caribbean so that he could gain some experience at sea. Living for nearly a year in close quarters, he came to enjoy the affectionate respect of the merchant sailors he sailed with, and whose wants and grievances he took to heart, and offered his generous sympathy. The connection between Nelson and the hardened sailors he impressed was marked by genuine regard and trust, and would forever influence the aspiring young officer's method of commanding men at sea.

Promotion to lieutenant was reserved for officers who had reached twenty. Nelson received his commission at eighteen. By then he had gained fighting experience, sailed to the Arctic, and around the Cape of Good Hope to the Indian Ocean. On the voyage to India he contracted malaria, and in a delirious state had a vision that he later referred to as a "radiant orb," which he took for a premonition that he would become a celebrated warrior for king and country. "My mind exulted in the idea," he later wrote. "Well then, I exclaimed, I would become a hero, and, confiding in Providence, I will brave every danger."

Barely twenty, and having attracted the attention and affection of subordinates and superiors alike, he was promoted to post captain. In 1793, as war commenced between Great Britain and revolutionary France, Nelson received his first command of a warship, the *Agamemnon,* and began his meteoric ascent to his exalted place in history. He distinguished himself in several encounters with the enemy, lost an eye fighting at Corsica, and earned the respect of the Mediterranean commander-in-chief, Jervis, who summoned him to the famous battle off Cape St. Vincent. During this period of arduous active service he formed many of the attachments with fellow officers of the line who would soon become Nelson's celebrated "Band of Brothers," the title borrowed from Shakespeare's *Henry V,* bestowed by Nelson on the generation of British officers who would lead the navy with distinction throughout the Napoleonic wars and beyond, but whose greatest distinction was that they had once served under the command of the gallant Nelson.

After the Battle of Cape St. Vincent, Jervis ordered Nelson to the Canary Islands to seize a Spanish ship anchored at Santa Cruz. In the difficult fighting that ensued, with Nelson in the lead and typically exposed to enemy gunfire, a canister of grapeshot shattered his right arm. The ship's surgeon performed a crude amputation without anesthesia, and within an hour, Nelson resumed command of the battle.

After a long and painful convalescence in England, Nelson returned to service in the Mediterranean. The French fleet at Toulon was preparing to carry Napoléon's army to some unknown destination. Jervis ordered Nelson to find out where, and gave him command of three battleships and five frigates. The French set sail and headed east on May 19, 1798.

Nelson's fleet, eventually joined by ten more battleships captained by some of Nelson's closest friends, crisscrossed the Mediterranean hunting Napoléon, but lacking a sufficient number of frigates, which serve as a fleet's scouts, he could not find them. Guessing that Egypt might be the enemy's destination, Nelson entered the harbor at Alexandria, near the mouth of the Nile River, on June 28. The French were not there, and Nelson resumed his frantic search of the Eastern Mediterranean. A few days later, Napoléon's army disembarked near Alexandria, where the French fleet rested at anchor in Aboukir Bay, having eluded their British hunters. Nelson would continue the search for more than a month, by which time Napoléon's conquest of Egypt was well under way. But he would find them, still riding at anchor in a long defensive line at Aboukir Bay, and in the first of Nelson's three greatest victories, utterly annihilate them.

Standard sea-fighting tactics in the age of canvass offered little chance to destroy an enemy fleet entirely. Two opposing fleets would sail parallel to each other in the same direction and engage in an artillery duel, firing broadsides at the hulls and masts of the enemy. Whichever side managed to hold the weather gauge, the windward position, and fire the most rapidly and accurately prevailed. But, more often than not, the losing fleet, recognizing the enemy's advantages, would hasten to escape with whatever number of its ships that had not been disabled by enemy fire. Nelson's genius was to dare a more dangerous outcome in the hope of completely destroying an enemy fleet by attacking its line head-on, closing in a tumult of crashing bows and yardarms, and attempting to encircle it. What they did not destroy by cannon fire, they would finish off with boarding parties using muskets, pistols, swords, and pikes. It was ferocious combat, which cost victor and vanquished much higher casualties than the old battle lines had caused. And the most dangerous place in the battle was the ship's quarterdeck, where the captain stood, totally exposed, an inspiration to his men. Nelson loved it.

British crews handling the ship's sails and guns, most particularly those who sailed under Admiral Nelson, were the best trained in the world. They were the most confident and capable under fire, and could fire cannon at a rate sometimes three times faster than the much less experienced crews of the French republic. Nelson was a demanding commander, drilling and drilling his crews to increase his advantages in battle. But he was a fair, generous, and inspirational master as well, going to great lengths to address the needs of his men, encouraging them to see challenges as great opportunities for prize money and glory, and imparting to them the sense of invincibility that he seemed to possess. They loved him, and it is not romantic overstatement to observe that their admiral loved them in return.

Even greater was the affection shared between Nelson and his subordinate commanders. The fog of war was evident and more confusing in sea battles. Ships communicated with the admiral's flagship by means of signal flags, which could often be nearly impossible to see in the gun smoke and chaos of battle, most particularly so in the kind of close-quarter combat preferred by Nelson. He took great care to cultivate the friendship of his subordinates, and to explain to them in detail his battle plans in advance of an operation. He emphasized to them what he intended to accomplish, and would leave much of how it would be achieved to them. Once guns were firing, he expected them to use their own initiative without waiting for his further instructions, to conform to the extent necessary to the overall line of battle he had given them, but seize opportunities where they presented themselves to destroy the enemy with the courage and daring he always showed in combat. "No captain can do very wrong," he told them, "if he places his ship alongside that of the enemy."

He inspired them to share his self-assurance by his demonstrations of confidence in them. And he saw to it that the rewards of glory and fortune won by daring and ambition were fairly shared. Most important, he did not shift the blame for mistakes and occasional failures to his subordinates, but assumed the responsibility for them himself. He gave his officers greater responsibility than they had ever possessed, and he never shirked his responsibility to them. This quality of command—daring, inspirational, confiding, and fraternal—renowned as the "Nelson touch," forged extraordinarily strong bonds of mutual trust and affection between Nelson and his officers. It made him the greatest commander of his age. And in the Battle of the Nile, it would destroy the French fleet.

The fight began at nightfall with only lantern light and the flash of gunfire to illuminate the battle. The British officers and crews knew what to do. Nelson ordered some of his captains to sail directly at the lead ships of the anchored French fleet, while the rest attacked the center of the French line. Once engaged, some of the British ships slipped past the enemy and anchored between the French sterns and the dangerous shoals to their rear, and there wreaked havoc and ruin on the enemy. When it was over, ten of thirteen French battleships were captured or destroyed, and the French flagship had exploded into splinters when its gunpowder magazine caught fire. Nelson hadn't lost a single ship. During the battle, which lasted nearly seven hours, he suffered a slight wound. He patiently waited his turn in line with injured sailors to be treated by the ship's surgeon, after which he wrote his dispatch to the British admiralty office informing his superiors of the victory his fleet had won. Britain rewarded Nelson with a peerage, Baron Nelson of the Nile. Lord Nelson attributed the honor and the victory to the fact that he had "the happiness to command a Band of Brothers."

Nelson would claim two other great victories, the first at Copenhagen, where he was subordinate to Commander-in-Chief Admiral Hyde Parker in an attack on the Danish fleet that Britain feared would soon join the Swedish fleet in alliance with Napoléon. Parker wanted simply to blockade the Danish ships, but Nelson wanted to take the fight to them as soon as practical by attacking the fleet at anchor in Copenhagen's harbor. Though outnumbered, and exposed to gun batteries on shore, Parker agreed.

The battle was much harder than Nelson expected. There was little room for maneuver in the harbor's shallow waters, and the battle became an artillery duel. Danish gun crews on ship and shore proved more proficient than anticipated, and subjected Nelson, his officers, and his crews to withering fire. Nelson was undisturbed. When Parker signaled to him to break off the battle and sail out of gun range, the insubordinate Nelson put the telescope to his blind eye and complained that he could not read his commander's signal. The fight raged on for a long while, until Nelson, having finally gotten the better of the duel, threatened to put the Danish ships to the torch unless their commanders surrendered. It was a difficult, costly, but still great victory.

His last and greatest victory, the epic battle at Cape Trafalgar near the port of Cádiz off Spain's Atlantic coast, occurred more than four years later. And it was at Trafalgar, Britain's greatest naval triumph, that "the immortal memory" of Horatio Lord Nelson claimed the eternal affection of the British Navy and nation.

Napoléon, now the master of continental Europe, intended to vanquish the one remaining power that threatened his ambitions, Great Britain. He planned to ferry an invasion force, 160,000 strong, staged at Boulogne on the French coast, across the English Channel and be the first man to conquer England since William I and his Norman invaders in 1066. To accomplish the daring enterprise he needed to assemble his navy to protect his crossing. He ordered his Mediterranean fleet, under the command of Admiral Pierre Villeneuve, who had fought Nelson at the Nile and escaped, to leave the Mediterranean port of Toulon, evade the British blockade commanded by Lord Nelson, and sail past Gibraltar and around the Spanish coast to rendezvous with France's gathering fleet in the English Channel.

Villeneuve did manage to escape the British blockade at Toulon, and Nelson, having initially wrongly guessed the enemy's course, turned his fleet around and chased Villeneuve in a legendary pursuit across the Atlantic to the Caribbean. One of his captains, Sir Robert Stopford, wrote in a letter home during the desperate search, "We are half-starved and otherwise inconvenienced by being so long out of port, but our reward is that we are with Nelson." The hunt, however, proved in vain. Nelson was still searching the West Indies for the French while Villeneuve was sailing his fleet back to Europe. When he arrived he fought a brief, inconclusive battle with a British squadron off the northwest coast of Spain, and added six more ships to his line.

Panicked at the prospect of the French fleet sailing north and forcing the English Channel, England prepared for invasion. But Villeneuve was no Nelson. He did not have the confidence in his ships' officers and crews that Nelson had in his. He feared they would be no match for the more experienced British. But most of all, he feared he was no match for Nelson. So rather than sail north, with Napoléon impatiently awaiting his arrival, Villeneuve raised his sails the second week of August 1805, and the combined French and Spanish fleet headed south for Cádiz.

Nelson had returned to England after his fruitless transatlantic search when he received news that his friend and early member of the Band of Brothers, Admiral Cuthbert Collingwood, had spotted the French and Spanish ships making their way into harbor at Cádiz, where Collingwood would remain to prevent the enemy from leaving until Nelson could join him. Less than four weeks later, H.M.S. *Victory,* flying the ensign of the great Lord Nelson, joined the fleet off Cádiz, where eight of his Band of Brothers awaited him as their commander. One of them, Thomas Hardy, captained the *Victory,* Nelson's flagship. Collingwood would serve as Nelson's second-in-command. All of them, as well as the captains of the rest of the British fleet of twenty-five battleships and four frigates, awaited eagerly to experience the Nelson touch when the admiral would share with them his order of battle. He would not disappoint them.

Upon his arrival, he invited half his captains to dinner aboard the *Victory,* and the next night the other half, and in an atmosphere of fraternal affection and trust, conferred with them about his plans, his most daring yet, to bring the combined French and Spanish fleets to battle and annihilate them. He intended to divide his fleet into two columns, the first to be led by the *Victory,* the second commanded by Collingwood aboard the *Royal Sovereign.* The two columns would hit and cross the gaps in the enemy line at two places, creating chaos in an attempt to encircle them. On the approach, the British ships, especially those leading the columns, with their bows and not their cannon pointed at the enemy, would be exposed to a merciless broadside from enemy cannon.

Even Nelson was surprised by his captains' enthusiastic reception of his plan. For all its danger, indeed, its stunning recklessness, it was the Nelson touch at its most audacious, and they shared its author's expectation of complete victory. They were completely confident in their commander and he in them. All that was left now was to wait for Villeneuve to work up the nerve to attempt to break out of the trap and make for the Mediterranean.

On October 19, he risked it. He was immediately spotted by a British frigate, and the signal reached Nelson that the enemy was sailing. Nelson ordered his fleet, spread out over miles of sea, to form together and chase the enemy. Two days later, they spotted the entire combined fleet nearing Cape Trafalgar at the entrance to the Straits of Gibraltar. Villeneuve, aware now that Nelson was in pursuit, panicked and ordered his fleet to turn with the wind and race back to the sanctuary of Cádiz. The maneuver was time-consuming and poorly executed, and disrupted the French line. Nelson, pacing the quarterdeck of the *Victory,* anxious for the battle to begin, saw that the moment he had dreamed of for most of his life had arrived.

As British crews hurriedly prepared their ships for battle, their commander-in-chief signaled them: "England expects every man will do his duty." Upon seeing Nelson's message, Collingwood complained that "we know well enough what to do." Indeed they did. Nelson had made sure they did, and that they had the skill, confidence, and his trust to do it well.

The combined fleet opened fire at 11:45, and Nelson responded by signaling, "Engage the enemy more closely." Nelson's column made for Villeneuve's flagship, the twelfth ship in the line, while Collingwood intended to cross the gap between the eighteenth and nineteenth ship. As they approached the still-disorganized enemy line, cannon opened up and raked their decks and rigging with a tremendous barrage. Nelson and Collingwood ordered their crews to lie flat on the deck, while their commanders remained upright on the quarterdeck, and pressed on to the great encounter. Collingwood was first to reach the enemy, fighting off several of the enemy ships at once, but managing to get behind their line, and open up his guns on their sterns. Nelson crossed the line not long after, taking fierce fire from several ships. He told his dear friend and the *Victory*'s captain: "This is too warm work, Hardy, to last for long." But the *Victory* managed to cross the line behind Villeneuve's flagship, firing a tremendous broadside into her stern as she passed. As it did, the next French ship in the line, the *Redoubtable,* rammed into the *Victory.*

The fighting was fierce, smoke-fogged, and confused, as Nelson had expected and desired. Everywhere British, French, and Spanish gun crews were firing broadside after broadside; in some instances two enemies were so close they set each other on fire. Several British and enemy ships became entangled, firing away furiously, locked in a death struggle. Casualties in the first two hours of battle were high, and the conclusion far from certain. The *Victory* and *Redoubtable* were locked together at the yardarms, as French sailors fired their muskets at the British from the sail rigging. Their commander ordered them to aim for British officers, and at 1:35, less than two hours into the battle, a French musket ball struck Lord Nelson in the chest. As he collapsed to the deck, he told his friend, "They are done for me at last, Hardy. My backbone is shot through." It was a remarkably accurate diagnosis. The wound was mortal. The ball had penetrated a lung and shattered two vertebrae. Hardy had his commander carried belowdecks, where the ship's surgeon could see to him, while he returned to the quarterdeck to do his duty, along with Nelson's other captains.

Recognizing that no treatment would prevent the inevitable consequence of the French marksman's fatal work, the surgeon did what he could to make his patient comfortable, and with Nelson's approval returned to treat the other wounded. Within a half hour, the battle turned to Britain's advantage, and Hardy retired belowdecks to visit the dying Nelson. "How goes the battle?" Nelson asked.

"Very well, my lord," his friend replied.

"I hope none of our ships have struck [surrendered], Hardy."

"No, my lord, there is no fear of that."

"Don't throw me overboard," Nelson pleaded.

"Oh, no, certainly not," the weeping Hardy responded.

The battle raged on before finally coming to a merciful end after seven hours of the most ferocious fighting imaginable. Two hours before the last shots were fired, Lord Nelson died in Thomas Hardy's arms, asking in his last moments, "Kiss me, Hardy," which the grieving captain obeyed by brushing his lips on his fallen commander's forehead. "Thank God I have done my duty," Nelson offered a few moments later, just before he breathed his last.

It was a tremendous victory. Eighteen of the enemy's thirty-three battleships were destroyed or captured. Napoléon would never again threaten an invasion of Britain. The enemy had suffered thousands more casualties than had the British. But the British had lost Nelson, and the loss weighed heavily, even balanced against their victory in the greatest sea battle in history. The men of the fleet, even the most hardened, wept when they learned the news, some inconsolably.

The frigate H.M.S. *Pickle* raced for London bearing the news. "Sir, we have gained a great victory," its captain informed his superior, "but we have lost Lord Nelson." England collapsed in grief.

Admiral Villeneuve, who eventually took his own life in attempted atonement for his defeat at Trafalgar, offered the wisest testament to Nelson and his Band of Brothers and their unsurpassed sense of responsibility to one another and to Great Britain's continued dominance of the seas: "To any other nation, the loss of Nelson would have been irreparable; but in the British fleet off Cádiz, every captain was a Nelson."

COOPERATION

John Wooden

*The modest man whose wisdom and evident decency
taught boys how to become winners and good men*

Bill Walton, the all-american center on ucla's champion basketball teams of the early 1970s, was a young man with strong views on a lot of subjects: the Vietnam War, politics, music, education, sports, and, most especially, on the subject of individual liberty. Young Bill was his own man. He would decide for himself how to think, what to say, how to dress, and how long to wear his hair. And if he chose to sport a beard, then that would be his decision and his decision alone.

His coach had opinions, too, although I think it's fair to say he expressed them with less drama, and less boisterously than did his star center. John Wooden was a modest, quiet sort of man, old-fashioned, fair, broad-minded, and tolerant but with as firm a grip on his convictions as Bill Walton had on his, even firmer. He led mostly by example. The instructions he gave—which many of the players who received them might have thought were rather quaint and outdated—were often delivered quietly with the homespun maxims he had learned from his father, or with verses of poetry that had impressed him, or by patiently repeated rituals.

He cared about his players, and paid strict attention to teaching them the small and big things that would help them become the best basketball players they could be, and, most important, the best men they could be. He would bench a player for using profanity or for criticizing a teammate or for treating an opponent disrespectfully. He expected his players to dress appropriately, be courteous to everyone, acknowledge their other teammates when they scored, and to refrain from showing excessive emotions on the court. He taught them dignity, based, as dignity is, on self-respect and respect for others. And he taught them not only the usefulness of teamwork, five men all playing their assigned roles, but the virtue of cooperation, and the sense of satisfaction it provided to an individual. He was a teacher, something many coaches claim to be, but not all really are.

The first practice of every season, Coach Wooden would spend a half hour or so teaching his players how to put on their socks and shoes. As a high school coach, he had noticed how players with wrinkled socks and shoes that were a half size too big got blisters on their feet and toes in the quick stops and starts of a basketball game. So he showed them how to roll up their socks, smoothing out the wrinkles before they put their shoes on, shoes he selected for them after making sure they were a half size smaller than they were used to wearing. After laboriously instructing them in this small manner of dressing one foot, while the players shot one another looks of amusement or impatience, he would wait until they could do it properly, and then he'd say, "Good. Now, let's do the other foot."

He never looked down on one of his kids. Differences in race, religion, privilege, or politics didn't make a person a better or lesser human being. He insisted that his players respect their teammates and the role played by each individual, starter or sub or bench rider, to make the whole greater than the sum of its parts. He loved them, all of them, he insisted, even if he didn't always like every one of them.

He admired self-confidence, and he liked players who had the courage of their convictions. But courage meant you had to be prepared for the consequences of your actions. So when Bill Walton showed up at practice one day with a beard he had grown during a ten-day break in the season, his coach, who had a rule about such things, asked him to shave. John Wooden worried that long hair and facial hair took too long to dry after showering; a player would leave the locker room and go outside with his hair and beard still wet, and might catch a cold. He had relaxed a little, but not much, the rule on hair length, considering how many of the male professors and administrators at UCLA had, in deference to the fashion of the times, let their hair grow over their collars. But he stuck firmly to his no-beards rule.

The outspoken, confident Walton believed this an unacceptable infringement on his liberty, and he argued that Wooden didn't have the right to make such personal decisions for his players. John Wooden liked and admired his star center. Their politics were different, of course, as were their views on personal appearance and behavior. Wooden had bailed Walton out of jail once after the young man had gotten himself arrested at an antiwar demonstration. That had saddened his coach, who told his player that he understood his strong beliefs, but didn't think getting arrested was a very good idea.

But there was much to like about Walton. After all, Walton was the linchpin of UCLA's championship teams in 1972 and 1973, a three-time national Player of the Year. Later, Coach Wooden wrote, "Bill was one of the greatest who ever performed at his position at every level of competition"; this from the man who had, a few years earlier, coached the great Lew Alcinder (who later changed his name to Kareem Abdul-Jabbar). He admired Walton's intensity, his hard work and intelligence. Walton was an academic All-American as well, which made his coach very proud of him. And he did sincerely admire Walton's determination to be his own man. That took strength and courage, admirable virtues in Coach Wooden's book. But again, you had to accept the consequences of your actions, the good and the bad, if you were truly to be your own man.

So the coach asked his player if he really felt that strongly about the beard. Walton replied that he did. "That's good, Bill. I admire people who have strong beliefs and stick by them, I really do. We're going to miss you."

Walton shaved his beard on the spot. He had the right to determine his own appearance, but his coach had the right to determine who would play basketball for the UCLA Bruins. And Walton wouldn't have missed playing for John Wooden, not for anything. John Wooden was the greatest basketball coach who ever lived, and one of the very best teachers in the game, and Bill Walton, smart young man that he was, knew it.

John Wooden was born in 1910, in the small town of Martinsville, Indiana. He was raised on his family's farm outside town, where he learned the values that would stand him in good stead his entire life, values he brought to coaching, as he brought them to every aspect of his life. The family home had no running water or electricity, and since these were the years of the Great Depression, the Woodens had little money. The four Wooden boys worked hard, following the example of their parents, but theirs was not a grim life. Their wise, loving parents made sure they had time to play and learn.

John Wooden reveres the memory of his parents, and believes their father, Joshua, was the best man he has ever known. Joshua Wooden taught his children by instruction and example all of life's most important lessons. His son John often recalls three of the most important ones:

1) Never lie, never cheat, never steal.
2) Don't worry about the past, you can't change it, but make every new day your master-piece.
3) And the lesson he took most to heart: Don't try to be better than someone else, just try to be the best man you can be.

When the Wooden farm went bankrupt in the 1930s, and the Woodens had to move back to town, his father's advice and example helped them through tough times without any of his children ever feeling unfairly deprived or beaten by life.

Indiana in the 1920s was as basketball crazy as it remains today. John Wooden first played basketball with his brothers in the family barn using a tomato basket, and wadded up old rags for a ball. Tiny Martinsville had one of the best high school teams in the state. John Wooden might have been the best guard who ever played there. From 1924 to 1928, he led the team to three state championship games, winning the title in 1927. He was an All-State player his sophomore, junior, and senior years. His prowess, work ethic, and intelligence on the court attracted the attention of college coaches, and he was recruited to play Big Ten basketball for Purdue University.

At Purdue they called the scrappy Wooden the "Indiana Rubber Man," in appreciation for the way he would throw himself on the hardwood, scrambling for loose balls. He had obvious athletic talent, but it was his intelligence, preparation, enthusiasm, and industry that made him a standout collegiate. With Wooden at the point, Purdue won two Big Ten championships, and in his senior year, a national title. He was a three-time All-American, and in 1932, he was named national Player of the Year, having scored 154 points in twelve games, an unheard-of total in those low-scoring days. In 1942, he was included in the Basketball Hall of Fame's All Time All-American Team (in 1960, he was admitted to the Hall of Fame as a player, and twelve years later as a coach, the first man to be admitted as both a player and coach). He was also an honor student. It was no surprise, then, when professional scouts sent word back to their head offices recommending a pro-ball contract for the Indiana Rubber Man.

John Wooden had other plans. His coach at Purdue, Ward "Piggy" Lambert, was another great influence on young John Wooden, and it was to Coach Lambert that he went for advice when the Celtics offered him a contract. Before they called, Wooden had accepted a job as an English teacher at a Kentucky high school, and he was torn about whether he should reconsider now that he had an offer from professional basketball that promised a substantially larger paycheck. Lambert asked him if his highest priority at Purdue had been an education or basketball.

When Wooden answered that it was an education, Lambert suggested that he already knew what to do.

Wooden had started Purdue as a civil engineering major, but he had discovered that a degree in his chosen field would require him to attend classes during the summer, when he had to work to earn money to defray his college costs. He switched majors to English. Wooden loved English poetry, particularly Victorian verse, as well as Shakespeare and Dickens. He had the character, education, and enthusiasm to be a good English teacher. So he became one.

Taking the job in Kentucky would also mean he could immediately marry his fiancée, Nellie Riley. She was his high school sweetheart, the first and only girl he had ever dated. He had fallen in love with her at first sight. He was an intensely shy person, and Nellie would help him come out of it, as she would help him develop into so much more as a basketball coach and a man. Theirs would be a marriage of extraordinary closeness and devotion lasting fifty-three years.

Even at his young age, John Wooden had long thought about what it means to be a success. Another fortunate influence on his life had been his high school math teacher, who had once asked him to define the word, whether it meant achieving fame and fortune, or something greater than material success. He hadn't stopped thinking about it yet, and never really would. His deliberations led to one succinct maxim that he still shares today with anyone interested in how this very successful man defines success. It's largely based in the wisdom his father had shared with him. Success is "peace of mind that is the direct result of self-satisfaction in knowing you did your best to become the best that you are capable of becoming." His ceaseless meditation on the concept of success also led to the development over fourteen years of John Wooden's most famous coaching and life lesson, the Pyramid of Success.

He determined to be the best English teacher and coach he could be. He taught for two years in Dayton, Kentucky, and coached all sports there. Then, he and Nellie moved to South Bend, Indiana, to a new teaching position where he coached three sports, basketball, baseball, and tennis, and remained for nine years. In his eleven-year high school basketball coaching career he posted a record 214 wins and 43 losses. As an English teacher, he lamented parents who thought their children were failures if they didn't earn a high grade. He always valued the average student who made the maximum effort to earn a C over the bright but indifferent student who effortlessly managed an A.

He joined the navy in World War Two, and after the war ended accepted the athletic director and head basketball coaching job at Indiana State University. In his first year of coaching, the team received its first invitation to play in the national tournament. The twelfth man on his team, who rarely played, was an African American. The tournament excluded black players then. And though Wooden probably wouldn't have played the young man anyway, he refused to tolerate bigotry, and kept Indiana State home.

His success at Indiana State—in two years under his leadership the team compiled a 44–15 record—led to coaching offers from two bigger universities, the University of Minnesota and the University of California, Los Angeles. John and Nellie preferred to remain in the Midwest; the excitement of living in glamorous L.A. had little appeal to two modest Midwesterners. He would have taken the Minnesota offer, but a winter storm prevented officials there from reaching him with the offer before UCLA had tendered theirs, which he accepted. When Minnesota called the next day with their offer, which he would have preferred to accept, John politely declined to renege on his commitment to the Bruins.

They didn't like California at first, neither John, Nellie, nor their two kids. It was too big, hectic, and impersonal for their small-town tastes. But they got used to it, and prospered. John wasn't particularly thrilled with the playing and training facilities at UCLA either. Their second-story gym was a musty, small, dirty, and antiquated place they had to share with the school's other sports teams. They played only a few games there until the fire marshals told them it wasn't up to code and the Bruins would have to play their home games in borrowed gyms. Before practice every day, John and the team managers would sweep and mop the court with especially large brooms and mops that John had designed. It would be many years before UCLA built the first-rate modern facility, Pauley Pavilion, they had promised John when he signed on as coach.

Long before the Bruins had a spacious, modern arena to play in, John Wooden had built the most famous dynasty in college sports history. The twenty-seven years John Wooden coached UCLA basketball would be something to see for fans of the game today, when high school players go directly to the NBA, or stay in college only a year or two before leaving for the fat salaries and glamorous life of the pros; when players concentrate on their individual stats and publicity with only a passing thought for their team; when making the highlight reel with a dazzling dunk is as good if not better than winning the game; when behind-the-back passes to the trailing player are preferred to forward passes to an open man; when players wear shoes that cost hundreds of dollars, droopy shorts, and tattoos. One of my great regrets is that I was stuck in a place where I didn't get to watch basketball during most of the greatest years of UCLA's success. But what a success it was.

John's practices were notoriously arduous and long. He wanted his players to feel in practice the same pressure they would feel in a game. Bill Walton, who, like most of his teammates, maintains the highest esteem and affection for Coach Wooden, remembers their practices as constantly structured around four laws of learning: explanation, demonstration, correction, and repetition. But John never yelled at or terrorized his players. He corrected them when they made mistakes, but he would never embarrass anyone. He would encourage them, again and again, to work as hard as they could to become the best they could. "Players need models more than they need critics," he said. "Coach taught us self-discipline," remembered Kareem Abdul-Jabbar, "and he was always his own best example."

In his first year as UCLA's coach, the Bruins went 22–7; the next year, 24–7, when they received their first NCAA Tournament bid under his leadership. Six years later, the team played its first perfect league season, 16–0, a performance they would repeat eight times in John's career there. In 1962, the Bruins made the Final Four, but lost in the semifinals. Two years later, they won the championship. They won it the next year, too. Two years later, in 1967, with Lew Alcinder, they did it again, and once again the following year, and the year after that, and the year after that.

Then, in 1971, during the Walton years, they really got hot. They began a winning streak that wouldn't end for more than three seasons, when they lost to Notre Dame, an astonishing eighty-eight consecutive victories, including three national championships (which, if you're counting, made seven in a row). No other team had ever come close to such a streak. In 1975, the Bruins played for the national championship again. Before the game, Coach Wooden told his team that this would be his last game. He was sixty-five and had coached for forty years, twenty-seven at UCLA. I don't know how the players took the news. But, as usual, they won that night. John Wooden had led the Bruins to ten national championships, another record no other coach is ever likely to own. He was the best basketball coach in the history of the game, and everyone will always know it.

Character is what made him great. His own was beyond reproach. But what made him truly special was how by his example and teaching he made such a lasting impact on the character of his players. "Be the best in whatever endeavor you undertake. Don't worry about the score," Bill Walton remembers his coach telling him, "don't worry about image. Don't worry about the opponent." He helped them become better basketball players by teaching them the meaning of success, and all its component parts. His fifteen-step Pyramid of Success cites enthusiasm and industriousness as the cornerstones, but in the foundation is cooperation. He wanted unselfish players, who loved to play the game, but loved the team just as much.

I suspect he regrets the way some teams today are identified as one player's team. When Shaquille O'Neal left the Lakers, all the sportswriters remarked that it was Kobe Bryant's team now, Kobe's responsibility to win or lose. It's as if Kobe played all five positions. I doubt John

Wooden thinks much of that kind of basketball. It doesn't necessarily win championships. It sure doesn't make for a more beautiful game. And it doesn't make a player a better man. "Always think of passing the ball," John Wooden told his players, "before shooting it."

"It's such a team game. It's a beautiful game when it's played as a team. To me, it's not beautiful when it's one individual working one on one and making a fancy dunk. . . . That may be what most of the fans seem to love, but I don't."

His early championship teams were led by some of the shortest players to ever win a title. "But size isn't always the answer," Wooden points out. "The players accepted their roles. . . . Maybe there were some other teams that might have been individually better, but as a unit these were very strong teams.

"I tried to explain to my players that every person has a role and every role is important. . . . Fill your role. What good is an engine if you lose a wheel."

At ninety-five, Coach Wooden says he can remember most of the hundreds of boys who played for him, even most of his high school players. He knows where many of them are today. And you can be sure that his players remember him. Age might dim your memories of someone who taught you to be a better basketball player. But you never forget someone who taught you to be a better human being.

PART THREE

Strength

What stronger breastplate than a heart untainted!
Thrice is he arm'd that hath his quarrel just,
And he but naked, though lock'd up in steel,
Whose conscience with injustice is corrupted.

—HENRY VI

COURAGE

Edith Cavell

The dedicated nurse and lonely woman who gave her life to save others

"HOW MUCH TIME WILL THEY GIVE ME?" THE ENGLISH NURSE ASKED her visitor.

"Unfortunately, only until tomorrow morning," came the reply.

She had prepared for the moment as she had lived her life, dutiful, disciplined, and prayerful. Pastor Le Seur, the Lutheran minister who brought her the grim news that the German military court which had hastily and in secret tried and convicted her had just as hastily arranged her execution, found her quite resigned to her fate and brave. She had expected the sentence when she had asked him how much time remained to her. She may have been surprised to learn that her death was imminent, but with her usual reserve gave little outward sign of her despair. Le Seur recounts that "her cheeks were flushed and a moist film passed over her eyes—but only for a moment."

Edith Cavell hardly looked the part of an enemy of the German state. She was quite small and slender, forty-nine years old, with a thin, often unsmiling mouth, graying hair, and perceptive gray eyes. She wore a nurse's uniform, her daily costume for twenty years. She had been described by many who knew her in her profession as a hardworking, capable, and dedicated nurse, and a stern, austere, and humorless woman. Clearly, she took her responsibilities seriously, but that she was formal and aloof, even severe at times, in her professional conduct should not be taken as evidence of a cold, passionless character.

A warm heart is not always a light heart. A demonstrative personality is not proof of passion nor is a reserved one proof of its absence. How more passionate a love could anyone possess than that of a person who risks and surrenders everything out of a sense of duty to others? However guarded it might be, such passion is genuine and courageous and uncommon, as was Edith Cavell.

She was born in 1865, the oldest of four children, in the Norfolk village of Swardeston, where her father was vicar of the local Anglican church. Her family was close-knit, although the children were raised strictly by their serious father. They had a comfortable home, with a lovely, large garden, but little money, and they lived frugally. The Reverend Cavell personally saw to his children's early educations because they couldn't afford a governess or tutor. By instruction and example he encouraged in his children a deep sense of duty to others. He could be stern and demanding, but he was not without kindness. His children loved and respected him. On Sundays the children were not permitted any form of recreation. Even reading was forbidden. They attended church services in the morning and afternoon, and listened attentively to their father's sermons on the necessity of self-sacrifice and prayerfulness in a virtuous life. Edith once remarked to a friend that her father's sermons were long and dull, but their lessons made an impact on her, as did her father's exemplary behavior. Before they sat down for their Sunday dinner, the Cavells always carried portions of their meal to poor families in the parish.

What her father lacked in warmth and humor was more than compensated by the loving and generous nature of her mother, who shared with her daughter a gift for drawing and painting, and a love of nature and children. Edith remained devoted to her mother all her life. Years later, Edith, who would never marry, remarked to a friend, "with a mother like mine to look after, and . . . my work in the world which I love, I am such a happy old maid that everyone would feel envious of me if they only knew." For all the strictness of life in her father's vicarage, Edith's childhood was a happy one, where, except on Sundays, the children were always laughing and playing outdoors, skating in the winter, playing tennis in the summer, and she always remembered it fondly.

As a teenager, she attended various schools that emphasized the moral training her father insisted upon, and where she was noticed for her virtuousness, her fine hand at painting, and her fluency in French. Upon graduation, Edith was recommended as governess to several English families. And in 1890, eager to see something of the world, and improve her French, she accepted a post in Brussels as governess to four children in a Belgian family, the Francoises. The Francoises were fond of Edith and she of them though she took very seriously her responsibilities for educating the children. The strict discipline she imposed, however, was softened by her evident affection for them.

During her holidays at home in Norfolk, Edith developed the only known romantic attachment of her life, to her second cousin Eddie, whom, it is said, she had hopes of marrying. And though Eddie returned her affection, he was not, apparently, the marrying kind, and never proposed marriage to Edith nor anyone else. But he retained a special place in her affections all her life.

Her position in the Francois household ended in 1895, when Edith returned home to nurse her father through a serious illness. The experience was the motivation for a change in careers. Reminded of the moral obligation to others she had been raised to accept, Edith decided that she would become a professional nurse. She went to London to be trained, and remained there for several years as a nurse in private care and at hospitals for the poor. In 1906, she became the matron (head nurse) of a hospital in Manchester, where her devotion and skill were much appreciated by her destitute patients and by the doctors with whom she worked.

For much of the profession's history, nursing was reserved for women in religious orders, who had little if any formal training. In England, all that changed with Florence Nightingale, whose superior care of wounded British soldiers sparked a movement toward professionally trained nurses. But in much of the rest of Europe, nuns still dominated the vocation. In Belgium, a farsighted surgeon, Dr. Antoine Depage, sought to change this, and looked for someone capable of running a nurses' training school at the clinic he had established in a Brussels suburb. One of the Francois children, who had grown up to become a woman of influence, recommended Edith. She accepted the position in 1907.

She was, by all accounts, a gifted and fair teacher and administrator. She is also remembered for being quite strict and demanding with her nurses. She insisted they work hard and long hours, be clean, and precisely punctual at all times. If one of her nurses showed up a minute or two late for work, Edith would impose an extra two hours of duty on the offender. She also insisted her nurses adhere to the highest ethical standards, and possess a firm sense of duty to others. It was here that Edith gained her reputation for aloofness and severity, although her record of generosity to people in need shows how shallow such observations can be. However much her nurses might have chafed at her rigid discipline, they profited by it. Under her guidance, they became gifted professionals. And although initially the Church in Belgium and much of Belgian society resented the idea of lay nurses doing work that had always belonged to the Church, the improved care provided by the professional nurses Edith trained changed their views, and the school became a great success that profoundly influenced the way Belgian hospitals were run, and patients were treated.

Dr. Depage, though he certainly appreciated the devoted and talented woman he had hired as matron of the school, nevertheless frequently clashed with Edith over decisions related to the school's operation and curriculum. He was a forceful, brilliant, and temperamental man, and Edith, who could be just as forceful and determined, and very independent-minded, refused to defer to him when she believed him to be wrong. By this time, she was lecturing not only to student nurses but to doctors as well, and she was quite confident in her knowledge and ability. During these confrontations, Depage's wife, Maria, who was fond of Edith, would calm her angry husband, and persuade him to accept Edith's position, even if he couldn't bring himself to agree with it. In return, Edith held Maria Depage in the highest esteem and affection.

In August 1914, Edith was spending her holiday in Norwich with her now widowed mother when they heard the news that World War One had begun. Belgium would be on the frontlines of the war, and though her mother tried to persuade her to remain safely in England, Edith refused, and made plans to return to Brussels. "At a time like this," she insisted, "I am more needed than ever."

Back in Brussels, the war raging, Edith insisted that the clinic, which had become a Red Cross hospital, treat all wounded soldiers without regard to nationality. Belgian, French, and German soldiers were all cared for by her well-trained nurses. When Brussels surrendered to the invading German armies, the German authorities removed their wounded to their own hospital, and ordered most foreign nurses to return to their own countries. For unknown reasons, they allowed Edith to remain.

In that first year of the war, the Germans quickly swept through Belgium, forcing the British, Belgian, and French armies south toward France. Hundreds of retreating soldiers were cut off from their armies by the swiftly advancing German troops. They hid in the Belgian countryside, seeking what shelter they could find. Many of those who were caught were shot immediately by German soldiers. So they took cover in the woods, in churches and convents, in the homes, cellars, and barns of sympathetic Belgians, and in Edith's hospital. It is a testament to the patriotism and courage of those Belgians who risked hiding Allied soldiers that they did so knowing that the Germans had announced they would shoot anyone helping enemy soldiers to escape. It's a testament to Edith Cavell's courage as well, and to her deep humanity.

In November 1914, a Belgian patriot, Herman Capiau, brought two disguised British soldiers, a lieutenant colonel with a broken leg and a sergeant, to Edith, and asked her to shelter them. She accepted the responsibility without hesitation or question, and she gave them beds and food and treated their wounds. When they were well enough to travel, Edith arranged for two

English civilians living in Brussels to escort them north to the Netherlands, from where they could make their way back to England.

Capiau was part of a Belgian underground organization that assisted Allied soldiers in escaping the country. He reported Edith's assistance to a Belgian aristocrat and his wife who led the organization, the Prince and Princess de Croy. A little while later, Prince de Croy visited Edith and asked if she would consider helping them aid other soldiers. Again, Edith immediately consented. Over the next nine months, she sheltered, fed, and treated as many as two hundred British, Belgian, and French soldiers in her hospital, and helped them escape. She gave them money, secured false identification papers for them, arranged for guides to lead them out of the country, and, if necessary, escorted them herself to another hiding place or to a meeting place. She was a British patriot, which no doubt encouraged her to take such risks. But more important, she felt, as she had felt all her life, a sense of duty to help those who could not help themselves, and to make whatever sacrifices her duty expected of her. It was no difference to her whether the object of her care was a sick patient or a soldier running for his life. She was a deeply compassionate woman, and she had the courage to remain so in the face of grave danger.

She managed to keep her secret work from most of the nurses she supervised. She did not want to endanger them, as she endangered herself. As the months wore on, Edith began to sense that her efforts had aroused suspicion, and would soon be discovered. She wrote her cousin and former suitor, Eddie, that she was helping the British war effort "in ways I may not describe to you till we are free." And she wrote her beloved mother that she feared she would soon be arrested. By the time the letter reached England, its prediction had come true.

A Brussels architect, Philippe Baucq, a member of Edith's underground railroad, was arrested first. When they raided his house, the Germans discovered various documents, some of which mentioned Edith's name. Prince de Croy came to Brussels from his country estate to warn his comrades that they were in danger. He visited Edith, told her he was going into hiding, and suggested she immediately do the same, and they would try to get her home to England. Independent and stubborn as ever, she refused, although she conceded that she expected to be arrested. Her friend Maria Depage had been a passenger on the ocean liner *Lusitania*, which had just been sunk by German submarines. She felt firm in her conviction that she must make the sacrifices necessary to do her duty. She had a responsibility to people who were depending on her, and she would not shrink from it. "Escape for me is futile and unthinkable," she explained.

A few days later, a German secret police officer, Otto Mayer, arrived at the hospital and took Edith into custody. They interrogated her for three days, without result. Finally, to induce Edith to confess, he informed her that more than thirty of her colleagues had been arrested and had confessed. They had not, but Edith believed the lie, and provided Mayer with all the information he required concerning her activities. Over thirty of her associates were arrested and brought to trial as well. Only two would be executed, Philippe Baucq and Edith Cavell. The rest would be saved by her death.

The Germans held her in solitary confinement for ten weeks. The only evidence of her guilt they possessed, in addition to her confession, was a postcard she had received from one of the British soldiers she had helped escape who had written to thank her. She was allowed to write and to receive letters. Without any sign of regret, she defended her actions to her correspondents with the simple justification, "Had I not helped, they would have been shot." That was all her conscience required for her to risk and sacrifice her own life. She had been raised to value other people's lives as much as she valued her own.

Her trial lasted two days. She was convicted on the morning of October 11, 1915, by a military court of "successfully conducting allied soldiers to the enemy of the German people." It was a capital offense, and, as the law required, she was sentenced to be shot. The law did not require the sentence to be carried out immediately, but the Germans were in a hurry. They feared the unfavorable international attention the execution of a middle-aged nurse, particularly one so selfless and brave, would cause them. They hastily arranged her execution for the following day.

The American and Spanish ambassadors frantically and repeatedly appealed for mercy on her behalf, but their appeals were rebuffed by the German military governor. She was allowed a visit by German Army chaplain, Pastor Le Seur, who offered to minister to her in her last hours. She politely rejected his assistance. He was a German Lutheran and she was a member of the Anglican faith. She did, however, accept his offer to arrange for an Anglican minister, Reverend Stirling Gahan, to visit her. Since the Germans would not permit an English clergyman to attend her execution, she accepted gratefully Le Seur's offer to support her at the end.

The Reverend Gahan, who was quite moved by the experience, recalled his visit to Edith on her last night. When he arrived at her cell, she was lying on her cot. She rose to greet him, pulling her robe on, and holding it to her. She was calm and resigned. Her life had been so hurried and not always happy, she told him, and she had welcomed an opportunity to do her duty for her country and the men she had saved. She also allowed that she was "thankful for these ten weeks of quiet to get ready." She accepted the justice of her sentence, and had "been kindly treated here. . . . Standing as I do in view of God and eternity, I realize that patriotism is not enough, I must have no hatred or bitterness towards anyone." She received communion, and sang with Gahan the popular Victorian hymn "Abide with Me."

> Abide with me; fast falls the eventide;
> The darkness deepens; Lord with me abide.
> When other helpers fail and comforts flee,
> Help of the helpless, O abide with me.

She had few possessions in her room: two vases of dying roses that had been sent to her by her nurses, a Bible, her prayer book, and *The Imitation of Christ,* the spiritual devotion written by a fifteenth-century monk. She had scribbled her most recent thoughts into her prayer book and in the flyleaf of the *Imitation.* She had also written many letters to her mother, her friends and loved ones, and to her nurses. To all she said a last good-bye, and asked them not to grieve too much for her loss. She had been prepared for death, and accepted it confident that she would leave this world for a better one.

The American ambassador who had failed to convince the Germans to show her mercy described touchingly the sentiments she expressed in her last letter to her nurses: "She had been a strong disciplinarian, a self-contained nature, which she had completely mastered, sternest always with herself; and in asking those girls, who may not always have understood her, O forgive what they may have considered her severity, she was with that touching confession telling them that she loved them more than they ever knew."

Pastor Le Seur arrived before dawn the next morning to accompany her to the place of her execution. He found her ready for the appointed hour, "all her little property [packed] with the greatest care in a handbag." She and Philippe Baucq were driven to the courtyard where the sentence would be carried out. Baucq had shaken the hands of his German guards and offered that he would "bear no grudge," and called out to his executioners that "we are all comrades." Le Seur gave Edith a final blessing, and she squeezed his hand in return. "Ask Mr. Gahan," she requested him, "to tell my loved ones later on that my soul, as I believe, is safe, and that I am glad to die for my country."

Then she was blindfolded and bound to a stake. A column of eight men fired the shots that claimed her life. All present would confirm that she died as she had lived, with the courage of a loving heart.

SELF-CONTROL

George Washington

*The self-made man who learned to govern himself before
he governed the great country that would claim him as our father*

THE COMMANDER-IN-CHIEF OF THE CONTINENTAL ARMY HAD DETER-
mined to strike Sir Henry Clinton's much larger British force while it
slowly progressed from Philadelphia to New York with its supply lines
stretched thin for miles. He gave command of the American advance forces to General
Charles Lee, a rather odd, experienced officer, formerly a soldier of fortune for several
European monarchs, who was notorious for his wanton lifestyle, excessive drinking, and
the rough company he preferred to that of polite society. His behavior toward his superiors was often impertinent, a reflection of the scorn he felt for anyone's military talents
save his own. He was argumentative, surly, and incapable of controlling the fiery temper
that had earned him an Indian name that translated as "boiling water."

Lee had denounced as foolish the decision to confront the British in New Jersey, and
at first refused the command of the advance forces. When the command was offered to
the young Marquis de Lafayette, Lee reversed himself and grudgingly accepted the assignment. His orders were to attack the rear of the British force, unless extraordinary and
unforeseen circumstances prevented him from doing so, and keep it engaged until the rest
of the Continental Army could arrive on the field.

The morning of June 28, 1778, broke hot and humid at Monmouth Court House in Free-hold, New Jersey. The thermometer rose to nearly one hundred degrees. Men on foot and horse-back stripped to the waist to seek some relief from the roasting heat. Even breathing was difficult. Before the day ended, many men and horses would escape death by musket ball and bayonet only to perish from sunstroke. With little guidance from Lee, his troops struck the British rearguard in an uncoordinated attack, with some units fighting while others remained unengaged. Confusion overtook the ranks as some troops, not knowing whether to advance or retreat, chose the latter course as a matter of prudence. Lee, apparently, did nothing to impose order on his bewildered soldiers, but replied to a questioning aide dispatched by the commander-in-chief to ascertain his progress, "Tell the General I am doing well enough." The general himself soon rode onto the scene to see for himself what Lee meant by "well enough."

The scene George Washington surveyed as he rode up beside his diffident subordinate shocked him and unleashed a Washington attribute that was much rumored about but infrequently witnessed—his colossal temper. Seeing the American ranks completely broken and in headlong retreat from the enemy, Washington shouted at Lee, "What is the meaning of this, sir? I desire to know the meaning of this disorder and confusion!"

"The troops," Lee responded, "would not stand the British bayonets."

"You damn poltroon," Washington countered, "you never tried them."

Washington, briefly but forcefully, did as much violence to Lee as one could do when using words as weapons. According to General Charles Scott, who was present at the encounter, Washington "swore on that day until the leaves shook on the trees." Washington was famous for his impenetrable reserve and unfailing civility, qualities that were hard purchased for someone whose temperament was by nature passionate and sensitive. He had to be mightily provoked into even minor lapses of self-control, but Lee's incompetence had been sufficient to do the trick, and the explosion that resulted was, to all who witnessed its fury, unforgettable.

The situation was desperate, however. The Americans were on the brink of a humiliating defeat, and Washington couldn't afford to lavish any more of his angry attention on Charles Lee. He ordered Lee from the field, and spurred his white charger into the thick of the retreating soldiers, shouting at them to "stand fast . . . and receive your enemy. The [army] is advancing to support you." He was everywhere at once, while British cannonballs tore up the earth all around him, beseeching, frightening, inspiring his fleeing soldiers to turn around and fight. His horse collapsed from exhaustion, and he quickly mounted another, impervious to the enveloping danger, undaunted by imminent catastrophe; he was as magnificent on that day as on any day of the long and costly war for American independence. "Never have I beheld so superb a man," Lafayette remembered. The soldiers, chastened by his example of courage, rallied, reformed their ranks, and charged the enemy. By the day's end, the Americans held the field, having inflicted twice as many casualties on the enemy as they had suffered.

At the Battle of Monmouth Court House, the Americans privileged to serve under Washington's command saw for themselves the essence of his extraordinary strength—his iron will, forged in the furnace of a passionate temperament that he disciplined by a supreme exertion of self-control. It is no exaggeration to acknowledge Washington as the father of our country or to suggest that by exercising the famous self-control with which he governed himself he virtually willed America into existence. In the storied annals of American history, only two men are indispensable to the salvation of our country, Abraham Lincoln and George Washington. It is arguable who was the most important, but it is beyond dispute that we could not have survived the absence of either at the moment their service was needed.

By the time he accepted command of the army from the Continental Congress on June 16, 1775, and rode immediately to relieve the American defenders at Boston, he was, in the observation of one witness at Philadelphia, "a complete gentleman." He hadn't always been, although from early youth he strove to earn the distinction.

He had first sought martial glory twenty years before in the French and Indian War. The twenty-two-year-old Washington, a surveyor and aspiring gentleman planter, had written to the governor of Virginia, Robert Dinwiddie, to offer his services as a soldier in an approaching conflict with the French, who were invading and building forts in lands beyond the Appalachians that the British crown claimed and called the Ohio country. Although he had no military experience, he was given the rank of lieutenant colonel and marched at the head of two companies of Virginia militia into Pennsylvania. There he would join Britain's Indian allies and confront the French at Ft. Duquesne, located at the site of the future city of Pittsburgh.

Forty miles from the fort, Washington discovered a French platoon encamped in a clearing. With forty Virginians and his Indian allies, Washington encircled the French and ordered the attack. The engagement was quick and decisive. When the French officer in command, Joseph Coulon de Villiers, Sieur de Jumonville, tried to surrender and explained that he commanded a diplomatic mission, Washington was unable to prevent Tanacharison, his principal Indian ally, from splitting the unfortunate Jumonville's head with a tomahawk, and ordering his braves to do likewise to the other French wounded.

Though the French were outraged, the account Washington sent to Dinwiddie made no mention of the atrocity, but simply noted Jumonville's death in battle. His small victory in the Pennsylvania wilderness was celebrated throughout Virginia, the other colonies, and in Great Britain, and helped make Washington's reputation as a man of military promise. Washington had ordered the first shots fired in the French and Indian War, the initial theater of the first truly world war, known in history as the Seven Years' War, and it was the first sign that the young Virginian might become a man of some importance.

Washington was promoted to colonel and given reinforcements that increased the number of his force to 350 men. He raised a crudely built fort not distant from the site of his recent victory, and prepared to face a larger detachment of French soldiers from Ft. Duquesne who were marching to avenge Jumonville. The location he chose for Ft. Necessity betrayed Washington's inexperience. It sat on a river bottom surrounded by wooded hills on three sides, giving the enemy higher ground and sheltered positions to make short work of Washington's defenses. On the morning of July 3, 1754, seven hundred French soldiers besieged Ft. Necessity. By the day's end, his situation hopeless, Washington surrendered.

The French permitted Washington and his troops to march back to Virginia on the condition that he sign a surrender agreement that consented to a prohibition of the building of new British forts in the Ohio country for a year, and acknowledged that Jumonville had been assassinated. This last condition caused him considerable embarrassment when he returned to Virginia, and he claimed that he had not understood the French word for assassination, and would have refused to sign had he known its import.

His humbling defeat didn't tarnish his growing reputation among Virginians. Ever sensitive to slights, he bitterly resigned his commission over a dispute about the payment of colonial officers, and when he learned that the British would not accept his rank as the equivalent of a regular army commission. But when General Edward Braddock and an army of British regulars arrived in Virginia in February 1755 to launch a campaign against Ft. Duquesne, he could not resist the allure of battlefield glory, and petitioned Braddock for a commission in his army. The general offered him a position as his aide with an honorary rank of colonel. Washington accepted, and though he quarreled with his superior on the march into Pennsylvania over tactics and the character and fighting merits of Americans, Braddock nevertheless regarded his intemperate young aide well. His confidence would prove to be well placed.

Although Washington's advice that Braddock divide his slow-moving column and march an advance guard ahead to meet the French proved unsound, the consequences of the misadventure occasioned the first vivid display of Washington's courage and coolness under fire. Nine hundred French and Indian soldiers ambushed Braddock as his troops crossed the Monongahela River. Washington, quite ill with dysentery, had initially remained behind with the main body of the army, but had just been carried by wagon to Braddock's side when the fighting commenced. It was a disaster. The smaller British force was immediately overwhelmed, and Braddock, who behaved with conspicuous bravery, was mortally wounded.

Washington, despite his illness, threw himself boldly into the battle. At first he tried to help Braddock rally his panicked soldiers, and when that effort fell short of preventing defeat, he galloped back to the rear and returned with the Virginia militia to attack the French flank. With a presence of mind seemingly impervious to danger, Washington was extraordinary. Through hails of gunfire, he imposed order out of chaos while two horses were shot out from under him and four musket balls tore his coat. He even managed to attend Braddock as the general breathed his last. His efforts secured an organized line of retreat and saved the army from total annihilation. For his efforts he was appointed commander of all Virginia troops.

The next few years were frustrating ones for Washington. He saw little significant action in the war, and he could not suffer with grace the lack of respect by British regulars for his commission and other inequities he viewed as insults to his honor. He complained constantly and bitterly to his superiors, criticized the performance and character of men serving under him, as well as British officers he felt didn't deserve to hold superior rank to his, and even sharply criticized his patron, Governor Dinwiddie, showing an ingratitude that was not the quality of a gentleman. When near the end of the war he marched with yet another column to Ft. Duquesne, he despaired over another lost chance for glory when the French evacuated and burned the fort before the British arrived. He resigned his colonial commission as a brigadier general in 1759, took a seat in the Virginia legislature, the House of Burgesses, and married an extremely wealthy widow, Martha Dandridge Custis, whose dowry would help him become one of the richest and most prominent men in Virginia society.

Though he had revealed in his time in uniform certain unattractive qualities of temperament that he had not yet learned to govern, he had made an attractive reputation for himself as a conspicuously brave, able commander, and a man of considerable merit. He prized his reputation above most accomplishments but was so overly sensitive to criticism and even imagined slights that he felt insecure despite the laurels that his courage and competence had won him. He could not restrain himself from an often unnecessary and excessive self-defense of his record and character. But he had never been one to resort only to protestations to secure his good name. He was tirelessly devoted to self-improvement as well. More self-aware than most, he knew he must control his passion and threw himself at a very early age into the challenge with the same unyielding determination that he displayed in battle.

When he next put on a uniform, he would not be the same person who had felt so deeply trivial insults. He would never be indifferent to criticism, but he would not allow himself to despair that its effect would destroy his reputation. His character would prevent that. He would be a complete gentleman, and his destiny, as he conceived it, would become inextricably linked to the destiny of his country.

His father had died when Washington was eleven years old. His relations with his mother were unpleasant. He was raised by his older brothers Augustine and Lawrence, primarily the latter, who at his death left Washington the estate he had built on the banks of the Potomac, Mount Vernon, which Washington, after his marriage, would greatly expand and improve. Yet despite the care and affection he received from his brothers, Washington felt keenly his lack of advantage as a fatherless youth, with no material resources of his own, little formal education, and a station in the polite society of colonial Virginia well below that of the vast landholding aristocracy. But he determined that he would rise to prominence in that society by merit and perseverance, and the waste of a single hour in that pursuit pained him.

At fourteen, he transcribed in a copybook the principles with which he intended to govern his manner and character, "110 Rules of Civility and Decent Behavior in Company and Conversation." Some of them seem rather comical and antique to the contemporary reader. "Spit not into the fire . . . especially if there be meat in it. Bedew no man's face with your spittle, by approaching too near to him when you speak. Kill no vermin as fleas, lice, ticks . . . in the sight of others." Other of its recommendations, however, are more serious principles of good character and a sense of honor. Perhaps the first and last of the 110 were the most important to Washington: "Every action done in company, ought to be with some sign of respect, to those that are present"; and, "Labor to keep alive in your breast that little spark of celestial fire called conscience."

He was intent on becoming a man of unquestioned dignity and he labored always to achieve the manners, appearance, and temperament that were its physical expressions. Nature aided him significantly in this endeavor. He grew to be six-feet-two, a full head above the average height of the time, and his physical prowess was formidable. He was quite athletic, lean and muscular, with notable strength, his posture impeccably straight but graceful rather than stiff. He mastered horseback riding so completely that no man of his time cut a finer figure in the saddle. He taught himself to dance with exquisite skill. His clothes were fine and neat but never flamboyant. He presented, as an admirer later observed, such an aura of command that "there is not a king in Europe that would not look like a valet . . . by his side."

He consciously groomed and comported himself and cultivated his manners to present that image to the world. He was unfailingly courteous and rarely uncivil to anyone, of higher or lower station. He was careful not to brag or be immodest in any way. But he kept a cool reserve and distance from others, and could remain inscrutably silent in the midst of heated disagreements among his peers. When an acquaintance suggested that his facial expressions often indicated what he was feeling, Washington corrected, "You are wrong, sir, my countenance never betrays my thoughts." He seems, somehow, to have anticipated that history would hold an august office for him, and how well he occupied that place would be for him the ultimate proof of his honor. He was quite aware of his faults as well as his strengths, but believed that human nature could be improved upon, and if not perfected, brought much closer to perfection than might have seemed possible at one's birth.

He was a keen observer of other people's character as well. He had seen the worst excesses of human nature in his days as a colonial officer—greed, selfishness, cowardice, laziness, fractiousness—and he knew that if his countrymen did not govern their character, their flaws would restrain the progress of the republic. But he never doubted that others could improve their nature, that the character of an entire country could be governed by example and by a firm, guiding hand. He would be that example.

During the years between wars, he became a man of great wealth and influence, who loved the life of the gentleman farmer, managing his estates with prudence and fairness, hunting fox and riding for hours, entertaining company with well-prepared food, excellent wine, and good conversation, watching from his veranda as the sun rose above the Maryland hills. It was always hard to part from his good life at Mount Vernon. But part with it he would for many, many years.

His patriotism was as genuine as his courage, and indispensable to his sense of honor. He had long resented the haughtiness that characterized British regard for American colonialists, and the restraints imposed on American trade and westward expansion. When the British Parliament attempted to discipline its unruly colonies by dispatching an army to subdue Boston, he pledged his fortune and honor to the cause of American independence.

It was no surprise that he was selected to command the Continental Army. He was not only the best man for the office but quite probably the only man capable of leading the undermanned, ill-equipped, poorly prepared army through the long eight years of strife, surviving one defeat after another, but remaining in the field, and winning just enough victories to break the will of the enemy. To do that his own will would have to be without equal. And it was. In defeat and victory, through the bitter, devastating winters at Valley Forge and Morristown, in the face of Congress's and the colonies' bickering, criticism, and appalling failure to provide adequately for his troops; despite the constant departures of troops whose enlistment had expired; surviving myriad disappointment and treachery—he willed himself, his starved, barefoot, ill-clothed, and poorly armed soldiers, and his country on and on and on until the opportunity for victory arrived at Yorktown and he seized it.

The self-control he mastered to shape his behavior and character had grown immense by his maturity, and its effect on his judgment and leadership proved an inestimable benefit to his country. Again and again, had he let his sensitivity to criticism, his passion for martial glory, his former impetuousness, his intense desire for honor overcome his judgment, his country would have been lost. But he never did.

After his calamitous defeats in Brooklyn and Manhattan, he realized that he must avoid full-scale battles with the superior British Army, no matter how glorious an opportunity was presented, unless the circumstances were distinctly advantageous. He knew that victory would be long and difficult to achieve, that he would suffer many setbacks and deprivations. But if he could keep his army in the field, they would, in the end, prevail, no matter how distant the end was. So he harassed the enemy, striking when they didn't expect, sometimes winning a small engagement, sometimes losing, but always marching off to fight another day.

Congress was a constant source of frustration, never responding adequately to his appeals for food and arms for his troops, or to his sound argument that they needed to support a professional regular army rather than rely on the poorly trained, short-term militia. Yet he accepted the ideal that the officers of a republican army must always defer to civilian authority, and he never once violated that trust.

He knew that the French fleet was indispensable to the ultimate success of their cause, and its repeated delays in arriving upset him, but he never betrayed his anger to the French lest they decide never to arrive.

At the end of the war, as unpaid Continental soldiers were on the brink of mutiny, and some of his officers as well as certain members of Congress were plotting a military coup to rob Congress of its authority and make Washington a dictator, he staged perhaps the most carefully crafted and inspiring public appearance of his career. On March 16, 1783, he addressed his officers, several of whom were complicit in the plot, at Newburgh, New York, where the army was then headquartered. Never had his civility been more complete, more appropriate to the circumstances.

He walked slowly to the podium, the very essence of modesty and composure, and retrieved the speech he had written from the pocket of his coat. In his prepared remarks he would express his sincere devotion to the men who had risked their lives and fortunes to fight beside him through the long, dark years of war. He assured them that he would always remain their greatest admirer and defender. And then he beseeched them for the sake of their country and their sacred honor to denounce anyone who "wishes to overturn the liberties of our country, and who wickedly attempts to open the flood gates of civil discord." But nothing in his address so moved his audience, as he knew it would, than the small gesture he performed before he read from his text. He glanced at the paper before him for a moment, and then paused to pull from his vest pocket a pair of glasses. Washington had become an old man under the tremendous strain of the endless war. No one had ever seen him wear glasses before. He put them on, looked upon his brothers in arms, and apologized. "Gentlemen, you will permit me to put on my spectacles, for I have not only grown gray but almost blind in the service of my country."

His officers were undone by the almost certainly planned demonstration of noble selflessness, and the virtuous modesty of the dignified presence who had for so long shared their dangers and sacrifices. Men openly wept at the sight. Major Samuel Shaw, who was present at the address, recorded the scene. "There was something so natural, so unaffected in this appeal as rendered it superior to the most studied oratory. It forced its way to the heart, and you might see sensibility moisten every eye."

The Newburgh conspiracy died when Washington refused to become a Napoléon, his ambitious nature and craving for glory subordinated to the will he employed in service to his country, and with a simple gesture reminded his men what they had all suffered so much to achieve. In November that year, he would bid them all a tearful farewell at Fraunces Tavern in New York City, and the next month, offer one last compelling demonstration of his fidelity to his principles and his country when he surrendered his sword and commission to Congress in Annapolis.

He returned to his beloved Mount Vernon, only to be summoned too few years later to preside over the Constitutional Convention that convened in Philadelphia to form a more perfect union, and provide a federal government, which Washington knew was necessary to improve the character of a nation that was otherwise intent on division among its squabbling states, and the reckless pursuit of narrow self-interest. He was unanimously elected president of the new republic for two terms, and as president contributed his policies and his example to the achievement of a strong, stable government. He kept us out of war between France and Great Britain, enduring vicious criticism for his neutrality, and built the institutions and precedents that would guide our country in perpetuity.

At the end of his second term, with another his for the asking, he left office voluntarily, establishing another precedent and teaching another character lesson to his countrymen. America would have no kings. The people would rule. But neither would we in the name of liberty conduct ourselves with such abandon that we would suffer the excesses of the French Revolution, where the cause of liberty, equality, and brotherhood descended into chaos and the cruelty of the guillotine, and ultimately into the arms of a waiting dictator.

He understood the nature of his countrymen as well as he understood his own. He knew we are all flawed, that we must always be alert to the danger of ungoverned appetites, and must strive to control and improve our nature. He understood his country at its birth needed a leader of towering honor, wisdom, and selflessness, whose appearance must fit the role as well as his character did. And through the constant application of his self-control, he inhabited that role as no one has again, and became, in fact, the father of our country. He imprinted his character on his nation, and in that sense we are all his descendants, a people famous for our constant struggle to improve. We are never so removed from the failings of our nature that we cannot stand more improvement, but neither are we so removed from Washington's magnificent example that we dare not dream we can achieve it.

CONFIDENCE

Elizabeth I

Raised in fear and uncertainty, but with the heart of a king,
she became the greatest ruler of her time.

ER BIRTH WAS A GREAT DISAPPOINTMENT TO HER FATHER. THE king's physicians and astrologers had assured him that his new queen was carrying a male child. He had risked his crown and his soul in order that he might have a male heir to succeed him. Henry VIII had thought himself cursed before, and now he felt ill-fated again with the birth of another daughter. He had risked all, separated from his wife and married another, been ordered excommunicated by the pope, seized all authority for the Church in England, risked the wrath of the most powerful king in Europe and his former wife's uncle, the Holy Roman emperor Charles V, thrown his kingdom into turmoil, lost the counsel of his wisest advisor, Thomas More, whom he would soon have executed, all this for the son he expected but was not given. All this for another daughter. Surely, he thought, God was tormenting him for his past misdeeds. But being cursed did not humble the king. It angered him, and his anger could be a ferocious thing. He must have raged tremendously at this new misfortune, at fate, at God, at his young queen, perhaps even at the newborn princess.

Queen Anne must have felt keenly the king's displeasure, and trembled at the thought of its consequences. She had replaced as queen the much loved Catherine of Aragon, for the express purpose of giving birth to a prince, and she had failed in this most important duty. She was not popular, and although her family, the Boleyns, were great schemers at court, she knew her future depended entirely on the king's favor. If she lost that, she would be doomed. The king had already begun to tire of her. He had dispensed with one wife who disappointed him, and had forced the Church in England to obey his will. What would stop him from ridding himself of her?

Into this perilous world, on September 7, 1533, Elizabeth Tudor, second daughter of Henry VIII, princess of England, was born. She was not greeted with a mother's joy or a father's pride. In her first experience of life, incomprehensible as it was to an infant, she met a terrified mother, an angry father, a resentful older sister, the ill will of Catholic monarchs throughout Europe, and the dangerous ambitions of scheming enemies everywhere. She would have to become an extraordinary woman to survive, much less become a queen.

Disappointed though Henry was, the infant Elizabeth was still the daughter of the king of England. She would receive the honors due a royal princess. She was christened with the lavish pomp and pageantry Henry favored for great occasions of state. He instructed Mary, his seventeen-year-old daughter with the former queen, to surrender her title, Princess of Wales. The title would belong, if only briefly, to Elizabeth. But the new princess of Wales would not enjoy her father's favor for long. Queen Anne twice more carried the king's child, and hoped for a male heir. She miscarried the first, and in 1536, gave birth to a stillborn infant son. Henry's rage hardened into contempt for the wife who had failed him. Anne Boleyn's fate was sealed.

She was tried on various false charges, convicted and imprisoned in the Tower of London, from where she would later be taken to her execution. Legend has it that as Anne's royal barge carried her down the Thames River to the Tower, and came in view of the king's residence, she held up the two-and-a-half-year-old Elizabeth and pleaded to Henry for mercy. The king refused to look at his wife and daughter, and he had no mercy to spare. Seventeen days later, Elizabeth was motherless and soon to be dispossessed of her title, Princess of Wales.

Henry married Jane Seymour, who, the following year, gave him his long-awaited son and heir, Edward, and died a few days later from the strain of childbirth. Henry next married Anne of Cleves, whom he soon divorced. Catherine Howard became his fifth wife, but she was a foolish young woman, who resumed a love affair with a former suitor. Henry had executed a wife for much less, and when Catherine's infidelity was exposed, she, too, fell to the headman's ax. He took another, much younger wife to be his sixth queen, Catherine Parr. She would be his last. The king was getting old, had grown fat, and suffered from various infirmities. He died three and a half years later in 1547.

Until her father's death, Elizabeth lived with her half brother and future king, Edward. As childhood companions, who were tutored and played together, they grew very close. Henry's frequent remarriages had little effect on Elizabeth, although when she was eight she is reported to have remarked to Robert Dudley, a childhood and lifelong intimate friend, that she would never marry. She lost all royal titles once Edward was born, and for a time avoided being the object of dangerous political intrigue. Henry treated her affectionately on the few occasions when they were together. Catherine Parr, her father's last wife, was a kind and loving stepmother, who made certain Elizabeth was well treated and given an excellent education. When Henry died, and Edward was crowned king, Elizabeth was sent to live with Catherine, now the queen dowager. Catherine soon remarried to Thomas Seymour, her brother's uncle, and eventually Elizabeth, without intending to, would find herself endangered by the politics of Edward's court.

For a time, though, her life was tranquil. She was attended by her governess, Kat Ashley, and a servant, Blanche Parry, who were lovingly devoted to her, and whom Elizabeth loved in return. Catherine Parr had arranged for a leading scholar, Roger Asham, to be Elizabeth's tutor. She was his prize student. She was a serious young girl with an inquisitive and retentive mind. She loved reading and languages. She studied history, philosophy, and mathematics. She could read and converse in Latin and Greek, as well as French, Italian, and Spanish. Raised a Protestant, as was her brother, she took great care in her study of theology, and became well versed in the religious arguments of the period that were dividing English society and causing political turmoil throughout Europe. She could read music and play various instruments and learned to dance exceptionally well.

She was growing into an attractive young woman, not classically beautiful, but striking. Tall and thin, she dressed plainly as a girl, often in simple black or white, with little jewelry or makeup. But her fair complexion and blazing red hair, her natural elegance, and her unusually mature composure attracted much favorable comment from admirers. She had a temper, which she kept in reserve as a girl but that would one day prove as potent, if not as dangerous, as her father's. She could ride a horse as well as a man. She was exceptional in every respect.

Thomas Seymour, Catherine Parr's new husband, took special notice of the adolescent Elizabeth. He was very affectionate with her, more attentive than was appropriate for a surrogate father. Elizabeth at first enjoyed the attentions of the handsome Seymour, but after a while, his increasing familiarity caused her to worry about his intentions. When Catherine died after delivering Seymour's child, the widower's interest in Elizabeth took a dangerous turn.

Thomas Seymour's brother, Edward Seymour, was lord protector of England. He governed

England while King Edward was still too young to manage the affairs of the kingdom. Thomas envied his brother's power and plotted to replace him. He intended to marry Elizabeth, kidnap the king, and marry him to a Tudor cousin, Lady Jane Grey, and have himself installed as regent. He asked the fifteen-year-old Elizabeth for her hand, which she refused, but her suitor persistently attempted to persuade her to reconsider.

When the plot was discovered at court and Seymour was arrested, Elizabeth, because of Seymour's marriage proposal to her, was implicated in the scheme. Her brother's affections for her were strained. Her servants, among them her beloved Kat Ashley and Blanche Parry, were arrested and sent to the Tower. She was investigated at great length by one of Edward's counselors. She took great care with her answers to his many questions, which were intended to trick some form of confession from her. Had she been less effective in her own defense she would have surely joined her loved ones in the Tower, and, perhaps, have eventually faced her mother's fate. She was just a girl, all alone, with no friend or advisor to rely on for guidance. But with great skill and courage she maintained her innocence and denied her interrogator any evidence that could confirm her guilt. She was certainly frightened. What person of her young age wouldn't be, especially one who had lost her mother to a king's lethal wrath? Her steadfastness in the face of such a serious threat, despite fears that would have paralyzed most adults, revealed her uncommon reserves of strength and confidence, the qualities of a king that she had inherited from her father. She would need them as she faced down even greater dangers in the menacing years ahead.

Elizabeth remained under suspicion, and for a time was not welcome at her brother's court. She stayed at Hatfield, the manor house her brother had given her, where she had lived with her devoted servants for much of her early life. By the time she reconciled with Edward, his reign was nearing its end. The fifteen-year-old king was dying of tuberculosis, and the future of the English monarchy was unsettled. Next in the line of succession was Elizabeth's older half sister, Mary. But Mary remained a devout Catholic. Edward and the powerful men in his court, led by the new lord protector, John Dudley, were Protestants, and were determined to keep the crown from Mary, although Henry's will had declared Mary his rightful heir after Edward, and Elizabeth after her.

To disinherit Mary, Dudley would also have to deny Elizabeth's legitimacy as an heir to the crown even though she, like her brother, had been raised a Protestant. So, as Edward lay dying, Dudley put in motion a scheme to secure the crown for the king's cousin, Lady Jane Grey. Dudley arranged for the young and naive Jane to marry his youngest son, Guildford, and intended to proclaim his daughter-in-law queen once Edward died. He also intended to arrest both Mary and Elizabeth. He summoned both sisters to court on the pretense of visiting their dying brother.

Elizabeth, sensing the danger that awaited her there, sent word to Dudley that she was ill and unable to travel. Mary, however, lacked Elizabeth's keen instinct for the hazards of court politics, and began the journey to Edward's court.

Dudley's plot was a bold and dangerous gamble, and far from a sure thing. English Catholics, who were still numerous in the north of England, strongly favored Mary's accession to the throne, as did many Protestants who believed Henry's wishes should be honored even if it meant a Catholic would wear his crown. A supporter with knowledge of Dudley's intentions reached Mary on her way to court and warned her of his plan. Mary quickly changed course and traveled north to rally support for her cause.

When Edward died, Jane Grey was proclaimed queen, and Dudley remained lord protector. The new queen's reign and Dudley's did not last long. Mary and her supporters marched into London only nine days later. Dudley, the child he had made a queen, and her new husband were sent to the Tower. They would all soon face the ax. Days before, Mary had summoned Elizabeth to join her triumphal procession to London. Elizabeth rode to meet her sister, and when she reached the royal entourage, dismounted and knelt before her sister and sovereign. Mary dismounted and bid her sister to rise, embraced her, and invited her to ride beside her into London.

The differences between the two sisters couldn't have been more striking. Mary, thirty-seven years old, looked older than her age. Her face was worn by illness, and the cares and worries of her unhappy life in the years that had elapsed since her father had his marriage to her mother declared illegitimate. Her appearance was neither pleasing nor regal. The tall, healthy red-haired nineteen-year-old who rode into London beside her had an air of command and gracefulness completely lacking in her dour sister's appearance. Mary was as willful as her younger sister, and intent on ruling her realm with religious conviction and discipline. But of Henry's two daughters, only Elizabeth exuded the self-assurance and dignity of a princess of England. The contrast couldn't have been lost on the multitudes who gathered to observe the royal march into London. Some might have suspected that the sight of sisterly camaraderie was something less than genuine. Surely, the younger sister must have suspected that the new queen's affection could prove as temporary as it was artificial.

Mary did not like or trust Elizabeth. She had resented her from the moment she was born to the woman who had taken her mother's place. Worse, Elizabeth was a Protestant, and Mary was determined to return England to the Catholic Church. For a brief period, she treated Elizabeth well. But soon after her coronation, Mary began negotiations with Spain to marry Emperor Charles's oldest son and heir to the Spanish crown, Philip. The prospect of a foreign monarch ruling England and helping Mary restore the Catholic Church to prominence excited much opposition among both Protestants and even some Catholics who wanted an English king on England's throne. Elizabeth became the object of both rebel conspiracies and her sister's suspicions. When a Protestant named Thomas Wyatt was exposed for plotting to overthrow Mary and replace her with Elizabeth, whom he planned to marry to an English lord, the queen was persuaded by her Catholic counselors to arrest her sister despite Wyatt's insistence as he was led to the executioner that the princess Elizabeth was innocent of treason.

Elizabeth was taken under guard to the Tower, along with Kat Ashley and her other servants. She was again a victim of changes in political fortune that were beyond her influence to affect. The queen's counselors urged a reluctant Mary to execute her sister for treason, though they lacked evidence of the crime. They saw Elizabeth's life as a threat to the queen and the Catholic restoration. Elizabeth, although she was more popular with the public than her sister, had no one to protect her except herself. She was terrified of the Tower, the place where seventeen years earlier her mother had been sent to her doom. When she was brought to its gates she refused to enter, insisting she was innocent of any crime. She had written to her sister, declaring her innocence and begging for clemency. The letter had only further incited Mary's anger. Elizabeth knew her life was in grave peril. She asked her jailor if the scaffold erected for Jane Grey's execution was still standing or had been taken down. She knew it might soon be used to bear another royal execution.

It is easy to appreciate how powerless Elizabeth must have felt as events seemed to carry her fate toward a conclusion she knew all to well. When kings and queens felt threatened by someone, they acted swiftly and without mercy, no matter if the object of their fears was a royal relation. Yet despite her fears, she stood her ground in the face of treachery, relying on herself alone to oppose the dreaded intentions of her sister's court. She wrote another defiant, argumentative letter to her sister. Mary, who had expected her sister to plead meekly for her life, again exploded in rage. But Elizabeth, despite the terrors she faced, and the grim, unhealthy circumstances of her imprisonment, knew that meekness seldom saved a royal's life in the violent times in which she lived.

It was Philip, her future brother-in-law, who saved her life, not out of mercy, but because he recognized Elizabeth's popularity would make her death more of a threat to his plans to add England's crown to his family's possessions than if she remained alive. He was as devout a Catholic as Mary and as intent as she was on restoring the Church in England. But he knew his marriage to Mary would be unpopular with many Englishmen, not just Protestants, who feared foreign domination. And he was determined not to make his marriage even more unwelcome by marrying a queen who had the blood of her popular sister on her hands.

Moreover, he intended to marry Elizabeth to one of his relatives so that in the event that Mary, who might prove too old to bear a child, died without producing a new heir, and Elizabeth succeeded her, England's crown would remain in his family. He persuaded Mary to treat Elizabeth with leniency, and Mary, desperate for the marriage, ordered her sister's release from the Tower on the eighteenth anniversary of Anne Boleyn's execution. People turned out in droves to witness and applaud Elizabeth as she journeyed to her new residence. Still fearful for her life, the public's affection cheered her and strengthened her confidence. She would never forget their love, and would, as events turned out, repay it many times over.

She was far from being free of danger. She was ordered confined and held under guard at a house in Woodstock. And as Mary and her husband began to restore the Catholic Church by burning hundreds of Protestants at the stake, Elizabeth knew her situation remained precarious. Those who rebelled against her sister's rule would make her ascension to the crown their cause. And whether such conspiracies would provoke her sister to order her arrested and executed or not, she knew there were many Catholics and potential assassins who thought her death was the wisest course of action to protect a Catholic queen.

For five years Elizabeth lived in danger and uncertainty. Mary's reign, for which she would be remembered as "Bloody Mary," was unpopular and a disaster for England. She went to war with France and lost England's last French possession, Calais. The war and the religious strife that she initiated bankrupted England, weakened its armies, and left it prey to the ambitions of the two most powerful kingdoms in Europe, Spain and France. It was an unhappy time for the queen herself, who, desperate for a child, thought herself pregnant for a time only to discover that her swollen belly had been caused by a tumor and not the growth of a healthy child. She died in the fifth year of her reign, childless, alone (Philip had left her and returned to Spain), fearful of threats to her crown, and unloved.

Legend has it that Elizabeth received the news of her sister's death and her accession to the throne while walking in a meadow near her residence. She is said to have knelt to the ground and pronounced in Latin, "*A Domino factum est illud et est mirabile in oculis nostris*" ("This is the Lord's doing, and it is marvelous in our eyes").

She was crowned queen as England approached ruin following the tumultuous reign of her sister. She was beset by foreign enemies, some of whom looked to her cousin, Scotland's Queen Mary, to take her crown from her. Her treasury had been depleted, her armies shrunk and demoralized, the country consumed by bloody religious turmoil. She was only twenty-five years old, and believed incapable of governing the country even if the times had been more tranquil than they were. Her counselors wished her to marry as soon as possible so that England might be governed by a prince's steady hand. She would have none of it. She ruled with the courage and confidence that had steeled her against the danger, misfortune, and uncertainty that threatened most of her young life. She told her subjects, "I may not be a lion, but I am a lion's cub, and I have a lion's heart."

She refused marriage to all suitors, although she would use the prospect of a wedding to one or another foreign prince to play Spain and France, enemies for much of her reign, off each other. She chastised her counselors and Parliament, who insisted on her marriage, noting that she was the head of state. "I am your anointed Queen. I will never be constrained by violence to do anything. It is monstrous for the feet to direct the head."

Early in Elizabeth's reign, the Spanish ambassador to England wrote to his king that the young English queen was "thoroughly schooled in the manner in which her father conducted his affairs. She is determined to be governed by no one."

She sought, mostly successfully, to reconcile religious factions. She restored the Church of England, but contrary to the advice of many of her counselors, she did not intend to persecute Catholics for their faith. She did not "desire to make windows into men's souls," she said. As long as Catholics remained loyal subjects, she would not trouble their consciences. Her pragmatic approach to religious questions restored peace in her kingdom.

Her financial policies began to replenish England's treasury as well, and she strengthened her armies and began to build the navy that would make England the dominant sea power for centuries. As her reign progressed, her confidence renewed the people's confidence in the monarchy and in themselves, beginning a golden era in English history, forever referred to as the Elizabethan Age. In commerce, education, the arts, and literature, England began to surpass much of Europe, became militarily more powerful and richer. Her subjects called her Glorianna or Good Queen Bess, and were devoted to her. Her reign would last forty-four years, one of the longest in English history, and she would be remembered as the greatest monarch England ever produced. She had but one husband, "the kingdom of England." They loved her for it, and she loved them in return.

At the moment of greatest peril to her rule, when her former brother-in-law, the Spanish king Philip, sent his mighty armada into the English Channel to invade England in 1588, thirty years into her reign, Elizabeth betrayed no fear or doubt. She rode a white horse to meet her army, and told them to have courage in the approaching battle. "Let tyrants fear. I have always behaved myself that, under God, I have placed my chief strength and safeguard in the loyal hearts and goodwill of my subjects. And therefore I have come among you . . . in the midst of heat and battle, to live or die amongst you all; to lay down for my God and for my kingdom and for my people, my honor and blood even in the dust. I know that I have the body of a weak and feeble woman, but I have the heart and stomach of a king."

Less than two years before her death, in what proved to be her great farewell address to her people, she spoke of her greatest blessing and her greatest strength. "Thou God has raised me high, yet this I account the glory of my reign, that I have reigned with your love. . . . You may have many a wiser prince sitting in this seat, but you never have had, or shall have, any one who loves you better."

It remains a marvel to this day, where this girl, who had grown up motherless and exposed to the cruel ambitions of powerful enemies, found the confidence to survive all its dangers, and then become the most assured, determined, wisest monarch to ever rule her country. Was it the people's love that had made it difficult for enemies to take her life and gave her such strength of will? Or was it the blood of the willful King Henry that flowed in her veins? Or was it, as I like to believe, the reaction of one who in early life could count on only herself for a defense against treachery, and having come to know herself well, and possessing the inner resources all of us can find if we only look, knew from the moment of her elevation to queen that no man could make a greater sovereign?

In her last days, she lay prostrate on the floor of her bedchamber, "meditating," she said, on her approaching death, when her chief counselor insisted that she "must go to bed." The great Queen Elizabeth looked at her loyal minister, with, I suspect, the hint of a smile, and advised him, "Little man, the word *must* is never used to princes."

RESILIENCE

Abraham Lincoln

*Born in poverty and obscurity, his heart burdened with grief, beset by criticism
and misfortune, he would not yield until he had saved the country he loved.*

I N EARLY DECEMBER, WILLIAM MCCULLOUGH, FORMERLY THE CLERK OF
McClean County Circuit Court in Bloomington, Illinois, and lately an officer in
the Union Army, fell in battle outside Coffeeville, Mississippi. Upon learning the
news of his death, his young daughter, Fanny, was overcome with grief. Mutual acquain-
tances approached an old friend of the McCullough family and asked if he might send
the distraught child a few kind words to console her.

Abraham Lincoln, president of the country then wracked by a terrible civil war,
picked up his pen and wrote to Fanny, offering her the sympathy and wisdom of one who
had, like her, grieved the loss of loved ones.

EXECUTIVE MANSION
WASHINGTON, D.C.

Dear Fanny,
*It is with deep grief that I learn of the death of your kind and brave Father; and, especially, that
it is affecting your young heart beyond what is common in such cases. In this sad world of ours, sorrow comes to all; and, to the young, it comes with bitterest agony, because it takes them unawares. The*

older have learned to ever expect it. I am anxious to afford some alleviation of your present distress. Perfect relief is not possible, except with time. You can not now realize that you will feel better. Is not this so? And yet it is a mistake. You are sure to be happy again. To know this, which is certainly true, will make you some less miserable now. I have had experience enough to know what I say; and you need only to believe it, to feel better at once. The memory of your dear Father, instead of an agony, will yet be a sad sweet feeling in your heart, of a purer and holier sort than you have known before.

Please present my kind regards to your afflicted mother.

Your sincere friend
A. Lincoln

Few condolences received by Fanny McCullough could have been offered with greater sincerity than were Abraham Lincoln's tender sympathies. He had known loss and grief all his life. Ten months before William McCullough's death, Lincoln had buried his eleven-year-old son, Willie, who had succumbed to typhoid fever. He was the second of Lincoln's children to die. An older son, Eddie, had perished twelve years earlier, at the age of three. Lincoln was a devoted, loving father, who preferred the company of his children to all other companions. Of his four children, Willie had been the most like him, sweet-natured, but with a serious side, and, like his father, highly intelligent with a love of reading, especially poetry. Lincoln had taken Willie with him on his travels as an Illinois circuit lawyer, experiences father and son had cherished. Despite the demands of his office, Lincoln would suspend his activities whenever possible to indulge in a few minutes of play with Willie and Tad, his youngest child.

For two weeks he and his wife, Mary Todd Lincoln, had kept a constant vigil at Willie's bedside. On the evening of February 20, 1862, a distraught Lincoln walked into his office and informed his secretary, John Nicolay, "My boy is gone. He is actually gone." As he gazed upon the peaceful face of his deceased child lying in state in the Green Room of the White House, Lincoln cried, "My poor boy. He was too good for this earth. God has called him home. I know he is much better off in heaven, but then we loved him so. It is hard, hard to have him die."

A witness to Lincoln's grief offered this sad portrait of the grief-stricken president: "He was his father's favorite. They were intimates—often seen hand in hand. And there sat the man, with a burden on the brain at which the world marvels—bent now with the load of both heart and brain—staggering under a blow like the taking from him of his child."

The burden on the brain she referred to was, of course, the heavy responsibilities of the Civil

War, responsibilities that Lincoln had only temporarily set aside to minister to his dying son. But they were awful responsibilities, shouldered by a man who was, in the view of many, the least prepared man ever to enter the presidency.

The war had begun poorly, with the Union's humiliating defeat at the first Battle of Bull Run in July 1861. From the fall of 1861, however, Union political and military successes brightened the North's hopes for a quick war, settled without the utter devastation and immense bloodshed that would eventually prove necessary before the South could be forcibly reunited with the Northern states. In the months after Willie's death, more successes would be achieved at the Battle of Shiloh, at New Orleans, and as General George McClellan, at the head of the Army of the Potomac during the peninsular campaign, drove Confederate forces back to their capital, Richmond.

But the South would soon strike back. Stonewall Jackson drove Union forces from the Shenandoah Valley, and threatened Washington. Robert E. Lee frightened the hesitant McClellan from the Peninsula, and Confederate forces inflicted a second humiliating defeat on the Union Army at Bull Run. Lincoln and the Union Army prepared for a longer, harder, bitterer war than either side had initially expected.

In the four years and one month of his presidency, Lincoln suffered a great many setbacks and trials. He realized, earlier than many of his generals, that a restrained war to constrict the South by naval blockade and attacks on Confederate forces in Virginia was destined to failure. The South would never come to its senses until it faced utter annihilation. In its place, Lincoln urged total war, with the aim of completely destroying Confederate armies and ruthlessly prosecuting the offensive even among civilian populations that supported the rebels. He encouraged his generals to pursue aggressively the unconditional surrender of the South, and agonized over every lost battle and every victory, such as those at Antietam and Gettysburg, when his generals allowed the defeated Confederates to escape destruction. He hired and fired five successive commanders of the Army of the Potomac, including the insubordinate and insecure McClellan, until he finally found two generals, Ulysses S. Grant and William Tecumseh Sherman, who shared his conviction that a tenacious and ruthless campaign of conquest was a terrible necessity.

How strange it was that the man who encouraged Grant, as he relentlessly pursued Lee's army through Virginia, to "chew and choke with a bulldog's grip," was of such tenderheartedness that he hated hunting because he could not bear to see an animal mistreated.

Lincoln was a man of many seeming contradictions. He was a fatalist, resigned to a divine order and personal destiny he could only dimly perceive, often in his dreams, which he believed prophesized future events. In one of the most difficult periods of his presidency, he observed that, "I claim not to have controlled events, but confess plainly that events have controlled me." And yet he was an ambitious man who looked for opportunities to succeed, and seized them. He had a passive personality, suffering stoically the rebukes of a bad-tempered and emotionally unstable wife, whom, arguably, he hadn't wanted to marry, as well as various other misfortunes. Yet as the elected leader of a war-torn country, he was inarguably a man of action, who pressed his generals to the attack and, though he lacked any real military experience, involved himself in the most minute details of strategy and tactics. "If General McClellan isn't going to use his army," Lincoln once remarked in frustration over McClellan's lack of fighting spirit, and not entirely in jest, "I'd like to borrow it for a time."

He was a man of immense compassion and legendary humor, who at times revealed a joyful zest for life's entertainments. Yet he was also a melancholy man, the term given to those who suffered, as he did, from chronic depression. They were deep depressions he suffered all his life, but each episode would pass, and he would be well once more. Hence his assurance to Fanny McCullough that she would feel happy again. His friend and former law partner William Herndon remarked that Lincoln "was a sad looking man; his melancholy dripped from him as he walked." Lincoln, himself, described to another law partner the symptoms of a depression he suffered after he had broken off his engagement with Mary Todd, and felt torn between guilt over his broken promise and the bleakness of a potentially loveless marriage: "I am now the most miserable man living. If what I feel were equally distributed to the whole human family, there would not be one cheerful face on earth. Whether I shall ever be better I can not tell; I awfully forebode I shall not. To remain as I am is impossible; I must die or be better."

He got better, as he had in previous bouts with what he called "the hypo." Even during his presidency, particularly after Willie's death and the bloody Union defeat at Chancellorsville, he had to beat back depressions that provoked thoughts of suicide. He appeared, at times, to be almost fragile. Yet he was one of the most resilient men who ever walked a public stage. That he was able to endure such torment, and yet live a life of astonishing accomplishments and dedication, and understand the symptoms of his suffering well enough to counsel other sufferers, is evidence of a remarkably resilient character.

He had in his life so many misfortunes that it would be impossible to attribute his melancholy nature to just one source, if it was attributable to his experiences and not a genetic disorder. He had a hard and poor childhood in the Indiana wilderness, a disapproving father, little education, and lonely isolation. A younger brother died in infancy. His mother, whom he dearly loved, died when he was nine years old. The object of his first, and some argue his deepest romantic attachment, Ann Rutledge, died quite young. A beloved older sister perished in childbirth. He suffered great anguish during the temporary estrangement from Mary Todd, often in the troubled marriage that followed, and, of course, after the deaths of his children. Each of these misfortunes plunged him into emotional darkness, as did many of the frequent failures he experienced as he pursued his ambitions to make something of himself.

His early attempts at business failed. He lost more elections than he won. He was defeated twice for the U.S. Senate by Stephen Douglas, a man who had once been a rival for Mary Todd's affections, and who would be his opponent in the 1860 presidential election. As president, he was seldom very popular. Many members of Congress, his own cabinet, and the public looked down on him as a homely, uneducated rube, who wasn't fit to hold any significant office in the great crisis. The South's willingness to fight to the death and the defeats that Southern resolve and General Lee inflicted on the North put a terrible strain on him. He aged dramatically in office, every new line on his sad face a testament to his personal suffering of the war's bloody carnage.

It was the bloodiest war in our nation's history. Almost every American family experienced its losses. The North lost 364,000 men, and 275,000 were wounded. The South suffered 256,000 killed in action and nearly as many wounded. Lincoln insisted on the ruthless prosecution of the war because he wanted it to end successfully and as quickly as possible. He worried that the country couldn't bear to suffer indefinitely its awful wages. And neither could the president. When war had dragged on for two years, fewer and fewer volunteers enlisted in the Union cause. Lincoln was forced to impose a draft to fill the ranks of his army. Violent antidraft riots, especially in New York City, further damaged his popularity and shook the North's confidence in his leadership. He was as certain of his defeat for reelection as president as was most of the public. Grant seemed stalled in the trenches outside Petersburg, Virginia, and the casualties he and Lincoln were prepared to accept in the bloody campaign against Lee's Army of Virginia shocked the North, and greatly aggravated the public's war weariness. Lincoln faced his old antagonist, the vain, pompous, and spineless General George McClellan, who promised a negotiated peace with the South.

William Sherman's conquest of Atlanta revived Northern morale and saved Lincoln's presidency. Eight months later the war would mercifully end, and Lincoln was vindicated. But how did this man persist? This tenderhearted man, whose long opposition to slavery began on a riverboat trip where he first witnessed and was tormented by the suffering of African Americans in bondage; a man who suffered pitiably from the tortures of depression; a man with an essentially passive nature; a fatalist who seemed to doubt the salvation religion promised; a man who could not bring himself to harm an animal. How did he persist in the most violent conflict ever experienced by Americans to pursue resolutely his goal of union to its long, bloody, and bitter end?

In his second inaugural address, delivered a month before Lee surrendered to Grant, he spoke of his and the nation's desire for peace, "that this mighty scourge of war may speedily pass away." Yet, he followed his prayer for peace with a warning of his determination to achieve his purposes sterner than has ever been uttered by any other American president: "Yet, if God wills that it continue, until all the wealth piled by the bond-man's two hundred and fifty years of unrequited toil shall be sunk, and until every drop of blood drawn with the lash, shall be paid by another drawn with the sword, as was said three thousand years ago, so still it must be said, 'the judgments of the Lord, are true and righteous altogether.' "

In other words, Lincoln, who later offered an eloquent promise to the South of a just peace, in this passage, where his psychological will becomes almost visible through the power of his rhetoric, warned Southerners that if they resisted, he would wreak such righteous devastation on them, far exceeding what they had already experienced, that they might never recover. He was a formidable man.

He used industry, humor, and an almost spiritual commitment to American ideals of liberty and equal justice to persevere. His humor, most of it directed at himself, had political and personal purposes. He used jokes to deflect criticism from opponents, assuage hard feelings, and evade politically delicate situations. When Stephen Douglas, during one of their famous debates, accused him of being two-faced, the homely Lincoln responded by asking, "If I had another face, do you think I would wear this one?"

He also used humor to help overcome misfortune and the losses of war, and the injuries they inflicted on him personally. He told a friend, at a low moment in the war, "I laugh because I must not cry." He wept bitterly when Willie died, but he was not destroyed by the loss. He recovered, as he had in the past, using the knowledge gained from his previous experiences of loss and depression to relieve even this most grievous suffering, and he carried on, no less resolved to finish the great and terrible work that had been given to him.

A friend once observed that his work methods were neither swift nor brilliant, but "exhaustive." Add to that quality wisdom and idealism, and you could fairly summarize his presidency. In the end, it was his idealism that saw him through the experience, and saw him through disappointment, heartbreak, and his melancholy. He believed in the Union because it promised liberty to all, governed by a rule of law that protected rich and poor alike. His resilience sprang from the strength of his conviction that America was "the last, best hope of earth." The South's secession threatened that promise, and he would not rest until he put it right. Do not "let your minds be carried off from the great work we have before us," he told an Ohio regiment. To another regiment, he said that the Union must be preserved, so that liberty could succeed, and that any father's child could come to live in this White House, "as my father's child has." And at Gettysburg, in his immortal address, he memorialized the fallen for having given "the last full measure of devotion," so that "government of the people, by the people, and for the people shall not perish from the earth."

Years before his presidency, in a discussion of slavery, he offered a short but as perfect a definition of democracy—the systematic expression of liberty that offered an "equal chance to all"—as has ever been offered. "As I would not be a slave, so I would not be a master. This expresses my idea of democracy. Whatever differs from this, to the extent of the difference, is not democracy."

He didn't start off to end slavery, though he devoutly wished its end. He ended slavery to preserve the Union, to preserve American liberty. The assurance in the Declaration of Independence that all men are created equal, that a man of humble origins, as he was, could make something better of his life, and that no law would impose an obstacle to his ambition, was his great cause. Liberty gave the Union meaning and necessity. If a state could leave the Union whenever it decided to deny liberty to some of its citizens, in violation of the law, then the sinful nature of man would result in complete disunity and the end of all liberty.

He would not have it. So he fought, suffered, endured, and led his country into a "new birth of freedom." He paid for his devotion with his life. During a brief moment of rest from his labors, a few days after Grant had accepted Lee's surrender, a deluded actor fired the true last shot of the war into Abraham Lincoln. His triumph taken from him, his sorrows at an end, the public's fickle favor now transformed into hero worship, he was lost to his country's further service. But we had him when we most needed him, when the nation required a second revolution to survive, and Abraham Lincoln had answered the call to become the second father of his country, and, perhaps, the greatest man this nation has ever produced.

INDUSTRY

Eric Hoffer

The longshoreman who became a philosopher
and explained the purpose of freedom

H E WROTE SO MUCH THAT YOU GET THE FEELING HE NEVER HAD an unexpressed thought, as if whatever occurred to his curious mind he wrote down in his ten books or in the hundreds of notebooks he left behind when he died. That is probably an exaggeration. He left unexpressed or vague some memories of his life. Even the date of his birth is argued. Facts point to the year 1898 as the day Eric Hoffer was born in the Bronx to German-immigrant parents. But for the thirty years of his life in which he was something of a celebrity, "the philosopher of the docks" always gave 1902 as the year of his birth.

Ah, well, what does it matter? He was a peculiar man, to say the least. He had no formal education. He never married. He lived alone almost all his life. Despite the success his books achieved, and the money they earned him, he never acquired much in the way of property other than his books and notebooks. In his writing, his reasoning was cool, controlled, unsentimental, and often quite dark. Yet his personality, when he was among the men he worked with on the docks, in interviews, with students, at public events where he spoke, was warm, gregarious, and colorful.

We need not explore whatever remains mysterious about him. He left us enough about the experiences of his life and his opinions to read, consider, and debate, as he would expect us to, and in many instances, to draw strength and guidance from as we seek, as he did, the wisdom to understand the potential for both good and evil in human beings and the societies we form. What more should we expect from a philosopher or any person who devotes so much of his time to developing and expressing opinions about human nature?

He was not, he argued, an intellectual. He was a longshoreman. He found purpose and dignity in his labor; and his thinking, so much of it insightful and original, was shaped by his experiences as a manual laborer, and the self-esteem a worker derives from his industry even though we may "feel that work is a curse."

He was a misfit, he acknowledged with pride. And he lived in a country, the real America, he claimed, built by misfits. In other countries, misfits took a different course because their work and lives lacked worth and meaning. They became fanatics for a hateful cause. But not here, and not his life.

His parents had immigrated to New York from Alsace-Lorraine, then a part of Germany, now of France. His father was a cabinetmaker, quite poor but well read. By the age of five, Eric Hoffer could read and write in both German and English, although he never attended a school. He had no brothers or sisters. His mother died when he was seven years old. That same year, Hoffer went blind. He does not know what caused his blindness. His family couldn't afford doctors so no explanation was ever provided. His widowed father, left with, as he put it, "an idiot child," hired a big, good-natured peasant woman from Bavaria, Martha Bauer, to look after his blind son.

Hoffer remembers being quite happy in those days, despite his blindness, which he attributes to Martha Bauer's love for him. She cooked for him, groomed him, talked and sang to him, cheered him so that he never felt distressed by his dismal childhood—poor, motherless, with an unaffectionate father, blind. Curiously, and in a rather matter-of-fact way, she suggested to Hoffer that he probably wouldn't live past his fortieth birthday since most of the men in his family died very young. Perhaps she meant to encourage him to make the most of his life before it ended abruptly. When his sight returned eight years later, as unexpectedly as it had disappeared, he felt an insatiable hunger for the written word, fearing he would lose his sight again. He lived near a secondhand bookstore, and claimed to have read every book in the store, much of them well beyond the reading level of a teenager. "Reading was my only occupation and pastime," he remembered.

When World War One ended in 1919, Martha Bauer, his one source of unstinting love, who was no longer required to care for young Eric once he recovered his sight, returned to her native Germany. The next year his father died, confirming in his mind Martha's warnings about the short life span of Hoffer men. He had a few hundred dollars left to him by his father, but little else besides his books and a few clothes. He had no relatives or friends who felt responsible for him or to whom he felt responsible. He was alone with no formal education or experience, no idea of how to take care of himself and make his own way in the world.

Lacking direction, he left New York and hitchhiked across country to California. When he arrived in Los Angeles's skid row in 1920, he lived, as he put it, "on the bum." He rented a room near the library and read all day long, until he had used up the money his father had left him. He had no idea how to find a job nor any particular inclination to try to make a living from his own labor. He sold his books and his clothes, and when that money ran out, he starved and waited to die. After five days without food, he walked into a restaurant and offered to wash dishes in exchange for a meal. From that day on, he worked to make a living.

But he wanted a living that suited him. He wanted to remain free of attachments and responsibilities that might keep him tied to one job and one place. He wanted to work when he needed to, and to take time for reading and thinking when he could afford it. For ten years in Los Angeles, he worked at various odd jobs, earning enough to cover the material essentials of life—food, shelter, clothing, and books. He required nothing else, and desired nothing else.

Near the end of the 1920s, still convinced that he would die by forty, he finished a job and decided to live on the little money he had saved until it ran out. When it did, after two months of uninterrupted reading, he began to contemplate suicide. He never explained the reasons for his dark turn of mind beyond the sense of futility he possibly felt contemplating his expected early death. For whatever reason, he went to the place he always went to in search of information, the public library, where he began to research various poisons. Having resolved to end his life a few years before he believed it would have ended anyway, he felt free of all cares, and all hope, he remembered. One day, having acquired the poison, he took a streetcar to the edge of town, walked a ways, and then took a mouthful of it.

He spit it out. He gave no reason for his change of plans, other than the poison had tasted awful. Then he walked back to town, packed up his books and clothes, and left skid row forever.

For the next ten years he lived a wandering life, mostly as a migrant farmworker, and when farmwork was out of season, he worked for the U.S. Forest Service or prospected for gold in the Sierras or held other temporary jobs. Or he took a little time off to read. He always read, acquiring books from libraries all over California. When he began this nomadic period of his life, he had looked for a large book with small print that would last him awhile on his travels. He happened upon one that served his purpose, the *Essays* of a sixteenth-century French philosopher, Michel de Montaigne.

The subject of Montaigne's studies and his writing was himself. He used his experiences—his travels, his desires, his disappointments and delights—and his observations of the opinions and behavior of others to arrive at certain truths about mankind. His conclusions, recorded in his *Essays,* inspired Hoffer to do the same. Henceforth, Eric Hoffer, dressed all his life in a workingman's clothes, living on the road or in spartan circumstances in the city, read, thought, and wrote about mankind, carrying the red notebooks and pencils with which he recorded his observations on human behavior in the various pockets of his jacket, and became a philosopher. Montaigne also stirred in him an appreciation for a well-turned sentence. Once he began to express his thoughts in writing, he never stopped. "My writing is done while waiting for a freight, in the fields while waiting for a truck, and at noon after lunch," he wrote to an editor to whom he had submitted an early essay, "Tramps and Pioneers," for publication. "Towns are too distracting."

He began seriously to study human nature and the subject that would be the theme of his first and most famous book, the impulses in people that attract them to mass movements. It was the absence of self-esteem, he reasoned, that caused some people to surrender their identities to mass movements, and explained how Germans and Russians could embrace the evil causes of Hitler and Stalin. While in America, the necessity of accomplishment, the spirit of pioneers who built something for themselves from a wilderness, gave people a sense of their own self-worth, and a craving to accomplish more, not just as a civilization but as individuals.

He came to love his country, though he admitted he was not a typical American. Here, freedom offered the means to self-esteem. And in the progress of our civilization, he saw the indispensable contributions of people like him, the misfits, the men he lived with in migrant camps up and down California. And he rejoiced in the discovery. They were people, like the pioneers who settled the country, who for various reasons didn't fit in with conventional society, but who, "shouldered enormous tasks, endured unspeakable hardships, and accomplished the impossible . . . because they had to. They became men of action on the run."

When the United States entered World War Two, Hoffer registered for the draft. He was in his forties at the time, and was rejected for physical reasons. In 1943, with the war draining manpower from American industry, Hoffer found an opportunity for steady employment in a job that suited his personality, his need for independence, and his desire to study and write. He moved to San Francisco, joined the longshoremen's union, and began work on the city's shipping docks, volunteering for the most difficult work available as a way to make his contribution to the war effort.

He would work on the waterfront for nearly a quarter century, renting a small one-room downtown apartment, close to the San Francisco Public Library. He kept his few possessions in his room: little more than his notebooks, his books, and a desk made from a plank of wood where he wrote.

He published his first book in 1951. *The True Believer: Thoughts on the Nature of Mass Movements* was a critical and popular success. He became famous for having discovered in his own experiences and the enormous range of his reading why people are attracted to movements such as Nazism and communism, and in our time, the cause of Islamic extremists, movements that hold individual human life in contempt. He found the roots of such monstrous causes in the frustration of people who, either denied or fearful of the responsibilities that come with opportunities for individual success, develop contempt for themselves and other human beings. "Unless a man has talents to make something of himself," he wrote, "freedom is an irksome burden. . . . We join a mass movement to escape individual responsibility, or, in the words of the ardent young Nazi, 'to be free from freedom.'

"To the frustrated, freedom from responsibility is more attractive than freedom from restraint. They are eager to barter their independence for relief from the burdens of willing, deciding and being responsible for inevitable failure. They willingly abdicate the directing of their lives to those who want to plan, command and shoulder all responsibility."

And this abdication of independence, Hoffer argued, bred a susceptibility to the worst impulses of human nature. "Passionate hatred," he observed, "can give meaning and purpose to an empty life. Thus people haunted by the purposelessness of their lives try to find a new content not only by dedicating themselves to a holy cause but also by nursing a fanatical grievance. A mass movement offers them unlimited opportunities for both."

Hoffer's insights might seem more obvious today but they were strikingly original at the time. Many American intellectuals of the 1950s and '60s still felt, as they did in earlier decades, that the future of humanity lay in the workers' collectives and the centralized, unaccountable governments of socialized countries, and not in the individual striving, failures, and successes of people in free societies. Hoffer brilliantly exposed the deception and the inherent immorality of such self-deluding ideologies, and he did it in a uniquely practical, clearly comprehensible, and very American style of writing. "A man is likely to mind his own business," he wrote, "when it is worth minding. When it is not, he takes his mind off his own meaningless affairs by minding other people's business."

His book was not just a sensation among the best-educated Americans but among people of all classes, races, and creeds. And his book was not just relevant for his times. His insights strike us as no less profound today as we try to understand how anyone could proclaim his or her approval and support for terrorists who murder innocents by the thousands in the name of Islam.

People, usually well educated, who felt sympathetic to socialists and other collective movements, and harbored an instinctive distrust of our own government and society, didn't always share the longshoreman's philosophy. And as he became better known, published more books, and became an outspoken defender of America, they liked him even less. But such people were then, and thankfully remain today, a distinct minority in our country, and though their opinions rise and fall in public approval, they have never commanded much support from the rest of us. Eric Hoffer spoke for us.

He was a magnificent spokesman for Americans. With a workingman's cap on his bald head and the clothes and manners of a laborer, large and powerfully built from years of physical toil, his very presence seemed a rebuke to the notion of a worker's paradise offered by socialism. And he must have riled members of the intellectual elite who, from the relative comfort of universities, governments, and editorial boards, believed they had the best interests of working people in mind. Depending on your point of view, he was either ahead or behind the times. He didn't seem to care. He didn't consider himself a nonconformist, however, whom he thought was anything but. "Nonconformists travel as a rule in bunches. . . . And woe to him inside a nonconformist clique who does not conform with nonconformity." He was just a longshoreman, who read a lot and wrote, and was proud of it.

When he spoke up for America, he did so out of respect, not just for the wonders of our prosperity—the modern cities, the technological marvels, the race to put a man on the moon, the abundance of American life—but for the people who made it all possible, many of whom would be considered by other societies as the outcasts, the lowly, the rejected. My favorite Hoffer passage is an essay from a later book, *The Ordeal of Change.* It is a stirring tribute to Americans, and to the drive for self-improvement and sense of self-worth that freedom aroused in us.

Only here, in America, were the common folk of the Old World given a chance to show what they could do on their own, without a master to push and order them about. History contrived an earth-shaking joke when it lifted by the nape of the neck lowly peasants, shopkeepers, laborers, paupers, jailbirds, and drunks from the midst of Europe, dumped them on a vast, virgin continent and said: "Go to it; it is yours!"

And the lowly were not awed by the magnitude of the task. A hunger for action, pent up for centuries, found an outlet. They went into it with ax, pick, shovel, plow and rifle; on foot, on horse, in wagons, and on flatboats. They went into it praying, howling, singing, brawling, drinking, and fighting. Make way for the people.

His books reached wider audiences and made more money. President Eisenhower hailed him as his favorite author. He became acquainted with other presidents, and other leading figures of his time. Despite his success as an author and his growing public acclaim, Hoffer continued to work on the waterfront, and stayed there, happy in his work for many years. In addition to his books, he wrote a newspaper column for a time, and held offices at the University of California at Berkeley and at Stanford University, where he charmed and infuriated students and professors alike with the formidable power of his reasoning about the truths of human nature and societies, and with the exuberance with which he talked and argued. In 1967, he gave an hour-long interview to CBS News, and it was one of the most-watched, most-reacted-to programs of the time. Yet his celebrity and prosperity didn't change him. "The main thing is not to take myself too seriously," he said. He just kept working, reading, and writing.

He wanted to work as a longshoreman until he died. But old age and its inevitable physical decline lets few of us work at such demanding labor. He retired from the docks, but not from thinking. He substituted a long daily walk in Golden Gate Park for his exercise on the waterfront. There he would silently form his observations into well-turned sentences. He gave up his column in 1970, because he didn't "want to die barking." As the years passed, he withdrew from public life, explaining, "Any man can ride a train. Only a wise man knows when to get off." But he kept writing in his notebooks and in a memoir that would be published after his death in 1983. Shortly before he died, President Reagan awarded him the Medal of Freedom, and recalled an earlier meeting with Hoffer. "I got some pretty good, sound and salty advice," he remembered.

Hoffer once summed up his life to an interviewer as "twenty years in the nursery, twenty years in the gutter, and twenty-five years on the waterfront." But perhaps the better description of and tribute to his remarkable and unlikely life is found in Hoffer's memoirs, where he contemplated the working of memory: "The remarkable thing is that it is the crowded life that is most easily remembered. A life full of turns, achievements, disappointments, surprises, and crises is a life full of landmarks. The empty life has even its few details blurred, and cannot be remembered with certainty."

He had many memories. The life of Eric Hoffer, longshoreman, would be a hard one to forget.

HOPEFULNESS

John Winthrop

*He left the security of his native country to face the dangers of an
unknown world, and shape the character of a new civilization.*

O
F ALL THE CARES THAT ENCUMBER US, FEW ARE MORE WORRYING
than those for the child we fear has gone astray. Like all good fathers, John
Winthrop worried about his children. In the England of his time, with its
worldly temptations and corrupted Church, a devout Puritan like Winthrop had much
cause to worry about his many children. And his worries were not limited to typical concerns for their health and future prosperity. Most distressing of all were the threats to
their moral character that abounded in the spreading sinfulness of seventeenth-century
England. And none of his children was at greater risk of sinning than his second son,
Henry.

An adventurous boy, he had braved the dangers of an ocean crossing to live for two
years in less-than-virtuous company in the British colony on the island of Barbados,
where, it seems, he acquired habits that God-fearing Puritans avoided. His return to
England had not encouraged a recovery of his former piety. He stayed for a time in London apart from his family, and with his similarly self-indulgent companions lived as mer-
rily as young men often do in the city, where decadence appeared more charming than it
did in the more sober society of rural Puritan communities. Without a profession, inde-

pendent means, or the permission of their families, Henry had courted and married his cousin Bess. Unfortunately, the responsibilities of marriage did not seem to mature him either. And his father worried that Henry might never become a respected, virtuous member of his community as long as he remained in England.

Puritans had begun to despair that they could ever restore righteousness to English society or godliness to the Anglican Church. For decades, through the reign of Queen Elizabeth and her successor King James I, they had held out hope that their example of piety and their increasing influence in the Church and government might yet awaken England to the urgency of halting its slide toward iniquity. Puritans did not believe in separating from society, no matter how wicked it became. They were instructed to be "in the world but not of the world." They should not love earthly pleasures more than they loved God, but neither should they shun the blessings God had bestowed on their lives. They felt a duty to make the most of their blessings, to enjoy them but not too much, to use their intelligence and talents to reach their fullest potential as contributing members of their society, and to encourage society to live faithfully in covenant with the Lord. This they had done to the best of their ability for many years, no one more faithfully than John Winthrop.

With the accession of King James's son, Charles, to the throne of England, many Puritans, including John Winthrop, worried that their efforts were if not futile at least unlikely to succeed for many years to come. King Charles meant to rule without the interference of Parliament, where Puritans held great influence. When Parliament refused him money for his policies, he dissolved it. When the next Parliament refused him, he dissolved it, too, making plain that Parliament sat at his pleasure. When a third Parliament, encouraged by its Puritan members, challenged his authority again, he ordered it adjourned, and refused to consider calling another.

Charles was married to a Catholic, and while he did not profess her faith, it was clear to the Puritans that he preferred that the Church of England emulate certain Catholic teachings and practices that they considered heresy and idolatry. And Charles considered Puritans with increasingly open hostility, and dispatched a good number of them to the Tower of London for resisting his sovereign authority. Charles, Parliament, and the Puritan faithful were on a collision course that would eventually lead to civil war and to the loss of Charles's crown and head. But that was many years later, long after John Winthrop had bid good-bye to England and established a new, godly community in the wilderness of America.

He didn't intend to break openly with England or the Church, but if Puritans were to live in these wicked times in a godly society, they would have to leave England. They would depart with the hope that the example of their communities in the New World would someday be the salvation of the old.

In 1629, Winthrop learned that a group of investors had formed the Massachusetts Bay Company to support an English settlement in America that would provide the company furs, tobacco, and other trading commodities. They were not the first such venture. Several other English companies had been formed to encourage the building of American colonies before the Spanish and French could claim the entire continent for their kings. Several years before, the Plymouth Bay Company had sponsored the pilgrims who disembarked from the *Mayflower* at Plymouth Rock. But there was something different about the Massachusetts Bay Company.

The authority or charter for such companies was granted by the king. All previous charters provided the colony with a governor but kept ultimate authority for governing the colony with a board of directors that remained in England, close to the king. The men who wrote the charter for the Massachusetts Bay Company neglected to include this protection of the king's authority. It made no mention of where the directors were to meet.

Neither the writers nor the king and his ministers noticed the unintentional oversight. But John Winthrop did. He knew that if the king or his ministers failed to correct the charter before the colonists sailed for America, they would leave with sole authority to govern themselves once they arrived. If the company's directors remained in England, their affairs would be closely monitored by the king. If he didn't approve the way the colony conducted its affairs, he could simply revoke their charter. They would return to England in failure or remain in America governed by whatever new authority the king imposed on them. But if the entire company sailed for America, few in England would have any idea what they did or how they governed themselves once they were there. They would, in effect, be independent.

Winthrop saw this extraordinary opportunity as a means to establish a colony that governed not only its own political and financial affairs but could enforce the laws of God as well as those of men. It was the means by which the faithful could form and keep a new covenant with God, free from the influences of kings, wayward priests, and heretics. In New England, they could build the society they believed was God's will. It was the opportunity all of Winthrop's work, contemplation, and faith had prepared him for. And he seized it.

John Winthrop and the other members of the Massachusetts Bay Company began in earnest to raise the necessary funds for the venture and to recruit families willing to brave the journey and build a new society. Most of the prospective settlers they accepted were Puritans, but they also accepted a few non-Puritans who wished to emigrate for purely economic reasons and possessed useful skills or knowledge for the building of a colony.

They discussed who would be the best man to appoint as governor of the enterprise. They considered four candidates, but it was little surprise when "by a general vote and full consent" John Winthrop was given the honor. He was the right man. Few members possessed a stronger faith. Few could exceed his example of living in the world but not of it. He had prospered by his tireless industry and superior intelligence, and was a comparatively wealthy and influential man. Yet his success had never threatened the care that he took to remain more devoted to the will of God than to the rewards of worldly accomplishment. No other member of the company was considered a more just, wiser, more compassionate, or upright man. And no other member possessed the breadth of his vision, and his practical but tireless conviction that it could be achieved.

He sold his possessions and bought provisions for the journey and for what would certainly be a difficult first year in New England. He had wanted to take his family with him. But his wife, Margaret, whom he loved dearly, was pregnant with their fourth child. He had four other surviving children from an earlier marriage that had ended when his first wife had died quite young. He decided that Margaret and all but one of his children would remain in England until the child she carried was born, the colony was reasonably well settled, and he had made provision for their shelter and safety.

His oldest son, John, would remain temporarily in London to serve as his father's agent in the event that the colony needed additional supplies or encountered misfortune and required assistance from England. He would take his son Henry with him, whom he loved as well as he loved all his children, and whose faith and character he hoped would grow in strength as father and son set about the Lord's work together. Henry's wife, Bess, was pregnant as well, and she, too, would remain in England until the happy day when John Winthrop could reunite all his family in the new, righteous society they would build together.

Despite the impression of Winthrop as a severe, humorless, religious zealot that popular histories inaccurately record, he was a man of great warmth and feeling, who was miserable when parted from his family. This would not be an easy separation, no matter that it was temporary, for either Winthrop or for the loved ones he left in England. He and Margaret were especially forlorn when apart. But Winthrop put his duty to God and community before his personal desires, and Margaret put her duty to her husband and his cause above her own comfort as well. They promised each other that every Monday and Friday between the hours of five and six they would pause from their labors and think of each other. In their hearts they would be as close as their bodies were distant.

On April 7, 1630, four ships carrying the first four hundred settlers of the Massachusetts Bay Company put to sea for the New World. Six hundred others would follow a little later. Forty-two-year-old John Winthrop and Henry sailed on the *Arabella*. Before they had raised sail Winthrop and his fellow Puritan emigrants had assured England that they were not embarking on this fateful journey out of a desire to separate themselves from their country or its church, but would remain faithful to both. They parted with "much sadness and many tears in our eyes," to carry the gospel to the New World and to obey the Bible's injunction to "be fruitful and increase in number; fill the earth and subdue it."

It was a long and miserable journey, lasting just over two months. They were beset by frequent gales, and the cold, rough seas of the North Atlantic, as is their habit, battered the small ships cruelly. Not all the pilgrims had been as prosperous as the Winthrops, and could not afford adequate provisions for the journey and their first winter in America. Sickness spread throughout the crowded passengers and crew. Many would not reach their destination, but find their graves in the cold Atlantic. Winthrop never despaired. He was not capable of despair. He tried by encouragement and example to keep the pilgrims' spirits as high as they could be, given the circumstances. He roused them from belowdecks into the open air for exercise and prayer. He settled disputes, helped provide for the neediest, and kept them focused on the great work that lay ahead. On Mondays and Fridays between five and six o'clock, he thought of Margaret. And he wrote a daily journal that recorded briefly but diligently their progress, the weather, and the difficult time they experienced.

At some point before they reached America, he wrote and preached the sermon "Model of Christian Charity," which has become one of the most memorable addresses in American history. He spoke of the new covenant that would be established in the New World and their responsibilities to it, of the perils they would face should they fail to keep faith with it, and the glory they would achieve if they remained true:

> The Lord will be our God, and delight to dwell among us, as His own people, and will command a blessing upon us in all our ways. . . . shall make us a praise and glory that men shall say of succeeding plantations, "may the Lord make it like that of New England." *For we must consider that we shall be as a city upon a hill. The eyes of all people are upon us.*

There was no city glimpsed by the passengers of the *Arabella* and the other three ships on June 12, as they sailed within view of Salem, just the remnants of a small, earlier settlement crowded near the shore by the vast tracts of forestland that covered New England. The starving, weak, sea-weary pilgrims saw a few huts and small cleared fields, and then the deep, endless forest, and they despaired. Some would decide right then to return to England. Others would soon make up their minds to accompany them. But not John Winthrop. He went to work to build his city upon a hill.

He organized the settlers into building parties to raise crude huts for shelter, to store their provisions, and to establish relations with the local Native Americans, who could help them learn to live in this wild and dangerous place. They had to clear and cultivate fields, grow what food they could, and barter with the Indians to supplement the inadequate provisions they had brought with them. He led, as always, by example, working alongside the lowliest of the settlers to build their shelters. As one of them recalled, "He presently fell to work with his own hands, and thereby so encouraged the rest that there was not an idle person then to be found in the whole plantation."

Three weeks after they arrived in Salem, Henry Winthrop drowned in a river. His father recorded the tragic event simply.

FRIDAY, 2 JULY, 1630
The *Talbot* arrived there. She had lost fourteen passengers.
My son, Henry Winthrop, was drowned at Salem.

There his journal stopped for the day, providing not the merest glimpse at the grief that must have afflicted him. He had rescued his wayward son from a life deprived of God's grace only to see him die almost immediately in the country where he had come to do the Lord's work. But if the pain of the loss caused him to doubt God's mercy or his cause or to lose hope in its achievement, he never hinted at it. He accepted God's will, confident that his obedience would give him strength to keep his hope.

He would have need of it, for the next months would be his most trying. He soon left on the *Arabella* to explore the New England coastline, looking for another, better place to build his city. He found it in Boston Harbor, and moved the community to the lands surrounding it, where they dug shelters in hillsides, erected wigwams as they had seen done in Salem, hacked out small clearings in the fields, put up a few rough buildings, traded with the neighboring Indians, and gave thanks for God's blessings. They could not hunt for large game. It is a difficult thing to shoot deer or moose with a flintlock musket, and it would be a while before they mastered it. They had no skill with bows and arrows. They had little time to cultivate crops that season. Their supplies were dangerously low. The immensity of the task before them was daunting to the stoutest heart. Two hundred of their number left on the ships back to England. Two hundred more planned to follow in the spring when the ships, they hoped, would return.

The remaining pilgrims prepared to endure a hard, long winter, bitter beyond their memory of the worst winters they had suffered in England. Many of them died, either by starvation or by viruses that spread quickly throughout the settlement, claiming the lives of entire families. Some simply froze to death. The weather was frequently stormy and colder than any had ever experienced. The first bad storm struck, cruelly, at Christmas. Worse storms followed. The settlement seemed perched precariously on the brink of extinction. Many who survived lost all hope; the dreams of a better life seemed to them a delusion that mocked their pious naivete.

John Winthrop wrote his wife to tell her of the misfortunes they had encountered, but assured her that he was where he wished to be, and that he could only be happier when she and his children had joined him. "I thank God I like so well to be here . . . and if I were to come again, I would not alter my course, though I had foreseen all these afflictions: I never fared better in my life, never slept better, never had more content of mind."

In February, just when all appeared to be lost, a ship bearing fresh supplies sailed into the harbor. Winthrop rejoiced and gave thanks. He had sent a letter to his son John instructing him to arrange immediately for new shipments of food and other provisions, and John had obeyed. But when the spring and more ships arrived, the disillusioned settlers departed. The company's investors who remained in England began to doubt such an ill-fated enterprise would turn a profit, and withdrew their support. Winthrop used his own money, the proceeds from the sale of his estates, to provision the colony.

In the fall of 1631, Margaret and his family arrived, bearing the sad news that two more of his children had died, including the daughter Margaret was carrying when he had left and whom he had never seen. He mourned their passing and gave thanks to the Lord for reuniting him with his family. He never for a moment lost hope in his vision.

Historians often view his vision of a religious community bound by law to God's will, a city set upon a hill, as in conflict with the spirit of individual liberty that has been the engine of American progress, the spirit of simply being left alone to succeed or fail by one's own industry and daring. But I see no conflict, for the spirit of the pious Puritan community is part of that almost instinctive American craving for personal liberty. Both spirits tamed the frontier, motivated our sense of Manifest Destiny, which claimed a continent and gave us that uniquely American sense of mission in the world, that we were born to prove that freedom works. Its essence is the faith that people who are free to pursue their self-interest unfettered by kings or governments will perceive their interests in an enlightened way, in a kinship of ideals, and will build a city upon a hill in which all are free to share in the opportunities and responsibilities of freedom.

In the years after his family joined him in New England, thousands of new settlers arrived and began to build the greatest civilization in history. Winthrop governed them with courage, resolve, wisdom, and faith for many years. Margaret died in 1647. Winthrop noted her loss in his journal simply, as was his custom. But he grieved deeply the loss of the woman whom he had loved so warmly, and regarded with such respect that he had never trusted or cared for another as much.

Nevertheless, at the age of sixty he married again, to Martha Coytmore, who bore him another son. Winthrop died a year later, hopeful to the very end.

PART FOUR

Understanding

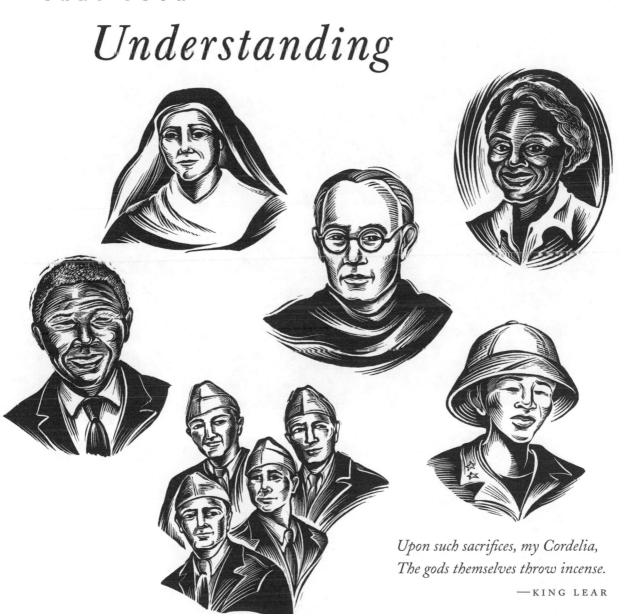

Upon such sacrifices, my Cordelia,
The gods themselves throw incense.

—KING LEAR

FAITH

Christian Guard at Hua Lo Prison

The enemy who helped me understand the power of my faith

"Bow!"

I heard this command shouted at me from the angry guard every morning for two very long years. The guard, whom we will call the Jerk, although we used an even less polite name for him, entered my small cell and ordered me to bow to him. It had become part of my morning ritual, like brushing your teeth. At six in the morning, a guard struck a steel gong fashioned from a piece of railroad track. I woke up in the twenty-four-hour-a-day glare of the naked lightbulb that dangled from my cell's ceiling, rose from the hard wooden board that served as my bed, folded what little gear I had, and listened to a half hour of Hanoi Hannah's propaganda while I waited to hear the jangle of keys that signaled the Jerk was on his way to bid me good morning.

The official purpose of his morning visits was to open my cell and allow me to set my waste bucket outside the door, which would be collected by whichever prisoner was assigned the duty of emptying the buckets that day. But the Jerk used the occasion to impress on me the difference in our stations. He represented the victorious army of North Vietnam. I was his defeated enemy, a luckless, cowardly agent of American imperialism, who had criminally dropped bombs on the people of Vietnam and their property, and whom the heroic Vietnamese people's defense forces had shot from the sky on a morning in October in 1967.

Since the Vietnamese considered American forces in Vietnam to be part of an illegal war against them, I was not entitled to any form of respect or to any of the protections granted prisoners of war under the Geneva Convention. I was not an enemy pilot and lieutenant commander in the United States Navy. I was a criminal, an air pirate. I was less than a dog. My life was entirely the concern of the representatives of the Vietnamese people to do with as they wished, and, thus, any claim I might assume to the rights of a captured soldier or even a human being was an insult to the people, their government, and to the Jerk personally.

So he felt it his duty to instruct me daily in the manner in which I should show deference to his country and to him. Every morning he would bark at me to bow to him. On most mornings, I would just stand there staring at him as if I didn't understand his order. That would prompt the next part of our morning ritual. The Jerk would swing his closed fist at my head and, more often than not, knock me to the ground. On days when for various reasons I wasn't up for the encounter and at his command made a small but noticeable bow, he hit me anyway.

The Jerk was one of the guards we called turnkeys. They occupied the second-lowest station of the prison organization, and were the least of our problems. Camp commanders and political officers were the most senior officials. After them were the interrogators, who by various means tried to force prisoners to provide them information about the American war effort or to make statements critical of our government, or propaganda statements confessing our crimes against the Vietnamese people.

The turnkeys were usually younger than the interrogators. They supervised the few activities we were permitted. They opened our cell doors to let us collect our two meals a day, and to wash up, and then they locked us back in. They escorted us to the interrogation rooms when our presence was required there, and, if ordered to do so, they would provide the interrogator with whatever physical assistance he needed to convince us to cooperate. They gave us our daily ration of three cigarettes.

They watched us to make sure we didn't break any prison rules, such as attempting to talk to a fellow prisoner or communicate with one another by tapping in code on the walls between our cells. We weren't even allowed to look at another prisoner. Our captors wanted to prevent us from drawing strength from the company of our fellow officers, or to know with certainty who and how many of us were being held as prisoners. Most of us, including me, were kept in solitary confinement, which was a terribly depressing condition to endure for any length, but we tried as best we could to maintain some form of contact with our comrades. We managed to communicate regularly by tap code, flashed hand signals when we were being moved past other cells, or by talking through the walls using our drinking cups, which we wrapped in our shirts to muffle our voices. The guards frequently caught men breaking the no-talking rule. They were never able, however, to seriously disrupt our communication system. But it wasn't from lack of trying.

Most of them treated us in the beginning with curiosity, and then, after they became accustomed to the strange foreigners they guarded, with indifference. Some of them grew to dislike us after a while, and to resent our manners, which we considered to be the most dignified behavior we could manage under the circumstances, but which they regarded as insufferable arrogance. Those guards, of whom the Jerk was the worst, would go to some lengths to make our involuntary stay in their prison even more of a trial than it already was.

The Jerk, when he wasn't ordering me to bow and knocking me around my cell, liked to amuse himself by disrupting my daily activities with other types of bullying. He would occasionally trip me on my way to wash up. As I had a broken leg at the time, falling was more than embarrassing; it hurt. He also liked to spill my food when he set it down in front of my cell. And he especially seemed to enjoy taking me, on a particularly hot and humid day, to the place where we washed, and as I looked forward to the little relief offered by bathing, he would laugh when I discovered that the cistern that held our bathing water was empty. These were, on the whole, minor disappointments to me. But his petty cruelty made me hate him as much as he appeared to hate me.

Interrogations were another matter. They could become something a great deal worse than humiliating. As noted, interrogators usually intended to compel us to give them militarily useful information, beyond our name, rank, and serial number, which the Geneva Convention stated we were obliged to provide, or to get us to sign some ridiculous statement that could be used to demoralize other prisoners. Sometimes interrogations were simply punishment meant to force an adjustment of a prisoner's attitude when his behavior had been considered uncooperative, disobedient, or disrespectful.

The means used to convince us to talk or change our behavior were various. At times we were simply asked questions. When we refused to answer them we were threatened with some unspecified punishment, but were then just ordered back to our cells and, for a time, forgotten. Occasionally, when they caught us communicating or breaking some other camp rule, we would be slapped around a little, and then sent to another, smaller, unventilated punishment cell, and put on restricted rations for a number of weeks. Sometimes we were forced to stand for many hours without relief, often through the night, and if we tried to drop to our knees or sit on the floor a guard would slap or punch us until we stood up again. Other times, we were made to sit for hours on a stool a few inches shorter than the chair our interrogator occupied, with our arms behind our back, trussed in ropes wrapped in tight loops around our biceps, and cinched around our waist. This was very uncomfortable, as you can imagine, and we would be left in this position for an extended period, sometimes a day or more.

In more serious moments, the ropes we were tied with became instruments of torture. They would force a prisoner's head down, and yank his arms painfully above it. I had also injured my arms, breaking both of them, when I had ejected from my airplane, and I dreaded rope torture more than most other forms of abuse. Some prisoners, but not I, were hung by their ropes on hooks in the ceiling of the interrogation room. Others, again not I, were kept for weeks in ankle stocks or leg irons. Often, our interrogators beat the heck out of us, sometimes more cruelly than on other occasions. A few men taken to interrogations were never again seen alive.

Like the turnkeys, our interrogators had different personalities, and they would treat prisoners with varying degrees of cruelty. Some of them were simply responding to orders from their superiors to obtain from us information or propaganda statements. They used only as much violence as necessary to comply with their orders. Others used a great deal more violence than necessary because they hated us, and enjoyed hurting us. We hated them in return. Their malice made the Jerk's petty brutality seem benign in comparison.

Hate is a condition of warfare familiar to every combat veteran. There are many noble qualities exhibited by soldiers in war. Love, compassion, courage, self-sacrifice have been expressed in the highest degree on all the battlefields of all the wars in history. But hatred, on both sides of a war, is ever present as well. You come to hate your enemies, and not in the abstract because you believe they serve some hateful purpose, but in reality, and individually. You hate them because they have harmed or killed comrades you have loved. You hate them because they are trying to kill you. And you hate them because it is your job to hurt or kill them, and hate helps you to do with your own hands the awful work of war. This is war's great tragedy, that no matter how just or necessary your cause, a part of you must become less human to serve it on a battlefield. It is a rare and magnificent soldier who can fight without hating any of his enemies.

For those of us held as prisoners of war, we needed more than hate to survive. We needed faith. Faith, first and foremost, in one another. We had faith that no matter how bad things got we could rely on the support and encouragement of our comrades to help us get through it. We relied on one another for guidance, for comfort when we were hurt and humiliated, for encouragement when our captors had forced us to do something we had struggled not to do. And we had faith that if the worst happened, our fellow prisoners would learn of our fate, and when they returned home would make sure our families knew what had happened to us, and that we had been brave.

We had faith in our country, that the American government and people who had sent us to Vietnam would not forget us but do everything possible to bring us home. And if we did not survive, we had faith that our country would honor our memory. I also had faith in the traditions of my own family, having been descended from a long line of military officers. My father and grandfather were both four-star admirals, and they taught me the duties of a naval officer, to have a sense of honor, and to rely on the traditions of honor and the self-respect gained from obeying them for the strength to get through whatever trials I might suffer.

Last, almost all of us had faith in God, even if when we arrived in prison we lacked a close affiliation with an organized religion. But in prison you needed to believe in a God Whose love for you was ever present. And you needed to believe in God to maintain, through all the horrors of war, a sense of moral responsibility to struggle to remain a human being.

Of all my memories of prison, many of which, it may surprise the reader to know, I recall fondly, the one I cherish most is a Christmas service we conducted in 1971. In 1970, our treatment had improved somewhat. We were no longer tortured routinely. But the most welcome change of all occurred when we were relocated to group cells. Twenty or more men were now kept together in large rooms. After years of solitary confinement, forced to remain in secret contact with our fellow prisoners, and subject to discovery and punishment at any moment, suddenly being allowed the company of other prisoners twenty-four hours a day was the most wonderful comfort imaginable. I doubt I have ever been happier than the day I moved into a group cell.

During the Christmas season our captors decided to allow us to conduct services in our cells, and even located a Bible for us to share with prisoners in other cells. I was appointed our cell's chaplain, and was given the responsibility for copying passages from the Bible before it was given to the men in the next cell. At this time, despite our joy at being allowed to live together in groups, many of us were in pretty bad shape. Some of us had been in prison for many years, and the inadequate diet, mistreatment, and other unhealthy conditions of imprisonment had taken a toll on us. That Christmas many of us were suffering from fevers or from injuries that had never properly healed and, in the cold of a Hanoi winter, could cause us considerable pain. We were a pretty wretched sight that Christmas night: crowded in our cell, with four bare lightbulbs in each corner of the room, some of us lying down because we were too sick or hurt to stand, some of us hobbling to our places on crutches, all of us shivering in the cold air.

Some of the prisoners in our cell had organized a choir. One of them had once served as the conductor of the Air Force Academy choir, and he led them in singing hymns of the season. Their voices sounded to us as rich and beautiful as those any cathedral choir could boast. We gave thanks for the birth of Christ, and for one another's company, for our families and for our country. I read from the passages I had copied: "And the Angel said unto them, Fear not: for, behold, I bring you good tidings of great joy, which shall be to all people. For unto you is born this day, in the city of David, a Savior, which is Christ the Lord."

We expected the guards to come into the cell at some point to force us to finish our celebration, and we all occasionally glanced at the bars on the cell's windows to see if they were watching us. But they left us alone. That Christmas service was as meaningful and encouraging to me as any I attended before or since. That night, in gratitude for the birth of my Savior, and the blessing He had granted me with the company of men I had come to deeply admire and love, I felt as close to God as I have ever felt. And that faith sustained me as no other could.

There was one other occasion during my imprisonment that moved me greatly as evidence of God's transcending love. During the time I was held in solitary, I was caught, not for the first time, communicating with my dear friend in the cell next to mine. For my transgression, I was kept overnight in a punishment cell tied very tightly in ropes.

The men in the lowest position in the prison organization, except that occupied by the prisoners, were the gun guards. These were usually Vietnamese soldiers who had some disability, either physical or mental, that prevented them from serving with combat units. They simply patrolled the camps, apparently to prevent an escape or some attempt at rescuing us, but they really had very few duties to perform. They rarely paid the least attention to the prisoners, and appeared to consider us with complete indifference, which was a welcome quality as far as the prisoners were concerned. We seldom paid any attention to them either.

On this particular night as I sat on the stool cursing my bad luck, and straining against the painfully tightened ropes, the door suddenly opened and a young gun guard I had occasionally seen wandering around the camp entered the room. He motioned to me to remain silent by placing his finger to his lips, and then, without smiling or even looking me in the eyes, proceeded to loosen the ropes that bound me. His kind action completed, he left without uttering a word to me. As dawn approached, he returned to tighten the ropes before he finished his watch and another guard might have discovered what he had done.

In the months that followed, I occasionally saw my Good Samaritan when I was moved from one part of the prison to another. He never allowed himself a glance in my direction, much less spoke to me, until one Christmas morning, when I was briefly allowed out of my cell to stand alone in the outdoors and look up at the clear, blue sky. As I was looking at the heavens, I became aware of him as he walked near me and then, for a moment, stood very close to me. He did not speak or smile or look at me. He just stared at the ground in front of us, and then, very casually, he used his foot to draw a cross in the dirt. We both stood looking at his work for a minute until he rubbed it out and walked away.

For just that moment I forgot all my hatred for my enemies, and all the hatred most of them felt for me. I forgot about the Jerk, and the interrogators who persecuted my friends and me. I forgot about the war, and the terrible things that war does to you. I was just one Christian venerating the cross with a fellow Christian on a Christmas morning.

I saw him again occasionally. But he never looked at me or attempted to speak to me. We never worshiped together again. But I have never forgotten him or the kindness he showed me as a testament to the faith we shared. That experience helped to form my lasting appreciation for my own religious faith, and it took the faith of an enemy to reveal it to me, the faith that unites and never divides, the faith that bridges unbridgeable divisions in humanity, the faith that we are all, sinners and saints alike, children of God. I became a better man, a stronger man, a more faithful man, who, for at least a moment, could love his enemies.

COMPASSION

Maximilian Kolbe

*The Polish priest who knew his mission was to give his life so
that another might live, and who thanked God for the privilege*

THERE IS SOMETHING MYSTERIOUS ABOUT HIS FACE, THE WAY HIS
gaze penetrates you. Photographs of him, as a young seminarian, a middle-
aged priest, a prematurely old man with a long white beard, aged by suffering, grip you and arouse your imagination. He looks directly into the camera lens, not shy,
but not arrogant either. What's the word for it? Imperturbable? Serene? Discerning? He
is handsome, but you have the sense his looks were formed more by character than bone
structure. His eyes are mesmerizing, as if there were light radiating from behind them,
rather than reflecting upon them. The effect of his slight smile on his expression is profound, like the Mona Lisa's, a suggestion of a secret possessed, and enlivens rather than
obscures his seriousness. The whole effect, as is often remarked, is luminous. For the
merely curious, his appearance might reflect some deeply felt passion, seemingly ethereal,
but possibly no less worldly than a scientist's pursuit of an elusive physical law or an
artist's obsession with the beauty of a summer garden. For believers, his face is beauty, and
its mystery no mystery at all, but revelation. When they gaze at the face of Maximilian
Kolbe they see holiness, nothing less.

There is to my mind something militant about him, not hostile, but purposeful and
single-minded. He had been a wild boy, a worry to his poor, devout parents. But a vision

of Mary, the Mother of God, had beckoned him to the faith and priesthood. She offered him two crowns, one of purity and one of martyrdom. He asked for both. Even as a child, "I always loved the 'Immaculata,'" he remembered. In the seminary he lay prostrate before the altar, and "promised that I would fight for her."

The ardor that invigorated his religious faith enlivened his patriotism as well. He was born in 1894, when his country, Poland, was little more than a geographic expression, its sovereignty lost to the encroachments of its stronger neighbors, Germany, Austria, and Russia. For a time in his youth, he felt destined to take up arms to rid Poland of foreign oppressors, and defend his countrymen's veneration of Mary from the degradations of imported cultures.

His pious parents, Julius and Maria, were weavers by trade, but hoped someday to devote themselves to the Church. When all three of their sons had been accepted into the junior Franciscan seminary in Lwow, Poland, where Raymond, their second, excelled at mathematics and physics, they announced their intention to enter religious life. Thus, Raymond felt encouraged to abandon his aspirations for a military career. He would wage spiritual war instead of a temporal one, and liberate the souls of his countrymen rather than their homeland. He was accepted by the Franciscan monks as a novitiate in 1910, and called Maximilian. Eight years later he was ordained a priest, and added Maria, for the Holy Mother, to his religious name.

An exceptional student, he studied theology and philosophy at the Jesuit Gregorian University and the Franciscan Collegio Serafico in Rome from 1912 to 1919, earning doctorates in both disciplines. While still a seminarian, he witnessed Freemasons demonstrate in Rome against the Catholic Church, and vowed to form a religious organization to thwart their attacks on the faith. With several other seminarians, he formed the Militia Immaculata, the Crusade of Immaculate Mary, with the purpose of "converting sinners, heretics and schismatics, particularly freemasons" to the love of Christ through the intercession of Mary.

Just as Maximilian was preparing for his holy crusade, he encountered the first of his many trials. "One day, while playing soccer I suddenly suffered a hemorrhage and felt blood come into my mouth. I stepped aside and lay down on the grass. . . . I spat blood for quite a time." He had tuberculosis, and would suffer its effects and a variety of other ailments for the remainder of his life. But he never let his chronic illness deter him from his holy purpose.

With one lung collapsed and the other badly damaged, he returned to Poland in 1919 to teach in a Krakow seminary. His country had been freed from foreign rule at the end of World War One, and he rejoiced in its liberation, attributing it to the blessings of Mary. He threw himself into the work of the Militia Immaculata, founding chapters throughout Poland, and publishing a monthly magazine, the *Knight of the Immaculate,* determined to make Mary the "Queen of every Polish heart." In a few years' time, the *Knight* was reaching over a hundred thousand of the Polish faithful, and Maximilian's crusade had grown too large for the confines of the small monastery where he resided.

He decided to establish a new monastery, the City of the Immaculate, near Warsaw, where "we shall practice obedience and we shall be poor, in the spirit of St. Francis." It, too, flourished, and within a decade had become one of the biggest monasteries in the world, with hundreds of brothers, priests, and seminarians. By the 1930s, his Militia Immaculata presses were printing 750,000 issues of the *Knight* monthly, and had begun publishing a popular daily newspaper. And, as he intended, his crusade affected the whole nation. Thanks in great part to the evangelizing and publications of the Militia, Poles of every class were becoming more religious and devoted to Mary. But Maximilian's was a restless faith. Success no more than illness could divert him from his mission to bring as many souls to Christ as were in his power to reach. Nor had he forgotten his promise to Mary many years before that he would accept a martyr's death. He left Poland in 1930 for the Far East, where new converts and, he believed, his martyrdom awaited him.

He founded a Franciscan monastery and seminary in Nagasaki, Japan. They lived in terrible poverty, spoke no Japanese, braved local suspicion and hostility, and, of course, flourished. He published a Japanese version of the *Knight,* and it and the monastery were nearly as successful as his ministry in Poland had been. He was wise enough not to displace Japanese customs with Western ones, but incorporated them into his proselytizing. He respected and became friends with many Buddhist priests.

His health declined, but not his ardor. "We will embrace the whole world," he pledged. He traveled to India and Siberia, intending to establish new monasteries, and then back to Japan, before illness forced him to return to Poland in 1936. The monastery he established in Nagasaki survived the nuclear explosion in 1945, and remains the center of the Franciscan ministry in Japan today. Though he was plagued by violent headaches, and his body was covered with sores, he was surprised that his expected martyrdom had eluded him. Yet he still sensed its approach, and still welcomed it.

Poland's brief episode of independence ended with Nazi Germany's invasion in 1939, and the beginning of World War Two. The German Army had occupied Father Kolbe's monastery, the City of the Immaculate. The monks and priests living there, including Father Kolbe, were arrested and deported to Germany in September of that year. They were released a couple of months later, appropriately on the Feast of the Immaculate Conception, returned home, and renewed their ministry. They continued printing monthly issues of the *Knight* and their various other publications, including some that were considered antithetical to Nazi ideology. And they established a shelter and hospital for Polish refugees, who numbered in the thousands, the majority of them Jewish. In what was perceived as a direct challenge to their Nazi rulers, Father Kolbe published a sermon under his own name in the *Knight:* "The real conflict is inner conflict. Beyond the armies of occupation and the catacombs of concentration camps, there are two irreconcilable enemies in the depth of every soul: good and evil, sin and love. And what use are victories on the battlefield if we ourselves are defeated in our innermost personal selves."

In February 1941, the Gestapo seized their printing presses and arrested Father Kolbe and his brothers. "Have courage," he told them, "we are going on a mission."

He was held at first in a Warsaw prison. A Nazi guard watched the little priest, dressed in his black cassock, hurry about the prison ministering to the other inmates. He stopped Father Kolbe and asked if he believed in Christ. "I do," Father Kolbe replied. Then the guard beat him. When he stopped, he asked him again, "Do you believe in Christ?" "I do," came the reply that incited another beating. Several times the question was asked, and the answer never changed. "I do. I do. I do." He was beaten for every answer.

In May, Father Kolbe was transferred to Auschwitz, dressed in a prisoner's striped uniform, and tattooed with the number 16670. He wrote to his mother to tell her where he was, and not to worry about his health, "because the good Lord is everywhere and provides for everything with love. It would be well that you do not write to me . . . because I do not know how long I will stay here."

Despite his one lung and failing health, he was given the hardest work, and supervised by the most sadistic guards. Although their reasons can be known with certainty only to their own wicked hearts, the guards seemed to feel a particularly cruel hatred for the frail priest. Perhaps it was because his example, so free of hatred, shamed them so, and rebuked their cruelty. He was put on a work detail pulling carts carrying heavy loads of limestone for the construction of a crematorium. The work was to be done while running. When he couldn't run fast enough the guards beat him savagely or set their dogs on him. He never cried out when he was attacked, but silently prayed for his attackers. When other prisoners tried to assist him, he waved them off. "Do not risk your lives for me," he told them. "Mary gives me strength."

He was later forced to cut and carry timber, and again routinely beaten when his pace slowed. One day a guard named Krott placed a great load of cut logs onto Father Kolbe's back and ordered him to run. When the priest fell, Krott viciously and repeatedly kicked him. Then he had him whipped, and left him unconscious in the mud. Several prisoners carried him to the camp infirmary, where he declined to be treated ahead of other prisoners.

All through his terrible ordeal he secretly carried out his ministry. He heard confessions, preached love and forgiveness, blessed the sick and dying, and prayed for them. When the desperately hungry prisoners pushed and shoved one another in the food lines, Father Kolbe waited for all to receive their meager ration of bread or soup before he took his. Often he went without any food. When he did receive his small portion, he shared it with others. Through all the horror and torture, no one remembers one instance when Father Kolbe doubted his faith or ceased to be an inspiration of love and salvation for others. When a prisoner asked him how he could constantly put the lives of others before his own, where everyone was fighting so hard to survive, he answered, "Every man has an aim in life. For most men it is to return home to their wives and families, or to their mothers. For my part, I give my life for the good of all men."

He was occasionally assigned the grim duty of carrying corpses to the crematorium. As he struggled with his terrible burden past other inmates, they heard him whisper, "Holy Mary, pray for us." He moved among new prisoners in his cell block, telling them, "I am a Catholic priest. Is there anything I can do for you?" When men crawled toward his bunk at night looking for some encouragement, some explanation of why they were made to suffer so much, he begged them not to hate their tormentors, but to rebuke their cruelty with good. "Hate is not creative," he counseled them. "Only love is creative." They called him "our little Father."

The camp commandant, Karl "Butcher" Fritsch, as his nickname and occupation implies, was an exceptionally cruel man. He ordered that the conditions and the treatment of prisoners be as harsh and as violent as required for men who should not be expected to live longer than two weeks. To discourage escape, he warned that ten men would be executed for every one who tried to escape. He was evil incarnate.

One day in July, a prisoner from Father Kolbe's cell block who had drowned in a camp latrine and not been found was believed to have escaped. All the prisoners in the block were ordered to stand at attention in the prison yard, under the hot sun, for the entire day. If the missing man was not betrayed or found by three o'clock that afternoon, ten of them would be taken to the starvation cell, and left naked in that underground dungeon where no light was admitted, without cover to protect against the cold, and without any food or water until they all slowly died. After many hours, and after many prisoners had dropped unconscious to the ground, weakened by hunger and the heat, Fritsch singled out his ten men. One of them, a member of the Polish resistance, Franciszek Gajowniczek, cried out in despair, "My poor wife. My poor children. What will become of them?"

Unmoved by the cries of the unfortunate ten, Butcher Fritsch stared at the small part of humanity whose lives and deaths were disposed of at his whim. Mercy was unknown to him. But before he turned away, one prisoner who had not been selected left the line, walked quickly toward him, and spoke to him. Fritsch didn't hear the words Father Kolbe spoke. "What does this Polish pig want?" he asked a guard. Father Kolbe repeated his request. He pointed at Franciszek Gajowniczek and said, "I am a Catholic priest. Let me take his place. I am old. He has a wife and children."

The other prisoners assumed that the priest's offer would only enrage the Nazi, who would condemn them both to death. They were stunned, and so, it appears, was the Butcher. For a long moment, he made no response, just stared at the little priest as if he could not comprehend what he had said. Evil incarnate had met love incarnate, and the sublime compassion, the higher ideals of someone he believed to be a member of an inferior race, must have thrown Fritsch into a moment, however brief, of doubt. A surviving prisoner remembered the scene. "From astonishment, the commandant appeared unable to speak. After a moment he gave a sign with his hand. He spoke but one word: 'away.' "

Gajowniczek returned to the ranks of the other prisoners. Father Kolbe was led to the starvation cell.

"I could only thank him with my eyes," Gajowniczek recalled. "I was stunned and could hardly grasp what was going on. The immensity of it: I, the condemned, am to live and someone else willingly offers his life for me—a stranger. Is this some dream. . . . The news quickly spread all around the camp. It was the first and last time that such an incident happened in the whole history of Auschwitz."

Another survivor remembered the effect Father Kolbe's self-sacrifice had on the other prisoner as "a shock filled with hope, bringing new life and strength. . . . It was like a powerful shaft of light in the darkness."

The sacrifice lasted two weeks. No cries were heard from the starvation cell, only the sound of men praying and singing hymns. As they grew weaker, the prayers were whispered. Their suffering was extreme. Desperate for water, the men licked the condensation from the damp walls of their tomb and drank their own urine. One by one, they slowly died in agony. But Father Kolbe continued his work. One inmate who was assigned the duty of removing corpses from the cell remembered the priest's lasting spirit of compassion: "At every inspection, when almost all the others were now lying on the floor, Father Kolbe was seen kneeling or standing in the center as he looked cheerfully in the face of the SS men. He never asked for anything or complained, rather he encouraged the others, saying that the fugitive might be found and then they would be freed. One of the SS guards remarked: 'This priest is really a great man. We have never seen anyone like him.' "

After two weeks, only four remained alive, and only one of them conscious, Father Kolbe. The cell was needed for other purposes. The order was given to inject each of the survivors with poison. Father Kolbe was the last to receive the lethal injection. As the executioner approached him, he smiled at him, whispered a prayer, and raised his left arm to receive the needle. When the inmate came to remove his body, he "found Father Kolbe leaning in a sitting position against the wall with his eyes open. . . . His face was calm and radiant."

His body was cremated the next day, which, as it happens, was the Feast of Mary's Assumption into heaven. Many years before, Father Kolbe had declared that he "would like to use myself completely up in the service of the Immaculata, and to disappear without leaving a trace, as the winds carry my ashes to the far corners of the world."

He had used himself up in service to God and mankind. But he left more than a trace behind. The winds carried the memory and the lesson of his sacrifice and compassion to the four corners of the world, inspiring millions to wage war against hatred with a militant love. He is revered as a saint not just by Catholics but by people of many faiths. His fellow Pole, Pope John Paul II, canonized him in 1981, calling him the "patron saint of our difficult century." Even in Auschwitz, the place of utter despair, his sacrifice was an encouragement to humanity. Those who saw it never forgot it. Franciszek Gajowniczek lived until he was ninety-five years old, fifty-three years after Father Kolbe had saved him.

"For a long time I felt remorse when I thought of Maximilian," he remembered. ". . . But now, on reflection, I understand that a man like him could not have done otherwise."

MERCY

Mother Antonia

*The wealthy Beverly Hills debutante who found
purpose and happiness in a Mexican jail*

A T 2 A.M. ON AUGUST 20, 2002, GOVERNMENT HELICOPTERS SWARMING low in the black sky used their floodlights to turn the night into day on the ground below. Two thousand federal and state police burst through the gates of the notorious La Mesa prison, "the black legend," in Tijuana, Mexico. Within an hour they had rounded up nearly an equal number of the most dangerous inmates—drug traffickers, organized crime bosses, murderers, and worse—handcuffed them, and loaded them onto buses bound for a new prison where the privileges that had made their incarceration at La Mesa a more than tolerable experience would be taken from them.

When the sun rose that day, bulldozers rolled into the prison yard and leveled El Pueblito, the little city that the more well-off prisoners had constructed to accommodate their wives and children. Over four hundred houses and little shops selling everything from tacos to DVDs to drugs were razed. The wives and children who had lived with the former inmates were moved from the prison to a Tijuana homeless shelter.

It had been a lawless and dangerous place. The prisoners in El Pueblito had created their own system of justice based on money, violence, bribery, and drugs. They lived with their families in homes of varying sizes, some with air-conditioning and other modern appliances. Crime bosses had continued to manage their enterprises with the assistance of, or at least without interference from, the prison authorities.

The other prisoners, as many as four thousand, who remained in La Mesa lived a far more desperate existence. Everything cost money in La Mesa, even a prison cell. If you couldn't afford one, you slept outside in a cardboard shelter or completely exposed. Cots, blankets, clothes, medicine, almost everything had a price. The unlucky were routinely victimized by guards and other prisoners, beaten, subjected to other forms of degradation, murdered. Mexico doesn't have a death penalty or even life sentences. But prison sentences are notoriously long for even minor offenses. Police corruption is prevalent, and many unlucky souls, including a good number of unsuspecting American tourists, found themselves subjected to the squalor and violence of La Mesa without ever having committed a crime. It was a hellish place where hope was as scarce as justice.

When the police and bulldozers left, El Pueblito reduced to rubble, the women and children gone, the remaining prisoners grimly adjusting to their changed circumstances, one woman remained behind with them—a tiny, aged, ill, bright-blue-eyed Madre Antonia. She was dressed, as always, in her pressed and clean nun's habit, standing just five feet two inches tall, feeling the aches and pains of her seventy-five years, short of breath and strength. And yet, she was unfailingly cheerful as she made her rounds comforting the afflicted, seeing to their needs, raising their spirits, giving them hope that one day the gates of La Mesa would open for them, and they would leave behind the nightmare lives they had lived and begin new lives, blessed by God and the Angel of Mercy He had sent to them.

She lives in a pink, ten-by-ten-feet cell, where she keeps a few treasured photographs of her children and grandchildren. She bathes there in a cold-water shower, behind a hanging sheet for privacy. She sleeps on a cot, with an oxygen tank nearby to help her when her weak heart won't let her catch her breath. When she was a girl, Mary Clarke had lived next door to Cary Grant, in a Beverly Hills neighborhood that was home to many Hollywood celebrities.

She is the daughter of an Irish immigrant, a kind, hardworking man with an innate sense of justice. Joseph Clarke grew up in a poor family in New York. His father died when he was an infant. He had only an eighth-grade education. But he became successful early in his career selling office products for a New Jersey company, married, moved to Los Angeles, and began a family. His wife, Kathleen, died giving birth to their fourth child, leaving three-year-old Mary and her older brother and younger sister motherless. When the Depression cost him his livelihood, he worked a variety of odd jobs, and cared for his children with tenderness. He remarried to a kind-hearted widow with a teenage son. He was offered his old job back when the economy improved, and became prosperous again. He moved his family into a large house in Beverly Hills, with movie stars for neighbors, and bought a summer house at the beach.

Mary attended good Catholic girls schools, dined in the best restaurants, wore expensive clothes, exhibited refined manners, and played tennis at the Beverly Hills country club. She was popular, had many friends, and became a beautiful young woman. Her lovely blond hair, good figure, lively personality, and mesmerizing blue eyes attracted the boys' attention, as well as that of studio executives, who offered her the opportunity to work in the movies.

Her father had imparted his compassion and sense of justice to her, making sure she was exposed to the hard lives of those less fortunate, and developed in her a sense of obligation to others. He had many Jewish friends, from whom Mary learned to feel empathy for the victims of Nazi persecution, beginning her lifelong affinity for the Jewish people.

When still in her teens, her strongest desire was to marry a good man and start a family. When World War Two ended she found the boy she thought was her soul mate, another Irish American kid, Ray Monahan, who had served in the Pacific with her brother. She was nineteen years old when they married in 1946.

She was barely twenty when she gave birth to her first child, a son, whom she named Joseph after her father. The delivery was long and difficult, and fatal to the baby she had wanted so much. His skull was crushed, and he died a few hours after his birth. She was devastated, and yet the loss didn't sour her on life or cause her to question God's love. On the contrary, it strengthened her faith and deepened her commitment to God. In her grief, she turned to her church for comfort and found it. She prayed every day, and always included prayers for her dead baby's soul in heaven, asking him to help her find the strength to endure misfortune. She still prays to him. Every day.

She recovered her strength along with her faith, and soon was pregnant with another child, a boy, whom she named James. Although she had pulled herself together after losing her first child, her marriage to Ray was another matter. They were often apart, and Ray began to gamble and develop other bad habits. He was failing as a businessman, and seemed equally ill-equipped for the responsibilities of a husband and father. They had another child, a daughter, whom Mary named for her mother, Kathleen. The Monahans moved to Denver, where Ray's family lived. He wasn't any more successful there than he had been in Los Angeles. He continued to gamble, was often absent from home, had a hard time making a living, and became angry and sullen. By the age of twenty-three, Mary was back in Los Angeles with her two children, separated from her husband, and working for her father to support her family.

The Monahans formally divorced in 1950. By that time Mary had fallen in love with Carl

Brenner, a tall, handsome, athletic man who was attentive and kind to her children. They married that year, and two years later she gave birth to their first child, Theresa. Four more children followed in quick succession. She longed to be a mother, living contentedly in a little white house with a loving husband and healthy, happy children all around her. Now, she had part of her dream. She had great kids. Both she and Carl were good parents. They had money. They lived in a nice home in suburban Los Angeles, and had a beach house as well.

But the marriage did not remain a happy one. Carl kept much to himself. He didn't discuss his work with her, had his own social life, and even took his vacations without his family. Mary kept working for her father's company. Her experiences in her first marriage had taught her the importance of having independent means of support. It wasn't easy having a career, caring for seven children, cooking and keeping a clean and comfortable home. She felt guilty about not devoting all her time to her children's care. But she did what she felt she had to do. When her father died in 1956, Mary inherited his business.

Her marriage never became a happy one. She suspected that Carl was not faithful. But she didn't want to be divorced again. She faithfully attended Mass with the children every Sunday, and remained close to her faith. But the Church doesn't recognize second marriages when the first spouse is still alive, and she was forbidden to take communion, which hurt her, but she accepted it, and stayed a devout Catholic. She and Carl went on as they were, not happy together, not in love, for twenty years. She was an excellent mother, and her children grew into happy and promising young adults.

She felt something more was missing from her life than an attentive, loving husband. She began to do a great deal of charity work. Her brother had suggested she become involved with an organization run by Maryknoll nuns that provided assistance to Korean war orphans. She threw herself into it, and quickly became indispensable to the charity. She solicited contributions from everyone she knew, and from many people who were strangers to her. She found ship captains who were willing to carry the cargo to Korea at no charge. And she stored growing inventories of food and medicine in her home until they were ready to be shipped. The work made her happier than she had been for a long time.

She was also involved with a children's hospital where her young nephew, suffering from leukemia, had been lovingly cared for before he died. And as the years passed, she took on more and more work for a variety of worthy causes. It gave her life a sense of purpose and meaning that was missing from her marriage and the work she had inherited from her father. Like her father had done with her, Mary made sure her own children were exposed to the lives of less fortunate people. She took them to slums, orphanages, and fields where Mexican migrants worked, and she often brought them with her as she hustled about her charitable work.

She became close friends with a Catholic priest, Monsignor Anthony Brouwers, who organized various relief missionaries around the world. She was inspired by his mercy and compassion for the hungry, lonely, and forgotten of the world. He was her mentor and spiritual counselor, who encouraged her to deepen her commitment to the faith that had always, through her broken first marriage and unhappy second one, sustained her. His dignity and selflessness worked miracles in the lives of those he touched, in Mary's life particularly. As he suffered without complaint through the painful cancer that was killing him, he never stopped encouraging her. Just before he died in 1964, he told her that the happy marriage she had always longed for, the perfect homemaker she thought she should be, were not God's plan for her. She was meant to be an angel of mercy. That was the happiness God called her to.

The year after Monsignor Brouwers died, Mary traveled to Tijuana with another priest to deliver bandages and medicine and other supplies to local hospitals there. Somehow, they ended up at the gates of La Mesa with donations for the prison infirmary. As she entered the prison, and walked through squalor and suffering, she knew that she had found her mission. She returned regularly with medical supplies, food, and clothing, drawn by the love she felt for even the worst offenders imprisoned there. She became a familiar and welcome presence in that terrible place, respected by prisoners and prison officials alike.

She sold her business in 1970. Two years later, Carl left her. They divorced a few months later, and Mary, depressed over the failure of another marriage, prayed for guidance to find her true purpose. Her five older children were grown and on their own. She took her two youngest children and moved to San Diego to be closer to Tijuana and La Mesa.

She knew she was called to a vocation in a religious order. She had wanted to join the Maryknoll sisters, but they only took women younger than thirty-five. Mary was nearing fifty. She couldn't find any missionary order willing to accept a middle-aged novitiate. Yet she knew it was God's will that she enter religious life. Her children knew this as well, and didn't oppose her intentions. In 1977, with no order willing to accept her, and with her bishop's permission, Mary dressed in the habit of a nun, took the name of Sister Antonia, in honor of her friend and inspiration, Monsignor Anthony Brouwers, and drove to Tijuana, a sister without an order. There she presented herself at the gates of La Mesa, asked to speak to the warden, and convinced him to accept her as a resident sister of mercy ministering to the least of God's children.

She first lived in a cell with other women. But the warden soon provided her with the tiny cell that has been her home for twenty-eight years, where she claims she has never "experienced one day of depression . . . never felt hopeless." She is Madre Antonia to the thieves, drug lords, murderers, and guards of La Mesa. They all love her and respect her. No matter how cruel their lives have been, no matter how sick, violent, hopeless they are, no matter how terrible their crimes, and they are among the most terrible imaginable, she loves them all. And they know she loves them.

For many of the prisoners of La Mesa, Madre Antonia is the only good thing in their lives. And her greatest gift, her best love, is the hope she gives them to find purpose and happiness in their own lives. She sees that they are cared for when they are sick, given clothes when they are naked, food when they are hungry, are seen by a dentist when their rotting teeth hurt them. She gives them blankets when they are cold. She kisses their cheeks and embraces them. She is fearless. She protects those who are preyed on by other prisoners. She breaks up knife fights and stops guards from hurting prisoners. No one dares defy her in her presence. She helps the wrongly convicted gain their freedom, and urges prison reforms on the authorities. When they are released she helps them find work. She convinces hardened criminals to confess and repent their crimes, and lead better lives. "They have to accept they are wrong," she says. "They have to feel the agony. . . . But I love them dearly."

She is in constant motion, even though age and infirmity have slowed her pace. No matter how tired she is or how ill she feels, she keeps busy with her mission, always cheerful, calling everyone, inmate or guard, her son or *mi amore.* She has changed their lives.

She started her own order in Tijuana, the Sisters of the 11th Hour, for older women who want a "second life" working in the Lord's name among His neediest children. She hopes the order will grow and continue her work when she is gone. She works with her fellow sisters outside the prison as well, running, among other good works, a shelter for the homeless and a hospice for women and children with AIDS. But every night she returns to La Mesa and her little pink cell, and works late into the night ministering to the needs of her flock.

Mother Teresa came to visit her and pay her respects. President Reagan wrote to commend her for her "devotion to a calling beyond the ordinary." It is surely that. An admiring priest observed, "You walk in her presence and you know you're in a different world. . . . She has that one-on-one relationship with God."

In 1994, on a Halloween night, the agony and injustice that made such a hell of La Mesa exploded in violence. Prisoners kept in a punishment cell block, where the conditions were appalling, had seized several guards and held them hostage, taken their weapons, set their own mattresses on fire, and started shooting from the windows. Police commandos had been summoned and were preparing to storm the cell block. The families of the rioting prisoners gathered at La Mesa's gate, and were crying in anguish for someone to save their sons from the violence and death that the police would soon deliver to them. Madre Antonia arrived to encourage the women to cease crying and start praying. Then she walked into the prison, smiling and humming a cheerful tune. The warden tried to stop her but she ignored him. She entered the dark building—the electricity had been cut when the riot started—and climbed the stairs to where her sons were. When she reached them, they begged her to leave. They were prepared to die, but they didn't want her to get hurt. She refused to leave. She prayed with them for God to spare them, and everyone who suffered the torments of La Mesa. She told them to lay their weapons down, and follow her out into the prison yard. No one dared defy her.

For almost thirty years she has lived happily amid violence, cruelty, and suffering. She has had friends murdered. She has grieved for prisoners whom she thought she had changed, but lost themselves again in a life of crime and degradation. She has seen children's lives destroyed, and experienced inhumanity at its worst. Yet she is content to have meaning in her life, happy to be of service. Late in her life, she found her true calling, mercy, and she is grateful beyond expression for the opportunity to give the last part of her life, the best part, to God.

She is there now, perhaps resting on the hard cot in her little cell, looking at a picture of her children or cajoling a guard to show a little mercy to the prisoner he intended to hurt or offering a few kind words of encouragement to someone who long ago gave up all hope of love. She is nearly eighty, and approaching the end that awaits us all. But who among us will ever be better prepared for that moment? The last thirty years of her life have been far from comfortable, but no one can say they weren't happy. Madre Antonia, formerly a beautiful Beverly Hills debutante, now a beautiful angel of mercy, might be one of the happiest people in the world.

TOLERANCE

The Four Chaplains

Four navy chaplains of different faiths and denominations who treated one another as brothers and gave the war-torn world an example of human solidarity

A N EXPERIENCE OF WAR IS A HARD THING TO FORGET. IN TRUTH, IT cannot be forgotten. But for the sake of their peace of mind, veterans, who once used both hatred of their enemies and love for their comrades to steel themselves against the horrors of war, must overcome some of their memories. They must find in the memory of intense friendships formed under fire, and the love and sacrifice that distinguish such friendships, the courage to let go of the old hatred. Only then will the worst memories of war that disturb our dreams recede into the darkness from where they came, and memories of compassion, devotion, and gratitude reconcile us to both the tragedies and the joys of life.

At a moving ceremony in Washington, D.C., on February 14, 2000, six former enemies came together, not to bury the past, but to honor human aspirations for peace and brotherhood that no war, no matter how cruelly fought, can extinguish. Ben Epstein, Walter Miller, and David Labadie had survived one of the worst American disasters at sea in World War Two, the sinking of the troop transport ship the *Dorchester,* off the coast of Greenland. Dick Swanson had been the sonar operator on the coast guard cutter *Comanche,* which rescued some of the survivors. Kurt Röser and Gerhard Buske had served on the German U-boat *223* that sank the *Dorchester.* All six men had come to Washington to honor the memory of four men who, for the sake of their beliefs, had died in the icy waters of the North Atlantic in the darkness of a February night in 1943.

Almost from the moment they perished, they became known as the "Four Immortal Chaplains," whose shared love of their fellow man, and obedience to God, stand as a moral witness to the qualities of tolerance and love for all God's children that are the first casualties of war.

Their bond had been stronger even than the strong bonds typically forged in the shared sacrifice of comrades-in-arms. They were of different backgrounds, different ethnic heritage, different religions. They were all Americans, but in America in those days, and still today, economic, ethnic, religious, regional, and political differences can fracture the unity of a country conceived in the belief in human equality. Yet they were all servants of God.

The Reverend George Lansing Fox was a Methodist minister. Of the four, he was the only one who had experienced war before. At the age of seventeen, he had escaped the misery of an impoverished and brutal childhood in Pennsylvania to serve in the ambulance corps on the frontlines of World War One. He had been seriously wounded and decorated for bravery. He came home partly disabled by his wounds, but rather than return to the father who had beaten and tormented him, he had sought refuge with another family, resumed his education, and answered the call to a religious vocation by studying to become a Methodist minister.

After his ordination, with a wife and two young children, he served as pastor to several different congregations in Vermont. He had overcome the initial coolness of his congregations to become a respected and popular pastor, but his ministry never provided much in the way of material compensation. His family lived happily but very modestly from one pastorate to another. He had become so popular in his community that he received offers of employment outside the church that would have greatly improved his standard of living. But Reverend Fox, although he worried about his family's security, lived for purposes he believed more important than the accumulation of wealth. He was an exceptionally kind man, a loving husband and father, who had a powerful calling to serve God in every aspect of life. So his family made do with what little they had, compensated by the deep satisfaction of his ministry and their love for one another.

When the Japanese bombed Pearl Harbor, George knew almost instantly that God would call him to serve again in his country's armed forces, this time as a chaplain seeing to the comfort and spiritual needs of the young boys who, as he had once done, would risk their lives to defend their country. He was forty-one years old and a man of the cloth. No one expected him to serve in another war. His son intended to enlist in the marines. No one could question his family's patriotism. But despite the arguments of his wife and neighbors, he felt he had a duty to go where his ministry was most needed. And so he enlisted in the army's Chaplains Corps in August 1942.

Clark Poling was the son of a famous evangelist and had grown up in quite different circumstances than had George Fox. His father's ministry and national reputation provided the Polings a very comfortable living. Even the death of Clark's beloved mother when he was only eight years old hadn't destroyed the happiness of his family. His father, the Reverend Daniel Poling, was married again to a woman who became a warm and loving mother to his children. Despite his small size, Clark had been a star halfback on his high school football team and president of his class. He was a well-liked, thoughtful, and earnest boy who took his religious faith seriously. No one was surprised when Clark decided to pursue a religious vocation as a minister in the Dutch Reformed Church. He had always been an idealist, in his childhood, in his religious studies, and in his ministry. He cherished the values of nonviolence and fellowship among all people, and believed the principles of his faith were compatible with other religions. As a college student, he had become close friends with a blind Jewish student. And as the pastor of a Schenectady, New York, church, he had felt it his mission to reach out to people of other faiths. As news from Europe in the 1930s brought word of Nazi atrocities against the Jews, Clark was stirred to establish bonds of fellowship with the local Jewish community, and several times he invited a leading local rabbi to speak to his congregation.

After Pearl Harbor, Clark felt obliged to give up his ministry temporarily to become a soldier. But his father, who had served as a chaplain in World War One, assured him that there was certainly no cowardice in serving as an army chaplain, reminding him that chaplains suffered a higher percentage of casualties in the last war than had soldiers. So Clark bid good-bye to his pregnant wife and young son, and went to war unarmed, but carrying a deep and abiding faith in God's love for all mankind.

Rabbi Alexander Goode shared Clark Poling's dedication to interfaith understanding and cooperation. He, too, had followed his father into religious life. His father had not wanted him to become a rabbi, but a civil engineer, in the hope that his son would enjoy greater material security than he had ever been able to provide his family as a rabbi, moving them from one synagogue to another.

He had known religious bigotry as a boy, having been bullied by other boys for being a Jew. But like Clark Poling, Alex Goode also perceived shared values in the Jewish and Christian traditions where others saw only differences and strangeness. And his love for America was based on his belief that our democracy was formed by those common values, and offered the best protection to them. As the rabbi for a synagogue in York, Pennsylvania, he had confronted the opposition of leading members of his congregation who resisted his efforts to promote understanding between Christians and Jews. He helped his synagogue form a local Boy Scout troop, but threatened to withdraw from the project until his congregation consented to open the troop to boys of all faiths and races. And he had been the subject of angry criticism within the Jewish community when he conducted joint services with a local Lutheran church, preaching the unity of Judeo-Christian values, and the importance of religious tolerance to the success of American democracy.

Nazi Germany's persecution of European Jews only strengthened his religious and political ideals. And it encouraged his decision to join in his country's defense when the war came to America. He, too, left his young wife and daughter to become an army chaplain.

Father John Washington was the oldest of his Irish immigrant parents' seven children. Raised in a tough Irish neighborhood in Newark, New Jersey, good-natured and fun-loving, he enjoyed singing and playing the piano. He was the kind of boy who impressed people as a born leader. He was a loving, dutiful son who looked out for his younger sisters and brothers. He had a ready smile, a quick wit, and obvious decency, and he could brighten anyone's day with a kind word or polite greeting. At his confirmation into the Catholic Church, when he must have been around eleven or twelve years old, he sensed the first stirrings of a religious vocation. As an altar boy, he felt called to the priesthood. His sense of a calling was made all the stronger by a childhood illness that nearly took his life. He had received the sacrament of the sick and dying, the last rites. When he recovered, he knew with certainty that God had some great purpose for him.

He was ordained a priest in 1935, and was as happy in his vocation as any man could be. He loved being a priest, and his parishioners in Kearney, New Jersey, loved him. Still fun-loving and good company, he was devoted to the needs of his flock, and resisted suggestions that he would rise in the Church hierarchy. He found his deepest satisfaction in pastoral work. He was a parish priest, and wanted no other job or life. But when the war came, his respect for the values of freedom and justice, which he felt both his faith and his country served, moved him to leave his parish to care for a larger flock.

He had tried to enlist as a navy chaplain, but a childhood accident had left him with poor eyesight, and the navy turned him down. He next tried the army, and felt it was not too great a sin to cheat on the eye examination, knowing as he did that God wanted him to share the sacrifices of the young Catholic boys who were off to Europe and the Pacific, from where many of them would never return. So, Father Washington kissed his worried mother good-bye and went to war.

All four chaplains were accepted into the chaplains school at Harvard University, where they first met. There they enjoyed the friendship of hundreds of clergymen of different backgrounds and faiths, all united in common service to their fellow man. No one's faith was treated as superior to another's. They heard one another's prayers, observed forms of worship different in custom and ritual but similar in devotion, offered witness together to the love of one God. It was a profound ecumenical experience for many of the men. Rabbi Goode and Reverend Fox became close friends there. So did many others, whatever their theological differences; they would soon provide spiritual comfort to men of many different faiths who faced hardship and death together. The annals of war offer witness to many men whose religious or racial bigotry were overcome by love for the soldier fighting beside them. And the men whose calling had taken them to chaplains school knew it was their responsibility to serve the brotherhood of men at arms by treating every soldier's faith and background with respect, by treating every soldier as one of God's children.

All four chaplains wanted to be assigned to combat units. And after chaplains school, they had petitioned their superiors to send them overseas. They grew frustrated waiting at stateside bases for orders that would take them to Europe or North Africa or the Pacific with men who were most in need of their services. They were at first relieved when each received orders to report to Camp Miles Standish in Taunton, Massachusetts, to prepare for deployment overseas. But they were all disappointed to learn that they had been assigned to serve as chaplains to soldiers who were not deploying to combat zones but to the Arctic wilderness of Greenland, where they would maintain two airfields and several army weather stations.

Nevertheless, they followed orders, said good-bye to their families, and prepared to embark on a rusty old luxury liner that had been pressed into service to transport troops, the U.S.A.T. *Dorchester,* bound from New York City for Greenland on January 23, 1943. While they were not destined for the war-torn continent of Europe, they would sail through the treacherous waters of the North Atlantic, where German U-boats hunted in "wolf packs" for American ships bringing men and materiel to the war.

They left in a convoy, escorted by three coast guard cutters, the *Tampa,* the *Escanaba,* and the *Comanche.* On board were 902 men: 595 soldiers, 171 civilians, a ship's crew of 132 men, and 4 chaplains—two Protestants, one Jew, and a Catholic. Most of the men on board were green recruits. A few were returning from leave, and had crossed these waters before. They were aware of the dangers that lurked in the dark seas of the North Atlantic, where the slow-moving *Dorchester* would be welcome prey for prowling German wolf packs. So did the *Dorchester's* captain, Hans Danielsen, a merchant marine officer.

When the convoy reached St. John's, Newfoundland, the men on board the *Dorchester* enjoyed a few hours of liberty before resuming their voyage to Greenland. Once they left St. John's, the ship would pass through the Strait of Belle Isle, waters known as "Torpedo Junction" by the soldiers and sailors who had braved them on previous crossings. Although before a U-boat could get them, they would have to suffer through a gale that tossed the old ship violently, and sent many men to the rails or to their bunks with seasickness.

From the moment they boarded, the four chaplains began their ministry, encouraging the frightened recruits, who had been warned that they were sailing on a suicide ship, organizing entertainment to relieve the boredom of the crowded ship's slow progress, and distracting the men from worrying over invisible dangers they could do nothing about. Each of the chaplains had a fine singing voice, and liked to exercise it, and they planned a sing-along for later in the trip. They were instantly friends, were often seen talking, joking, and laughing together, and conferring about their responsibilities and how they would organize their ministries once they arrived in Greenland. They respected one another as fellow servants of God, and enjoyed one another's company.

They had attractive personalities and were relaxed and comfortable around the men, who were just as comfortable around them. Men would seek out one or the other chaplain for advice or spiritual comfort without regard to the church he represented. Nor did any of the chaplains restrict his ministry only to those soldiers who were members of his faith or denomination. They were all joined in the same cause, all soldiers facing the same dangers, all praying to the same God.

On the afternoon of February 2, when the storm had subsided and the men recovered from their nausea, the sonar operator on the coast guard cutter *Tampa* picked up the distinctive ping of a U-boat, and signaled Captain Danielsen that the convoy was being stalked. Danielsen ordered navy gunners to take their battle stations, and prepare to fire at any wake that might be caused by a submarine. The *Dorchester* was just one day's sail from Greenland and safety. When the chaplains learned that a U-boat was hunting the ship, they kept the news to themselves but planned religious services for that evening.

Around six-thirty, as the men were lining up in the ship's mess for dinner, loudspeakers broadcast an urgent warning from Captain Danielsen. The men were informed of the nearby U-boat, and ordered to sleep that night fully dressed, with coats and gloves, and, most important, with their life jackets on. To calm the alarm the men were feeling, the chaplains organized a party. Father Washington played an old piano and with the other chaplains led the men in song late into the evening. As the good priest finished the final chords of the last song, the men left for their bunks, grateful to have enjoyed a few hours' diversion from the terror that would trouble their sleep that night. Despite their fear and the captain's warning, most of them wouldn't sleep in their life jackets. Sleeping would be hard enough, and it was too hot belowdecks to find any rest dressed from head to toe.

Sometime after midnight, with the *Dorchester* only 150 miles from its destination, the captain of U-boat *223* waited for four other U-boats to join him as he prepared for combat. Looking through his binoculars, he could not make out how many Allied ships were in the foggy darkness ahead of him or how well protected they were. As the minutes slowly passed, he feared his submarine would soon be spotted and fired upon by the convoy's escorts. He gave the order to fire torpedoes at the largest of the ships he could see. At 12:55 A.M., February 3, 1943, one torpedo struck the *Dorchester* amidships, well below the waterline. Water flooded into the ship. It was a fatal wound. She would sink in less than half an hour.

Captain Danielsen knew instantly that his ship was sinking, and gave the order to abandon ship. Many men had already been killed in the initial explosion. Many more were wounded. The ship's power was out, and it had lost radio contact with its three escorts. Desperate men, many without life jackets or warm clothes to guard against the cold Arctic wind and waters, raced through darkness to get up on deck and into lifeboats. Many were certain that death was at hand.

The ship had been struck on its starboard side, which was listing into the water, and the lifeboats secured on that side were unreachable. The port-side lifeboats were quickly dropped into the sea, and men began to scramble down ropes to board them, capsizing some of the boats when too many men crowded into them. Some life rafts floated away from the ship before men could board them. Only 230 of the men would survive. Six hundred and seventy-two men would never see their homes again. All was chaos and despair, except for the four men who calmly walked among them trying to give them courage, leading them to lifeboats, treating the wounded, and saying prayers for the dying. When one sailor on deck tried to return to his cabin to retrieve his gloves before he found a seat in a lifeboat, Rabbi Goode stopped him, gave him the gloves he was wearing, and told him to go. Men raced everywhere on deck looking for life jackets before they jumped overboard. Each of the chaplains surrendered their life jackets to men who had none. Not one of the chaplains asked the man to whom he gave his jacket, and, in effect, his life, if he was a Catholic or a Protestant or a Jew. One of the soldiers who jumped overboard and floated in the freezing black water amid sounds of agony from dying men remembered that the sight and voices of the chaplains "were the only thing that kept me going." Another who had witnessed the chaplains give away their life jackets recalled the sacrifice as the "finest thing I have seen or hope to see this side of heaven."

As men in lifeboats and floating in the water pulled and swam away from the sinking ship, they beheld one last sight of the four men whose loving devotion to God and man had saved many of their lives. When the *Dorchester* rolled over, the four men climbed up on the keel. There they stood, holding one another's hands, praying to their one God together, as the water rose around them. Just before the ship slipped beneath the waves, the chaplains raised their arms in the air, still holding hands, and sang a sailor's hymn, ready to meet together their God.

Several years later, President Harry Truman presided over the dedication of the Chapel of the Four Chaplains, a place of worship for people of all faiths that Clark Poling's father had worked to have built as a monument to the courage of the chaplains and the dreams of brotherhood they had given their lives to defend. Or, as President Truman put it, "to teach Americans that as men can die heroically as brothers so should they live together."

FORGIVENESS

Nelson Mandela

*The prisoner who forgave his jailer, and helped
his countrymen forgive one another*

IT WAS AFTER ONE O'CLOCK WHEN THE PHONE RANG. NO ONE CALLS LATE at night with good news. James Gregory stirred from his bed to answer it. A callous policeman curtly informed him, "Your son is dead." No explanation was offered or condolence expressed, just a summary instruction to come to the police station.

Twenty-three-year-old Brent Gregory had been returning home from a night out with friends in Cape Town when he crested a hill in his small Toyota and drove into the back of a semitruck that was stopped in the road with its lights out. He had been a good boy, the pride of his parents. In the days following the accident, James Gregory sank deeply into grief, nearly senseless to the rest of the world. He could not accept the burden of his tragedy. It was too hurtful, freighted with too many regrets, too many "if onlys" and "what ifs" and "I wish I hads". Life from then on would be something less than it once was, and there was nothing, he believed, that he could do to recover his purpose and enthusiasm. He lost his faith in God. He spurned the attempts of friends and associates to comfort him. He was beyond consoling. No words, no assurance of eventual recovery could ease the pain. You do not recover from losing a child. You never forget. Never. After the funeral, he had rudely chased friends, ministers, and associates from his house. A day later he couldn't even remember having done so. He was lost in grief.

A neatly addressed, brief condolence note arrived from the one man whom Gregory knew could understand the torment he was suffering. Six days after the funeral, seeking distraction from his anguish, Gregory decided to return to work. Shortly after he arrived he was summoned to the house where the author of the condolence letter resided. The man was waiting to greet him as he entered, and for a moment stood wordlessly staring at his friend, as if to read the pain on his face. Then softly, he suggested that they walk together in the garden, as they had done so often in the past. Taking him by the arm he led Gregory outside, where they walked together awhile in silence. As they made their way to the tree where they often rested in the shade, the man spoke to him for the first time that morning. "It has happened. It is a terrible thing," he observed.

"Let's remember the good times we both had with Brent. He was a wonderful child and I have a picture of him sitting here reading his Bible, discussing passages with me. He cared, and in a situation like this, that is a quality so rare."

Then he began to address the pain that they suffered in common. "Time will heal physical wounds, inflicted wounds, yes, but time will not heal the invisible wounds. People will mean well when they offer kind words, but they cannot know. . . . It is important to remember that they mean the words even if they cannot feel them."

His words had the comforting effect they did because the grieving father knew that the man who offered them spoke them from a heart that had been broken as his was now. Twenty years earlier his own son, Thembi, also twenty-three years old, had been killed in a car accident. Gregory had brought him the news, told him he was sorry, and then in deference to his friend's preference to grieve in solitude, he had left him alone, standing through the night, not eating, not sleeping, not weeping or speaking, just staring out the window at the night sky. Gregory returned the next day, and asked if he still preferred to be left to grieve alone. "No, stay," came the reply. Gregory attempted, sincerely if vainly, to comfort him, acknowledging that he could not begin to understand the pain of such a terrible loss. He had wished he could have done something more for his friend, but their circumstances would not have allowed it.

A few days later he bore more bad news. His friend would not be permitted to attend his son's funeral. The government had denied his request. It must have been a hard thing to tell a friend he must bear another cruel injustice. But it was his job. James Gregory was a jailer. And his friend, Nelson Mandela, was his prisoner.

Nelson Mandela believes "no one is born hating another person because of the color of his skin, or his background, or his religion. People must learn to hate, and if they can learn to hate, they can be taught to love, for love comes more naturally to the human heart than its opposite."

Nelson Mandela taught James Gregory to love what he had once hated. And there is no doubt that as he walked with Mandela in the garden the week after Brent died, he loved the man who tried to comfort him, the man who had been prisoner for so many years. And he loves him to this day. I think Gregory would acknowledge that Nelson Mandela has been one of the most important influences in his life, at least as important an influence as a father is to a son.

That their friendship should seem so remarkable, so astonishing to us is attributable to the hard, cruel history of the country where they were born: South Africa, during the long years of apartheid when black South Africans were treated as subhuman by the ruling white minority. But it isn't astonishing to Mandela. He is a man who respects anyone who respects him, who gives kindness to those who are kind to him, who loves as well as he is loved. That the history of his country has in recent years changed so much for the better, that South Africa has been saved from the ravages of racial hatred is due, in large part, to Mandela's noble character, among whose virtues has been the ability to forgive the wrongs done to him and his people, because he believes truly that love is the natural condition of the heart, and that hatred is as much a burden to the hater as it is to the hated.

Rolihlahla Mandela was born on July 18, 1918, in a small village near Umtata in the black homeland of Transkei. The English translation of Rolihlahla is, appropriately enough, "trouble-maker." His father, Henry Mandela, was a principal advisor to the chief of the Thembu people. His great-grandfather had been a Thembu king. The name Nelson was given to him by a teacher on his first day of elementary school, apparently in memory of Lord Nelson.

His family lived in a traditional thatched hut. He spent his early childhood happily in the countryside herding cattle, hunting, and fishing, and was the first child in his family to attend school. He was only nine years old when his father died, and he was sent to live at court as the ward of the Thembu chief, and was raised to become an important person in the affairs of his people. The stories he heard from his father and at the Thembu court about his ancestors, Xhosa warriors with a long history of defending their homeland from European invaders, are said to have inspired in Mandela a zeal to liberate his people from their subjugation to white rule. He was expelled from the university he attended after he joined a student protest. Soon after, he left the Thembu court and moved to Johannesburg to escape the future his guardian had planned for him and the arranged marriage that awaited him.

He soon completed the course credits for his bachelor's degree, and at the suggestion of the man who would become his lifelong friend and comrade, Walter Sisulu, he joined a Johannesburg law firm as an apprentice, and was eventually admitted to the bar. With Sisulu and Oliver Tambo he joined the African National Congress (ANC), which was founded in 1912 to advocate the creation of a multiracial democracy in South Africa. The ANC had met with little success and in the opinion of Mandela and his colleagues had become too acquiescent in its ineffectiveness. They determined to change it, and in 1944 they formed the ANC Youth League, which they hoped to use to transform the organization into an active mass movement.

As a young Johannesburg lawyer, Mandela observed firsthand the inequities that were the daily lot of black South Africans, where even the few rights they were accorded were often ignored if they inconvenienced white South Africans, those who were of English ancestry and the Afrikaners, who were descended from the early Dutch settlers who had fought for South Africa's independence from England. But the indignities blacks had suffered in the segregated country would become far more severe in 1948, when the Afrikaners' National Party came to power and imposed the apartheid ("apartness") system.

Under apartheid, blacks were forced to live in designated neighborhoods, and then later to be moved, often forcibly, to crushingly poor black homelands. They attended vastly inferior schools. Universities that were once open to all races were now closed to blacks. They were at all times, in ways large and small, made to feel as if they were a lesser form of human existence, and that was exactly how the leaders of the National Party viewed them. A black South African, a kaffir, the word for "nigger" to an Afrikaner bigot, had no guarantee that he even possessed an inviolable right to life. Killing blacks was no great crime to many Afrikaners of the time, and lives were often taken for no greater offense than speaking boldly to a white man. Apartheid was institutionalized hatred.

Mandela rushed to fight this injustice. He and Walter Sisulu and Oliver Tambo quickly distinguished themselves as rising ANC leaders. Their means of protest were strictly nonviolent but increasingly effective and noticed. In 1952, Mandela led the Defiance Campaign, a mass protest of apartheid that earned him his first arrest. He was charged and convicted of violating the Suppression of Communism Act, given a suspended sentence, and forbidden to attend any public gatherings or to leave Johannesburg for a month. His contest with the government had begun. He was making a name for himself, and the men who ruled South Africa were adept at vanquishing promising black leaders before they could pose any serious threat to apartheid. Throughout the 1950s, he was often arrested, banned from public activities, and occasionally jailed.

In 1960, the antiapartheid protestors in the black township of Sharpeville staged a huge rally in opposition to the pass laws that restricted where blacks could travel in South Africa. South African police fired indiscriminately into the crowd, killing sixty-nine people—men, women, and children. Many of them were shot in the back. After the massacre, the government declared a state of emergency and banned the ANC. The ANC responded by abandoning their strict non-violence policy and establishing an armed wing of resistance, the Umkhonto we Sizwe (Spear of the Nation), or MK. Nelson Mandela became its leader. The MK planned a campaign of economic sabotage and violence against government offices. Political assassinations were not permitted nor was taking innocent life.

Oliver Tambo left the country to work on behalf of the ANC from exile. Mandela went into hiding as he organized armed resistance. His success, and the failure of the authorities to apprehend him, earned him the title the "Black Pimpernel." In 1961, he escaped South Africa and traveled throughout Africa and Europe seeking support for the MK, and training for MK guerrillas. He returned the following year, and was immediately arrested, tried, and imprisoned on Robben Island, a bleak speck of land off the coast of Cape Town, where hope was banished.

In 1963, he was brought back to Johannesburg to stand trial for treason and sabotage along with other ANC leaders who had been arrested in Rivonia, a prosperous Johannesburg suburb. The Rivonia trial excited the passions of both black and white South Africans. To white South Africans, the accused were communists and terrorists who planned a campaign of murder and mayhem to drive whites from the country they had settled and into the sea, and who should be hung for their crimes. To blacks, the government in one fell swoop had decapitated the leadership of the only organization that might conceivably bring justice to South Africa. All the South Africans, including the accused, knew the leaders were on trial for their lives. They were charged with capital offenses and they very likely would hang for them.

Amazingly, Mandela and the other defendants didn't deny the charges, but explained that they had reluctantly turned to a campaign of sabotage when the government had left them no peaceful recourse to prosecute their grievances. Mandela, who conducted his own defense, argued that an all-white judicial system could not possibly try black opponents of the system fairly. His riveting closing statement from the dock has become one of the most celebrated speeches in modern political oratory: "I have fought against white domination, and I have fought against black domination. I have cherished the ideal of a democratic and free society in which all persons live together in harmony and with equal opportunities. It is an ideal which I hope to live for and achieve. But if needs be, it is an ideal for which I am prepared to die."

He did not have to die for it. He and the other accused were sentenced to life imprisonment and sent to Robben Island. It would be twenty-seven years before Nelson Mandela was freed, and his country about to become the place he dreamed it would be.

James Gregory came to Robben Island by a different route. He, too, was raised in the country, on his family's farm in the Natal. His closest boyhood friend had been a Zulu, Bafana, who taught him to hunt and fish, and the virtues of genuine, race-blind friendship. Gregory was closer to Bafana than probably any other person he had ever known. The Zulu boy had even saved Gregory's life once, when he had been bitten by a poisonous snake. But Gregory had been sent away to school while still quite young, and never saw his Zulu friend again.

In school his Scottish surname earned him the animosity of his Afrikaner schoolmates, who teased and bullied him and, often as not, received a punch in the nose for their trouble. He had been expelled from a series of schools for fighting, and when he finally completed high school he decided he had had enough education. He went to work as a traffic policeman in Cape Town. At school he had entered a new world, predominately Afrikaner, where hatred for kaffirs seethed. The same bigotry prevailed in law enforcement ranks, and after a time, Gregory forgot the natural tolerance he had known as a boy playing in the wide freedom of the bush with his friend Bafana, and accepted as just and proper the misunderstandings, lies, and cruelty that white Afrikaners used to oppress the black majority. Like the Afrikaners, he thought the Rivonia accused should have been hung, for they threatened the lives and freedom of every white South African. He had been taught to hate, and it crowded from his heart the lesson of love he had learned from Bafana.

In 1966 he accepted a position in the penal system, and the following year with his wife and three small children boarded the boat at Cape Town bound for the small island that lay on the hazy horizon. His primary occupation on Robben Island would be censoring the prisoners' mail, both incoming and outgoing, because of his facility with what his superiors called kaffir languages, Zulu and Xhosa. He looked forward to the job and new life with equal parts apprehension and curiosity. He knew famous political prisoners were incarcerated there, and though he did not believe himself to be a wantonly cruel man as many of the wardens and guards at Robben were, he nevertheless considered the prisoners, particularly Mandela, to be black terrorists. He held them in the contempt he believed they deserved.

Life on Robben Island was harsh for prisoners. They worked long hours in the hot summer sun and cold winter wind quarrying limestone and breaking large rocks into smaller ones. Political prisoners were segregated from the general prison population. They were not allowed to communicate with one another or with the outside world with any regularity, although they managed to anyway. The food was awful, their seven-by-eight-feet cells cramped, the verbal and physical abuse constant and often brutal. Guards were known to urinate in their food. One prisoner had recently been buried up to his neck while a particularly abusive guard urinated on his head.

When Mandela first arrived there, he had been ordered to trot in leg irons from the boat dock to the prison. He refused. A guard warned him that his life was nothing on Robben, and any white man could kill him without a fuss. Mandela assured him that there would be quite a fuss if he so much as raised his fist in anger to him. He was not an easy man to scare, and an even harder man to force any indignity on. Mandela, a proud man, to be sure, insisted on his dignity. His was no more than any person was entitled to, and he would not accept any degradation without challenge. He was the acknowledged and most famous leader among the ANC prisoners on the island; indeed, he became the most famous political prisoner in the world. But something more than the prospect of unfavorable publicity restrained his captors; there was simply something in his character that was superior to his oppressors', and they knew it.

James Gregory knew it, too, from the moment he first glimpsed the man who would become his close friend. Mandela was taller than most, and straight-backed. He carried himself with confidence. The deference the other prisoners showed him enhanced his stature. He was a man to be reckoned with even if you thought him a kaffir.

Before Gregory was introduced to the prisoners he would oversee, the warden and guards instructed him in the customs of the maximum-security facility. He was at all times to remain distant and authoritative in manner and speech with the prisoners; to tolerate no infraction of prison rules; to show them no kindness, no courtesy, no respect, for they deserved none. When it came time to begin his duties, the guard who would introduce him to his wards summoned him with an indifferent "Right, Gregory, let's go meet the kaffirs." Mandela was talking to a small circle of comrades, his back to the new guard. "This here is Nelson Mandela," Gregory's colleague indicated. Mandela turned around, looked Gregory in the eyes, and with a smile offered a polite "Good morning. Welcome to Robben Island." "Good morning," Gregory replied. And then, for reasons he did not understand at the time, Gregory offered a friendly Zulu greeting he had known as a boy in the Natal, before he had been taught to hate: "I see you."

Mandela gave respect to those who showed him respect in kind. For all the terrible sickness of the heart that the culture of bigotry imposed on the bigot, Gregory was not a bad man. Mandela, an astute judge of character, must have sensed that about him, perhaps from that first unexpected Zulu greeting. Slowly at first, but inevitably, they came to respect each other. Mandela's evident decency, his courage, and his steadfast righteousness evoked Gregory's memory of his childhood friendship. In the twenty-three years that followed, in several prisons, they grew close. Gregory came to understand the justice of Mandela's cause and to sympathize with it. They shared confidences together, commiserated over life on the island, the strains on their families, and the absurdity of people who believed skin color to be a character trait. And though Mandela was an intensely private man who did not pour out his troubles to anyone, Gregory grew to understand his friend and prisoner as well as he understood any man, and know when his confidence was wanted and when it was not.

They walked together, talked together, drank tea together, and celebrated holidays together. He helped Mandela communicate with his family and followers with minimal censorship. He carried messages from him to the outside world. In later years, in a mainland prison, he would even take Mandela in the trunk of his car out the prison gates and into the wide world for a moment of freedom. He felt embarrassed when he was required to supervise Mandela's visits with his wife, and did whatever he could to afford them some measure of privacy. And when both men suffered grievous losses, they were a comfort to each other.

As apartheid began to crumble, Gregory escorted Mandela to meetings with the South African president that would eventually lead to Mandela's release and then to a genuine multiracial South African democracy. On the day Mandela was finally released in 1990, Gregory was with him. They embraced when they parted, a note from Mandela in Gregory's pocket: "The wonderful hours we spent together the last two decades end today. But you will always be in my thoughts." Gregory wept as he watched his friend walk through the prison gates, and raise his arm in the ANC's clenched-fist salute to the cheering crowd who waited for him. Gregory retired from the prison not long after. The absence of Mandela hurt too much for him to continue there. But he rejoiced three years later, as he watched from seats reserved for special guests, as Nelson Mandela was inaugurated the first truly democratically elected South African president.

He had come to love the man whom he had wrongly believed to be his enemy. And Mandela had learned to forgive Gregory as an agent of the government who oppressed him, and see him as a man, not a color, a man whose personal decency earned his respect and friendship. Love, you see, comes more naturally to the human heart than hatred. Nelson Mandela brought that same wisdom, that same generous, forgiving spirit to the country he loved, and by his sacrifice and devotion and unassailable dignity opened South Africa to the love he knew it yearned to possess.

GENEROSITY

Oseola McCarty

She washed laundry for a living, and had few possessions,
but by the end of her life she was the richest woman in town.

SHE SAID SHE KNEW THE DIFFERENCE BETWEEN NEED AND WANT. FOR seventy-five years she worked from early in the morning until ten or eleven o'clock at night washing and ironing other people's clothes. You aren't paid much for washing clothes. She never bought anything on credit, though. She never needed to. "I try not to spend money I don't have," she said, "buying what I can't afford." She didn't need much—enough food to eat, simple clothes to wear, a little something to put in the collection plate on Sundays—and she made enough money for that. She lived in a small wooden frame house in Hattiesburg, Mississippi, with an old black-and-white television, a radio, and a tattered Bible. She never owned a car, and never learned how to drive. She walked to the grocery store once a week and two miles to the Friendship Baptist Church, where she had attended Sunday services since she was a little girl. The summer gets pretty hot in Hattiesburg. She didn't seem to mind. She didn't have an air conditioner until recently, and then she would use it only when visitors called. She had everything she needed, and enough money to pay for it.

She had enough money to do what she wanted, too. And what she wanted was to help other people. So she gave away most of the money she saved. She knew other people's dreams were bigger than hers, and if they needed help to make them come true, she wanted to give it to them. She left some of her money to her church, and some of it to a few of her relatives. She left most of it to the University of Southern Mississippi, in a scholarship trust for deserving students who couldn't afford a college education. The university was only three miles from her house, but she had never visited the campus. No one there had ever done anything for her. She wasn't paying anyone back for helping her. She just wanted to help a few kids go to college, and so she did.

Oseola McCarty, "Miss Ola," to her friends and family, had decided to make out her will when she had to stop taking in wash because she had become too crippled with arthritis to do the work anymore. She was eighty-six years old then, and she knew it was probably time to put her things in order. So she met with her bankers, and told them what she wanted them to do with her $250,000 after she passed away. The biggest share, the money for the scholarship fund, came to $150,000. That's a pretty generous gift. Maybe it's not a fortune in this age of billionaires. But it is an awful lot of money for an old woman who washed and ironed clothes for a living. She built her fortune over seventy-five years, a few dollars at a time. And she just gave it away. "I just want it to go to someone who will appreciate it and learn," she said. "I'm old and I'm not going to live always." People were shocked. Most folks respect frugality, and Miss Ola was frugal. Not many people are as generous as they are frugal. But she was.

She was born in 1908, in Shubuta, Mississippi, deep in the Jim Crow South. Her mother and father weren't married. She knew who her father was, but he wasn't a good man. He didn't want anything to do with Ola and her mother. And they didn't want anything to do with him. "He never did nothing for me," she remembered, "and I didn't care nothing about him."

Her grandmother, the daughter of a slave, raised her. She was a widow. Her husband died when Ola's mother was a little girl. He died shortly after he broke his back carrying cut timber at a sawmill. Her grandmother raised five children, and then Ola, alone on their little seven-acre farm. "Because she was a widow woman she didn't get a chance to . . . sit back like most women did," Ola recalled. "She had to work, trying to raise her children, trying to feed them and keep them clothed, send them to school. They didn't get much education, but they tried [to] get a little so they could read and write."

She called her grandmother Mama, and her mother Mama Lucy. When her mother got married, she and her husband moved around a lot and Ola stayed with her grandmother. Little Ola watched how hard her grandmother, her mother, and her aunt and uncle had to work to make a poor living from their farm. But she was happy. Her grandmother loved her, and she loved her grandmother.

When Ola was eight, the family left their farm and moved to Hattiesburg, where her mother and aunt took in washing. Her stepfather drowned in the great flood of 1927. He had climbed a tree to escape the raging waters, but after a long while there, with no one to help him, he got tired and weak from hunger and simply dropped out of the tree and disappeared into the water. After he died, Ola's mother moved in with them, and helped with the washing and ironing. They didn't have a washing machine. They used a rub board, an old washtub over a wood fire, and a hand wringer, and then hung the clothes on a line to dry. Ola worked, too.

She attended Eureka Elementary School in Hattiesburg until the sixth grade. When she came home from school, she worked with her grandmother and aunt until bedtime. She had watched her grandmother wash and iron, and knew how to do it. So she did. "[My grandmother] just trained me how to do whatever she done," Ola told an interviewer. "I just loved my grandmother to death and everything I'd see her do I tried to do it."

When her aunt got sick and needed an operation, Ola left school to help take care of her and work in the family's laundry business. She had once dreamed of becoming a nurse, and wearing a starched white nurse's cap and dress. She thought it was the most beautiful attire she had ever seen. She wished she had continued in school so she could have trained as a nurse, worn a smart-looking uniform, and helped people. But she didn't regret the hard work she did as a child, and continued doing for the rest of her life. "All the rest of the family was done and married and gone from home, and that left everything on my grandmother . . . and so I had to help her."

No one ever gave them a thing. Not even during the Depression, when times were awfully tough, and money hard to come by. They never got any help from the government. "My grandmother tried, but they wouldn't give her nothing. They said we was able to work . . . and that's the way it was." They worked their way through it, never complaining, never bitter over their poor lot in life. They had each other, and enough work to put food on the table and a roof over their heads. And they were happy.

"We loved to work," Ola later recalled. "My whole family was workers, just like I worked when I was able to. I worked all the time, night and day. Anything I wanted, I'd see it, I'd go at it, and get the money to pay for it. . . . I didn't owe nobody nothing. Nobody."

When she was still in school, Ola walked into the First Mississippi National Bank with a few dollars she had saved and wanted to put away for safekeeping. Since she didn't know about compound interest or how to invest, she put her money into a checking account, even though she didn't plan to draw anything from the account. Later on, a bank teller recommended she open a savings account, where her money would earn interest. Every month from that day until her arthritis forced her to stop working in 1994, she put each dollar she didn't need to spend in the bank, and began to build her fortune.

She never married. "I had a few boyfriends, but not many," she remembered. She and her grandmother were devoted to each other. When her grandmother's health started to fail, Ola took care of her, and didn't have time left for boys. She didn't mind. She liked that her grandmother needed her. When a stroke had locked up her grandmother's jaw, Ola was the only person who could pry it open. The old woman didn't want anyone else to help her. And Ola didn't need anyone else to feel useful and wanted. She and her grandmother, her mother, and her aunt lived in their little house in Hattiesburg, working night and day, happy together.

Her grandmother died in 1944 from a stroke. She had had two strokes before that. She was seventy-five years old, and worn out from so many years of hard work. Her death hit her granddaughter hard, although they all saw it coming. But for Ola, death was "hard to get acquainted with."

She and her mother and aunt continued as they had, taking in laundry for the families of Hattiesburg, working into the night, going to church on Sundays, keeping one another company, and saving their money. Her mother died in 1964 of breast cancer. Her aunt followed three years later. They left Ola a little money, which she added to her savings. Their deaths were hard on Ola, too. She was alone then, with no one for company, and she mostly kept to herself. She was a quiet and private person. When she wasn't working, she read her old Bible, watched a little television, and listened to the radio. Except for trips to the grocery store and church, she seldom left her house. But she loved the springtime, and enjoyed a solitary walk to look at all the flowers. Folks kept bringing their laundry to her. She washed and ironed for three generations of some families. She was always grateful for the work, and enjoyed it. "Hard work gives life meaning," she explained. "Everyone needs to work hard at something to feel good about themselves. Every job can be done well and every day has its satisfactions."

She worked another twenty-seven years after her aunt died. By that time she had invested her money in several different Hattiesburg banks. Trustmark Bank, the last place that held her savings, encouraged her to invest in certificates of deposit and money market accounts, and her fortune grew faster than it had in a savings account. Two nice ladies who worked there, Nancy Odom and Ellen Vinzant, did a lot more than provide financial advice. They encouraged her to make plans for the day when she couldn't work and would need someone to look after her. They also persuaded her to buy a window air conditioner, although Ola didn't really think she needed one. She was used to the Mississippi heat.

They started Ola thinking about what she would do with her $250,000. She didn't have any plans for her retirement. She had never traveled much, never had a need to, and had been outside Mississippi only once in her life. She had gone to see Niagara Falls, and that was enough sightseeing for her. She knew she wanted to leave a little inheritance to a few cousins, and to leave some money to Friendship Baptist, but she didn't know what she should do with the rest of it.

She had a young cousin, Albert, who had wanted to go to college but didn't have enough money for the tuition. His father had died when he was very little and his mother had struggled to make a living. Ola had contributed several hundred dollars to his college fund so he could attend Southern Mississippi, and the gift had made her feel good. It seemed right to her to help someone get the education she never had.

She told her friends Nancy and Ellen that she had decided to leave most of her estate to the school. They had her talk to the bank's trust officer, Paul Laughlin. "She said she wanted to leave the bulk of her money to Southern Miss," Laughlin recalled, "and she didn't want anybody to come in and change her mind." Laughlin called a lawyer for whom Ola had washed and ironed laundry, and he talked to her to make sure the gift had been her idea. She assured him it was. So they worked it out. "I can't do everything," she said. "But I can do something to help somebody. And what I can do I will do. I wish I could do more."

When Southern Miss announced her gift, the news spread far beyond Hattiesburg. Her generosity gained the attention of the entire country, and beyond. Television networks sent camera crews to Hattiesburg to cover the remarkable woman and her astonishing gift. *The New York Times* reported the story on its front page. Newspapers all over the country published similar accounts. *Time* magazine ran a profile of her. So did *Newsweek, Life,* and *People* magazine. Even the foreign press reported the story. Ola became a celebrity, and despite her natural shyness, she seemed to enjoy it. Folks from all over the world wrote to tell her they had been inspired by her kindness. People added their own donations to the scholarship fund she started. The founder of CNN News, Ted Turner, promised a billion dollars to the United Nations, explaining he had been inspired to do so by the example of Ola McCarty.

The simple decency of Oseola McCarty, the shy, modest washerwoman who had saved a fortune and given it away, struck a deep chord in people. As we hustle along making money, conspicuously consuming, accumulating all sorts of things we don't need, going into debt, she reminded us that happiness isn't a commodity with a price tag. Selfishness won't purchase it no matter how big a house you live in, how nice a car you drive, how many toys you have, how easy your life has been. You have to give something away to be happy. You have to give yourself away. Oseola

McCarty lived a simple life. She worked hard for it. And she gave everything she had away. In a sense, she gave all her work, all her life to others. People want to touch that kind of person, see if a little of the happiness can rub off on them.

President Clinton invited her to the White House and gave her a medal. Harvard University gave her an honorary degree. The United Nations gave her an award also, and when she wouldn't go to Paris to receive it, they came to Hattiesburg. People from all over sent her things: letters, poems, new Bibles, nurse's caps, little crafts they had made commemorating her gift. An artist in New Jersey sent her a portrait he had painted of her. She flew on an airplane for the first time in her life. Hattiesburg celebrated Oseola McCarty Day. The last years of her life were as much fun as the first eighty-six had been hard. Hundreds of people wanted nothing more than to be her friend or say they had met her once. She enjoyed herself but all the fuss about her giving her money away puzzled her. "It wasn't hard," she explained. "I didn't buy things I didn't need. The Lord helped me and he'll help you, too." She said she was "blessed."

Stephanie Bullock, also of Hattiesburg, was the first recipient of an Oseola McCarty scholarship. She calls Ola her honorary grandmother. She is reported to have done well at Southern Miss.

Ola died in 1999, four years after her gift was announced. She spent the last few weeks of her life in her modest home, where she wanted to be. Thousands of people who never met her mourned her passing, and vowed to make their lives a little richer by giving something of themselves to others. I guess they thought Ola knew something they didn't or had forgotten sometime ago when their work had become nothing more than a means to a lifestyle.

A good life, Ola told them, was any life that you could be proud of. "A lot of people talk about self-esteem these days. It seems pretty basic to me. If you want to feel proud of yourself, you've got to do things to be proud of. Feelings follow actions." Oseola McCarty lived a modest life, but she knew a few things, important things, that many people with more advantages never learn. She knew self-respect has a greater value than wealth or fame. She knew hard work is more satisfying than a life of unearned leisure. She knew generosity makes us happier than acquiring possessions we do not need. She knew that feelings follow actions, lived her life accordingly, and died a proud and happy woman.

PART FIVE

Judgment

This fellow's wise enough to play the fool,
And to do that well craves a kind of wit.
—TWELFTH NIGHT

FAIRNESS

Dr. Martin Luther King, Jr.

*From a jail cell he wrote a letter that is one of the most celebrated documents
in American history, and summoned his country to the cause of justice.*

THEY WERE GOOD MEN. MEN OF FAITH. MEN OF CHARITY. TOLERANT men. Concerned men. Respectable men. Men with a sense of civic responsibility. They could reasonably claim to be among the more enlightened people of their community, compared with some of Birmingham's leaders, and some members of their congregations, and their bigotry and brutality. They were the pastoral leaders of Birmingham, of white Birmingham, anyway, eight distinguished clergymen, Methodist, Episcopalian, Baptist, Presbyterian, Catholic, Jewish. In the city of the blind, they were one-eyed kings. They were good men, no doubt. But they were wrong.

They had in their time criticized segregation and the violence used to maintain it. They recognized that Birmingham should change the way it treated the 40 percent of its citizens who were African American. But their liberal moderation did not make right their opposition to antisegregation demonstrations planned by civil rights leaders from outside Birmingham.

They were wrong to counsel patience; wrong to counsel silence; wrong to counsel respect for unjust laws. They were on the wrong side of justice and, as it turned out, the wrong side of history. And while they might have believed themselves to be acting in a responsible and fair manner, their concept of fairness was something less than objective.

A full, honest explanation of fairness would be given in response to them by the civil rights leader whose judgment and tactics they doubted, and whose interference in Birmingham's affairs they intended to discourage. An authentic appeal for fairness would come from a Birmingham jail cell, from the pen and heart of Martin Luther King, Jr.

The largest industrial city in the South, a gritty, tough steel town and stronghold of the Ku Klux Klan, it had been nicknamed "Bombingham" for the eighteen bombings that had occurred in black neighborhoods over the previous six years. All of them remained unsolved by Birmingham police, led by the police commissioner and ruthless foe of integration, Theophilus Eugene "Bull" Connor. In 1961, when the Freedom Riders came to town, Bull Connor's police not only failed to protect them (Connor had given the police the day off because it was Mother's Day), they probably conspired with the white mobs who set the buses on fire and beat the emerging passengers.

Such tactics had begun to worry the business community and other leading citizens of Birmingham. Most of them were committed segregationists, but murder and mayhem were bad for business, and they worried Birmingham's reputation for violent public bigotry was drawing too much national attention and threatening its future prosperity. Something had to be done, and that meant Bull Connor would have to be relieved of his public office.

Bull Connor had always been a reliable bigot. In his first inaugural address as commissioner in 1957, he had promised to defend the status quo. He responded to Supreme Court decisions ruling official segregation unlawful by arguing, "These laws are still constitutional and I promise you until they are removed from the ordinance books of Birmingham and the statute books of Alabama, they will be enforced in Birmingham to the utmost of my ability and by all lawful means." He was also prepared to resort to unlawful means when he felt it necessary to keep black people in their place. When a court decision desegregated Birmingham's parks, Connor closed them. When libraries were ordered to integrate, all their chairs were removed. No part of Birmingham society was integrated while Bull Connor ran the town. Schools were segregated. Lunch counters were off limits to black diners. Water fountains and restrooms were for whites only. Jobs in the steel mills went to whites first, as did all the promotions.

The very local merchants who now worried that Connor was hurting their profits had long insisted on second-class citizenship for their black patrons. They were glad to have Connor, a crude but useful man, help them keep Birmingham segregated. But times were changing, and while few city leaders wanted segregation to end, it would have to be maintained by more subtle means than Bull Connor was equipped to employ.

So, in early 1963, Birmingham decided to make a change. An election was held that terminated the three-member commission that ran the municipal government, on which Bull Connor served as commissioner of public safety, and elected instead a mayor. Connor didn't accept this change in his status quietly. He ran for mayor, and when he was beaten by a more moderate segregationist, Albert Boutwell, he and the other commissioners refused to leave office. The courts would have to decide which of the two city governments was lawful. Nevertheless, for the more practical citizens of Birmingham, even some African Americans there, things were looking up in Birmingham. With a little peace and quiet, a more reasonable accommodation between black and white Birmingham might be achieved.

Birmingham resident and founder of the Alabama Christian Movement for Human Rights, the Reverend Fred Shuttlesworth, was not inclined to wait. His previous efforts to integrate Birmingham had met with little success. In 1963, he turned for help to the Southern Christian Leadership Conference (SCLC), led by the thirty-four-year-old pastor of Atlanta's Ebenezer Baptist Church, the most famous and inspirational civil rights leader in America, the Reverend Dr. Martin Luther King, Jr.

Plans for a Birmingham protest campaign originated in a defeat, the first defeat for the SCLC and Dr. King since Montgomery's bus boycott in the mid-1950s. They had tried for more than a year to desegregate public facilities in Albany, Georgia. Disagreements among civil rights leaders during the campaign had contributed to the failure. So, too, had the lack of careful preparation and the failure of the protest to affect the city's commercial interests. Some demonstrators resorted to violence. And Chief of Police Laurie Pritchett was careful to ensure that the Albany police acted with restraint, and refrained from doing anything that would earn the protestors greater sympathy and national attention.

Albany remained segregated. The campaign was recognized as a failure not only by the civil rights leadership but by the nation. The movement urgently needed a success to reenergize their efforts.

When Fred Shuttlesworth called the SCLC to offer them an opportunity, they seized it. A protest campaign in Birmingham would be a difficult challenge. Success was far from assured, and there was a real danger that people would get hurt. But if Birmingham, the hardest nut in the South to crack, could be integrated, progress for the civil rights movement would accelerate throughout the South. Congress and the White House would feel pressured to pass meaningful civil rights legislation.

This time, they prepared more carefully. Dr. King preached in scores of meetings of the principles and methods of nonviolent protest. He recruited volunteers who were willing to go to jail peacefully. They picked their targets wisely, using the economic power of Birmingham's African American community, which constituted two-fifth's of the city's population, to force change by boycotting city businesses during the second-busiest shopping month of the year, the Easter season. And they proceeded with greater prudence, wisely postponing the campaign until the mayoral election was over to avoid encouraging more white support for Bull Connor's ambitions.

Many opinion makers thought it wise to let the new mayor try to calm racial divisions. *Time* magazine called the protests "ill-timed." There seemed to be a general sentiment that Birmingham could be changed without marches and other protests, perhaps more slowly than preferable, but without the risks, ill will, and violence that might be caused by trying to rush things too quickly. More than a few black citizens in Birmingham shared that sentiment, and resisted calls to join in marches. Nevertheless, Dr. King and his associates were determined to proceed.

On April 3, the campaign began with sit-ins at lunch counters and the release to the press of the "Birmingham Manifesto," which called for the desegregation of all downtown department store lunch counters, restrooms, and water fountains. A march on city hall began three days later, and several dozen marchers were arrested. The next day, more marchers were arrested, one of whom was attacked by police dogs. There were kneel-ins at white churches and sit-ins at the library. The economic boycott of downtown merchants had an immediate effect.

On April 10, the city obtained a court order forbidding King and Ralph Abernathy from marching, to prevent the possibility of "bloodshed and violence." Dr. King chose to disobey it, arguing, "We cannot in all good conscience obey such an injunction which is an unjust, undemocratic and unconstitutional misuse of the legal process." And he decided that he and Abernathy, along with the other volunteers, would go to jail. Many of the protest's organizers urged him to remain free to help raise bail money for those who could not afford to buy their release. But Dr. King insisted he had a moral obligation to participate in the suffering he had asked others to accept. "I have to make a faith act," he told his colleagues. On April 13, Good Friday, he and Abernathy were arrested as they marched peacefully.

He was kept in solitary confinement. He could not meet with his lawyers or call his wife, who had, a few days before, given birth to their fourth child. He had no mattress, pillow, or blanket. This was his thirteenth arrest. But he had survived worse. He had been stabbed. His home and family had been threatened with bombs and bullets. He had received death threats on a near daily basis since the beginning of the Montgomery bus boycott in 1955. He had courage, and had grown tough in the struggle.

Soon after he entered his jail cell, he happened to see in the Birmingham newspaper a statement by the leading white religious leaders of Birmingham, the eight good men described at the beginning of the chapter, criticizing the demonstrations as "unwise and untimely." Like many Birmingham citizens, they were encouraged by the election of the new mayor, and worried over the violence that might result from protests organized by outside agitators, especially when they included the most famous agitator of them all, Martin Luther King. "Just as we formerly pointed out that 'hatred and violence have no sanction in our religious and political traditions,' we also point out that such actions as incite to hatred and violence, however technically peaceful those actions may be, have not contributed to the resolution of our local problems. We do not believe that these days of new hope are days when extreme measures are justified in Birmingham." They ended their statement by urging "our own Negro community to withdraw support from these demonstrations."

No doubt they believed they acted with nothing but the best of intentions for white and black Birmingham. Some of them, surely the Catholic bishop and Jewish rabbi, had experienced prejudice themselves. I'm sure they would not have proceeded in such a manner if they thought it unjust, unfair to black and white alike. But it was unfair, terribly unfair. And Dr. King in a magisterial response, the "Letter from Birmingham Jail," called them to account, and called his country to the cause of justice.

As a statement of the principle of equality under the law, as a promise and a demand of fairness from one man to his fellow human beings, it has no equal. The sentiments are, of course, the animating principles of our Declaration of Independence and our Constitution, but these had long been compromised by the treatment of African Americans, first in bondage, and then under Jim Crow. In his letter, Dr. King eloquently and passionately expressed the unacceptability of waiting patiently for the sun to rise on another day when the promise of American freedom was not extended to every American.

Over the next several days, he wrote his letter, nearly seven thousand words long, on scraps of paper and in the margins of newspapers, which were smuggled out of his cell to his colleagues. He wrote and rewrote until he had delivered to the press and public one of the most admired American public documents of the twentieth century. "My Dear Fellow Clergymen," it began. Recognizing that his correspondents were "men of genuine good will and your criticisms sincerely set forth," he promised to respond in patient and reasonable terms. They were reasonable terms, and undeniably fair, but patient they were not.

We have waited for more than 340 years for our constitutional and God-given rights. . . . Perhaps it is easy for those who have never felt the stinging dark of segregation to say, "Wait." But when you have seen vicious mobs lynch your mothers and fathers at will and drown your sisters and brothers at whim; when you have seen hate-filled policemen curse, kick and even kill your black brothers and sisters; when you see the vast majority of your twenty million Negro brothers smothering in an airtight cage of poverty in the midst of an affluent society; when you suddenly find your tongue twisted and your speech stammering as you seek to explain to your six-year-old daughter why she can't go to the public amusement park that has just been advertised on television, and see tears welling up in her eyes when she is told that Funtown is closed to colored children, and see ominous clouds of inferiority beginning to form in her little mental sky, and see her beginning to distort her personality by developing unconscious bitterness toward white people; when you have to concoct an answer for a five-year-old son who is asking: "Daddy, why do white people treat colored people so mean?"; when you take a cross-country drive and find it necessary to sleep night after night in the uncomfortable corners of your automobile because no motel will accept you; when you are humiliated day in and day out by nagging signs reading "white" and "colored"; when your first name becomes "nigger," your middle name becomes "boy" (however old you are) and your last name becomes "John," and your wife and mother are never given the respected title "Mrs."; when you are harried by day and haunted by night by the fact that you are a Negro, living constantly at tiptoe stance, never quite knowing what to expect next, and are plagued with inner fears and outer resentments; when you are forever fighting a degenerating sense of "nobodiness" then you will understand why we find it difficult to wait. There comes a time when the cup of endurance runs over, and men are no longer willing to be plunged into the abyss of despair.

Then he sternly challenged them as religious leaders who had failed their vocation. It was a harsh but fair indictment.

So often the contemporary church is a weak, ineffectual voice with an uncertain sound. So often it is the archdefender of the status quo. Far from being disturbed by the presence of the church, the power structure of the average community is consoled by the church's silent and often vocal sanction of things as they are.

But the judgment of God is upon the church as never before. If today's church does not recapture the sacrificial spirit of the early church, it will lose its authenticity, forfeit the loyalty of millions, and be dismissed as an irrelevant social club with no meaning for the twentieth century.

Finally, he rebuked them for commending the police force for keeping "order" and "preventing violence": "One day the South will recognize its real heroes. . . . One day the South will know that when these disinherited children of God sat down at lunch counters, they were in reality standing up for what is best in the American dream and for the most sacred values in our Judeo-Christian heritage, thereby bringing our nation back to those great wells of democracy which were dug deep by the founding fathers in their formulation of the Constitution and the Declaration of Independence."

Nine days after his arrest, Dr. King was released. So were the others jailed with him. Supporters of the cause had managed to raise sufficient funds to post bail. The protests continued. More arrests were made. Bull Connor, at the urging of city leaders, had initially acted with more restraint than he could usually manage. But when, at Dr. King's urging, black children, high school age and younger, marched without their parents, Connor could stand no more. He turned police dogs and high-pressure fire hoses on the children. The television broadcasts of these brutal tactics shocked the nation. The demonstrations grew in number and intensity. Connor, by returning to form, had helped the cause he so despised. The protests succeeded, and Birmingham began to desegregate. Dr. King had his much-needed victory.

The cause was far from over, of course. A long, hard road still lay ahead. The Birmingham home of the Reverend A. D. King, Dr. King's brother, was bombed after the agreement was reached. Four months later, the Ku Klux Klan planted a bomb in a Baptist church in Birmingham, killing four little girls. Many other acts of violence were committed against members of the civil rights movement. Dr. King himself was murdered five years later, on the balcony of a Memphis motel.

But they would wait no longer, no matter what. From Birmingham on, the tide was irreversible until America, at least in the construction and defense of its laws, if not in the hearts of every one of us, arrived at the place Dr. King had summoned us to, that exalted place that had been the highest ambition of our Founding Fathers and the highest value we recommend to the rest of the world; the place where all people are recognized as equal, and endowed by their Creator with inalienable rights.

African Americans recognize the debt they owe Dr. King's courage, wisdom, and unshakable sense of fairness. But Americans of European descent owe him a greater one. At the cost of his life, he helped save us from a terrible disgrace, the betrayal of our country, and the principles that have ennobled our history. And that is a debt we must happily bear forever.

HUMILITY

Dwight D. Eisenhower

How an obscure army officer from rural Kansas made the most important decision of World War Two and saved the world from Nazi tyranny

HE WALKED AMONG THEM FLASHING HIS FAMOUS SMILE, THE PICture of confidence and easy charm, shaking their hands, patting their backs, cheering them, asking in his broad Midwestern accent: "Where you from, soldier?"

"Texas . . . Montana . . . Indiana . . . New York."

"What kind of work did you do?"

"Steamfitter, sir . . . farmer . . . drove a cab, sir . . . went to school, General."

"Anybody from Kansas?"

"Yes, sir."

"Go get 'em, Kansas."

"Don't worry, General, we'll take care of this thing for you."

As the men of the 101st Airborne Division lifted their gear, packs weighing over a hundred pounds, and lined up to board the waiting aircraft, and he shook the hand of their commander, Brigadier General Max Taylor, one young soldier stopped just before he entered the plane, turned, and snapped a crisp salute. Supreme Allied Commander General Dwight David Eisenhower returned the salute and smiled. Then he turned away, walked to his car, and wept.

"It's very hard," he said, "to look a soldier in the eye when you fear you are sending him to his death."

It was seven o'clock in the evening, June 5, 1944. The men to whom he had just bid farewell were part of the initial stage of Operation Overlord. Three airborne divisions, over twenty thousand men and boys, boarded hundreds of transports that would ferry them across the English Channel. Droning through a barrage of antiaircraft fire, they would make their way to Normandy, where they were to parachute to the earth while German machine-gun rounds and tracers tore through the night sky. Those who made it safely to ground were supposed to secure the right and left flanks of the Allied invasion from the aroused German Wehrmacht. As he knew while he had walked and joked among them, many of them, maybe most of them, would never return.

At 6:30 the next morning, D-Day, over 150,000 soldiers would hit the first of five beaches, the British and Canadians at Juno, Gold, and Sword; the Americans at Utah and Omaha. Over five thousand ships would carry them, their armor, supplies, and fifty thousand vehicles of every description over sixty to a hundred miles of gray and stormy seas. Eleven thousand aircraft would support them. The first ships would soon put to sea. There was no turning back now. One man, and one man alone, had made the now irreversible decision to launch the greatest air and seaborne invasion in history, Dwight David Eisenhower.

Despite his cheerful repartee with the departing paratroopers, and their bravado, no one was sure the landings would succeed. Casualty estimates ran as high as 75 percent. June 6, 1944, was to be the most fateful day in the history of the twentieth century. The future of the world hung in the balance. And no one knew how it would turn out. They had planned it meticulously and trained exhaustively. They had achieved unquestioned air superiority over the Luftwaffe. They had nearly eliminated the U-boat threat. They had studied the German defenses as best they could. Morale was high. They were resolute, and steeled for the terrible toll in dead and wounded that would inevitably result. But nothing in war is certain, except the occurrence of the unexpected. Disaster was as likely as success. Churchill himself, who had never been keen on a cross-Channel invasion, confessed his worry to Eisenhower that the "flower" of English and American youth would die by the many thousands. "I have my doubts," he fretted. "I have my doubts."

They believed they would face formidable opposition, the Atlantic Wall. The Germans' best general, Field Marshal Erwin Rommel, the "Desert Fox," had recently been given command of the defenses. When he had arrived at his command he was shocked at how inadequate they were. But he swung into action to improve them. Mining the beaches everywhere, planting obstacles on every beach, strengthening pillboxes where German machine guns would rain fire on the invaders, moving more artillery and mobile forces to the coast. He had managed to move one of his best divisions, the 325th, to the high cliffs over Omaha Beach. And he begged Berlin for more men and munitions to reinforce his other positions. "The only possible chance will be at the beaches," Rommel argued. "That's where they are always the weakest."

Somehow, over the course of the next few days, the Allies had to land a million men on those beaches. Once they were there, especially on Omaha, it would be their own ingenuity, fortitude, and courage that got them off the beaches. They could use some luck during the landings. But the weather was threatening to make a hard job almost impossible. The invasion had been scheduled for the day before, but Eisenhower had to postpone it because a gale had whipped the Channel into a frenzy, and air support couldn't see through the clouds. The meteorologist, whom Eisenhower trusted, had told him that there might be a small window of not perfect but tolerable weather on the sixth. At 4:15 A.M., on the fifth, he asked his senior commanders for their opinion. Some argued to launch. Others recommended another postponement. Eisenhower paced the floor, his head down, an ever-present cigarette between his fingers. After what seemed like five minutes to one observer, he looked up and said simply, "Okay, let's go." And so they went.

The generals and admirals rushed from the room to their various posts to set events into motion. Eisenhower was left alone in his house with his thoughts and cares. There was nothing more he could do now except worry. He had made his decision, and there would be no turning back. When they had planned Overlord, he had told his friend Omar Bradley, who would command the American invasion force, "This operation is not being planned with any alternatives. This operation is planned as a victory. . . . We're throwing everything we have into it, and we're going to make it a success." Now, he could just whisper to himself, "I hope to God I know what I'm doing."

The astonishing thing was that he did know what he was doing. Before the war, before he received the four stars he wore on his shoulder, fifty-three-year-old "Ike" Eisenhower had never commanded so much as a platoon in battle. His appointment as supreme commander, Allied Expeditionary Force was a surprise. Although Eisenhower had commanded the Allied invasion in North Africa, everyone believed that General of the Army and U.S. Chief of Staff George C. Marshall, the man who had sent Eisenhower to North Africa, would command the invasion of Europe. But President Franklin D. Roosevelt did not feel he could spare Marshall, whom he relied on, from Washington. And so the decision was made to give it to the man who had served on his staff and who had impressed the hard-to-impress Marshall, as he had impressed all his bosses, with his intelligence, hard work, and strategic vision.

Although there were some senior officers who criticized his performance in North Africa,

Eisenhower had proved capable enough. Marshall trusted him because he knew Eisenhower shared, and had helped develop and stoutly defend his concept of how the war should be fought: Europe first, and then the Pacific, and an invasion of France as soon as practical. Besides, Ike's personality, his patience, courtesy, and charm, were suited to one of the most important aspects of the supreme commander's job—diplomacy.

Not all the leading figures in the Allied cause were as modest, collegial, and selfless as Ike. Some of them were downright prima donnas, like the vain British general Field Marshal Bernard Montgomery, who was never satisfied unless he received more glory and attention than any other general in the field; the prickly Free French General Charles de Gaulle, whose arrogance and sense of entitlement vastly exceeded the size of the force he commanded; the great Winston Churchill, whose sense of destiny, vast knowledge and experience of warfare, and potent personality could overwhelm the brightest star in his presence. Eisenhower would have to soothe their egos, take their criticism, settle their disputes, guide them, encourage them, disappoint them, defend them, and keep them all working in harness together. Like Marshall, he knew victory would have to be a team effort. The Allies would have to be far more unified than they had been in the last war, when jealousy, bickering, and suspicion had contributed to the deaths of the best part of a generation of the British and French. Many of the senior Allied commanders who were subordinate to him believed themselves his superior in experience and ability. Perhaps they were in some respects. But, as events turned out, no man could have done the job better.

He was born on October 14, 1890, the third of David and Ida Eisenhower's seven sons, and raised in the old cattle town Abilene, Kansas. His parents were poor, and had little in the way of luxuries. They had to struggle for the bare necessities of life. His father had a potent temper that he would pass on to his son Little Ike. Never very talkative, he taught his sons self-discipline with a belt across their backside. He was a decent man, hardworking and responsible, but tough. Eisenhower's mother was devoutly religious, and though strict, she was a wise and dedicated mother, whom Eisenhower would always remember as the greatest influence of his life. She was also quite a firm pacifist who viewed war among the greatest of sins.

His childhood, as he remembers it, was a happy one, with his many brothers to play with in the wide-open spaces on the edge of the Great Plains. He learned discipline, self-reliance, and humility. He was a good student, encouraged by his parents to regard education as the means that would provide a better life than they could presently afford. He was also a promising athlete, excelling at baseball and football. His qualities as an athlete and scholar won him a place at West Point in 1911. All the Eisenhower boys would do well. They had been raised well.

When he graduated from West Point, in the middle of his class (which included several men who would hold senior commands in World War Two), America had not yet entered the war that was then raging in Europe. When two years later President Wilson ordered Americans to the trenches of World War One, Ike, a young captain, hoped he would have his first opportunity to serve in combat, and was bitterly disappointed to be left stateside training troops. He had been given a wartime promotion to lieutenant colonel but that, like his dreams of combat experience, ended with the armistice. He reverted to his peacetime rank of captain. He was soon promoted to major, and would remain in that rank for much of the years between the two wars.

The war's end, and the widespread opposition in America to any future involvement in a European conflict, resulted in a substantial reduction of the size of the army. Millions of Americans were under arms while the fighting continued in Europe. The peacetime army would seldom exceed 200,000 men. Opportunities were few, and promotions rare. Eisenhower held a number of less than glamorous assignments, and had little hope of ever having a memorable military career as a combat commander. But he made the most of all his jobs, worked hard, showed a lively intelligence, and earned the trust of his superiors. He was also a man of towering ambition. He was no limelight seeker, but he did crave accomplishment. That his ambitions were unlikely to be realized given his circumstances did not cause him to despair, however. As he always did, he applied himself completely to his work, and he moved along.

He did earn prestigious assignments, first with his friend (and personality opposite) the flamboyant George Patton, with whom he promoted the development and use of armored tanks to avoid ever having to endure the bloody stalemate of trench fighting again. What he considered his most fortunate assignment began in 1922, when he served in the Panama Canal Zone as chief of staff to Brigadier General Fox Conner. Conner was a brilliant military scholar, strategist, and tactician, and, impressed by his young staff officers, undertook to improve Major Eisenhower with a first-class education in military theories and their practical application, as well as in much of the Western classics. Conner was also one of the few American officers, one of the few Americans, in fact, who believed another European war was not far off. He recognized that the last war was greatly hindered by the lack of Allied unity, and he impressed on Eisenhower the critical importance of improving coalition warfare in the next one.

After his service in Panama, Eisenhower won a prestigious assignment to the army's Command and General Staff College at Ft. Leavenworth, where he graduated first in his class. He was marked as a promising young staff officer, which gave him entry into the rarified ranks of the war department. He was assigned as an aide to then Army Chief of Staff General Douglas MacArthur, and accompanied MacArthur to the Philippines as his chief of staff when the imperious general undertook the formation of the Philippine defense forces as Japanese militarism threatened Asia. When he returned, four years later, near the outbreak of World War Two, he was given the first (and brief) command of his career, a battalion of the 15th Infantry Division, at Ft. Lewis, Washington, and promoted to colonel, the highest rank he had hoped to attain.

By June 1941, he was serving as chief of staff to the commanding general of the Third Army in San Antonio. There he began to analyze the immense changes that would have to be imposed on the organization and training of the army when it mobilized to fight another world war. Eisenhower devised the Third Army's battle plan in carefully conceived and full-scale war games that were held that year against the Second Army. His Third Army won, and Eisenhower found himself promoted to brigadier general and transferred to the war department to work for the brilliant, demanding, and starchy George Marshall.

Eisenhower had by this time become quite adept at serving difficult bosses. MacArthur was an infamously difficult and exasperating superior. He remembered Eisenhower, however, who would eventually hold an equivalent command to his, as the best staff officer he ever had. Marshall was less eccentric than the flamboyant MacArthur, but as strict, formal, and unsympathetic with his hardworking subordinates as they come. He immediately recognized Eisenhower's unique abilities as a military strategist, gifted staff officer, and skilled diplomat. He recognized, as well, that his sincerity and total devotion to achieving the task at hand without regard to who earned credit made him uniquely suited to coalition warfare. The job proved to be Ike's most fortunate assignment. He became Marshall's protégé, and the logical choice to assume the Allied command of the North African campaign. By 1943, after Roosevelt, Churchill, and Stalin conferred in Tehran, Roosevelt gave him four stars and command of the entire Allied force in Europe.

In a letter to his wife, Mamie, shortly after he received the command, he wrote of its impact on him. Ambitious though he surely was, he expressed such natural modesty and sincere devotion to duty that it seems unlikely to have come from the pen of a man who in a period of a couple years had ascended from obscurity to the greatest military command in the history of warfare.

I am human enough to want the official approval of my past action that such an unusual advancement implies—but anyone worthy of high command is so concerned with the enormity of the tasks, for which his own faculties so frequently seem pitifully inadequate, that what the world calls success or promotion does not loom up as particularly important. . . .

Loneliness is the inescapable lot of a man holding such a job. Subordinates can advise, urge, help and pray—but only one man, in his own mind and heart, can decide "Do we, or do we not?" . . . No man can always be right. So the struggle is to do one's best; to keep the brain and conscience clear; never to be swayed by unworthy motives or inconsequential reasons, but to strive to unearth the basic factors involved and then do one's duty.

His duty was daunting and nearly impossible, and its effect on him grave and burdensome, but he faced it with the same courage and selflessness as the boys he ordered to France. He was, in many respects, more like his troops than his fellow commanders. He came from the same background, was raised with the same values, was dedicated, patriotic, responsible, and saw the war not as an opportunity for glory but as a cause to defend the right against wrong, to save freedom from tyranny. He was, of course, marked by genius, but that did not make him a complicated man, just a very capable and determined one. He was as simple as the soldiers who loved him, and as good. That is the character which made him a great man, where others relied simply on their brilliance or daring to achieve.

By D-Day, he was drinking fifteen to twenty cups of coffee a day, and smoking four packs of cigarettes. He suffered from high blood pressure, terrible headaches, and insomnia. He worried, got depressed, kept his game face on and his smile aimed at the world. He wouldn't betray any doubts. He held his diverse group of commanders, with their conflicting ambitions and temperaments, together, and kept them focused on their job. No matter how great the person was, Ike patiently steered him to the job he was needed for. He had no need of flattery or comfort or any unnecessary perks or attention. When he first arrived in London he was given a lavishly furnished mansion at a fashionable address. He hated it, and chose for his quarters a two-bedroom house in a London suburb, which he became quite fond of. He worked around the clock. He got ready, carefully, exhaustively, and then he said, "Okay, let's go."

He had taped a statement for the troops that was broadcast at every embarkation point and to the press.

Soldiers, Sailors and Airmen of the Allied Expeditionary Forces: You are about to embark upon the Great Crusade toward which we have striven these many months. The eyes of the world are upon you. The hopes and prayers of liberty-loving people everywhere march with you. . . .

Your task will not be an easy one. Your enemy is well-trained, well-equipped and battle-hardened. He will fight savagely. . . .

I have full confidence in your courage, devotion to duty and skill in battle. We will accept nothing less than full victory! Good luck! And let us all beseech the blessing of Almighty God upon this great and noble undertaking.

In his shirt pocket he carried another statement, to be issued in the event that the landings failed, at the cost of untold thousands of lives. There would be no blame shifting if it did. No complaints about the weather, incompetent subordinates, mistakes in combat out of the commander's control. It was a direct and plain message. He consulted no one when he wrote it. "Our landings . . . have failed to gain a satisfactory foothold and I have withdrawn the troops. My decision to attack at this time and place was based upon the best information available. The troops, the air, and the Navy did all that bravery and devotion to duty could do. If any blame or fault attaches to the attempt it is mine alone."

The paratroopers had a hard time of it. In the cloud cover, many of the pilots dropped them far from their destinations. Units were widely scattered and taking fire from the enemy in small groups. But somehow they re-formed and did their jobs. The landings went better than expected, except at Omaha, encountering lighter opposition than they had planned for. The Germans had thought the landings would occur farther north, in Calais, and hadn't deployed as many forces as Rommel had argued they should. Rommel himself was in Berlin celebrating his wife's birthday. He never believed the Allies would invade in such bad weather.

At Omaha, the bombers that were supposed to take out the enemy pillboxes and artillery widely missed the mark. The strong tides and high seas pulled and swamped many of the landing craft. They couldn't get any armor on the beach. Machine guns and mortars rained down on the GIs, who were totally exposed. The only cover they could find were mounds of sand kicked up by enemy shells. They had to climb the high cliffs and get at the enemy's fortified positions themselves, under absolutely withering fire. As Omar Bradley peered through his binoculars at what he thought was an irreversible debacle in the making, he thought he would have to call it off, and not order any other men onto the beach to die with the ones he had already sent. But he didn't. They took their beating and did their job. They were magnificent. By the end of that first day they were in France to stay. Casualties hadn't been as high as Eisenhower had feared they would be, but five thousand dead soldiers will make you weep just the same. And there would be more to come. In a letter to Mamie, a grateful Eisenhower recounted his first visit with his soldiers in Normandy. "[They] . . . are indescribable in their élan, courage, determination and fortitude. They inspire me."

On June 7, Eisenhower boarded a British ship and crossed the Channel to observe the follow-up landings after the initial assault. He asked the skipper to bring the ship closer to the beaches for a better look. The obliging captain ran the ship aground in his effort to comply with the supreme commander's wishes, knocking Eisenhower and the other brass accompanying him to the deck. Worried that the officer would be reprimanded, he wrote to the British sea lord, took responsibility for the mishap, and asked that the skipper not be punished.

The war in Europe lasted another ten months. They all kept at it. When Hitler threw the last of his reserves in a huge offensive through the Ardennes Forest, entrapping the 101st Airborne at Bastogne, Ike, unlike many of the other Allied commanders, saw it as the opportunity for finishing the war. He ordered his friend Patton to race the Third Army north, and the war was over in three months.

Seven years later, General of the Army (retired) Dwight David Eisenhower was elected president of the United States. Many well-educated, sophisticated Americans thought him to be poorly qualified for the job, and none too bright. He was not an eloquent man. He often jumbled his syntax and tortured the language. They mocked him for it, but he didn't seem to care. "They think I'm stupid, but honest," he remarked. He wasn't stupid and he was immensely popular with the American people, many of whom he had commanded in the most dangerous sacrifice of their lives. And why wouldn't they love him? He was one of them, simple, modest, hardworking, decent. Oh, he was a genius as well. That's obvious now. And not all of America's soldiers were geniuses. But collectively, as a generation, they did possess genius. They might have been humble, but after they had helped save freedom for the world, at great personal cost, they came home to build the prosperous, powerful, decent America we live in today. And smiling Ike Eisenhower was their leader.

GRATITUDE

Tecumseh

The great Indian leader who lost a war but taught even his enemies how to live

EIGHT HUNDRED AMERICANS CHASED THE BRITISH ENEMY DOWN A wooded ravine. Moments before, they had quickly overwhelmed the small enemy force guarding British artillery across the Maumee River from Ft. Meigs. The battery had inflicted four days of punishing bombardment on Major General William Henry Harrison and his besieged garrison at Ft. Meigs. Harrison had sent word to General Green Clay to divide his relief column of Kentucky militia in two. Clay's second-in-command, Colonel William Dudley, was to seize and destroy the British cannons and then quickly cross the river to the fort before the enemy counterattacked. Had the Kentuckians followed Harrison's orders to the letter, they would have been remembered more for their courage than their poor judgment. But after they had spiked the guns, Dudley's men were unable to resist the opportunity for a greater victory and set off after the escaping enemy.

Death waited in the forest.

Roused by the sound of gunfire, a much stronger force of Indian warriors, encamped with British soldiers under the command of Colonel Henry Procter, rushed through the woods to meet the unsuspecting Americans. Within minutes Dudley's column was routed. Many of the Kentuckians threw their rifles away as they raced back to their boats. An untold number were surrounded and killed or captured before they reached the riverbank. Dudley was killed and scalped. Most of those who reached the river were surrounded and only a few managed to escape. Those who surrendered were dragged back through the woods to the British encampment.

At the camp, the prisoners were made to run the gauntlet, as two long lines of braves struck them with tomahawks, rifle butts, and clubs. Colonel Procter, a man of little honor and less courage, watched the slaughter with indifference. Forty Kentuckians had been killed, and the rest soon to follow, when the Shawnee chief who commanded the Indian warriors galloped into camp, sprang from his mount, and screamed, "Are there no men here?" He grabbed two of his warriors, threw them to the ground, and stood between the others and their terrified prisoners. "You are cowards," he rebuked them. Chastened, they backed away. Then he turned to Procter, and angrily demanded why the colonel had not tried to prevent the atrocity. "Your warriors cannot be controlled," Procter answered. "You are not fit to command," the disgusted chief responded. "Go away and put on petticoats."

Not for the first time had his character proven superior to the men he fought beside and the men he fought against. Everyone knew that the great Tecumseh, fearless warrior and visionary, steadfast leader, did not tolerate torture or murder, or suffer intentional harm to be done to innocents. He was a man of honor. Even his enemies knew that, especially the man who had fought him the longest, William Henry Harrison.

By 1768, the year of Tecumseh's birth, the Shawnee had long been a wandering tribe pushed ever westward from their hunting lands by the relentless march of American settlers over the Appalachians, the land speculators who encouraged them, and the saber-carrying soldiers, the "Long Knives," who protected them. They had fought the encroaching white men for decades. Allied with the French in the French and Indian War, Shawnee braves had joined in the ambush and destruction of British general Edward Braddock's army as it marched through the Pennsylvania wilderness to take the French fort at the site of the future city of Pittsburgh, giving a young colonial soldier, George Washington, his first major experience of battle. Shawnee war parties raided homesteads on the Virginia and Pennsylvania frontiers during and after the war.

In the war for American independence, the Shawnee at first intended to remain neutral, but American aggression soon forced their alliance with the British in battles along the Ohio River Valley frontier. Fifteen-year-old Tecumseh got his first taste of battle in a skirmish with Kentucky militiamen who had crossed the Ohio to attack Shawnee villages. He had accompanied his brother and guardian, Chiksika, to the battle. The fighting was fierce and Chiksika was slightly wounded. The young Tecumseh was unnerved in his first encounter with organized bloodletting, and fled the battle. It was the only time in his life his courage failed him.

In a later raid near the end of the war, the Shawnees attacked the crew of a flatboat on the Ohio River. All but one of the crew was killed in the encounter. The lone survivor was dragged ashore and burned at the stake. The atrocity left a deep mark on Tecumseh, who, though he was too young to intervene in the victim's behalf, denounced the murder after it occurred, and swore he would never again remain silent in the face of such an injustice.

He had been raised from birth to be a warrior, and an unrelenting foe of white men. He would live and die determined to defend Indian land from the insatiable appetites of American settlers. In the course of his crusade, he became the greatest Indian leader of his time. Many would argue, including Americans who fought him, that he was the greatest war chief of all time.

He was the fifth child and third son of the Shawnee war chief Puckeshinwa, and his wife, Methoataske. At the moment of his birth, near today's Springfield, Ohio, a comet streaked across the night sky, an auspicious sign that the baby was destined for great things. Puckeshinwa named him Panther Crossing the Sky—Tecumseh—and looked forward to the time when the child would begin his journey to greatness by fighting alongside his father. But that day would never come. Puckeshinwa fell in battle in 1774, fighting the militia under the command of the British governor of Virginia, Lord Dunmore, at the Battle of Point Pleasant. His oldest son, Chiksika, was one of the warriors who carried the fallen Puckeshinwa from the field. Before he died, the proud warrior made his son promise never to forget his duty to fight the white invaders and to raise young Tecumseh to be a brave warrior.

The treaty that ended the American Revolutionary War did not bring peace to the Ohio frontier. Shawnees, with the encouragement, if not always the support, of the British continued to resist the western expansion of the new American nation. Keeping his promise to his late father, Chiksika took special care of his younger brother Tecumseh. He taught him to hunt and fish, and to learn the fighting skills of a Shawnee brave. He raised him to revere the memory of their courageous father, and the virtues he had exemplified as a warrior who preferred death to dishonor. He instilled those virtues in Tecumseh by example, becoming a young war chief whose skill and courage in battle earned the respect of his tribe's elders. Tecumseh idolized him.

The time Chiksika spent with Tecumseh, taking the boy on long journeys well beyond the villages of their tribe, greatly exceeded the attention he gave his other siblings. Puckeshinwa had left six children and a wife pregnant with triplets when he died. Methoataske delivered the triplets several months after her husband's death, one of whom died in infancy. A few years after their birth, Methoataske left the village with her youngest daughter, and returned to her own people, the Creek. Her remaining children were left in the care of the oldest and married daughter, Tecumpease.

Of the two surviving triplets, one would also become a distinguished member of his tribe. But that was far from evident during his childhood. He was given the name Lalawethika, the Rattle, or Loudmouth. He was a disagreeable child, made all the more miserable by his mother's absence. He was fat from overeating and laziness, and unattractive, with a drooping right eye he had accidentally poked with an arrowhead. He was ungainly, an object of derision to the other children of the village. He fared poorly at the games Shawnee boys played to emulate the warriors they would become. He could not hunt or fish well. He was a poor marksmen and an ungraceful rider. His lack of skills, however, did not encourage any humility in the boy. He was boastful and complaining. The greater his failings, the more boastful and annoying he became. Most people preferred to avoid him, including his oldest brother.

A skilled hunter, Chiksika helped provide for his younger siblings. But with the exception of Tecumseh, he didn't spend much time with them. Both he and Tecumseh were close to Tecumpease, who acted as their surrogate mother. Tecumseh attributed his honesty, which as an adult would earn the respect of friend and foe alike, to his older sister's virtue and innate decency. She, too, was an implacable foe of the white settlers who stole their land, but she never used her hostility to excuse a lack of virtue and humanity. Fierce warrior though he was, their father had been a civilized man and Tecumpease and her brothers would live their lives as he had lived his. Although she cared for Lalawethika as she cared for her other brothers, she, too, found little to like in the child. Chiksika could barely stand the sight of him. Tecumseh kept his true feelings for his younger brother to himself, and treated him with courtesy and sympathy, though they were not close as children.

As Americans pressed new claims on Shawnee lands north of the Ohio River, Indian fighters Benjamin Logan and George Rogers Clark raided Shawnee villages to drive the tribe farther west. Shawnee warriors grew impatient with their tribal elders, who counseled caution in the face of the advancing enemy. They were drawn to the combative leadership of young militants like Chiksika, who in the late 1780s led a small band of braves south to make common cause with other tribes against the settlers and soldiers that kept pouring through the Cumberland Gap. Tecumseh, though still a teenager, left for war with his brother. He wouldn't return for three years.

Chiksika's band joined Cherokee warriors in raids on settlements throughout the frontier in Kentucky and Tennessee. Tecumseh took part in the battles, growing in confidence and skill with every encounter with the enemy. In the summer of 1788, they prepared to attack a small fort in eastern Tennessee. On the morning of the battle, Chiksika announced he had dreamed he would not survive the battle. But his premonition had little effect on his courage as he led the attack. As they advanced on the fort, Chiksika was mortally wounded, and died in Tecumseh's arms. The disheartened Shawnee braves broke off the attack, and most of them soon returned to their village in Ohio. Tecumseh refused to join them, and with a small band of braves continued to raid white settlements in the south. When he returned to his village in 1790, he was no longer Chiksika's younger brother. He was a leader of men at war, and on his way to becoming the leader of the Shawnee nation and a growing confederacy of Indian tribes that would become the greatest threat to the expansion of the American empire ever posed by Native Americans.

When Tecumseh returned to his tribe, he found that they had been forced by American raiders to relocate to the northwestern corner of Ohio and northeastern Indiana, crowded with several other Indian nations in an ever-shrinking part of what would come to be called the Old Northwest. The Americans had built a fort at Cincinnati, which encouraged settlers to press farther and farther west. By 1790, the government was demanding that the Shawnees and other tribes sign peace treaties that ceded even more of their lands to the Americans. When they refused, the governor of the Northwest Territory ordered an army into the field to compel them. A large force of Shawnees, Miamis, Chippewas, Potawatomies, Delawares, and Ottawas destroyed it.

Tecumseh had arrived home just after the American defeat, and when Governor Arthur St. Clair ordered an even larger army to avenge the defeat, Tecumseh led his small band to join the coming battle. This army, too, was routed by a broad alliance of Indian tribes led by the great Miami war chief Little Turtle, and encouraged by the support of British garrisons that still remained in parts of the Northwest Territory. Six hundred of St. Clair's soldiers were killed. It was the worst defeat ever inflicted on an American army by Indians. Tecumseh had played an important but not leading part in the battle. Still a young warrior, he was not yet considered a tribal leader. But his courage and skill were gaining the respect of his tribe, particularly among the young warriors who felt emboldened by the victory over St. Clair to reject peace overtures from the Americans that some of the older Indian leaders were inclined to accept.

When the United States Constitution was adopted, and a strong national government elected, the fortunes of war shifted against the Shawnee and their allies. President George Washington dispatched a famous Revolutionary War veteran, General "Mad Anthony" Wayne, to the Northwest Territory to subdue the victorious Indian alliance. Stationed at Ft. Washington, Wayne methodically built and trained his forces over two years. When they took to the field, they advanced slowly, carefully protecting their supply lines so they wouldn't be short of munitions, horses, and other provisions when they brought the Indians to battle.

In August 1794, the numerically stronger and better-armed Americans met what remained of the alliance near the eastern end of Lake Erie. The Battle of Fallen Timbers, as it came to be called, was an unqualified victory for the Americans. They proved a much more capable and steadfast force than the Indians had faced before. Tecumseh had led a small party in the battle and had fought heroically, exhibiting all the courage and inspirational leadership he would become famous for in the years ahead. But the defeat was a bitter one nonetheless. Another of Tecumseh's brothers was among the casualties. And the important support the British had provided the Indians was finished as well. When the routed Indians sought refuge with a British garrison stationed at Ft. Miami, they were refused. During the battle, Tecumseh had fought for the first time the man who would become his greatest adversary, William Henry Harrison, then a young lieutenant in the U.S. Army.

The defeat resulted in the 1795 Treaty of Ft. Greenville, which ceded most of Ohio to the Americans. The alliance of tribes that had showed much promise as a resisting force to American expansion disintegrated, the tribes returning to lands guaranteed them by the treaty. A relatively small number of Shawnee refused to accept the treaty's provisions and follow the Shawnee chief, Black Hoof, to the small holding of land designated for their use. They were encouraged by a new leader, who denounced the chiefs who had made their mark on the treaty. The land, Tecumseh argued, belongs to all Indian people, and cannot be given away by one or a few tribes, surrendering the birthright of all. He established his own village with the surviving members of his family, and the young warriors drawn to his defiance, and refused to move. Though the years following the treaty were largely peaceful, and Tecumseh offered assurances that he did not intend to make war against the Americans, neither would he or his braves consent to the American government's repeated demands to submit to American authority.

Little time elapsed before the settlers grew discontented with the land granted them under the Ft. Greenville treaty. They forbid the Shawnee hunting privileges in lands below the Greenville line, but ignored the demarcation to build new settlements north of the line. Under pressure, their complaints to American authorities ignored, the tribes began to migrate farther west into Indiana. Tecumseh remained. And in councils with other Shawnee clans as well, other Indian tribes argued that only a reestablished and larger alliance of Indian tribes could check the relentless Americans and secure for Indians the ability to live their lives independently and with dignity.

In the early years of Tecumseh's diplomacy, most Indians, although impressed by the young chief's oratory, refused his call for an Indian confederacy. The Americans were too numerous and strong. Ohio had recently become the seventeenth state in the Union, and a new governor had been appointed by President John Adams. He was a capable and energetic administrator, who possessed what seemed to the Indians nearly dictatorial powers, and a willingness to exercise them to subdue any incipient Indian revolt. He was knowledgeable about the customs and inclinations of the tribes of the Northwest. He had fought them as a young lieutenant in Mad Anthony Wayne's army. While he understood and may have sympathized with their plight, and surely knew that the treaty violations were entirely committed by the Americans, Governor William Henry Harrison was devoted to his country's western expansion, from sea to shining sea. Instead of enforcing the boundaries established by the treaty, he pressed the tribes to legally surrender additional millions of acres of their land, and make room for the inevitable.

One man declined to accept his misfortune as inevitable, and beginning in 1805 was attracting the attention of Harrison as a serious impediment to American ambitions. Tecumseh was becoming a great man to the Shawnee and to admiring warriors in other tribes. Despite all the twists and turns of his eventful life, where he had seen the villages of his people burned, their lives ruined by starvation, alcoholism, and other depredations inflicted upon them by their would-be conquerors, and his closest relatives killed by Long Knives, he never lapsed into despair but accepted the difficulties of their lives with grace and courage. There was something in his character that repelled despair, finding in life, with all its many tragedies, a reason to be thankful for the very fact that he could remain true to himself. He was the kind of person for whom life was a gift that could not be diminished by suffering, and it gave him a unique strength, a confidence that was superior to most people's. Tall and sinewy, with an erect bearing, a superior skill at arms, exuding a sense of command, and possessing a gift for oratory that earned him admirers even among his enemies, he was renowned as a capable provider and protecter of his clan, whose leadership had an ever-broadening appeal to neighboring tribes. But the spark for the Indian confederacy he encouraged came from an unlikely source.

Until then, his ne'er-do-well brother, Lalawethika, had remained true to his nature, contributed nothing of value to the clan, and become an alcoholic. But in 1805 he claimed to have received a vision from the Master of Life, in which he was charged with leading the Shawnee away from the customs and dependency imposed on them by the white invaders, and refuse the implements whites used to subdue them, such as alcohol, white clothes, metal pots, and various trade goods. He called on the tribes to purify themselves by returning to their old traditions. His name henceforth would be Tenskwatawa, or Open Door, but he became known to the white settlers as the Prophet.

Most of the Shawnee were taken by surprise by the Prophet's sudden conversion, including, one supposes, his brother Tecumseh. But when the Prophet predicted the arrival of a solar eclipse (which he had probably learned of in a British almanac), great numbers of Shawnee warriors and those of other tribes were persuaded to join the new spiritual movement and move their families to Tecumseh's village. When the village grew too large to accommodate all its new members, Tecumseh moved their followers to a new and larger village in Indiana, which the worried settlers called Prophetstown.

Tecumseh, whether he believed in his brother's divine calling or not, knew that the movement the Prophet had started served his larger purposes of forming a new pan-Indian alliance. With his brother, he began to summon warriors to the great cause that awaited them, the final battle with their enemies that would determine once and for all to whom this country belonged.

At about this time, according to the historian of Native Americans, Lee Sultzman, Tecumseh delivered an address to his people as he prepared them for the coming struggle that has become famous not only as a measure of his own character, but as a code of honor that merits respect and emulation.

So live your life that the fear of death can never enter your heart. Trouble no one about their religion; respect others in their view, and demand that they respect yours. Love your life, perfect your life, beautify all things in your life. Seek to make your life long and its purpose in the service of your people. Prepare a noble death song for the day when you go over the great divide. Always give a word or a sign of salute when meeting or passing a friend, even a stranger, when in a lonely place. Show respect to all people and grovel to none. When you arise in the morning give thanks for the food and the joy of living. If you see no reason for giving thanks, the fault lies only in yourself. Abuse no one and no thing, for abuse turns the wise ones to fools and robs the spirit of vision. When it comes your time to die, be not like those whose hearts are filled with the fear of death, so that when their time comes they weep and pray for a little more time to live their lives over again in a different way. Sing your death song and die like a hero going home.

Tecumseh the hero traveled wide, recruiting other Indian peoples to his great alliance, which he believed would rival the white nation's federation, called the Council of Seventeen Fires. Most of the Northwest tribes had already rallied to him. More would follow.

The worried William Henry Harrison summoned him to meet at the federation capital in Vincennes, Indiana, warned him not to take up arms, and to submit to the government's authority. Though Tecumseh assured Harrison that he did not intend to break the peace, he would not submit to the further theft of Indian lands. In their first encounter, Tecumseh sat himself on a bench next to Harrison, and proceeded to move the governor closer and closer to the bench's edge, instructing Harrison that this was what it felt like to be an Indian powerless to stop his enemies' ceaseless territorial ambitions. Violence came close to exploding in that first conference. Angry words and misunderstood movements caused both whites and Indians to reach for their weapons. Harrison himself drew his sword and Tecumseh grasped his tomahawk before the governor caught himself and urged his guests to recover their civility.

Though they parted on better terms, neither his first nor his second conference with Harrison in 1811 dissuaded Tecumseh from building an Indian nation to rival Harrison's. "Hear me," he told his adversary, "we shall have a great council at which all the tribes will be present. . . . I am the head of them all." Both men knew they would be enemies for life. But they had come to respect each other as well. Harrison would later remark that Tecumseh was "one of those uncommon geniuses which spring up occasionally to produce revolutions, and overturn the established order of things. If it were not for the vicinity of the United States, he would, perhaps, be the founder of an empire that would rival in glory Mexico or Peru."

Harrison did not, however, feel an equal respect for the Prophet. He knew that Tecumseh had left their conference to travel south to rally Cherokee and Creek to his cause. He anticipated that another war with Britain, the War of 1812, was imminent, and he was determined to strike a blow against Britain's probable Indian allies when the opportunity presented itself. With Tecumseh away, and his brother in charge, Harrison marched an army to Prophetstown. Though Tecumseh had warned his brother to do nothing to break the peace before he returned, the Prophet decided his moment of glory was at hand, and ordered warriors to meet the enemy in battle, assuring them that the Master of Life would grant them victory. Such are the idiosyncrasies upon which history often turns. A flawed man with a reckless ambition too great for his meager talents, a great man whose attention was temporarily distracted, and an enemy who understood the character of his adversaries; and, thus, the only native resistance with the genuine potential to thwart the Manifest Destiny of the United States ended in a moment.

The warriors who ran into battle at the Prophet's command were defeated in detail at Tippecanoe Creek. Prophetstown was burned. Thirty years later, William Henry Harrison, "Old Tippecanoe," would be elected president of the United States. Tecumseh returned to find his dreams of a pan-Indian nation destroyed. He angrily confronted his brother. "You have destroyed what has taken ten years to build." Had the Prophet not been Tecumseh's brother, the Shawnee would have killed him. But he would live a long life in disgrace.

Tecumseh's life would last but two more years. Never having despaired over the vicissitudes of life, he would not do so now. He arose in the morning and gave thanks for the joy of living. As war between America and Britain began, Tecumseh rallied his followers to the British flag. He fought, as always, with courage and skill. The British made him a general, gave him a sword and a uniform. He defeated the American army at Detroit, and in the rout at Ft. Meigs. His fellow commander in the field was far from his equal in character or generalship. He could not convince Procter to return to finish the siege of Ft. Meigs, and when Commander Perry defeated the British fleet at Lake Erie, and the American army under the command of Harrison pursued the retreating British and Indian forces into Canada, Tecumseh could not convince Procter to stand and fight.

When he finally convinced the nervous British officer to confront the American force at the Battle of the Thames in Ontario on October 5, 1813, Procter and his soldiers fled the field after the first volley was fired. Tecumseh dispensed with his sword and British officer's jacket, and charged, as always, into the thick of the battle. When a musket ball shattered his right leg, he told his braves to leave him. He kept fighting until a crowd of American soldiers surrounded him. He sang his death song and died like a hero going home.

HUMOR

Mark Twain

He became the most famous person in the world, and he helped Americans live up to their promise by making us laugh at ourselves.

ASPIRING YOUNG AMERICAN AUTHORS, AS THEY WORK IN A DARK, sparsely furnished basement apartment or shabby motel room or drafty attic, have, for lack of regular meals and other creature comforts, only hope for sustenance. They are nourished by the hope that at the end of their poverty and suffering, they will have laid claim to the most prized goal in the world of American literature: the great American novel. As popular-culture clichés go, the above is one of the more durable, at least it was when I was young. I suppose it still is, of course, with certain modernized improvements to the picture of the struggling artist. The old manual typewriter and the crowded stacks of an ancient library are replaced with a laptop computer, wirelessly connected to Google. All authors of serious American fiction were romanticized into having accepted as their personal holy grail the great American novel that others had tried to write, sometimes came close to writing, but had always just missed. Pity, it isn't true. It's such a romantic notion.

Nearly 230 years since the birth of our nation, there is a large library of great novels written by Americans. But to perpetuate the myth of the missing singular, we might argue that none has yet to achieve the distinction of being *the* great, the one book that our unique history and genius deserve as their representative accomplishment, the art that sums us up, explains us to the world and to ourselves, the good and the bad, the extraordinary and the very ordinary attributes of our particular branch of humankind. That is quite a thrilling ambition for any American, a demanding muse for any artist of our culture. But I wouldn't take it as an awful disappointment to know that someone has beaten you to it. For someone has, and quite some time ago. The great American novel was published in 1885, after seven years of intermittent writing. Its title is *The Adventures of Huckleberry Finn*. There had never been one as good before, and there has never been another as good since, or more American. Until he was twenty-seven years old, the man who wrote it had been known as Samuel Langhorne Clemens. Thereafter, he was Mark Twain.

The story, I assume, is well known to you. Young Huck, the happy-go-lucky, uncivilized son of an abusive, alcoholic father, takes flight from his troubles with a fugitive slave named Jim, traveling together by raft on the exciting, mysterious, and ever-changing Mississippi. The setting of *Huckleberry Finn* is a river town in the antebellum South, where society's moral code approved the institution of slavery as biblically sanctioned and condemned those who would violate its cruel customs. Among the worst of sins was to give aid to a runaway slave. In their adventure, Huck comes to love Jim, who is a better father to him than the man he was cursed to call by that name. Yet, Huck is tortured by the fear that he would be damned for helping Jim escape bondage. In the central scene that serves as the story's moral resolution, Huck, after a long time wrestling with his conscience, concludes, "All right, then, I'll go to hell."

Rebellion was Twain's salvation. Rebellion against social injustice, against the weaknesses of human nature, against life's cruelest misfortune, against the heart's own crimes. When confronted with the choice between what others thought was wrong but conscience insisted was right, "All right, then, I'll go to hell," was the rebel's answer. Twain led no great protest movement, enlisted in no underground army, ran for no office, joined no political party. He was, as has often been remarked, a "great noticer" of people, places, and things, and he told their stories, or variations of them. He told them with as much humor as he was capable of conceiving—humor that was, as it turned out, more entertaining and more meaningful than that of anyone before or since. He was the funniest man alive, and he made good use of the talent. "The human race has only one effective weapon," he argued, "and that is laughter."

He told tall tales, or at least improbable ones, and yet his books, particularly *Huckleberry Finn*, were astonishingly realistic. With a capacious memory, an eye for the telling detail, and an ear for the music and liveliness of speech, he rendered the people and places of his stories, no matter how far-fetched, with an authenticity that was unequaled. He was from the center of the American continent, a place he both loved and whose character he understood, both its virtues and its sins. Before Twain, American literature had been imitative. With its stately prose, flowery dialogue, and above-it-all, heavy-handed narrative, it sought to mimic European, particularly English, novels. Twain was an original. He was American. He sounded like an American, listened like an American, and wrote like an American. His characters spoke like Americans spoke, particularly Americans in the nineteenth century, and particularly those Americans in the small town nestled between the bluffs of the mighty Mississippi River, his place, his Hannibal.

He was an American, a fact he was grateful for and proud of, but never conceited about. Human nature is flawed, wherever it resides, and he felt its flaws keenly in others and in himself. He knew his country was building a civilization better than the celebrated civilizations of the past, but that some aspects of human nature could never be changed. Human beings are apt to do as much bad as good. But Twain knew something else. They were apt to be funny as well, awfully funny. I think it could be fairly said of Sam Clemens, and the alter ego that was his great achievement, that he didn't like people generally, but loved them well enough individually. And they loved him back. "An American loves his family," Thomas Edison once observed. "If he has any love left over for some other person he generally selects Mark Twain."

His family moved to the town of Hannibal, Missouri, in 1839, when he was four years old. His father, John Marshall Clemens, was a severe and distant man to his family, and a frustrated, determined failure. Always striving for prosperity, in one venture after another, always respected by his neighbors, he never succeeded. According to his son, "he never demonstrated affection for wife or child." Whether he was by nature a cold man, or disappointment had made him so, his son, whose boyish antics and high spirits would never be permanently subdued by age or failure, could not find a way to communicate with him, to reach his hardened heart. His father seldom beat him, but just as seldom were there expressions with word or gesture of paternal affection.

We can guess that young Sam, whose mischievousness was as natural to him as breathing, couldn't help but try to entertain his father into a better humor, though without much success. All that would have ended when Sam was eleven, and his father died of pneumonia at the age of forty-nine, asking in his last moments for the embrace of Sam's oldest sister, Pamela. Death, in those days a frequent experience for even the young to witness (two of the seven Clemens children had preceded their father in death), had a profound influence on Sam's personality, and the way he viewed life. The last mortal act of the austere man who was his father, who couldn't manage an encouraging smile for his children, had been a request for the comfort of a loving daughter's embrace. Sam, the "great noticer," must have found the unexpected display of affection somewhat redemptive of his father's flaws, and filed it away in his acute, retentive memory, from where it might someday be recollected and put to good use.

His mother, Jane Lampton Clemens, was a much livelier presence. Although no more given to displays of affection than her husband, she was considerably more fun-loving, a colorful, enthusiastic plunger into life's joys and challenges. She was religious, which his father had not been, and worshiped an exacting and sometimes vengeful God, who intervened directly in human affairs to reward the righteous and punish the wicked. But as with most other activities, she took considerable enjoyment from her devotion. She loved lively, bombastic preaching and a rousing hymn. She loved parades, music, dancing, and storytelling, and was quite gifted herself in that last occupation, her admiring son remembered. She had an arch and ironic sense of humor, and was as often amused by her son's mischief as she was distressed by it. Sam, by his own account, had drowned nine times before he learned to swim. When informed by her son of one of his near fatal mishaps, Jane Clemens remarked with a laugh, "People who are born to be hanged are safe in water."

"My mother had a great deal of trouble with me," he remembered, "but I think she enjoyed it."

She was a loving mother. Sam had been born two months prematurely (arriving ahead of schedule, it was said, so he could enjoy Halley's comet, then tracing the night sky, a once-in-every-seventy-five-years occurrence) and was sickly as a small child. She nursed him with an intense devotion, although the bizarre frontier remedies she employed to cure him were little comfort to her ailing son, which he would someday recount for the great amusement of his audiences. But he loved her, and deeply admired her, and inherited from her the seeds of his own genius. The rest he got from Hannibal and the river.

He would recall his hometown as a boy's paradise, not a spiritual paradise, exactly, and certainly not an unblemished community of God-fearing people, free from vice and worse occupations, but an idyllic place for a barefoot boy with high spirits and a sense of adventure. The river, the woods, the hills and caves, and, beyond them, the wilderness were the ideal environment for fun-loving kids with little in the way of wealth but with the riches of active imaginations. They played their games amid nature's ample offerings, told one another stories to frighten and amuse themselves, and secretly indulged their young vices (minor ones, to be sure, such as smoking and especially mischievous practical jokes, but mostly frowned upon just the same, by some folks more than others).

The steamboats that stopped for a day or two in Hannibal supplied news of the world beyond the hamlet's knowledge and as varied a display of human nature, in all its goodness and sinfulness, as a boy could comprehend.

Sam Clemens noticed all of it, and memorized it, and learned an occasional lesson about his own character's susceptibility to temptation. Most of it he just enjoyed. Among his many Hannibal friends were the models for the novels that evoked that time and experience, like his first love, Laura Hawkins, and the free-spirited, good-hearted son of the town drunk, Tom Blankenship, the models for Becky Thatcher and Huck Finn, respectively. Sam, himself, we assume, was the model for the clever, conniving, but genuinely good-natured Tom Sawyer, whose adventures in one of Twain's most popular books emphasized the idyllic aspects of his hometown, while *Huck Finn* conjured up a few of its darker qualities. He listened as carefully as he looked, and his skill at re-creating the sounds of Hannibal and the color of its citizens' speech as well as its picturesque qualities gave his fictionalized accounts their honesty. As Huck commented about his biographer, "Mr. Mark Twain, . . . told the truth, mainly."

Missouri was a border state, where the white population believed slavery was practiced more humanely than in the Deep South. Slaves in Hannibal were considered fortunate by their masters to have escaped the brutal conditions of plantation life in Mississippi or Georgia or South Carolina. That it was by nature an inexcusably inhumane institution, whether practiced by kind, indifferent, or cruel masters, seems not to have troubled the conscience of most Missourians. It would come to trouble Sam Clemens, however. As a boy, Sam would later confess, "I was not aware there was anything wrong with it." But he enjoyed at an early age the friendship of slaves, and the affection he felt for them, and they for him, shaped his conscience, which eventually ceased to accept the great lie that sustained Southern culture: that a person with a darker complexion was less human than a white person.

He spent summers on his uncle John Quarles's farm, a place he loved, "a heavenly place for a boy," he remembered, with its abundance of good food, wide-open spaces, and cheerful playmates. Along with his cousins, his closest companions on the farm were his uncle's slaves, and it was there that he first "got my strong liking for the race and my appreciation for certain of its fine qualities." He never saw his uncle John mistreat a slave, if you overlook the fact that bondage itself, no matter how gently practiced, is nothing less than institutionalized mistreatment. Sam was charmed by the society of slaves, by their speech, their singing, and their folktales. Slave children like Mary and Jerry Quarles became his best friends.

But the person he admired above all was the family's most trusted slave, old Uncle Dan'l, "whose heart was honest and simple and knew no guile." Uncle Dan'l was like a father to the children on the farm, both black and white. He looked after them, taught them about nature, charmed them with songs, the Negro spirituals Twain would love all his life, and held them spellbound with his repertoire of ghost stories and tall tales. His stories, probably more than any other experience, influenced Twain's fiction, in which Uncle Dan'l would become Jim, the good man for whom Huck was prepared to go to hell to save. As an old man, Twain would recall the loving figure and good company of Uncle Dan'l, and attribute to that good man's character and the warmth of his friendships with the slaves on the Quarles farm his affection for the African American race. Because of them, he remembered, "The black face is as welcome to me now as it was then."

His affection for slaves and his view of slavery were not entirely shaped by the comparatively happy circumstances of his uncle's farm. He once saw his father beat a slave girl for being disrespectful. On another occasion, he witnessed a white man throw a chunk of iron at a slave's head, killing him on the spot, for the crime of performing a chore incompetently. And he never forgot the wretched look on the faces of twelve slaves, chained together for transport to a Southern slave market, and from there to the brutal miseries and harsh toil of plantation life. These images haunted Twain's imagination, gave his stories their moral power, and sharpened his appreciation for the weaknesses of human nature. Nineteenth-century humor was, for the most part, meant only to entertain. Except for Twain's humor. His humor, in his stories and lectures, entertained as well. Indeed, he was the greatest entertainer of his time. But he had another, more important purpose: to teach us about ourselves, to expose our humanity, its faults and saving graces, for our own moral scrutiny.

Three years after his father died, Sam Clemens gave up formal education to help alleviate his family's poverty, and began his rich and varied career. "I worked," he later wrote, "not diligently, not willingly, but fretfully, repiningly, complainingly, disgustedly, and always shirking work when I was not watched." He first worked as an apprentice to a local printer, before his older brother Orion offered him a job on the newspaper he owned, the *Hannibal Journal.* Although he was hired to set type at the *Journal,* he soon began contributing humorous stories under the pen name Rambler, and, with his unerring nose for trouble, took aim at some of Hannibal's more prominent citizens, to his brother's and Hannibal's regret. "My literature attracted the town's attention," he observed, "but not its admiration." A few years later, at the age of seventeen, the Rambler began to ramble, beginning the life of wandering that he would never cease entirely.

He left first for St. Louis and then east to New York, Philadelphia, and Washington, and back west to St. Louis again, and then to Keokuk, Iowa, where Orion had moved and opened a printing shop. Unable to earn a living wage from his brother, and "wild with impatience to move," Sam accepted an offer from the Keokuk newspaper, the *Daily Post,* to supply entertaining letters describing his journeys, at five dollars apiece, his first employment as a professional writer. At twenty-one he boarded a steamboat for New Orleans, from where he intended to travel to South America to make his fortune. But, as the saying goes, life is what happens when we're busy making other plans. Sam Clemens didn't go to South America on that trip, although he would eventually travel virtually the entire world in the course of his long, adventurous life. But first he would become what every Hannibal schoolboy dreamed of becoming, a steamboat pilot on the Mississippi River.

On the way to New Orleans, Sam met an experienced pilot, Horace Bixby, a tough, tempestuous, but fair man who, after much persuasion and the promise of five hundred dollars, agreed to teach him his profession aboard the *Colonel Crossman.* For the next four years, as an apprentice and then as a licensed pilot in his own right, Sam Clemens made his way in the wondrous world of the Mississippi, where thousands of steamboats carrying every manner of cargo and human character made the river the most fascinating thoroughfare in the world. He learned to steer a steamboat through all the dangers of that wild, always changing river, with its submerged sandbars and fallen trees, powerful currents, and various other hidden perils. In the constant search for a safe channel to pass through, steamboat men would drop a knotted rope into the water until it reached two fathoms (twelve feet), and then call out the words that signaled safe water to the relieved pilot: "mark twain."

In 1858, Sam's beloved younger brother, Henry, joined him on the river, on the steamboat the *Pennsylvania,* where Sam had been contracted out by Bixby to work under the supervision of a bullying and cruel man, William Brown. Sam hated him, and when he ended his watch and retired for the night he would forget the responsibilities of a cub pilot. "Instead of going over the river in my mind as it was my duty, I threw business aside for pleasure, and killed Brown. I killed him every night for months."

One day Brown, who had failed to heed an order from the captain, blamed the mistake on Henry, and when Henry called him a liar, the pilot picked up a piece of coal, with which he intended to strike the boy. Sam rushed to his brother's aide, broke a chair over Brown's head, and proceeded to beat him senseless. Expecting to be fired for the offense, he was instead transferred to another boat when they reached New Orleans. Henry remained on the *Pennsylvania* for the return trip to St. Louis. Sam followed two days behind on board the *Alfred T. Lacey.*

Before they parted company, Sam offered his younger brother some professional advice. In the event the boat met with disaster, Henry should keep his head, help the women and children into the lifeboat, and not take a place there himself. "It is summer weather, and the river is only a mile wide . . . you can swim ashore without any trouble."

Just as the *Pennsylvania* reached Memphis, Tennessee, its boilers exploded, breaking the burning boat in two, and killing nearly two hundred passengers and crew. Henry was seriously hurt, his body broken by falling steel debris, his features burned and his lungs scalded by the escaped steam. Rather than swim for shore, and the immediate medical care he needed to survive, he made his way to a raft that had been launched to help rescue survivors. There he languished in the summer sun for eight hours, too injured to be of much use, but, or so Sam Clemens believed, determined to put the safety of the passengers ahead of his own, as his older brother had taught him.

By the time Sam reached him, Henry was in terrible shape. When the pain of Henry's burns and injuries was beyond bearing, Sam asked that a doctor administer morphine to his brother. The distracted doctor gave him too much. Henry lapsed into a coma and died before the next dawn. Sam blamed himself. He had talked Henry into joining him on the river. His fight with Brown (who had been killed in the explosion) had cost him his position on the *Pennsylvania*, where he might have helped save his brother or at least shared his fate. He had encouraged Henry to help others before he saved himself, and, thus, he felt responsible for Henry's heroism, which resulted in his brother's long hours of untreated suffering on the raft. And he had asked that Henry be given what he now believed was a fatal draft of morphine. For the rest of his long life, Sam felt bitterly responsible for Henry's death, a death that surely he deserved more than his "blameless" little brother, "the light of my life." His brother's fate and his own escape from the tragedy confirmed his dark view of the world, where the good can have no guarantee of a happy, long life and the wicked often prosper.

Sam Clemens's life on the Mississippi ended in 1861, at the outset of the Civil War. He fought briefly and, by his own admission, gutlessly for the Confederacy before lighting out with Orion for Nevada territory. There he tried his hand at prospecting for silver and gold, which he failed at, and, more successfully, wrote humorous sketches for the Virginia City newspaper, first under the pen name Josh, and then, in the name that would become the most famous in the world, Mark Twain. His stories often caused him trouble, and one of them, it is said, resulted in a duel with a victim of his sharp pen. As an observer, who must have been at one time Twain's target, protested, "He is a Bohemian from the sagebrush, a jailbird, bail-jumper, deadbeat, and alcoholic," to which Twain might have responded, "Amen, brother," before he beat another hasty retreat to some other unsuspecting town.

He left Nevada for California, where his pen again got him into trouble with local authorities. But he had also made the acquaintance of one of the most popular humorists of the time, Artemus Ward, who encouraged him to write. Twain gave Ward one of his stories, "The Celebrated Jumping Frog of Calvaleras County," who had it published in the New York *Saturday Evening Press.* Its success and the success of his public lectures regaling San Francisco audiences with a hilarious account of a recent trip to the Hawaiian Islands marked the moment that Sam Clemens of Hannibal, Missouri, printer's apprentice, steamboat pilot, prospector, and confessed ne'er-do-well, would hitch his fate to the quickly rising, brightly shining star of Mark Twain, the riotously funny scourge of the pompous, the proud, and the dishonest. Many of those who were victims of his satirical wit, which always included himself, laughed as hard at his jokes as those few who managed to escape its reach. A commission from California's largest newspaper, the *Alta California,* to chronicle his trip to Europe and the Holy Land, which would be published in book form as *The Innocents Abroad,* spread his fame permanently around the world. With its publication, he became the most popular author and public speaker in the country, and much of the rest of the world.

Mark Twain moved east, met the love of his life, Olivia "Livy" Langdon, the daughter of a wealthy coal dealer from Buffalo, New York, and married her. The couple settled briefly in Buffalo in a fine house his father-in-law purchased for them. From there they moved to Hartford, Connecticut, where they remained for twenty years, in a large and exotic house that managed to reflect its owner's personality. They had four children; their oldest and only son died before he was two years old, leaving his grieving father to fight off another of life's tragedies with his most reliable weapon, his humor.

The years in Hartford were Twain's happiest, most productive, and most prosperous. These were the years when he published some of his best and most popular works: *Tom Sawyer, The Prince and the Pauper, Life on the Mississippi,* and *Huck Finn,* his masterpiece. He was the most famous man in the world, beloved by his family and his adoring public, who couldn't get enough of his opinions on any subject, any more than the author could get enough of sharing them. "I have never tried . . . to help cultivate the cultivated classes," he wrote. "I was not equipped for it either by native gifts or training. And I never had any ambition in that direction, but always hunted for bigger game—the masses. I have seldom deliberately tried to instruct them, but I have done my best to entertain them, for they can get instruction elsewhere."

Whether he even knew it or not, he was as a speaker and writer as instructive as he was entertaining. He helped Americans see the strengths and the foibles of our own peculiar, promising, but imperfect nature. He helped us see it because he recognized in himself those very same flaws and strengths. He helped encourage in us an honesty about the injustices we had committed or allowed to exist, and a desire to repair them. He made being human seem both a trial and a privilege, and a very funny joke. "God created man," he said, "because he was disappointed in the monkey."

His admittedly dark view of human nature would have caused many others to shout denunciations at the world. Twain laughed at it, and made the world laugh back. "I have had a 'call' to literature, of a low order—i.e. humorous," he wrote his brother Orion. "It is nothing to be proud, but it is my strongest suit." As he often treated any personal fact, Twain exaggerated his own modesty. He knew humor to be life's most necessary tonic, and employed to take the sting out of human folly and misfortune, "to blur the craggy outlines, and make the thorns less sharp and the cruelties less malignant."

He adored his family, the wife he considered his best friend and most trusted counselor, and his three talented and beautiful daughters, especially his oldest daughter, Suzy. He was happiest in their company, though he was often apart from them. He made and spent a considerable fortune, as his genius did not extend to the world of financial investments. Approaching sixty, he went bankrupt and was forced to travel the world for seven years giving lectures to restore his fortune. He managed to pay off his debts to every one of his creditors, earning the renewed admiration of his wide public. But during these wandering and worrisome years, Suzy died from meningitis, devastating Twain. On her gravestone he had chiseled a verse from a poem father and daughter had both loved, and recited to each other.

> Warm summer sun
>   Shine kindly here,
> Warm southern wind
>   Blow softly here,
> Green sod above
>   Lie light, lie light—
> Good night, dear heart,
>   Good night, good night.

That touching glimpse into the heart of a grieving father, as affecting as it is, and as demonstrative of the depth of Twain's love, does not, however, fairly represent the way Twain continued to take on the world and make some better sense of it in the wake of his beloved daughter's death. "I bear it as I bear all heavy hardships that befall me," he wrote a friend, "with a heart bursting with rebellion."

The remainder of his life was filled with other equally heavy hardships. Livy, who had long suffered ill health, died eight years later in 1904. He missed her terribly, yet he persisted in his chosen profession to make the world and himself laugh, he persisted in being Mark Twain, the irrepressible rebel. Beloved friends began to pass from this world. Age and infirmity slowed his step and frustrated his natural restlessness. Yet at his seventieth birthday party, in a famously comical speech to a large assembly of friends and admirers, he gave no sign that old age had disappointed him much. He offered his secrets for a long life, "by sticking strictly to a scheme that would kill anybody else."

I made it a rule to go to bed when there wasn't anybody left to sit up with; and I have made it a rule to get up when I had to.

In the matter of diet . . . I have been persistently strict in sticking to the things which didn't agree with me until one or the other of us got the best of it.

I have made it a rule never to smoke more than one cigar at a time. . . . It has always been my rule never to smoke when asleep, and never refrain when awake.

When others drink I like to help; otherwise I remain dry, by habit and preference.

I have never taken any exercise, except sleeping and resting . . . it cannot be any benefit when you are tired, and I was always tired.

I have lived a severely moral life. But it would be a mistake for other people to try that, or for me to recommend it. Very few would succeed.

Having reached seventy, he declared, he need no longer accept unwanted social invitations or concoct some lie to get out of them. Now, he need only observe, "I am seventy, and would nestle in the chimney corner, and smoke my pipe, and read my book, and take my rest, wishing you well in all affection, and that when you in return shall arrive at pier No. 70 you may step aboard your waiting ship with a reconciled spirit, and lay your course toward the sinking sun with a contented heart."

But his heart wasn't contented, and he remained too restless to indulge for too long the comforts of his chimney corner. His humor took a darker turn as the loss of loved ones weighed heavily on his heart, but he was still trying to laugh, his favorite rebel yell. And he still tried to make the world laugh with him as he pierced the fog covering some hard truth about life and human beings that might have frightened us if anyone else had pointed to it. He kept close to his friends, played his favorite game, billiards, whenever he could, paraded the streets in his white flannel suit, and kept writing.

He lived first in New York City after Livy died, and then in a house in Connecticut, where he formed a little society of young ladies who doted on him, and whom he doted on in return. When another daughter, Jean, died from an epileptic fit, the loss finally vanquished his heart. A few months later, on April 21, 1910, he, too, died, just as he promised, as Halley's comet again lit the night sky. I suspect he expected his timely exit as one last, amusing joke to make us think one last kind and amusing thought about the great Mark Twain, the man who made us think more honestly, and more hopefully, or at least more amusingly, about ourselves even as he ridiculed our pretensions and other deficiencies. Few have ever been able to accomplish the feat of being brutally honest about human nature without depressing those who claim membership in the race. George Bernard Shaw called it the ability "to make people who would otherwise hang us, believe we are joking."

He encouraged us to rebel against injustice and cruelty and falsehood, even when they were our own creations. "I have no color prejudices nor caste prejudices nor creed prejudices," he once assured an audience. "All I need to know is that a man is a human being, and that is enough for me; he can't be any worse."

He once explained to his dear friend, the noted editor William Dean Howells, how he managed to sustain his powerfully affecting combination of disdain for and sheer delight in the antics, passions, accomplishments, failures, and sins of mankind. "Ah, well, I am a great and sublime fool. But then I am God's fool, and all his works must be contemplated with respect."

Howells returned the favor in the eulogy he delivered at his friend's funeral. "I wish we might show him frankly as he always showed himself. We may confess that he had faults, while we deny that he tried to make them pass for merits. He disowned his errors by owning them; in the very defect of his qualities he triumphed, and he could make us glad with him at his escape from them."

COURTESY

Aung San Suu Kyi

She was the Burmese wife of an Oxford don who came home to free her people,
and oppose the tyrants who jailed her with courage and decency.

PHOTOGRAPHS SELDOM DO JUSTICE TO HER ARRESTING, ALMOST WRAITH-like beauty, her composed serenity, and the exquisite gracefulness that can settle an anxious crowd, and befuddle the powerful, angry men who occasionally meet with her in yet another futile attempt to bend her to their will. No camera lens could capture such an affecting portrait and the opposite qualities it conveys to observers at close quarters: delicacy and fortitude, stillness and purpose, tranquillity and passion, sympathy and outrage. One simply can't forget the experience of meeting her. She has reached her sixtieth birthday, alone in her house on a Rangoon lake where she has spent most of the last sixteen years. Though it has been a while since I last met her, I know that the years will not have dimmed such loveliness, no more than they could have exhausted her courage and tenacity.

In Burma, where brutality and violence are common, as a few corrupt men hold an entire people hostage to their greed and power lust, people extend the most elaborate courtesy and sincere kindness to every acquaintance, whether an intimate friend or a complete stranger. It is, for a man of my rougher manners and impatience, mystifying, a fragile hothouse flower that blossoms in the most extreme conditions, inexplicable and enthralling. A Western visitor might be tempted to describe such politeness as quaint, and obviously out of place in the harsh and cruel environment that Burma's rulers have attempted to impose on their country's culture. But that would miss their power when employed in the service of humanity. In Burma, courtesy is a rebellious gesture to a ruling elite that has tried to terrorize such refined kindness from their culture, and make a world where only power matters, where there are only the fearsome and the fearful.

Common among Burmese courtesies is the polite address of *Oo* ("uncle") or *Daw* ("aunt") to people distinguished by their station or age. Thus Aung San Suu Kyi is addressed as Daw Aung San Suu Kyi by almost all Burmese except those who rule the country and keep her imprisoned. They avoid such common courtesy when dealing with the woman who has for so long resisted them and who they wish would just disappear. I imagine they resent even more the title by which she is most commonly referred to by the vast majority of Burmese who love her and feel protected by her. To them, she is simply the Lady.

Suu, as she asks Western visitors to call her, never reciprocates discourtesy. She is a practicing Buddhist who refuses to hate those who hate her because, she says, she cannot fear what she doesn't hate. When she meets with regime leaders to listen to their offers of conditional release from house arrest or to discuss her demands that all political prisoners be released, she addresses them as "Uncle," and politely pours their tea for them. I, too, have been the beneficiary of her kindness.

On the first occasion when I met her, I found her waiting for me in the residence of the American chargé d'affaires, seated on the sofa, dressed in a *lungyi,* the traditional Burmese sarong, her hair fastened into a bun and decorated with a flower. Very slightly built, a few inches over five feet, and weighing no more than a hundred pounds, she sat quite straight and poised as I entered the room. She rose to greet me, and I bid her to remain seated, which she ignored, and waited for me to take a seat before she returned to hers. We made our introductions, and she instructed me to call her Suu (I wasn't sure if Daw was her first name at the time or an honorific, and until she instructed me otherwise I several times addressed her by her full name, with Daw preceding it). She was drinking tea as we talked, and when I reached for the teapot to pour a cup for myself, she gently brushed my hand away, and poured it for me.

She spoke in a soft voice with a British accent she had picked up at Oxford University, which she had attended and where she had lived for much of her life before she returned to Burma. Her gentility, however, did not obscure the passion she felt for the cause that kept her in Burma: the liberty of her people. I asked about her discussions with the regime, and she briefly summarized their substance. Curious, I asked her how she could control her anger in their presence. She asked me what I meant.

"How do you deal with them? Don't you find it difficult considering what they have done to you and to your country?"

"How do I deal with them?"

"Yes."

"Quite like I am talking to you. Civilly. I address them as 'Uncle.' "

I smiled at that, imagining the scene, the stern military men, grimacing in their exchanges with her, attempting to intimidate her with their solemnity and machismo, and Suu Kyi smiling her lovely smile as she called them Uncle and poured their tea. I had met some of those men. They were rough customers. They certainly lacked her gentility and subtlety. I had struggled to control my temper with them, and had even abruptly and angrily walked out of a meeting with one of them. I couldn't conceive of anyone less likely to be described as avuncular than them. But whether they merited such courtesy or not, Suu Kyi extended it to them because she knew that even though they had the guns and all the power, her cause was just, and that distinction was reinforced by her manners and their lack of them. I imagine they felt it, too, and it must have frustrated them immensely. They are used to frightening people. She must have made them feel ridiculous.

She is the daughter of General Aung San, the "father of Burma's independence." He had fought to free Burma from the British Empire, and then to free it from the Japanese. He is Burma's greatest hero. When Suu Kyi was two years old, in 1947, as Burma approached its first free elections and the formal recognition of its independence, Aung San was murdered by political rivals. The people of Burma revere his memory, as does his daughter, whose face, manner, and courage evoke that memory in every Burmese heart.

Her mother played an active role in the Burmese government for many years. In 1960 she was posted as ambassador to India, where Suu Kyi attended high school. While she lived in India she studied and deeply admired the life and philosophy of Gandhi, though I doubt she imagined at the time that she would one day become one of the Mahatma's most famous disciples. Suu Kyi left New Delhi in 1964 to attend Oxford.

While there she met, fell in love with, and married a British scholar of Asian cultures, Michael Aris. When she accepted his proposal, she made Michael promise "that should my people need me, you will help me do my duty by them." It was a promise both husband and wife kept, at great personal cost, for the twenty-seven years of their marriage.

For the first sixteen of those years they lived a comfortable, rewarding, and happy life together. Their first son, Alexander, was born in 1973, their second son, Kim, four years later.

Michael was an Oxford professor, and Suu Kyi stayed at home with her children and worked on a biography of her father. When the children were a little older, they traveled Asia together, as both Michael and Suu Kyi furthered their studies of Asian cultures. She returned frequently to Burma to visit her mother. In 1988, Suu Kyi received word that her mother had suffered a stroke. She raced to Rangoon to be with her. She has not left the country since.

When her father was assassinated, senior Burmese military leaders formed a junta to crush Aung San's vision of a democratic Burma. Led by General Ne Win, they would rule Burma until the year Suu Kyi returned. Suu Kyi arrived home at the beginning of the Rangoon spring, when Burmese students were staging large-scale and nationwide demonstrations to protest the military dictatorship.

The junta reacted to the protests with the means they understood best—brute force. They murdered somewhere between three thousand and ten thousand peaceful demonstrators, and then suggested that the victims had resorted to violence and were responsible for the terrible casualties. Hardly a soul in Burma or anywhere else believed them. The international outrage that resulted from their reign of terror convinced Ne Win to resign his office, dissolve his government, and ostensibly retire from public life. A new government was formed with many of the same tyrants from the previous regime, and with Ne Win still in charge while he pretended to enjoy his retirement from behind the gates of his luxurious home. A few months later the new government was replaced with another junta. A few of the ruling generals had apparently disagreed about how far to accommodate the nation's demands for freedom, and that prompted the last coup d'etat. Again, Ne Win was believed to have played a decisive role.

On the last day of the violence, Suu Kyi released to the public a letter she had sent the regime, demanding the formation of an independent organization to prepare for free elections. The following day she addressed a massive rally and assumed the leadership of what she called "the second struggle for independence." She told the cheering thousands, "I could not, as my father's daughter, remain indifferent to what is going on." The Burmese recognized in her the savior her father had been. From the moment she stood before them, they would recognize in their hearts no other leader as legitimate. She traveled the country, drawing larger and larger adoring crowds. The growing crowds and the world's focus on Burma forced the regime to schedule parliamentary elections, but they forbid public campaigning and, calling her a foreigner because of her marriage to Michael, ruled Suu Kyi ineligible as a candidate.

She ignored them, formed a political party, and ran for office. Tensions mounted as it became clear to the regime that Suu Kyi's extraordinary popularity was a threat to their continued rule. As she walked at the head of a huge campaign march, a squad of visibly agitated soldiers appeared and blocked the marchers' progress. As the crowd tried to press past the soldiers, they raised their rifles, and the commanding officer prepared to give the order to fire. Betraying no evidence of fear, Suu Kyi told her colleagues to step away from her, as she brushed past the soldiers who aimed their rifles at her, and walked directly toward the officer. She stood before him, perfectly still, without uttering a word, and looked him straight in the eyes. He returned her stare, and then ordered his soldiers to hold their fire.

As word of her heroism spread throughout the country, the regime decided to resort to more familiar tactics. They arrested her and many of her followers. Suu Kyi was placed under house arrest, while some of her associates were tortured. Whatever the tyrants thought to accomplish by violence, they were soon to be disappointed. Evidently, they assumed that they would win the election by intimidation. Had they thought otherwise they would have canceled it or never agreed to allow elections in the first place. On May 27, 1990, millions of Burmese went to the polls and gave Aung San Suu Kyi's party one of the greatest democratically elected mandates in the history of free elections. She and her party won 82 percent of the vote, 392 seats in Parliament. The regime, to their complete surprise and embarrassment, could only claim 10 seats. Suu Kyi was the elected leader of her country.

She would not, however, be permitted to assume her office. The regime, it seems, would only accept the results of elections it won. Suu Kyi remained under house arrest. Other election winners were arrested and sent to the notorious Insein prison. Beatings, murder, and arbitrary arrests resumed. Many Burmese feared for their new leader. But the international publicity Burma received resulted in worldwide admiration for the woman now seen as Burma's Gandhi. The secretary-general of the UN demanded her release, as did representatives of many nations, not all of them democracies. Even the thugs that ran Burma worried that killing or seriously hurting her would cause them even more difficulties.

They decided that the best course was simply to get her out of the country, but they couldn't forcibly eject her from Burma or they would make her an even more potent force on the world stage, and she would remain a hero to the Burmese people, who would rally around her. They had to convince her to want to leave. So they kept her under arrest, and refused to allow her family to visit. They were dealt a considerable setback in 1991 when the Nobel committee named her the winner of the Nobel Peace Prize. She did not leave Burma to receive it. Her sons, Alexander and Kim, accepted it on her behalf. In a statement she had smuggled to the press at the time, she explained her steady, almost cheerful resistance to the regime's attempts to frighten her. "It is not power that corrupts but fear," she wrote. "Fear of losing power corrupts those who wield it, and fear of the scourge of power corrupts those who are subject to it."

She remained unmoved by the regime's threats, in her small, run-down villa by the lake. Occasionally to protest her treatment and the suffering of her associates she would go on hunger strikes until the regime promised some accommodation. By 1994, she was allowed to meet with UN representatives, visiting members of the U.S. Congress, and foreign reporters. Later that year she began discussions with a senior regime leader, Khin Nyunt, who, while hardly an enlightened reformer, might have understood that she was never going to go away, and the world would never let them dispose of her by their usual means.

The regime would not agree to accept the election results or to schedule new elections, which Suu Kyi would win by just as large a margin. They insisted that Burma must have a new constitution, which was in the process of being drafted, before another election was held, and they were intent on assuring that no constitution would ever be finished. It was an excuse to hide their fear of her. They did let Suu Kyi travel outside her house a little, and to meet with some of her supporters. In Christmas 1995 they allowed Michael and her sons to visit her. It was the last time they would be together.

In 1996, with still no progress toward elections, Suu Kyi and her party called on the international community to impose economic sanctions on Burma, and new political demonstrations were held. So the regime cracked down again, with their usual blunt force. Demonstrators were beaten, her supporters thrown into prison, and Suu Kyi again confined and isolated in her home. They let her out again the following year, in yet another comical attempt to spruce up their international image. But the regime warned Suu Kyi not to attempt to leave Rangoon or to join in rallies with her supporters. She ignored them, politely but firmly, and was again arrested.

That same year Michael learned he had terminal cancer. The Burmese government refused to grant him or their sons a visa so that Suu Kyi could be with her dying husband. If she wanted to say good-bye to her husband, she would have to leave Burma, and not expect to be allowed to return. She stayed. Both husband and wife kept the promise they had made when they were married. She would serve her people, and he would help her. Michael died in 1999. Suu Kyi, still under house arrest, grieved alone.

The years since Michael died have passed in similar fashion for his widow. The world still demands her release. Regime officials have occasionally knocked at her door to discuss some possible improvement of the situation if she will only stop trying to lead her people to freedom. Whenever they have released her from house arrest, she has resumed meeting with her associates, traveling the country to rally her supporters, and making speeches demanding the release of all political prisoners and the scheduling of new elections. She once remained in her car for nine days when security forces stopped her as she traveled outside the city on her way to meet with supporters, and she refused to turn around. (One must never mistake her good manners and delicate beauty for a lack of will and strength.)

The regime has always reacted true to form. They have beat up her followers, thrown many of them in jail, placed Suu under house arrest again, and denied her contact with the outside world.

They released her in 2002, as a United Nations representative tried to encourage negotiations between her party and the regime aimed at a political settlement of Burma's sad troubles. She was willing, as always, to show her persecutors every courtesy and to entertain a polite willingness to consider their concerns as they discussed the future of their country. "Confrontation," she told a *Time* magazine reporter, "comes about because there is no other way to settle differences. If there is a channel open for settling differences, there should be no need for confrontation." She informed the authorities when and where she intended to travel. And when she was asked how cruelly she had been treated by the regime, she responded, "I have never been treated cruelly."

But the regime, the bullies who are destroying the country and are so afraid of this one small woman and her implacable determination, would not acquiesce to any plan that might result in their long-overdue loss of power. As Suu Kyi campaigned in the north of the country, a group of government hired goons with clubs surrounded her motorcade and beat to death dozens of her supporters. They managed to hurt her physically on that occasion, and rumors are rampant that some of the regime's leaders intended to have her killed and blame the murder on her supporters, but Khin Nyunt intervened at the last moment to stop it. This time she was briefly held in Insein prison, a terrible place where the incarcerated are treated as animals. Not long after, the regime itself was in turmoil, as hard-liners cracked down inside and out. Khin Nyunt was expelled from the government, arrested, and imprisoned. He has not been heard from since. Bowing to the outrage and demands of the world, the junta released Suu from prison, and placed her again under house arrest.

In an article that sheds much light on her purpose and wisdom, Suu Kyi described the Japanese tea ceremony, recalling a display in the exquisite art of preparing and serving tea in delicately beautiful porcelain bowls that she witnessed years before. The master exhibited the beautiful objects in a room that had been spoiled with a garish, modern carpet. "The tea ceremony," she said, "illustrated the necessity of removing all that is ugly or disharmonious before reaching out to beauty . . . to acquire truly good taste one has to be able to recognize both ugliness and beauty is applicable to the whole range of human experience."

Recently, reports have surfaced that the tyrants are again considering the release of Burma's national heroine. Perhaps they will soon knock at the door of her home again. I have no doubt that when they do she will receive them with perfect courtesy, not that they deserve it. But she does not extend her courtesy as a sign of respect for them or their power, but to show, yet again, that they cannot make her become the only type of person they understand, one of the fearful or one of the fearsome. She is merely, steadfastly, reaching out to beauty to banish ugliness from her sight and the lives of her countrymen.

PART SIX

Creativity

Glendower: I can call spirits from the vasty deep.

Hotspur: Why, so can I, or so can any man;
But will they come when you do call for them?

—HENRY IV

ASPIRATION

Ferdinand Magellan

He left the service of one king and won the support of another
so that he could pursue an ambition as big as the world he discovered.

HIS AMBITIONS WERE AS BIG AS THE WORLD, AND THE WORLD WAS bigger than he thought it was. His is not a happy tale, though it is undoubtedly a heroic one. Its details offer as much evidence of a man's conceit and cruelty as they do his tremendous courage and daring ambition. Yet despite the hero's tragic flaws, few had ever aspired to so great an adventure or possessed the tenacious will its achievement required. The story ends badly for the hero, who does not live to enjoy the recognition of his singular accomplishment. But history has celebrated his triumph and immortalized his legend. As well it should. For in the age of discovery, the age of Columbus and da Gama and Balboa and Cabot, who preceded him, and Cartier and Drake and Hudson and Cook, who followed him, Ferdinand Magellan claimed the most daunting and marvelous prize. By the greatest feat of seamanship in history, he was the first European to go around the unknown world.

He was born Fernão de Magalhães in 1480 to a family of minor nobility in the mountainous north of Portugal. He and his brother Diogo were offered a place in the royal court in Lisbon as pages to Queen Leonor in the year Columbus set sail from Spain for the world beyond the Atlantic Ocean. At court, the young Magellan received an excellent education in the arts and sciences as well as the martial arts. He was also exposed to accounts of Portuguese and Spanish adventurers who had sailed through the Mediterranean Sea and then traveled overland, fighting through Muslim resistance, to reach the fabled cities of the East Indies. While he was still at court, Vasco da Gama had rounded the Cape of Good Hope off the southern tip of Africa and sailed into the Indian Ocean, charting a sea route to India. The successes of these brave explorers nurtured Magellan's own dreams of great adventures, and the glory and fortune that were their rewards.

In 1505, he joined the fleet of the first Portuguese governor of India, and over the course of several years' service became a skilled navigator and a brave and capable soldier. He fought in many battles off the coast of India and East Africa, in which he suffered wounds, earned respect, and rose to the rank of captain. In 1511, he fought in the battle for Malacca, in Malaysia, which established Portuguese supremacy in Asia. Following the battle, Magellan is reported to have explored the Moluccas, in what is today Indonesia, which were then known in Europe as the Spice Islands. Their name explains their value. They offered Europeans a great treasure, a seemingly endless supply of pepper, cinnamon, ginger, nutmeg, and cloves to flavor and preserve their bland diets. Until Vasco da Gama's success opened a new route to the East, the trade in spices had been controlled by Arabs. Now, Europeans claimed the trade, and the courts of Europe, served by many brave and enterprising soldiers of fortune, were constantly searching for a faster route to the prized Spice Islands. Whether Magellan had indeed reached them while he was in service to the Portuguese crown, there is little doubt that like all adventurers of the age, he held them as the richest prize on earth, and surely dreamed of sharing in the wealth and reputation they offered.

Magellan returned to Lisbon and the court of King Manuel I in 1512. The following year, he was off to Morocco in the mightiest fleet ever assembled by a Portuguese king, to lay siege to the fortress city of Azamor. In the many battles that ensued, he fought bravely in combat, often hand to hand, and took an Arab lance in his leg that left him with a lifelong limp. With Azamor safely in Spanish hands, he returned home in 1514, and personally petitioned the king for an increase in his pension. Manuel not only rejected the request but accused Magellan of leaving the army without permission and profiting from a corrupt financial bargain that sold captured livestock to the enemy, and ordered him to return at once to Morocco. When the charges against him were eventually dismissed, Magellan appealed once more to his king for a pension that recognized his long and dangerous service to the crown, and was again rejected.

Denied the king's generosity, the determined Magellan sought instead to enlist his support for an adventure that would earn him the wealth and fame he yearned for. Columbus's voyages to the New World had proven conclusively that the world was round. And in 1513, the intrepid

Vasco Núñez de Balboa had crossed the Isthmus of Panama and stood on the shore of what he called the South Sea, and claimed all the lands it touched for the Spanish crown. Magellan believed that a passage between the Atlantic Ocean and that uncharted sea to the west, and through it a western route to the Spice Islands, existed at the unexplored end of the South American continent. He was determined to locate it.

Manuel, who, for various reasons, held the persistent Magellan in low regard, again refused to support his ambitions. As he prepared to leave Manuel's court, the disappointed Magellan kneeled to kiss the hand of his sovereign, as custom required. Manuel withdrew his hand, and turned his back on him, a humiliating gesture of contempt that the proud soldier would never forget. Magellan left Lisbon, renounced his Portuguese citizenship, and offered his services to Manuel's rival, the young Spanish king Charles I. Charles, though over thirty years younger than Manuel, had the more discerning eye for opportunity. He accepted the offer, and agreed to supply Magellan with ships, arms, and provisions for the incredibly dangerous but potentially lucrative adventure.

In 1494, Pope Alexander VI had drawn a line through the Atlantic Ocean from the North to the South Pole. Everything east of the line, including India, belonged to Portugal; everything west belonged to Spain. Alexander charged the kings of each country, and their armies, with spreading Christianity on their respective sides of the invisible line. The Treaty of Tordesillas between Spain and Portugal ratified the papal edict. What no one knew was how wide the world truly was, and left in dispute was whether Portugal or Spain could claim the Spice Islands. Magellan argued that by sailing a western route around the world, and avoiding the Portuguese-controlled Cape of Good Hope, he could claim the islands and their invaluable treasures for Spain.

On September 10, 1519, five small ships, the *San Antonio*, the *Concepción*, the *Victoria*, the *Santiago*, and the *Trinidad*, carrying 265 men, a sizable arsenal of arms and munitions, and a less-than-adequate store of food and water, left the Spanish port of San Lucar de Barrameda for South America. The ships' captains were Spaniards. The fleet's ultimate destination was kept secret from the ships' crews, who believed that they were sailing for South America, and not for the unknown world beyond its shores. It would not have been possible to find a crew willing to embark on such a perilous, if not impossible, journey. Their Portuguese commander, Ferdinand Magellan, sailed aboard the *Trinidad*, flying the imperial standard of Spain, the flag of Castile. Only one of the ships would ever return.

During the months of preparation for the voyage, an emissary of King Manuel, Sebastián Alvares, had tried with promises, flattery, threats, and insults to revive Magellan's former loyalties to his native country. He warned Magellan that his fleet's Spanish officers and crews would never submit to the authority of a Portuguese commander, and that he should abandon the expedition, for it would surely end in disaster or disgrace. When Magellan, who cherished his aspirations more than his former patriotism, rebuffed the appeals, the disappointed emissary reported to Manuel that despite Magellan's disloyalty, "his heart was true as to what befitted his honor and conscience."

It wasn't long before Magellan had cause to remember Alvares's warnings about mutiny. The captain of the *San Antonio* and inspector general of the little fleet, Juan de Cartagena, had been ordered by King Charles to serve as his eyes and ears, and to report any violations of His Majesty's instructions or other signs of disloyalty by Magellan. Cartagena believed his royal charge gave him authority equal to the fleet commander's, which only exacerbated the natural antipathy, jealousy, and distrust that Spanish captains felt for the opportunistic Portuguese adventurer who presumed to give them orders. Only a few members of the expedition were tied by genuine bonds of loyalty to their commander, among them Magellan's own son Cristóväo, his Malaysian slave, Enrique, and an Italian adventurer, Antonio Pigafetta, whom Magellan had ordered to record a secret account of the expedition. Magellan further inflamed the situation by expecting his orders to be followed without hesitation or explanation.

Magellan received word that King Manuel had dispatched two Portuguese ships to intercept his fleet and arrest him. In order to avoid capture, he ordered his captains to sail south along the western coast of Africa rather than immediately head west for South America. He declined to inform his captains of the reasons for this detour through dangerous and mostly uncharted waters. Two weeks of fair sailing were followed by two months of foul weather that battered the ships and threatened to crash them upon the rocks. When the storms finally subsided and the lack of winds left the fleet drifting helplessly in the prostrating heat along the equator, Cartagena and the other Spanish captains, except Juan Serrano on the *Santiago,* plotted mutiny.

In conference aboard the *Trinidad,* Cartagena accused Magellan of serving Portugal's interests by intentionally misdirecting the fleet, and announced that he would no longer take orders from the Portuguese commander. Magellan ordered two loyal members of his crew to seize the rebellious captain and clap him in irons. Cartagena called on his fellow mutineers to kill Magellan, but, for whatever reason, they declined. At the behest of the captains who had, for the time being, decided against mutiny, Magellan released Cartagena from his shackles, relieved him of his command, and ordered him confined aboard the *Victoria*, where the embittered mutineer nursed his dreams of vengeance.

Three weeks after the aborted mutiny, fortune smiled on the tiny armada as favorable winds arrived to carry the ships across the Atlantic to their first destination in the New World, Rio de Janeiro. Two weeks later, with fresh provisions, the fleet embarked on its mission to locate the elusive passage to the other side of the world. The search proved more difficult than Magellan had imagined. Every possible passageway to the west was explored only to frustrate the explorers and their impatient commander with another dead end. Even more troubling, the farther south they sailed the colder and stormier the weather. On March 31, 1520, five long months after they had left Spain, Magellan ordered his ships to anchor in the harbor of San Julian in Argentina, to wait out the southern winter. Another five months would pass before they resumed their voyage, during which disaster would again strike, leaving Magellan to pursue his dream without the assistance of three of his captains.

The approach of the brutal Antarctic winter, and the long months of isolation and short rations it would entail, bred insubordination among the men, many of whom had had enough of Magellan's ambitions, and wished to return to Spain. Others argued that the armada should wait out the winter in the warmth and other comforts of Rio de Janeiro. Magellan refused, insisted that they would never return until they had found their passage to the west and circumnavigated the world, and chastised the officers and crews for their lack of courage and dedication. Suspecting that his Spanish captains were planning another, far more serious mutiny, Magellan planned to strike first.

He informed the officers and crews of the two ships that remained loyal to him that the mutineers intended to murder him on Easter Sunday, April 1. The plotters used longboats to communicate their plans, and when the crew of one of the boats, which belonged to the captain of the *Concepción*, Gaspar de Quesada, foundered in the swift current, Magellan ordered the crew of the *Trinidad* to rescue them and bring them aboard his ship. Magellan plied the men with drink and food, and persuaded them to confess the plot. Then he prepared the *Trinidad* for action.

That evening, Quesada and Cartagena secretly boarded the *San Antonio*, arrested its sleeping captain, attacked the ship's master loyal to Magellan, seized the ship, and enlisted its crew in their conspiracy. In a few hours, the rebellion had spread to two other ships, Quesada's *Concepción* and the *Victoria*, with Captain Luis de Mendoza in command. The captain of the *Santiago*, Juan Serrano, knew of the conspiracy, but again chose to remain neutral.

Magellan, believing he only faced one mutinous captain, learned the following morning that the rebels had seized three of his ships. The odds were greatly against his survival. But he would not be dissuaded from his great purpose. He had come to find the undiscovered passage to the west, and he would not let any misfortune—foul weather, Portuguese pursuers, failed explorations, vast, uncharted distances, exhausted supplies, hostile natives, or mutiny—deter him. He would go around the world or die trying.

He sent a longboat of fifteen secretly armed men to the *Victoria* on the pretense of negotiating the rebels' demands. Mendoza allowed them to come on board. Magellan's emissaries presented the *Victoria*'s captain with a letter demanding his surrender. Mendoza laughed and threw the letter overboard. The officer Magellan had placed in charge grabbed the rebel captain by his beard and cut his throat. As he fell to the deck, another fifteen of Magellan's men in a second longboat stormed the ship. The crew quickly surrendered, and the mutiny on the *Victoria* was ended.

The fate of Mendoza, signaled by the hoisting of Magellan's flag on the *Victoria*, convinced Captain Serrano on board the *Santiago* to abandon his neutrality and come to his commander's defense. Magellan now had three boats to the mutineers' two, and quickly formed a blockade of the harbor, trapping the *Concepción* and *San Antonio*. The odds had turned in his favor. He expected captains Quesada and Cartagena to realize that they might meet the same fate as the dead Mendoza, and surrender. They chose not to. Either their vanity would not let them submit to their Portuguese enemy or they remained confident they could fight their way through the trap or they feared they were doomed even if they did surrender. For whatever reason, they chose to fight.

When night fell, Magellan ordered one of his men to secretly board the *Concepción* and cut the anchor cable. When the current carried the drifting ship within range of the *Trinidad*, Magellan ordered his ship's cannons to open fire. Grappling hooks dragged the rebel ship to the *Trinidad*'s side, and Magellan's crew swarmed onto the *Concepción*'s deck and made short work of the rebel opposition. Most of the crew immediately surrendered. Quesada and his loyalists were arrested. Aboard the *San Antonio*, Cartagena watched as his fellow mutineers were subdued, then he swallowed his pride and offered Magellan his surrender.

The mutiny at an end, Magellan exacted a swift and terrible justice on the mutineers. He ordered Mendoza's body to be torn to pieces, which were then impaled on stakes and displayed for months as a lesson to any who might harbor thoughts of rebellion in the future. A few other mutineers were hideously tortured to death. Forty others were sentenced to death, but Magellan granted them clemency. Quesada was not among them, however. Magellan ordered the condemned captain to be beheaded by his own servant. Cartagena and a priest who had conspired with him were spared execution. Magellan planned an even worse fate for them.

When the armada left San Julian the following August, Cartagena and his fellow conspirator were left behind, marooned on a little island in the harbor, with barely any provisions, where, we can assume, they lingered for many desperate weeks before hunger, the elements, or hostile natives ended their suffering. Their plaintive cries for mercy followed the ships out of the harbor as they resumed the voyage south. Now, the surviving members of the expedition sailed toward an uncertain future less afraid of the dangers that might await them than they were of the man who commanded them.

Nearly a year had passed since they had left Spain. Magellan had expected to have reached the Spice Islands by now. They had survived many dangers. But worse dangers and many more months of terrible hardships still lay ahead. Magellan's fleet had been reduced to four ships. Before the winter had ended and they left San Julian, Magellan had ordered the *Santiago* to scout for the passage that no European had ever seen but which Magellan knew he would find. As she descended a river in the false hope that it would lead to the way west, a sudden storm destroyed her. Weeks passed before the stranded and starving crew was rescued.

By mid-October, after suffering more harrowing late-winter storms and further delays, the armada had rounded the end of the eastern coast of South America, and Magellan spotted a calm and lovely bay. He ordered the *San Antonio* and *Concepción* to investigate whether it might be the opening to the elusive strait. As they often do in the inhospitable Antarctic climate, a gale rose out of nowhere and swept the *Trinidad* and *Victoria* out to sea. It drove the other two ships toward the shore and out of sight of their commander, who presumed them to be lost. All day and night, Magellan battled to save his last two ships from the savage storm. As dawn broke, and the weather temporarily subsided, a lookout on the *Trinidad* spotted two sails on the horizon. The *Concepción* and *San Antonio* had survived. And they had found the strait to the great ocean in the west. The explorers named it the Strait of All Saints, but posterity named it the Strait of Magellan, for its discoverer.

Many of the men argued that having made their important discovery, they should return to Spain, and leave it to some future expedition to navigate it. Magellan, whose satisfaction at having found what it seemed only he believed existed we can only imagine, remained determined to reach his final destination, the Spice Islands. He ordered his ships to sail west into the gray and forbidding waters of the strait. A few days later, the *San Antonio,* the largest of the armada's ships and carrying most of its provisions, tacked east and raced for home. Magellan was powerless to stop the deserters. He pressed on, fixed as always on his impossible dream.

Thirty-eight days later, having again survived the horrors of brutal winds, freezing temperatures, and treacherous waters, and having performed what is still regarded as the most impressive achievement of navigation in all of history, Magellan brought his remaining three ships safely through the strait, where they beheld the endless expanse of the largest ocean in the world. The proud and impassive Magellan was reported to have wept at the sight. Known until then as the Western Sea, which few Europeans had ever seen, Magellan, in appreciation for the calmness of its waters and the gentle breezes that carried them west, bestowed on it the name the Pacific ("peaceful") Sea.

No European had ever sailed from its eastern shore. It was wrongly believed to be a smaller ocean than the Atlantic. Magellan was convinced that the Spice Islands were only a few days' sail from the strait he had just navigated. In reality, he was about to cross the largest expanse of water any human being had ever sailed. Three and a half months would pass before Magellan would reach the Philippine Islands.

As gentle trade winds carried them north, the ships followed the coastline of Chile for nearly a month before their commander gave the order to head west for Asia. The northwest course he followed would carry him safely past coral reefs and other unseen dangers that might have destroyed his ships, but they also kept the ships beyond sight of islands where they might have replenished their stores of water and food. Within a month, his crew was starving. Two weeks later they began to die.

The Italian Pigafetta recorded their misery in the journal Magellan had ordered him to keep: "We ate crumbling biscuits infested with grubs, and drank water filthy and stinking. . . . We ate [leather strips] from under the yardarms, sawdust and rats. The gums of the men swelled so much they could not chew."

Scurvy claimed dozens of lives. The survivors lay prostrate in the heat, many unable to stand, their teeth falling from their bleeding gums, the stench of death filling their nostrils. Few had the strength to continue. Most were resigned to dying. Even the dauntless, determined Magellan gave in to despair at times and raged at his endless misfortune. Yet he pressed on and on and on.

In January they happened upon a small uninhabited island where they found fresh water and a little food. But they had only completed a third of their Pacific voyage. Within a few weeks their torments returned. Every day Magellan strained his eyes to the west, searching in vain for the distant image of land and salvation, nurturing the hope his crew had long ago abandoned. Every day he was disappointed.

Finally, on March 4, the only man strong enough to climb the rigging to keep a lookout spotted land in the distance. A few hours later the explorers, barely more than shrunken skeletons, made landfall at Guam in the Mariana Islands. They had crossed the Pacific Ocean, the first human beings to have done so. Through unimaginable danger and suffering, struggling for eighteen months to survive the terrors of a strange and nameless world, having overcome mutiny and desertion and shipwreck and death and every natural disaster conceivable, they had succeeded. They had crossed the largest body on earth, traveled 42,000 miles whereas the famous Columbus had only braved 8,000 miles to ensure his immortality. Theirs was the greatest achievement of the age. And the one man who believed it could be done, who had compelled his reluctant, terrified men to pursue the aspiration they believed was unattainable, who, through the force of his will, had realized a dream too big for others to chase, Ferdinand Magellan, would only know the private satisfaction of having done what no one else would have dared to do. The glory and wealth that should have been his reward for so historic an achievement would go to others. He would never see home again.

Three days later, their terrible thirst and hunger over, the ships stores filled with fresh provisions, they sailed for the Philippine Islands before making their way to their final destination. They arrived on the sixteenth of March. Within six weeks, Magellan had converted a local chieftain to Christianity and allied himself with the new convert's tribe and against his enemies. Before he departed for the Spice Islands, he promised his ally that he would give battle to a rival chief on the island of Mactan. Magellan prepared to march ashore on April 27, with only a small force of sixty men, confident that God, Who had seen him through so many worse dangers, would protect him again, and certain that his small number of soldiers was sufficient to frighten the thousands of primitive islanders. Those islanders with their leader, a warrior called Lapu Lapu, were calmly awaiting his arrival. Magellan had sent the rebel chief a warning that he must submit to Spain's authority or face the wrath of Magellan's well-armed soldiers. The self-assured Lapu Lapu taunted in response, "Come across whenever you like."

A coral reef prevented the ships from bringing Magellan's soldiers as close as he intended, and from where the enemy force would be within range of the ships' cannons. Magellan's men struggled through the deep surf in their armor, carrying muskets, crossbows, lances, and swords. The islanders were armed with spears, arrows, stones, and bamboo shields strong enough to repel musket balls and crossbow darts. By the time they reached the shore, Magellan's men were exhausted from wading through the water in heavy armor. The affair was over within an hour.

Realizing they were terribly outnumbered and that their crossbows and muskets had no effect against the islanders' shields, most of his men desperately fought their way back to the reef, where they could be rescued by longboats. Magellan fought on with only ten men beside him, surrounded by thousands of closing warriors. His foot was pierced by a poison arrow, which he wrenched free. He was speared in the face, and his right arm was severely wounded. He plunged his lance into the breast of a charging native, but the wound to his arm prevented him from pulling the lance from the body of his fallen foe. He grasped for his sword but could not draw it from its scabbard before an enemy sword slashed his leg, and he dropped to his knees in the surf. At the sight of his distress, scores of warriors rushed to finish him off, cutting him to pieces.

The remaining members of his expedition, greatly reduced from their original 265, set sail for the Spice Islands, leaving Magellan to be buried where he died. Having too few men to manage three ships, they scuttled and burned the *Concepción*. A gale blew Magellan's flagship north toward Japan, where she was captured by a Portuguese man-of-war and lost. Only the *Victoria* made it home to Spain, laden with a full cargo of cloves from the Spice Islands, a treasure great enough to earn the expedition a profit, despite its terrible losses. Only eighteen men were aboard her when she arrived to a hero's welcome. The captain of the *Victoria*, Juan Sebastian del Cano, was hailed as the man who had rounded the world for Spain, and enjoyed the acclaim and wealth that Magellan had dreamed would be his.

Antonio Pigafetta was among the survivors, and only when his journal was published some years later would Magellan receive the recognition he deserved. The author, like the captain he had come to admire above all other men, knew that history would not deny Magellan the immortality he had so justly earned. He wrote: "In the midst of the sea he was able to endure hunger better than we. Most versed in nautical charts, he knew better than any other the true art of navigation, of which it is certain proof that he by his genius, and his intrepidity, without anyone having given him the example, knew how to attempt the circuit of the globe which he had almost completed."

That, Pigafetta was certain, was more than enough to assure that his master, the man who proved equal to a most extraordinary aspiration, would never be forgotten. Because he had dared to sail around a world bigger and more dangerous than anyone imagined, without ever looking back, "the glory of Magellan will survive him."

DISCERNMENT

Leonardo da Vinci

He was a scientist who painted masterpieces as part of his grand ambition to see all that was visible in nature.

T HOUGH HE WAS RAISED IN HIS FATHER'S PROMINENT HOUSEHOLD, the boy had received merely a rudimentary education, which was not surprising given his status. He was the illegitimate son of a Florentine lawyer and a servant girl. And although he was well cared for by his father's family, and throughout his childhood had no legitimate half siblings to compete with for his father's favor, he could not expect to be raised, as would a legitimate son, to become a prominent gentleman of his city. He could read and write, and had shown a considerable aptitude for arithmetic. Greek and Latin, however, were the core of a classical education, the latter being the language of serious scholarship, and he had no working knowledge of either language. He was tall, athletic, and remarkably handsome, with an exquisite singing voice and a skilled hand for playing musical instruments. But he had a more uncommon gift than a lively intellect, physical beauty, or musicianship. He could see more than others could see, because he looked more intently and inquisitively than others looked, because he knew how to see. And with the knowledge about form and function he obtained through the employment of his incomparable power of concentration, and applied with the dexterity of his hand, he could draw. He could draw, in the words of an art critic centuries later, "like an angel."

So at the age of fourteen, he was taken by his father to the studio of Andrea del Verrocchio and apprenticed to the master goldsmith, painter, and sculptor, whose inventiveness and painstaking craftsmanship was favored by the patronage of the Medicis, the ruling family of Florence, the capital of the early Renaissance. With his well-deserved renown as a sculptor, his appreciation for the vitality and feelings of his subjects, and the extraordinary care he took with their execution in bronze or paint, Verrocchio was for a time the city's most influential artist. Some of the greatest artists of the Renaissance exhibited elements of Verrocchio's genius, including Botticelli and, indirectly, Michelangelo, whose own master's artistry had been influenced by Verrocchio.

The boy could have had no better master, but, it can be fairly said, his greatest teacher was experience, which he observed with his own eyes and recorded in charcoal, chalk, pencil, and paint faithfully and with unequaled skill. He would never need to rely on others' experience. His education had not bred him to revere the classic artworks of the Greek and Roman age as the achievements of the highest aesthetic, the aesthetic rediscovered, reborn, in the Renaissance. He would draw, paint, and sculpt life as he observed it, as much of life as was visible to the human eye, without compromising his observations by imposing on them or his art the standards of expression of a past age.

Around 1473, Verrocchio accepted a commission to do a painting, the *Baptism of Christ,* for the Convent of San Salvi in Florence. The work was executed in oil, a rarely used medium in Florence at that time, and was innovative in both its composition and the modeling of its figures. In most of its parts, the sharp boniness of John the Baptist, for example, the painting is regarded as stiff and inelegant, a little rough around the edges, and the figures seem frozen in their poses. But two of its details stand out: the great perspective depth of the distant landscape in the painting's background finely integrated with the figures in the foreground, which was achieved with a sophisticated blending of colors; and one of two kneeling angels holding Christ's garment in the left corner of the painting.

The blond angel farther left is the most striking figure in the composition. Unlike the angel to its right, who gazes at some middle distance away from the scene, with a look that is either indifferent or entirely absorbed in inscrutable contemplation, the blond angel is intent upon the baptism, neither anxious nor distracted, a look that appears at once both natural and sublime. Though kneeling and respectful, it is not a passive figure, but conveys energy in the twist of its head, the turn of its shoulders, the bend in its posture. It is a body exhibiting very natural human movement. The angel alone makes the painting remarkable, unusually expressive and vibrant. There can be no doubt that it is the work of a master. But it was not done by Verrocchio's hand.

He had let his young apprentice, then twenty or twenty-one years old, paint the angel and the landscape in the distance. Their collaboration in the *Baptism of Christ* was proof that the pupil had eclipsed the master. For as influential and admirable an artist as Verrocchio surely was in his time, the young Leonardo da Vinci was immeasurably superior in vision and skill, and was destined to become the most influential artist of his age, among the most influential of all time.

Even among the recognized geniuses of history, few can be said to be without any equal. Leonardo is one of those few. There is little argument among art historians that he deserves this singular distinction even though only seventeen of his paintings, several of them unfinished, exist for us to admire today. Arguably his greatest painting, *The Last Supper,* is a ruin of its original glory. We have the few paintings, though, and we have hundreds of his drawings in pencil and pen, superior by far in the stunning accuracy, clarity, and expressiveness of their representations, and we have the thousands of pages of his notebooks, which contain the many, various products of the vast range of his intellectual curiosity.

It was not Leonardo's single ambition to become the greatest painter of his age or the greatest artist. Those were the ambitions of lesser geniuses. His ambition was all-encompassing. He intended to observe, comprehend, and explain nature with drawings, painting, and sculpture—not some of nature, such as the workings of the human body, for example, but all of it. He wanted to understand everything that his penetrating eye, his extraordinarily disciplined observation, could discern. No one could achieve such complete knowledge, not even Leonardo da Vinci. He would lament later in life, "I have offended God and mankind because my work didn't reach the quality it should have." But he tried, and in trying could claim a breadth of accomplishment unrivaled by any other human being before or since. Every human being can take from his genius the satisfaction that it was a human being, one of us, who achieved this and not the revelation of a divine intelligence.

There was virtually no field of inquiry he did not pursue. He was a scientist of every discipline, an artist of every medium. He was anatomist, botanist, biologist, physicist, aerologist, astrologist, paleontologist, mechanic, painter, sculptor, architect, engineer, mapmaker, designer of pageants, and more. He left Florence in 1482, thirty years old, leaving behind two unfinished commissions (so much of his work was unfinished, owing to his diverse interests, which often distracted his attention from projects he had undertaken, and to his striving for perfection, which would cost him years in completing a painting). He appealed to the duke of Milan, Ludovico Sforza, for employment in a letter advertising his abilities as a military engineer, and his plans for mobile bridges, "cannon, mortars, and light ordnance of very beautiful and useful shapes, quite different from those in common use," catapults, battering rams, scaling ladders, what today we would call cluster bombs, and ships that resist fire and shelling. He also had designed plans to divert rivers, to tunnel under enemy fortifications, and even to build an armored tank.

All these creations of his hyperactive mind were conceived in service to an endeavor—war—that he loathed. In later years, he would draw a design for a submarine (like his tank, centuries before the first prototype was constructed) but would keep the plan secret lest anyone actually use it to harm another. He was, after all, a vegetarian who couldn't bear to destroy a living creature to feed his appetite. Needing work, he simply cataloged a few of his many inventions from the great vault of his knowledge that he thought would be of some interest to a prospective employer. Of his other abilities, should they prove useful to the duke, he acknowledged, "I can execute sculpture in marble, bronze or clay, and also painting, in which my work will stand comparison with that of anyone else whoever he may be." He was, to understate it, very interested in how things worked, how everything worked. He was a useful man to a duke or a king. Wherever an employer's primary interest lay—war, art, science, building, pageantry—Leonardo was his man.

I think it can be accurately said that Leonardo, whether or not he would agree, was a philosopher before he was an artist, scientist, or engineer. Central to his genius was his conception of a theory of knowledge that employed both science and art, to see, comprehend, and reveal the way nature worked. At the beginning is the eye. The eye may experience through sight, if it is perceptive and unimpeded, all that is knowable. Then, the hand, particularly one as dexterous and that answered so faithfully to the command of the mind as did Leonardo's, will describe the knowledge, not in words, but convey it, represent it, in pictures.

Leonardo was well read, and his notebooks, which he began in earnest to write around 1490, proved him to be a skillful and engaging writer. The notebooks are written backward from left to right, and have in our day as in the past given rise to speculation that they contain a secret code that, if it were broken, would reveal a secret conspiracy of some kind or a powerful insight unknown to history. They do contain many powerful insights, but none of them was intentionally obscured from the reader. Leonardo was left-handed, and while it was not common, he probably found it easier and more efficient to record his observations in what was called "mirror writing," because it could be read from right to left in a mirror's reflection. He never meant to keep his notebooks secret. Near his death he sought assurances from his closest associates that they would be published. That so many of them weren't published for centuries after his death and their potentially great influence lost to scientific inquiries of the age was not his intention but the result of their disorganized, almost random and difficult-to-organize state, their wide dispersal and forgotten location.

Despite the prodigious quantity of his writing and the substantial library he collected, he felt literature to be a lesser art and a less useful medium of instruction. His notebooks, crammed though they are with tens of thousands of words, are lavishly illustrated with drawings, his ideal form of instruction.

Everywhere Leonardo went he carried a pad of paper stuck in his belt, always at the ready for a quick sketch of an observation or discovery. He would reach for it as he studied the flight of birds, and then conceive in his sketches the aerodynamics of flight, and designs for machines that would give men wings. He attempted once or twice to put his designs to the test, to no avail. But in his notebooks you can find drawings for gliders, helicopters, and flying contraptions of all kinds, so advanced in their concepts that they were beyond the imagination not only of his contemporaries but the greatest minds of later centuries.

How things moved and why was an intense lifelong interest. He saw the laws of mechanics at work everywhere in the movement of the stars, the flow of a river, the reach of a human arm toward another. He would grab his notebook as he dissected cadavers to discern the working of muscles, and use the knowledge to infuse the figures in his paintings with a natural force, expressiveness, and grace. He had no need to idealize the human form as the Greeks and Romans had, and his younger contemporary Michelangelo did, with incredible musculature that fantasized beauty by contorting reality, the "bag of nuts," as he derided it. The body as he saw and understood it was more expressive and more perfect in its form and function than could be improved upon by a fanciful flight of artistic imagination. "The human foot," he wrote, "is a masterpiece of engineering and a work of art." He was as interested in and perceptive of nature's deformities as he was its special beauties, as meticulous in his drawing of the grotesque as he was painting God's splendor. And in his investigations of the body's inner workings, the soft machinery beneath the skin, he paid particularly close scrutiny to the eye, to understand how sight was obtained.

He would draw the fossils he discovered in rocks on his long and frequent hikes outside Florence, and then glean insights into the movement of mountains and the ages of the earth before man. He would study the movement of water, learn its properties, and understand its power. With that knowledge he would propose canals and hydraulic machines for a variety of purposes. The canals he designed in Milan are in use to this day. Little of the known world escaped his eye or his hand.

Scattered throughout his notebooks are the observations of a treatise or essay on painting that a close disciple organized after his death. In the introduction he mocks learned men who try to record knowledge through writing, and scorn the importance of art as revealed knowledge. "They will scorn me as an inventor and a discoverer," he wrote, "but . . . they have invented and discovered nothing. They do not realize that my works arise from unadulterated and simple experience, which is the one true mistress, the one true muse. The rules of experience are all that is needed to discern the true from the false; experience is what helps all men to look temperately for the possible, rather than cloaking oneself in ignorance."

Nothing, he thought, could be fully learned from books. Trying to acquire a complete understanding of a subject from a musty Latin text was a fool's errand to him. "Anyone who conducts an argument by appealing to authority is not using his intelligence," he argued. "He is just using his memory." Experience, seeing the thing for yourself, and taking pains to make sure you see it clearly was the only sure way to acquire knowledge. "Although nature commences with reason and ends in experience it is necessary for us to do the opposite, that is to commence with experience and from this proceed to investigate the reason."

To understand and explain nature, the artist is the best scientist. The artist has the keenest eye. The artist does not describe. He reveals. "All visible things were brought forth by nature," Leonardo explained, "and these, her children, have given birth to painting. Therefore we may justly speak of it as the grandchild of nature and as related to God." Geometry and mathematics reduce the world to its particular dimensions, but only a painting represents the same reality and more. Painting deals "with the quality of things which constitutes the beauty of the works of nature and the ornament of the world."

There is simply too much of Leonardo's genius to do justice to him in this short chapter. So with your indulgence I will limit my poor attempt at further describing him to a brief and untrained appreciation of his painting, to the Leonardo we can experience in particular in his two greatest paintings, *The Last Supper* and the small portrait of the wife of a prominent Florentine citizen, Francesco del Giocondo, which is the most famous painting in the world, the *Mona Lisa*.

It was the custom for ages to render depictions of the Last Supper at the moment when Jesus turned bread and wine into a living sacrament. The scene is always still, substituting lifelessness for reverence, the figures of the apostles frozen to represent a respectful understanding of the divine gift their Savior was bestowing on them. There is no action. The seated figures are all portrayed in isolation, side by side, distinguished from one another but not very different in temperament or emotion from the others, or even from the figure of Christ.

Leonardo conceived the scene differently, choosing a moment of surprise and tension, when Jesus announces that one of them will betray Him that evening. And knowing that the apostles were human, and would not have comprehended the prophecy-fulfilling purpose of the moment but have reacted with alarm, denial, and anguish, Leonardo visualized the authentic moment. His composition was strikingly original. The apostles are divided into two groups of six, on each side of Jesus in the center of the painting. Judas, a darkened figure, sits in the right corner at the end of the table, clutching the purse that holds his thirty pieces of silver, confronting the accusations of an angry Simon Peter and a distressed John. The apostles crowd into one another, straining, gesturing, questioning, beseeching, each figure a character portrait in himself, but the whole scene is tumultuous. The apostles' comprehension of Christ's announcement is depicted as a wave moving from those closest to Jesus to those farthest from Him, sparking the distinct passionate reaction of each apostle. The action in the painting becomes almost audible to the viewer. You can almost hear the apostles shout, question, and deny.

"Who, Lord?"

"Not I, Lord."

"It cannot be true, Lord."

"Tell us who would do this, Lord, and we will seize the traitor."

Jesus sits serenely in the midst of the unleashed passions of His disciples, unaffected by them. He has anticipated his apostles' reactions, but is beyond the reach of the commotion, fixed on His great redemptive purpose, the salvation of humanity. He is about to begin His passion, and though He occupies human form, He is unmistakably, authentically divine. He transcends the scene. Your eye is strongly drawn to Him. The perspective of the painting draws you unavoidably to the center of the composition, Christ's head, impervious to the chaos that surrounds Him.

Judas, too, is a little distant from the action, his features obscured in the shadow of guilt, evading envelopment in his fellow apostles' emotions, intent on his treachery.

Leonardo began the painting in 1495, on a wall in the dining room of the Convent of Santa Maria delle Grazie in Milan, Italy, and finished it three years later. It is an immense painting, fifteen by twenty-nine feet. Fresco paintings were done on wet plaster, and had to be executed quickly. Leonardo, always striving for perfection, worked more slowly, carefully. He painted with oil, in a richer, more varied palette than offered by egg tempura paints typically used for frescoes, and experimented with a dry plaster base he invented. But moisture soaked into the base, and it began to flake almost as soon as the painting was complete. Within fifty years it was almost a ruin. Early attempts at restoration did more harm than good, although in recent times some of the damage has been repaired. The magnificence of the painting as it was upon its completion, however, has been lost forever. But the perfection and originality of the masterpiece inspired the awe of Leonardo's contemporaries, and set a new standard for composition that influences historical painting to this day. The full splendor of the work may not ever be recovered, but what remains of its observable brilliance, its energy, the naturalness of its figures, the riveting transcendence of Jesus Christ, might never be equaled.

The liveliness of the figures of the apostles in *The Last Supper* is portrayed in the naturalness of their motions. In Leonardo's most famous painting, the *Mona Lisa,* the subject is still and yet her liveliness is even more vivid and more natural. It is a small, beguiling portrait, only thirty by twenty-one inches, of a young woman whose grace and mystery are captured completely by the painter. The first thing you sense about the *Mona Lisa* is that there must have been an extraordinary connection between the subject and her painter. Leonardo is said to have spent four years painting this single face, and the result of his intense dedication speaks to the love—and there is no other word for it—that he devoted to the work. It was his favorite painting, and he kept it in his possession for all but the last few years of his life. The effect of its liveliness is so profoundly engaging that those who have had the privilege of viewing it have remarked that Mona Lisa seems as alive as they are, as if they are actually seeing Leonardo's model as he saw her, studying her as he did, and as she studied Leonardo, rather than observing a flat image painted in two dimensions on a panel of wood.

How did he achieve this effect? We know the techniques he used, but it's hard to say if technique alone produced her mesmerizing mysteriousness. The refinement of perspective, linear and atmospheric, which Leonardo had so completely mastered helps make her so responsive to the viewer. The landscape on the horizon is higher on her left side than on her right. Thus, when the viewer looks first from one angle and then the other, her expression appears to change, which subtly alters her character.

But the most important skill animating the portrait is Leonardo's ability to excite our imagination, engaging the viewer with the subject as she engages us. We cannot be certain what she is thinking, what emotion she expresses. Her smile is either about to widen or about to vanish, and our curiosity enlivens both ourselves and the portrait. The corners of the mouth and the eyes are the most expressive attributes of a portrait, and Leonardo executed them with great skill using the technique called sfumato, which he didn't invent but completely mastered. The corners of her eyes and mouth are not crisply outlined but blurred, subtle changes in color giving them form, while leaving much to the enthralled imagination of the viewer. Sfumato is also used to great effect on her dress and robe. The haziness it achieves seems natural to the eye, the way living things are perceived at a glance, more voluptuous, breathing, moving, living. That, of course, is part of Leonardo's genius. He knew not only how to paint the eye, but, in his intense study of anatomy, he learned how the eye worked, how it perceived. He painted her in a way that took into account more than how the portrait should look at us, but how we would look at her.

The other technique used so skillfully in the portrait is chiaroscuro, which, again, Leonardo uses to give her a more natural or real appearance. Rather than render her features with a clear outline, he models them using contrasts between light and shadow. Look at her hands, for instance; they are fuller, more sensitive than the hands in other portraits painted by even great artists. You fully expect them to feel, if you were allowed to touch them, as supple and warm as your own hands. The illusion is so perfect that you half expect that to touch her would elicit a reaction from her.

The whole effect of this remarkable portrait seems, in the end, to depend on a unique bond, a sincere affection, between painter and subject that anticipates a third party's curiosity. It is as if they share a secret joke between them and part of their amusement is deciding whether we can guess it or whether they should share it with us. We are all, Leonardo, Lisa, and the viewer, present at the moment of creation. It is the creation of science and art, the greatest expression of Leonardo's theory of knowledge.

Leonardo worked for the duke of Milan for about sixteen years, during that time executing some of his most famous works, including *The Last Supper*. War drove him back to Florence, where he painted the *Mona Lisa*, and from there to Venice and Rome and back to Milan. He worked under the patronage of the great families of the Renaissance, the Medicis and the Borgias, another duke, a king, and a pope. Celebrated as the greatest artist of his time, he would accept a commission here and there and leave many of them unfinished. Some of them might have rivaled his greatest works, but the perfect ideal he pursued took years of study and preparation to achieve, and some other commission, some other discovery, would draw him away.

In the last few years of his life he accepted the generous patronage of the king of France and devoted admirer Francis I, who gave Leonardo a comfortable house and income near his court at Fontainebleau. A stroke had left Leonardo partially paralyzed by then, and his hand would not obey his mind's command. But his eye was as discerning as ever, and the king valued his counsel. He died there in 1519, sixty-seven years old.

The church where he was buried in France was destroyed centuries later, and the resting place of the great Leonardo da Vinci's remains is no longer known. Many of his paintings, and all of his sculptures, however few pieces he may have completed, have been lost to the ravages of time and the carelessness of men. We have the seventeen paintings that have not been lost, many of his notebooks, and many splendid, truly enlightening drawings. But even these cannot represent the whole of his legacy and genius.

Like his grave and his missing masterpieces, we might fear we can never locate his entire genius. But then we need only to look around us, to see the world we live in, which has been rendered comprehensible by advances in technology that even he could not have imagined, to know how little escaped his experience of it, and how much of it he discerned. To look at how much is expressed in a child's smile or the savage beauty of a flooding river or the graceful arc of a swooping hawk, and to understand the force that achieved the effect, is to know a little more of his genius. For once upon a time, long ago, Leonardo's discerning eye observed the same experience, and informed his mind that bid his hand to reveal its mysteries to us.

CURIOSITY

Charles Darwin

*His curiosity and courage helped him to discover the history of nature,
and start an argument that has continued for 150 years.*

THE INDOLENT, FRIVOLOUS BOY HAD FOUND A NEW PREOCCUPATION to fritter away the hours of his days, and lead him further astray from his studies and the prospect of ever becoming a respectable Victorian gentleman. So it had always been for his fifth child, Robert Darwin despaired. Sports and other idle pastimes, and a lazy mind with an eccentric curiosity, which had produced no accomplishment of merit, had made his son a disappointment. Robert Darwin had suffered the frustration of his son's failed medical education, and in a last attempt to give the boy direction, sent him to Cambridge University. But the boy again became bored with his classes, and preferred to spend his time outdoors, walking, riding, shooting, playing with dogs, and pocketing little things for his various collections. Now, another typically insignificant pursuit had become the boy's newest obsession: insects. Collecting beetles had become something of a fad in upper-class English society in the 1820s, and influenced by his cousin's enthusiasm, the boy had once again neglected his studies for the pleasure of collecting and studying bugs. What next, the father must have thought, what next?

What next was a revolution.

It would be hard to fault the man for failing to glimpse for his ne'er-do-well son the future he would one day claim. The boy would soon embark on the journey that would provide his curious mind with the information to discover the most important basic premise in biology. It would prove an accomplishment so extraordinary that it would make Charles Robert Darwin the most celebrated, controversial scientist of his age, the father of modern biology, and the man who explained the "mystery of mysteries."

He had never really been an idle boy, despite his father's concerns, just a little distracted and a bit of a daydreamer. He was prone to pursuing those subjects that engaged his curious intellect and the activities that aroused his warm heart, while ignoring those that did not. In his autobiography, published after his death, he remarked that he had "much zeal for whatever interested me." He enjoyed geometry, which he had been taught by a private tutor. He enthusiastically practiced experiments in his older brother Erasmus's improvised chemical laboratory in a garden toolshed. The Reverend Samuel Butler, the headmaster at the Shrewsbury boarding school he attended between the ages of nine and sixteen, disapproved of his interest in chemistry, and rebuked young Darwin in front of his classmates for wasting his time on such a disreputable pastime.

He was a poor student by his own admission. He had little interest in Greek and Latin and the other elements of a classical education. But he was fond of certain literature: Shakespeare's historical plays, the poems of Lord Byron, and the odes of Horace. He was captivated by a book, *Wonders of the World,* to which he attributed his early interest in exploring remote regions of the world.

He loved the outdoors, a passion that was excited on hikes during his family's summer vacations in North Wales. And though he was a somewhat awkward child, he was physically robust, a strong swimmer and a swift runner, and good at sports. He liked to hunt and was a practiced shot. He fished often as well. Both pursuits would conflict with his affection for animals. All his life he was exceptionally fond of dogs, and they of him. His greatest passion, however, was collecting things—minerals, stones, seashells, birds' eggs, insects, stamps, coins, plants, and other odds and ends.

He was born on February 12, 1809, in Shrewsbury, Shropshire, in the English Midlands, the second son of Robert and Susannah Darwin's six children. His mother, the daughter of the famous pottery manufacturer Joseph Wedgwood, died when Charles was barely eight years old. His father, Robert, was a physician, and while he appears to have been at times a stern and disapproving man, his son recalled him as "the kindest man I ever knew and whose memory I love with all my heart." Robert Darwin was a skilled doctor and a man of considerable practical sense, who had, his son observed, "a theory for almost everything that occurred," which surely influenced how Darwin approached his scientific inquiries, which varied from the practice of his times. He would begin every inquiry with a hypothesis, and then root out discoveries either to confirm or disprove it. His paternal grandfather, Erasmus Darwin, was also a physician, who enjoyed an international reputation not only as a man of medicine but as a poet, inventor, and biologist, and an early theorist of the possibility that species of life did not remain immutable from their creation but evolved by acquiring new characteristics. His grandson would someday provide further proofs of the theory of evolution, and it was his particular genius and curiosity that would provide the reason for it.

In 1825, Darwin recalled, "As I was doing no good at school, my father wisely took me away at a rather earlier age than usual, and sent me to Edinburgh University with my brother, where I stayed for two years or sessions." Robert Darwin packed him off at the age of sixteen to be trained in the family profession at the medical college in Edinburgh with the reproach ringing in his ears: "You care for nothing but shooting, dogs and rat-catching, and you will be a disgrace to yourself and all your family."

Charles Darwin considered his professors and classes at Edinburgh "intolerably dull," and geology so much so that it nearly bred in Darwin a permanent and fateful dislike for the study of the science. Had he kept his vow to avoid any further study of geology or developed out of boredom a similar aversion to other sciences, the pace of human understanding of natural history would have been much delayed.

Three friendships spared history of the loss of an extraordinary scientist. A freed slave from Guyana, John Edmonstone, who taught taxidermy to Edinburgh's medical students, became Darwin's friend and not only helped improve his taxidermy skills but fueled his imagination with tales of the natural wonders of South America. The curator of Edinburgh's Natural History Museum, William MacGillivray, also took an interest in the genial and naturally curious young Darwin. MacGillivray offered more practical and engaging instruction in the study of natural history than Darwin's dull Edinburgh professors could manage, and he also encouraged the boy to make a habit of taking copious notes of his observations. A zoology professor, Robert Grant, also succeeded where other professors failed in exciting Darwin's interest in his field by taking long hikes with him, and teaching him to spot and dissect interesting marine specimens. Darwin also profited from joining a science club, the Plinian Society, where members debated the study of natural history, and where Darwin encountered his first serious discussion of the theory of evolution, a subject then considered by much of English society to be heretical.

Added to the tediousness of his classes was his emotional unsuitability for the practice of medicine. Darwin could not stand the sight of blood or stomach observing surgical operations performed on patients in a time before the use of anesthesia. He would not follow his father and grandfather into the profession, as became apparent to his father by the end of Darwin's second year at Edinburgh. In 1827, an exasperated Robert Darwin ordered his son home to Shrewsbury. He had determined that the Church offered the only suitable profession for his wayward son with his curious but undisciplined mind, and that fall sent Charles to Cambridge University to study for the Anglican priesthood. At the time, Charles welcomed the idea, and imagined that the life of a country parson offered abundant time and opportunity to pursue his interests in natural history.

Once again, his formal studies were of little interest to Darwin, and though he proved a successful student at Cambridge, his chief interests, as always, remained outside the university lecture halls. And once again those outside interests saved him from an undistinguished life. Beetle collecting, his new passion, offered valuable instruction in the methods of scientific inquiry, and it introduced him to one of the most consequential friendships of his life. His cousin and fellow beetle enthusiast, William Darwin Fox, recommended to Charles a Cambridge botany professor, the Reverend John Stevens Henslow, as a sound source of advice on the intriguing world of beetles. Darwin immediately developed a deep respect for Henslow's talents as a superior naturalist, and Henslow was drawn to Darwin's own passionate interest in the natural world, as well as his sincerity and amiable companionship. Under Henslow's tutelage, Darwin began to blossom as a naturalist. He enrolled in Henslow's botany class, and was so often seen accompanying Henslow, deep in conversation, on scientific excursions into the country that he soon became known as the "man who walks with Henslow."

Henslow undertook not only to further Darwin's interests in the natural sciences but to ensure that he prospered, as he never had in the past, in subjects that didn't particularly engage his curiosity. He taught him math and theology, subjects required for a degree, as well as botany. Henslow also introduced Darwin to a professor of geology, Adam Sedgwick, who repaired the damage Edinburgh had done to Darwin's interest in the subject, and who took him on a geological tour of Darwin's beloved North Wales, firmly impressing on Darwin an awareness of the infinite discoveries to pursue in the field of geology.

Darwin's discussions with Henslow encompassed every subject of interest to the natural scientist: geology, biology, zoology, entomology, mineralogy, chemistry, and increased immeasurably Darwin's knowledge in the subjects of greatest interest to him. By the time he received his degree at Cambridge, with honors, no less, his favorite tutor recognized in him the characteristics of a potentially brilliant natural scientist. In the years ahead, the world would recognize how well placed Henslow's faith had been.

After he left Cambridge in June 1831, Darwin was not in any particular hurry to take holy orders. His fascination with beetles had cost him the affection of his fiancée, Fanny Owen, a Shropshire girl and friend of Darwin's sister. Fanny had become exasperated with the exorbitant time Darwin devoted to beetles at her expense, and had recently broken off their engagement. No doubt he was thrown off balance by the unfortunate turn of events, but had found solace in the quiet pleasures of the hobby that had cooled Fanny's passion for him.

At home in Shrewsbury, he received a letter from Henslow informing him that his friend and tutor had recommended Darwin as a gentleman companion to navy lieutenant Robert Fitzroy, the captain of the H.M.S. *Beagle,* scheduled to depart Plymouth in December for a two-year expedition to chart the coastline of South America. When he had been at Cambridge, Darwin had fallen completely under the spell of Alexander von Humboldt's seven-volume *Personal Narrative of Travels to the Equinoctial Regions of America,* which provoked in Darwin an intense yearning to explore the rain forests and other marvels of South America. Lieutenant Fitzroy desired that a well-bred man of scientific learning accompany him on his expedition to explore their mutual interests in nature, and to serve as a suitable guest at his dining table. Darwin desired to be that man.

His father had his doubts, and at first denied his permission. But Henslow and Robert Darwin's brother-in-law, Josiah Wedgwood, persuaded him that the adventure would not be the colossal waste of time he feared it would be. He consented, and agreed to pay for his son's passage. Charles traveled to London to offer his services to Fitzroy and discuss the details of their expedition. Before they departed, it had been decided that the original two-year voyage would be lengthened to an around-the-world voyage, adding explorations of various island chains on the Atlantic and Pacific coasts of South America, as well as Australia, to the itinerary.

In his letter to Darwin, Henslow had apprised him of his recommendation by stating, "I consider you to be the best qualified person I know. . . . I state this not on the supposition of your being a finished naturalist, but as amply qualified for collecting, observing, and noting anything worthy to be noted in natural history. . . . The voyage is to last two years, and if you take plenty of books with you, anything you please may be done."

Henslow was right. Darwin was not a finished natural scientist, and he would follow his tutor's advice to bring an ample supply of scientific texts with him to assist his inquiries. Among them was the recently published first volume of Charles Lyell's *Principles of Geology,* which Henslow had recommended to him. But he had also cautioned his pupil not to accept Lyell's general principle, uniformitarianism, which proposed that the earth was very slowly but constantly changing, and that the natural events that worked to produce these changes had not proceeded any slower or faster than they worked today. Lyell's critics, who were numerous, rejected his view as an offense to Christian theology, which disputed that the hand of providence was visible in nature.

Darwin thought the expedition was an opportunity to collect interesting geological, botanical, and biological specimens for England's leading scientists to examine. What neither Darwin nor Henslow suspected at the time was that the great things Henslow had assured Darwin he could achieve would include the young man's discovery of the proofs for a startling hypothesis, and his rise to preeminence in the field of natural history.

At eleven o'clock on the morning of December 27, 1831, the *Beagle* left Plymouth bound for Brazil, with the naturalist Charles Darwin on board. He was embarked on his great voyage of discovery, and would not return for five years.

His first discovery aboard the *Beagle* was the realization that he suffered terribly from seasickness. He spent much of the early part of the voyage confined to his hammock in the small cabin he shared with a few of the ship's officers. He recovered in time to disembark at the ship's first port of call, St. Jago, in the Cape Verde Islands, off the coast of Africa. During his exploration of the island he noticed a band of seashells embedded in a cliff forty-five feet above sea level, indicating that the cliff had once been underwater. From this discovery he deduced that the volcanic island's present height had been caused by receding waters and not by a sudden rise in elevation, confirming Lyell's view of constant geological change over an immense period of time. From that moment forward, Darwin acknowledged, he would observe nature "as if he had the eyes of Lyell."

Six weeks after departing St. Jago, the *Beagle* sailed into All Saints Bay in Brazil, and with the generous accommodation of Captain Fitzroy, Darwin began his exhaustive inquiries into the natural history of South America. Darwin was left ashore for weeks, traveling for hundreds of miles by horseback and foot deep into remote regions, collecting thousands of specimens of plants, minerals, fossils, insects, and wildlife, while Fitzroy surveyed and charted the coastline, and later rendezvoused at a specified place and time with the wandering scientist. Darwin explored his first rain forest in Brazil, recalling the experience as a "chaos of delight." He rode the pampas of Patagonia with gauchos. He discovered the fossils of large extinct mammals in Argentina and Uruguay, where there was no evidence of climate change or sudden catastrophe that could explain their extinction. He puzzled over the coloring of wild cattle herds in the Falkland Islands. He encountered a primitive tribe of natives in Tierra del Fuego. He raced to save his small exploring party's boat from being dashed upon rocks by a wave caused by a falling glacier in the Beagle

Channel. On his twenty-fifth birthday, he received the honor of having the highest peak in Tierra del Fuego named for him by Captain Fitzroy. He sailed the Strait of Magellan in April 1834. He climbed the Andes, where he discovered seashells in high mountain passes, and where he was attacked by swarms of biting insects, the probable cause of a recurring disability that plagued him the rest of his life. He witnessed a massive earthquake and a resulting tsunami destroy the city of Concepción in Chile, and raise the elevation of the land.

He filled his small cabin and any other available space on the *Beagle* with his specimens, filled his notebooks with detailed observations, and whenever the opportunity presented itself he sent his collections to Henslow on a returning ship.

On September 15, 1835, he first glimpsed Chatham Island in the Galápagos archipelago, six hundred miles off the coast of Ecuador, where his greatest discoveries awaited him. In that small cluster of nineteen volcanic islands, Darwin made his most important collections of tortoises, marine iguanas, and the small finches, later to be known as Darwin's finches, that would eventually illuminate the mystery of mysteries. Each bore different physical characteristics particular to the island on which they bred.

From the Galápagos, the *Beagle* sailed for Australia, New Zealand, and other islands and atolls of the South Pacific, where Darwin added to his collections, taking a particular interest in barnacles, and examined the coral reefs so prevalent in the warm waters, which, he theorized, contrary to contemporary views, had grown upward from a sinking sea floor.

He returned to England in October 1836, and discovered that he had become a celebrity. His old friend and mentor, Henslow, had shared some of his specimens and geological observations with England's leading naturalists, who regarded his expedition as a triumph of science. He lectured on his discoveries before the most distinguished scientific societies, and worked with various authorities in the scientific community to catalog his collections and prepare their findings for publication as *The Zoology of the Voyage of the H.M.S. Beagle.* A well-known ornithologist from the London Zoo observed that the small birds Darwin had brought from the Galápagos were not, as Darwin believed, different breeds of birds, but distinct species of finches. He was admitted as a fellow of the Royal Geological Society. In January 1837, he delivered his first lecture to the society, in which he theorized that the South American land mass had risen in elevation over an immense period of time, while the ocean floor subsided, and that the animal life there had, for reasons he had not yet grasped, adapted to the change. His lecture excited much debate and won him even greater acclaim.

His greatest growing interest, however, was explaining how species adapted to change. His experiences had taught him that species were not immutable, but he had not yet determined how their changing characteristics, or "transmutation," occurred. That was the mystery of mysteries. The theory of evolution, which Darwin called "descent with modification," was not original to him, but had been speculated about and debated for some time by the scientific community. His grandfather Erasmus had argued the notion. But no one had yet explained how the transmutation occurred. His finches would prove the key to unlocking the mystery. But it would be some time before Darwin found the nerve to publicize his theory, aware, as he was, of the enormous controversy it would provoke.

In 1838, he experienced the first onset of the intestinal disorder and heart ailment that had probably been caused by his misadventure in the Andes, and which would leave him a semi-invalid for much of his life. He also found the woman, his cousin Emma Wedgwood, who would make him the comfortable and tranquil home that eased the disease's discomforts and allowed him the peace and quiet to concentrate on his notebooks, and the revolutionary ideas they would engender. Contrary to advice his father had given him, he shared with Emma his ideas of evolution. They were anathema at the time to Christian theology, for they suggested that whatever role God had played in the creation of the universe, the progress of earth proceeded according to natural laws and not to providence, and Emma reacted with alarm to the ideas. But from the moment they married in 1839, she provided him, along with ten children, the emotional support to pursue his inquiries in the happy sanctuary of their home in Kent, Down House. The publication that year of Darwin's *The Voyage of the Beagle* established his reputation as a popular author and assured his liberty from material need by supplementing the generous income his father had provided him. He had no need to divert his attention from his scientific inquiries to provide for his family's security. He was at liberty to devote his energy and intellect to his great purpose.

Darwin's immensely curious and focused mind had already led him to the brink of discovering the means of evolution by the time he married Emma. He had happened to read a book by a respected economist, the Reverend Thomas Malthus, *Essay on the Principle of Population,* which argued that human populations increase beyond their means and must compete to survive. Malthus's insight into the laws of economics, though flawed, struck Darwin as compatible with what he had observed at work in nature. He hypothesized that the survival of a species depended on the improvement of its members' physical characteristics to a changing environment, and that only those members with the most adaptable characteristics would survive over time.

For years in the comfort of his study at Down House he corresponded with animal breeders, examined the specimens he had brought from the Galápagos, and added new observations to his copious notebooks to support the theory that others would later and somewhat mistakenly refer to as the "survival of the fittest," but which he termed "natural selection."

The theory of natural selection, the key to the mystery of mysteries, attributed the transmutation of species that were capable of prospering in slowly but inevitably changing environments to the breeding of those members with the most adaptable characteristics. Thus, the ecologies of the various Galápagos Islands had favored the survival of tortoises or finches or any other living thing with the most advantageous physical traits. And their ability to produce offspring to which they passed on their traits ensured that over time these traits would become the dominant characteristics of the species.

The idea of natural selection, while still capable of inciting debate, no longer shocks us. But it was a shocking notion, indeed, in Victorian England. Darwin kept his views largely to himself for years. He worked assiduously on his study of natural selection, and patiently gathered support for it. He drafted in 1844 an unpublished essay that explained his revolutionary theory, but discussed his efforts with only a few intimates. He enumerated the reasons for his reticence, which included his doubts that his view would be accepted by fellow naturalists, his worry that he would be branded an atheist, which he was not, and his concern that the scandal his theory would cause would hurt his family and friends. He spent much of his time for many years preparing for publication a four-volume study on the different species of barnacles he had collected on his voyage.

In 1858, twenty-two years after he had returned to England, and decades after he had arrived at his explanation for evolution, Darwin unexpectedly received a letter from a young natural scientist working in Indonesia, Alfred Russel Wallace, who informed him that he, too, had arrived at the same conclusions concerning evolution that Darwin had. The event provoked Darwin into action.

He prepared a paper on natural selection that would be read with a paper submitted by Wallace to a scientific society in London on July 1, 1858. One year later, he expanded his paper into a book titled *On the Origin of the Species by Means of Natural Selection.* The first edition sold out the first day of publication. The resulting uproar consumed the attentions of Church and science for years. A meeting to discuss Darwin's theory occurred at Oxford University on June 30, 1869. His friend Henslow presided over the debate, and two other close friends, the marine biologist Thomas Huxley, who would earn the reputation as "Darwin's bulldog" for his ardent support of his friend's theory, and the botanist Joseph Hooker, defended Darwin from his critics. The critics at that debate included the archbishop of Oxford, Samuel Wilberforce; the anatomist and director of the natural history department of the British Museum, Richard Owen; and the captain of the *Beagle,* Robert Fitzroy. Contemporary accounts suggest Darwin's friends carried the day, the most memorable point of the debate being Huxley's devastating ridicule of Archbishop Wilberforce's criticism. Darwin, who was acutely suffering the effects of his chronic illness, did not attend.

He was a shy, modest, and kind man, who took great solace in his family and home. He never traveled outside Great Britain again, and seldom left Down House. He was genial and nonconfrontational by nature. He did not take pleasure in the controversy and criticism his ideas provoked, but neither did they trouble him so much that he abandoned his views and subsequent research. He wrote three more books on natural selection, each one controversial. Even many of his critics would acknowledge that he was the leading natural historian of his time.

By the end of his life he had produced volumes on all matter of natural history, including the effects of earthworm waste on soil. Many of his interests were pursued in the comforts of his own garden and in his well-supplied study. He was, by all accounts, a happy man, despite his disability and his grief over the loss of three of his children. Much of his happiness must be attributed to the devotion of Emma, and the friends and fellow scientists who defended him so often and effectively against attacks, and much of it was surely also attributable to his confidence in his own ideas, to knowing he was right. His curiosity and courage had led him to an undiscovered truth, and there must be great satisfaction in that.

Regrettably, although he never rejected the existence of God, he did admit to having become an agnostic on the subject, influenced by the apparent randomness and inevitable processes of nature. The evolution of all life on earth, including man, was and still is, in some quarters, considered an affront to the belief that the progress of the human race over time bears the unmistakable sign of the divine spark in our nature. But why can we not be content in our faith with the understanding that God's divine intelligence, which exists beyond time and space, and has left us to choose by the exercise of our free will whether to accept His grace or reject it, could have left nature to work its physical changes upon us? Let the earth spin on its axis, the galaxies expand, and nature change according to its own laws.

We have a second nature, a moral nature, that is not determined by ecological change but by the workings of our conscience. Is not our conscience and its effect upon our will enough confirmation for the believer that God, the Creator, has endowed us with the divine spark of His love to improve, if we so choose, our second nature in service to Him? It is enough, I believe, for anyone who can see in our struggle to be good a divine purpose, as we may still glimpse in the wonders of nature the divine intelligence that created it and set it all in motion.

When he began his voyage, Darwin was not an experienced scientist. He was a man with curiosity, courage, and good sense. "I worked to the utmost during the voyage," he later wrote, "from the mere pleasure of investigation, and my strong desire to add a few facts to the great mass of facts in natural science." It is hard for me to appreciate the history he made without seeing in its accomplishment the hand of providence, as I have seen it in the accomplishments of other human beings whose lives have spared us from ignorance or the ravages of illness or the evil that some of our species have done to others of us. God is not indifferent to our suffering nor has He left us bereft of hope that we might triumph someday over evil or the calamities of nature or the flaws in our own hearts.

God, nonbelievers claim, cannot be credited with the good in history without crediting Him with the evil as well, and with the sometimes cruel effects of indifferent nature. Why? To believe and follow God is our choice. Not all will follow. Our principal belief is in our salvation not in this life but the next. Man and nature, even at their cruelest, cannot deny us that, nor the gloriousness of His creation, a gloriousness that human qualities like curiosity have led us to appreciate with humility and awe. Time and the laws of nature do not expose the absence of God, Whose proofs are a matter for the heart to contemplate, a matter of faith.

Darwin helped explain nature's laws. He did not speculate, in his published theories at least, on the origin of life. He did not exclude God, for Whom the immensity of time is but a moment, from our presence. The only undeniable challenge the theory of evolution poses to Christian beliefs is its obvious contradiction of the idea that God created the world as it is in less than a week. But our faith is certainly not so weak that it can be shaken to learn that a biblical metaphor is not literal history. Nature doesn't threaten our faith. On the contrary, when we contemplate its beauty and mysteries we cannot quiet in our heart an insistent impulse of belief that for all its variations and inevitable change, before its creation, in a time before time, God let it be so, and, thus, its many splendors and purposes abide in His purpose. Even Darwin, the professed agnostic, curious man that he was, must have felt the attraction of that faith when he ended *The Origin of the Species* with the following testament to its effect: "There is grandeur in this view of life, with its several powers, having been originally breathed into a few forms or into one; and that, whilst this planet has gone cycling on according to the fixed law of gravity, from so simple a beginning endless forms most beautiful and most wonderful have been, and are being, evolved."

ENTHUSIASM

Theodore Roosevelt

*He led one of the most eventful lives in American history
and did it all with the delight and eagerness of a six-year-old boy.*

HISTORY IS OFTEN A CONTRARY CHARACTER WITNESS FOR THE MEN and women whose actions it records. Someday it would record that the war which our hero gloried in and which glorified him might have been as much his creation as it was the enemy's, perhaps even more so. Of course, that particular history would have to compete with the history he would himself write. Our hero was a man of many interests and talents. Library shelves would eventually groan under the weight of his forty books, many of them with multiple volumes. And no one expected him to leave the true record of the war, in which his own exploits figured so prominently, to the pen of some fussy scholar safely ensconced in his study, as far removed from the memory of that war as he had been from the actual drama when it occurred. He would make sure Americans were provided a true account of the necessary and glorious adventure, America's little war with Spain, that he was *deee-lighted* to have joined. And he was just the man to provide it to them, making sure, of course, to include a full account, accurate in every thrilling detail, of the events that began at dawn on July 1, 1898.

As the bugles sounded reveille that morning, and the summer sun began its ascent, promising another day of sweltering heat and humidity for the swamps and jungles of Cuba, an American artillery barrage signaled the start of the battle. Brigadier General

H. W. Lawton, commanding the U.S. 2nd Infantry Division, had begun his assault on Spanish forces entrenched in fortified positions on a small hill, El Caney. The battle plan directed two other divisions, Brigadier General J. F. Kent's 1st Infantry and Major General "Fightin' Joe" Wheeler's Cavalry Division, to march through a thick jungle and hold a position at the foothills of San Juan Heights. There they were to wait until the 1st Infantry finished its assault on El Caney and joined them for a massed attack on the heavily fortified Heights. Beyond them lay their ultimate objective, the city of Santiago, a Spanish stronghold. The assault on the Heights and siege of Santiago were expected to be the decisive battles of the war in Cuba. Spain's position would become hopeless if Santiago were taken, and the war could be concluded just a few short weeks after the American invading force had first reached Cuban shores.

On the eve of the battle, General William Rufus Shafter, who commanded the invasion force, learned that General Wheeler had contracted yellow fever as had Brigadier General Young, who commanded the division's 2nd Brigade. Colonel Leonard Wood, a regular army physician who had won a Medal of Honor fighting Apaches, was promoted to brigadier general, and assumed command of Young's brigade. Wood's previous command, the brigade's First U.S. Volunteer Cavalry Regiment, popularly known as the "Rough Riders," went to Wood's subordinate and friend, who was promoted to colonel.

The promotion was appropriate. The young volunteer colonel, in his tailored Brooks Brothers uniform, had almost single-handedly raised the regiment himself, supported it financially, and had recruited most of the Rough Riders, a curious mix of Eastern aristocrats, Western ranchers, buffalo soldiers, and Indians, whose flamboyance was only equaled by their zeal for combat. Many of the Westerners in the regiment had been in a fight or two before. Few of the Eastern officers and men had seen any action more dangerous than the playing fields of their Ivy League schools. Their colonel, a Harvard man and politician from New York City, had been in a few scraps in the years when he had escaped sorrow by fleeing to the badlands of North Dakota, where he had a ranch, and where a few outlaws had been surprised to discover that the nearsighted Eastern dude, with the high-pitched voice, was a lot tougher than he looked.

In a furious battle, less than a week before, the Battle of Las Guasimas, the very same dude had proven his mettle to the Rough Riders. He had led them with the cool assurance of a veteran soldier, and with conspicuous bravery, though it was his first experience of combat. To borrow the animal metaphor he used, he had shown them how Theodore Roosevelt behaved "when the wolf rises in the heart."

Within moments of the opening American salvo, Spanish gunners on San Juan Hill, the highest promontory on the opposing ridge, answered with a barrage of their own. Shells began to rain down on the Rough Riders, killing a number of them. Wood and Roosevelt ordered their troopers into the cover of the jungle, and when the Spanish shelling ceased two hours later, they moved as quickly as they could through the thick mud and oppressive heat. Snipers' bullets ripped through leaves and tree limbs, dropping troopers in their wake. They splashed across a creek through a hail of bullets, and hustled into the clearing on the other side at the foot of the San Juan Hill. When they looked up to the hill's crest they saw a blockhouse, other fortifications, artillery, and soldiers filling several lines of trenches. It was a formidable position to assault from below. A great many Americans would die trying.

To their right, on the other side of a little creek, lay Kettle Hill, where they were to take up their positions and wait with the rest of the division for the 1st Infantry to begin the charge up San Juan, and for Lawton's 2nd Infantry to complete their assault on El Caney and join them. As his troopers crawled through the tall grass, they soon realized they were exposed to fire from little Kettle Hill, where Spanish soldiers were unexpectedly entrenched and armed with deadly German Mauser rifles. Roosevelt, the only man on horseback, barked at his troops to take what cover they could. In his memoirs, he recounted, "the Mauser bullets drove in sheets through the trees and the tall jungle grass."

The Rough Riders had been ordered to remain and support the main assault on the ridge after it began. But Roosevelt knew his present situation was untenable. Other regiments took up their positions to the left and right of Roosevelt's troopers. The fire grew so intense that Roosevelt dismounted and stretched flat on his belly, making himself a less conspicuous target than was his usual tendency. His best officer, Captain Bucky O'Neil, formerly the sheriff of Prescott, Arizona, was cut down by a Mauser just after he had bragged that the Spanish bullet had never been made that could kill him. They remained there for two hours, as other units took their positions in front of them, hunkered down in the teeth of the withering fire.

The 1st Infantry began its slow, treacherous ascent up San Juan Hill as a frustrated Roosevelt watched his men being slaughtered in their exposed positions. He dispatched one messenger after another to find General Wood and ask for permission to lead a charge up Kettle Hill. Just as the first messenger turned to carry out the order, he collapsed in Roosevelt's arms, bleeding from a fatal bullet wound. The next three messengers all returned, having failed to reach Wood. Roosevelt, as was his habit, was about to take matters into his own hands, when a courier handed him a message instructing him to support the assault. The circumstances being as urgent and lethal as they were, Colonel Roosevelt intended to do a bit more than just support the assault. He intended to lead it. And so, he later recalled, "my crowded hour began."

Galloping in front of his lines, he called his men to move forward. When one man seemed reluctant to follow, Roosevelt shouted at him, "Are you afraid to stand up when I am on horseback?" When they reached a regular army cavalry unit, cowering under heavy fire at the base of Kettle Hill, he ordered them to stand up and charge. They refused. He was not their colonel. He was only a volunteer officer, and they weren't going to get themselves killed for someone whose authority they needn't obey. So he ordered them to get out of the way and let his Rough Riders through. With a cheer, the Rough Riders began to run up the hill. Their gallant colonel spurred his little horse in front of them as a hail of Mauser bullets whistled through the heavy air around him. When he and his orderly reached a barbwire fence a few dozen yards from the top, he quickly dismounted, climbed through the wire, raced to the crest, and with his pistol shot the first Spanish defender who dared oppose him. In a moment, the other Rough Riders crested the hill, along with the regular troopers who had been shamed into action. The Spanish defenders fled toward Santiago.

The triumphant Roosevelt looked to his left to see the infantry struggling under merciless Mauser and artillery fire to take San Juan. He directed his troopers' fire at the enemy blockhouse from where Spanish riflemen were murdering Americans below. When the infantry resumed their charge up San Juan, he scrambled over tangled bales of barbwire and began to run down Kettle Hill to join them. When he turned around, only a few of his troopers were with him. He turned back, cursed at his men, and ordered them to follow. By the time they reached the top of San Juan, the battle was over. The surviving defenders had also retreated toward the walls of Santiago, a mile away. Eighty-nine Rough Riders had been killed in the assault. Miraculously, he was not among them. But they had given a good account of themselves. As soon as the war correspondents sent their dispatches to their newspapers, Roosevelt would become a national hero, and was nominated for a Medal of Honor. He surveyed the awful carnage, the torn earth, the battered defenses, his brave fallen comrades, the trenches filled with enemy dead, and pronounced himself delighted with the day.

Santiago, itself, wouldn't fall until after the Spanish Caribbean fleet had been sunk in Santiago Bay by American warships, and the surrounded city had endured two weeks of sporadic American artillery fire. By August, with both Cuba and the Philippines lost, the Spanish government accepted the terms of a cease-fire. Roosevelt had to wait several weeks, while his troops were being decimated by yellow fever, before ships arrived to carry them to Long Island and home, his "crowded hour" at an end.

Or so he thought. In truth, his entire life, before and after the Battle of San Juan Heights, was as crowded with breathtaking activity and stunning accomplishments as any life it has ever been my pleasure to admire. He wasn't quite forty years old when he returned from Cuba. And a cursory glance at his life before Cuba will leave the most industrious, accomplished, and high-spirited reader shamefaced for priding him or herself on her enthusiasm for life.

There has only been one TR, and there will never be another.

He was born into the aristocratic Roosevelt family in 1858. He was small and sickly, terribly nearsighted, and plagued by asthma that left him chronically breathless. His father, who was the greatest influence on his life, and whom he loved more than any other, took him for carriage rides in the evenings so that the cool night air might restore regular breathing to his gasping child. Despite the crowded duties of the respected and civic-minded reformer, the older Roosevelt never deprived his son of loving attention. He massaged the boy's back, calmed his fears, and encouraged him to defy his physical handicap, build his willpower, and strengthen his body. The dutiful son complied, and pushed himself with exercise, sports, and sheer bloody-minded determination to begin his lifelong crusade to become a vigorous, exuberant outdoorsman.

He marveled at the natural wonders of the world, becoming quite a gifted natural historian and budding ornithologist. He accrued a vast collection of natural specimens, particularly birds, which he happily killed for science and the pleasure of the hunt. (His acute hearing enabled him to distinguish different birdsongs from great distances.) He swam and fished and hunted and rowed and hiked and rode on horseback whenever he could. His mind was as eager as was the body he willed to health. He traveled widely with his parents, and committed to his impeccable memory everything he observed. He was a voracious reader, and could devour several books in a day on every subject imaginable, from natural history to military science. He built a library that would rival a university's. And he forgot nothing. Years later he would amaze dinner guests by reciting without mistake a poem or essay he had read decades before.

By the time he entered Harvard College, he possessed knowledge of some subjects that surpassed the learning of his professors. In his senior year, he wrote a treatise on the naval history of the War of 1812 that would become his first published book, and was studied at the United States Naval Academy well into the twentieth century. His mother, whom he doted on, had come from a Southern seagoing family, and had raised him on thrilling tales of adventures at sea. His own service would be in the army cavalry, but his first and last military love would always be the navy.

He was a companionable young man, if somewhat eccentric, and easily made friends, who were drawn to his high spirits and his vibrant, fascinating conversation. But he didn't share the indulgences of the other privileged youth who followed their fathers to Harvard. He had, to be sure, a romantic temperament, but he was a scrupulously moral boy. He did not smoke or drink, and would never offend God and womankind by pressing unseemly affections on a young lady. And he could not abide, under any circumstances, indolence.

In his second year at Harvard he suffered the biggest blow of his young life. His beloved father, Theodore Roosevelt, Sr., died of stomach cancer. His son was emotionally distraught, almost unbalanced at times, in his inconsolable grief. "I think I should almost go crazy," he worried. But within months he had steeled himself to his duty, which he always conceived in noble and romantic imagery. "My duty is clear—to study well and live like a brave Christian gentleman."

He spent a few weeks before the start of his junior year living in Maine's north woods with a rugged outdoorsman, lumberjack, and hunting guide, Bill Sewall, who became his lifelong friend. He was still a skinny kid, with thick spectacles. His constitution looked fragile to those who didn't know him, but he impressed the older man immediately, carrying as much in his pack on their hunting trip as Sewall, sharing the chores, keeping the pace in their canoe, hiking for endless distances through all kinds of weather, swimming in freezing water, and falling exhausted into sleep beneath the stars.

When he graduated magna cum laude from Harvard in 1880, he really got busy. He married the beautiful Massachusetts debutante with whom he had fallen hopelessly in love, Alice Hathaway Lee. He attended Columbia law school, studying for the profession he would never practice. At twenty-three, he was the youngest man ever elected to the New York State Assembly, where he immediately won widespread recognition as a brash and scathingly outspoken scourge of corrupt machine politics. Two years later, he won his third term with more votes than any other legislator received, and was elected leader of the Republican minority. In the summer of 1883, he bought land at Oyster Bay on Long Island, where he intended to build an immense home with Alice. When it was completed, he called it Sagamore Hill. He also traveled to the Dakota Territory that summer and bought two cattle ranches, leaving Alice behind, pregnant with their first child.

The following February, tragedy again struck. His beloved mother died. A few hours later, in the same house, the wife he adored died after giving birth to their daughter, Alice. He wrote in his diary that devastating evening, "The light of my life has gone out." He ended the epitaph he wrote for Alice's funeral with, "For joy or for sorrow my life has now been lived out." But it hadn't. His greatest accomplishments still lay ahead. "It was a grim and an evil fate," he wrote a friend, "but I never have believed it did any good to flinch or yield for any blow, nor does it lighten the blow to cease from working."

He quit the assembly that summer, commissioned the construction of his house on Oyster Bay, left his infant daughter with his sister, and traveled to Chicago as a delegate to the Republican National Convention, which nominated a man he despised, James Blaine, for president. He left Chicago for his ranches in the badlands, where he remained, on and off for two years, with his friend Bill Sewall. Within weeks of his arrival he had stood up to the local bullies, who thought him a ridiculously pampered Eastern snob. He rambled on horseback, shooting various game on long and arduous hunting expeditions. And he firmly established his local celebrity when he single-handedly chased, apprehended, and marched fifty miles to the nearest jail a gang of hardened outlaws who had stolen a boat he owned.

He returned to New York and politics in 1886, ran for mayor of New York City, and was beaten. That December, he married Edith Kermit Carow, a childhood friend, and moved with his new wife and two-year-old daughter to Sagamore Hill. He and Edith would add five more children to the family. In 1889, he was appointed a U.S. Civil Service commissioner in the administration of President Benjamin Harrison, serving in the office for six tumultuous years as he further enhanced his reputation as a crusading, rhetorically inflammatory political reformer who never saw shades of gray, mistrusted compromise, and woke up every day armed for the good and ready to fight the wicked. In 1895, he brought his by now famous zeal for reform to the notoriously corrupt New York City Police Department as a police commissioner. He often walked a beat at night searching out evildoers, some of whom happened to be policemen.

In 1897, he resumed his career in federal government as an assistant secretary of the navy, where he completely overwhelmed the aging, hapless secretary, John Long, with the fantastic, frantic pace of his industry, and his determination to wrest Cuba from Spain's control. He agitated, schemed, and prepared for the war he knew must come. When it did, after the U.S.S. battleship *Maine* exploded in Havana Harbor (probably by accident), the Pacific Fleet, and its commander, Admiral Dewey, were already in the Philippines and ready to sink the entire Spanish Pacific fleet in Manila Harbor. Roosevelt had sent them there, prepared for action, without bothering to inform Secretary Long. Then Roosevelt quit the navy, raised the Rough Riders regiment, trained with them in Texas, and went to Cuba to live his crowded hour.

Over the course of the preceding twenty years, he had also written and published thirteen books, including his influential four-volume history, *The Winning of the West*. He would write twenty-seven more, and die while working on another.

One would be forgiven for experiencing the fatigue the subject never seemed to suffer from even this bare recitation of the first part of Roosevelt's life. But fatigue is not something Roosevelt particularly troubled himself about. He had a lot left to do.

Three months after he returned from Cuba he was elected governor of New York. In a little more than a year, the reforms he was trying to ram through the legislature so alarmed the party bosses, they decided the best thing to do was get him out of the way by putting him on the ticket with the popular incumbent president, William McKinley, who was running for reelection in 1900. The vice presidency had few real responsibilities, and the bosses figured Roosevelt could do little harm to their ambitions in the largely ceremonial office.

McKinley's chief advisor and masterful political strategist, Mark Hanna, was worried, however, knowing that the vice president was the constitutional successor to the president should the latter die in office. But few vice presidents ever succeeded the president they served under, and he went along with the plan. When McKinley won the election, with Roosevelt as his vice president, Hanna groused to party leaders, "Don't any of you realize that there's only one life between this madman and the White House?" In September 1901, his fears were realized when an anarchist named Leon Czolgosz shot and killed McKinley in Buffalo, New York. Now, Hanna lamented, "That damned cowboy is in the White House."

At forty-two, Roosevelt was the youngest man ever to serve as president, and he was, as always, a hurricane of activity and sweeping ambition. In 1899, he had lectured the members of Chicago's Hamilton Club on the morality of individuals and nations. "I wish to preach, not the doctrine of ignoble ease," he told them, "but the doctrine of the strenuous life; the life of toil and effort; of labor and strife." It was his personal code of conduct and his governing philosophy. "A mere life of ease," he warned, "is not in the end a very satisfactory life," for people or for nations. It corrupts individuals and governments and "ultimately unfits those who follow it for serious work in the world."

Experience had taught him to be a shrewd political pragmatist, but in his heart and public speeches he was ever the moral absolutist, who loved a good fight, seeing in every struggle a clear contest between good and evil. Intent on purging party bosses of control over political patronage and government policy, he infused the creaky machinery of government with his own prodigious energy. He brought the first successful antitrust suit against a monopoly of J. P. Morgan and other powerful railroad barons, the first of forty similar lawsuits. Over the objection of management, he negotiated an end to a huge coal miners' strike, and established himself as an ardent foe of avaricious Wall Street financiers and labor bosses who approved violence to secure their goals. He passed laws to improve the safety of food and drugs. He imposed sweeping regulations on interstate commerce. He claimed millions of acres of pristine wilderness for a new national park system.

His conduct of American foreign and military policy was even more energetic and forward-looking. He built up the navy and threatened Germany and other European powers, which had designs on colonies in the Western Hemisphere. He fomented a rebellion in Colombia that gave birth to the Republic of Panama, from which he secured the rights to dig his big ditch, his grand Panama Canal, which would make America a great sea power in two oceans. He negotiated a peace treaty between Russia and Japan, for which he won a Nobel Peace Prize. When an American, Ion Perdicaris, was taken captive by a Moroccan thug, Mohammed el-Raisuli, he sent the sultan a blunt one-sentence warning. He wanted "Perdicaris alive or Raisuli dead." He got Perdicaris alive. Hugely popular, he was reelected to a second term by an immense margin. Near the end of his last term, he sent his huge new navy, "the Great White Fleet," around the world to show Japan and Europe and Americans that the United States was now and would forever remain a great world power. When Congress balked at providing him the funds for this global show of strength, he dispatched the fleet to Asia, and told Congress they would have to come up with the money to bring the ships back.

He was the first president to ride in an automobile, submerge in a submarine, fly in an airplane. He was the first to travel outside the country and the first to invite a leading African American, Booker T. Washington, to dinner at the White House. To every endeavor, personal and political, he brought the full measure of his zest for life. He railed at his opponents with the most colorful invective imaginable. They had backbones of chocolate éclairs and bananas. They were malefactors of great wealth, a mobocracy, muckrakers. And he ascribed to his resolute determination to forge a new nationalism of great power and purpose the American nobility of Lincoln and Washington.

Amid the constant demands of politics and his ambitious governance, he found time for his six rambunctious children, chasing them around the White House they had filled with their laughter, games, toys, and substantial animal menagerie. He took frequent hikes in the park, rode horseback as often as possible, swam in the Potomac River, and boxed with professional fighters in the East Room, suffering cuts, bruises, and the occasional cracked rib. He shook every hand extended to him, kissed every infant presented him, and pronounced to one and all that the whole experience of being Teddy Roosevelt was just "bully!" "The President," a British diplomat observed, "is about six." His secretary of state, who had once worked as personal secretary to Abraham Lincoln, exclaimed approvingly that Roosevelt was "more fun than a goat."

He left office in 1908, following the election of his friend and chosen successor, William H. Taft, and soon departed for an extended safari in Africa. When he returned with a great quantity of trophies, and the notes he would use to publish yet another book, the allure of politics seized him again. Angry that Taft had allowed the political bosses to recover their control over government, TR ran for the party's presidential nomination in 1912. He won all of the primaries, but party leaders gave the nomination to Taft anyway. So he ran for president as the head of a new progressive party, the Bull Moose party, a metaphor for the vigor of their candidate, promising a "square deal" to all Americans. He lost, but not by much. Near the end of the campaign, while he gave a speech in Milwaukee, a deranged potential assassin fired a pistol at his chest. The bullet passed through a copy of his typically long speech folded in his breast pocket and his metal eyeglass case before it came to rest near his heart. Knowing he had been wounded but not mortally, Roosevelt milked the moment for all it was worth. The doctors looked at the bleeding wound, and urged him to leave immediately for the hospital. TR waved them away.

In considerable pain but thrilled with the drama of the occasion, he informed his audience that he had just been shot, "but it takes more than that to kill a bull moose. The bullet is in me now, so I cannot make a long speech." No one need worry about him, he assured his awestruck listeners. Even if the worst were to happen, "no man has had a happier life than I have led, a happier life in every way." With his matchless industry, courage, and irrepressible enthusiasm for a life that was a "great adventure," Theodore Roosevelt had willed himself and his country to greatness.

After the 1912 campaign, he left for one more great adventure with his son Kermit on the River of Doubt in Brazil's Amazon jungle. He contracted malaria and nearly died. When he recovered he had lost some of his vitality but hadn't surrendered an ounce of his enthusiasm. He wrote more books, gave more speeches, planned to run for president again, and urged his country to join the Great War raging in England. When America did enter the war, he offered to raise a regiment of volunteers and lead them in combat. President Wilson refused the offer. Crushed, he watched as his four sons left for the big adventure, wishing he could join them. When his youngest child, Quentin, was killed over France in an airplane, the old bull moose finally met an opponent too formidable to overcome, though he struggled mightily to do so. He replied to a condolence letter by acknowledging his grief to the correspondent, yet stressed that no father could have asked more for a child. Quentin had "had his crowded hour, he died at the crest of life, in the glory of the dawn." But family and friends worried that the loss, as well as effects of the fever he had suffered in the Amazon, were draining too much of his enormous life force. He was often observed in the stables at Sagamore Hill, patting the little pony that had belonged to his dead son.

Still he tried to outrace his sorrows. He published his last book, *The Great Adventure,* began work on another, and plotted a final run for the presidency in 1920. He died in his sleep from a coronary embolism on January 6, 1919. He was only sixty years old. The vice president of the United States, Thomas Marshall, expressed the nation's admiration for the man who had fired their imaginations with notions of greatness, delighted them with his joyous exuberance, and captured their hearts by embracing them in the warmth of his immense love for life, for people, and for his country. "Death had to take him while sleeping," Marshall observed. "If he had been awake, there would have been a fight."

There was only one TR, and there will never be another.

EXCELLENCE

Wilma Rudolph

She survived poverty, racism, and polio to become the fastest woman on earth.

THIS WAS WHAT THEY HAD COME TO SEE. IN A MOMENT, THEY WOULD rise in unison as the shot from the starter's pistol echoed in Rome's Olympic Stadium. They wanted to see if the graceful, regal-looking American girl with the impossibly long legs, whom all of Europe was calling La Gazelle Noire, the Black Gazelle, could do it again. Her previous successes had astonished them. But this race, the 400-meter relay, should prove the greatest challenge. She would anchor the team, running last among the four sprinters from Tennessee State University. Except for her, the Americans hadn't had a lot of success in the 1960 Olympics. The four German sprinters were favored, anchored by the blindingly fast Jutta Heine, who had arrived in Rome having never lost a race. Should the American team pull it off, in the oppressive heat and humidity of that early September afternoon, no one would ever deny that the twenty-year-old Gazelle was the fastest woman on earth. That had been the great ambition she had first confided to her coach, to be the "fastest woman on the track on earth," only a few years after she had proved her doctors wrong, and walked.

Blanche and Eddie Rudolph had already welcomed nineteen children into the world when little Wilma arrived on June 23, 1940, two months ahead of schedule. Blanche had fallen down and almost immediately gone into labor. Weighing a little over four pounds at birth, Wilma Glodean Rudolph wasn't expected to live long. That the newborn survived those first perilous weeks was an early indication of the strength she would employ to see herself safely through the many crises of her childhood.

Blanche and Eddie were extraordinary parents, hardworking and devoted to their children. But with twenty-two children (two more were born after Wilma), and each parent holding more than one job, Eddie as a railroad porter and handyman, Blanche a laundress and housekeeper, it was hard to give much attention to any individual child. Wilma would need a lot of attention, and would have little prospect of finding much help outside her family. The family's poverty and the injustices of the segregated South offered scant encouragement to the Rudolphs as they looked to their community in rural Clarksville, Tennessee, for the care that their lively but chronically ill daughter needed. But they did the best they could; for as poor as they were, they were rich in virtue, and gave their struggling child the love and encouragement she needed to believe she might one day be a healthy, happy little girl.

When Blanche came home to the Rudolph's crowded house after a long day toiling for wealthy white families, cooked dinner for the family, and finished sewing their clothes from used flour sacks, she often spent the last minutes of her day nursing little Wilma through the latest illness that had befallen her. Whatever childhood sickness afflicted any Clarksville family never passed without visiting Wilma. She suffered measles, mumps, chicken pox, and the whooping cough before she was four years old. Colds and the flu constantly plagued her. She spent most of her early childhood in bed. Clarksville's only hospital was reserved for white people, and there was only one black doctor in town. Blanche nursed Wilma with the various home remedies she was expert in administering, wrapping her little girl in blankets to sweat the fevers out of her.

Shortly before her fifth birthday, Wilma became very sick with scarlet fever and pneumonia in both her lungs. Again, she was not expected to survive. Her family covered her in blankets, plied her with the usual remedies, comforted her, and prayed. But the illness persisted. Even as the crisis began to abate, a strange symptom occurred that caused her worried family even greater alarm. Wilma's left leg began to twist to one side. When her parents encouraged her to move it, she told them she couldn't. The doctor was called, and after examining her briefly, he informed Eddie and Blanche that their daughter had been stricken with polio, for which there was then no known cure. If she survived, he warned them, she would never walk again.

Thus afflicted, Wilma Rudolph's life was, for all practical purposes, over. She was, despite her illnesses, a naturally happy child, sweet-natured and bright. But no one should have expected her to survive such a difficult childhood with those qualities intact. She would never be able to play as her brothers and sisters played. She might not even be able to attend school, and have to depend on her overburdened parents for her education. The therapy and medical care she needed, if she was to have any chance to learn how to live with some measure of independence, to be able to get around a little with crutches and a brace, would have to be provided by her family, and free of charge by the one overworked, generous, and kind doctor in town who would consent to treat black patients, and a black medical college fifty miles away in Nashville.

Human beings can endure great hardship and they can summon reserves of strength they never imagined they possessed. But this was an awful burden to place on such small, slender shoulders. And Wilma, almost from the moment of her diagnosis, fell into despair. Forced to remain at home when she reached school age, left to cry alone in her bed through the day, still plagued by frequent colds and bouts of flu, she felt the acute anguish of those who have lost hope. The worst times, she recalled, were the mornings, when she would press her face against the window and watch her brothers and sisters walk to school, and feel the terrible loneliness descend upon her again as she began another long and dreary day. "I was so lonely," she remembered, "and I felt rejected. I would close my eyes, and just drift off into a sinking feeling, going down, down, down."

Her family saved her. Their constant encouragement and care helped Wilma to overcome her despair, and summon such a great quantity of strength and courage, and an almost superhuman power of concentration, that she would in time become known as their miracle child. She attributed those qualities to the great fortune of having a loving family. "The doctors told me I would never walk," she wrote in her autobiography, "but my mother told me I would, so I believed my mother." One day, as Wilma felt the onset of another illness, she decided she would begin to fight. "Enough! No more taking everything that comes along, no more drifting off, no more wondering."

Every Saturday, Wilma and her mother made the trip to Meharry Medical College in Nashville, for heat therapy and massages, a two-hour round-trip, riding in the back of the bus as the laws of Jim Crow required. As the staff manipulated her paralyzed left leg, Wilma would bite her lip and fight back tears from the pain. Her mother watched her doctors and nurses carefully, and learned how to do therapy at home. She taught her other children how to do it as well. Four times a day, every day, either her mother or one of her older siblings would massage Wilma's leg, and then her mother would wrap it with a blanket and hot water bottle. Wilma, too, took responsibility for her rehabilitation, spending the hours she was alone at home doing exercises to strengthen her leg, bearing the pain they caused her with a growing confidence that she would walk again. Slowly, very slowly, she began to improve.

At first she could just hop on one leg to get around the house. By the time she was seven she had learned to walk with a leg brace and crutches, and was able to attend school for the first time. But her schoolmates, as children sometimes do, treated her disability as an object of ridicule. Maybe the fact that she was, through no fault of her own, different from other children frightened or intimidated them a little, and they reacted by making fun of her. Or maybe they simply succumbed to that aspect of human nature that urges us to seize opportunities to belittle others to prove our own superiority, which we must all guard against. Whatever their reason for hurting her, and she did suffer from their mistreatment, they could never prove themselves to be stronger than the tough, determined little girl they had laughed at.

Wilma fought every day for the next two years to learn to walk without crutches and brace. At first, she would attempt to stand for a moment or two without them, a little more each day. Then she began to take a few faltering steps unassisted. Finally, just before her tenth birthday, she decided to demonstrate to one and all that she had beaten polio.

On a Sunday morning she accompanied her family to church. When one of them held open the church door to allow Wilma to enter, she told them all to go in without her, and she would follow in a moment. Once her family had entered, she took off her brace, left her crutches on the ground, and walked with a limp into the church and up the aisle to the pew where her family was seated. Everyone she knew was there. Heads turned and hearts gladdened. Wilma had shown them all.

From then on she used her brace as little as possible, wearing special orthopedic shoes to walk. By the time she turned twelve, she and her mother had returned the brace to Meharry so that it could be given to a child who needed it. Not long after that, her mother happened to look out a window to watch her children shooting a basketball at the old peach basket they used for a hoop. There, jumping and running barefoot with her brothers and sisters, her orthopedic shoes tossed aside, was Wilma. For years she had watched her siblings play the game she had come to love, and dreamed of joining them. She was finally healthy, and could join in games just like any other kid.

During the long years of her rehabilitation, when few outside her family ever believed that day would come, Wilma had developed into a young girl with extraordinary reserves of strength, and had learned to pursue goals that were beyond the reach of most people with a tremendous intensity of resolve and concentration. She was not just a normal, healthy kid. She was special, and she knew it. Now that she had beat the odds and learned to walk again, she decided to focus her formidable strength on becoming an athlete. She intended to play basketball, and she intended to play it well, and not just well, but better than the children she had watched when she was still in her brace. Better than the best players on her school's team. She would play it with greater speed, agility, skill, and determination than any other girl in Clarksville had ever played it.

In the seventh grade, she pestered the coach, Clinton Gray, to let her join the girls' team at the all-black Burt High School. And then she pestered him to let her play. For the first two seasons she sat on the bench and seldom saw any playing time. The coach only let her play in the final minutes of the game when her team was well ahead. He might have thought that a girl who had been crippled for most of her life wouldn't have the endurance and speed to keep up with the other players. But he watched her in practice, and noted how much harder she worked than the other kids, how she focused more intently on her conditioning and on the endless repetition of the drills, how she kept dribbling, shooting, and running when her teammates were exhausted. Her coach called her Skeeter, he told her, because she was "little, fast, and you always get in my way."

In her third season, after she again begged Coach Gray to let her play, he let her start a game against a talented opposing team. For the first time, spectators saw Wilma Rudolph's stunning speed and athleticism. She was a speeding, pivoting, dribbling, shooting whirlwind, and her astonished teammates raised the level of their games just to keep up with her. They clobbered their opponents that night, and they would clobber one after another team in the weeks ahead. From that game on, Wilma was the star player on the best girls' basketball team in Tennessee. She made the all-state team twice. She once scored forty-nine points in a single game. In her sophomore year, she took Burt High School to the state finals, after scoring twenty-six points against their strongest rivals in the semifinals. The team they faced in the finals was not nearly as talented as the team they had just defeated. Wilma and her teammates made the mistake of assuming they would win. They lost their focus, and took their eye off the game ahead as they dreamed of celebrating a state championship. They were beaten, and Wilma was crushed. But she had learned a valuable lesson.

There are four things necessary to excel at a sport, or anything, for that matter: skill, concentration, willingness to struggle, and love. She had the skill. She loved basketball. And she had long ago proved that she could concentrate on her objectives, and struggle through the worst challenges life could throw at her. But in that game she had forgotten she must struggle to excel, and let her confidence and lack of respect for her opponent distract her. She would never make the same mistake again.

Despite the defeat, the referee in the game had seen something impressive in their star player. Ed Temple coached the women's track and field team at Tennessee State University. The Tigerbells, as they were called, had a growing reputation, as they were becoming one of the most dominant track and field teams in the country. He invited Wilma to his summer camps, and she eagerly accepted. Before the summer was out she had proven to be a very swift sprinter. "I don't know why I run so fast," she told Temple, "I just run." She said it made her feel like a butterfly in the wind. When classes resumed that fall, Wilma left high school every afternoon to practice with the Tigerbells.

When she was only sixteen, she made the American women's track and field team in the 1956 Olympic Games, which were held in Melbourne, Australia. She had nearly reached her full height, but was still a skinny kid, too skinny. At only eighty-nine pounds, she was gangly, all arms and legs, and she looked malnourished, as if a stiff wind would blow her away. She failed to survive any of the qualifying heats for the 100- and 200-meter races. But she did qualify for the 400-meter relay. She didn't run the anchor leg, but she and her teammates performed well enough to bring home a bronze medal. Wilma was delighted with the accomplishment, of course, but knew that she was capable of accomplishing much more than third place, even if it was third best in the world. And she knew if she struggled hard enough, and employed all her powers of concentration on her goal of being the fastest woman in the world, then she would, in fact, *be* the fastest woman in the world. Only someone who had never known her would have doubted it.

Four years and forty pounds later, at twenty and a healthy 138 pounds, she left with several of her college teammates for Rome. Her reputation as a sprinter was growing, but few fans of the sport were confident she would win a medal in individual competition. Jackie Robinson had predicted she would one day set a world record. But most thought that day still lay in the future. She was only twenty, after all, and could not be expected to have already reached the top of her game. Tennessee State had the best track team in the country, and the American 400-relay runners were all Tigerbells. They were expected to do quite well, and Wilma might win another medal in that competition. But even then, her teammate Lucinda Williams was considered the faster runner. In the individual races, the 100 and 200 meters, all anyone could talk about was the West German sprinter Jutta Heine, who had never lost a race. She, and not Wilma, was hailed as the fastest woman in the world.

In the early track competitions things didn't go very well for the Americans. The world's fastest runner, Ray Norton, was expected to win easily a gold medal in the 100-meter dash. He failed to win a bronze. Neither had any Tigerbell won a medal before Wilma's first race. The only American who was making any news in Rome was a young boxer from Louisville, Kentucky, and he was making a lot of it. Nineteen-year-old Cassius Clay had knocked down one opponent after another on his way to winning a gold medal, and eventually to becoming the most famous person in the world, Muhammad Ali.

Another bit of misfortune struck the Americans on the day before Wilma's first race. During a practice run for the 100 meters, Wilma had stepped into a hole in the infield and sprained her ankle. As she had learned all her life, and would later recount, "the triumph can't be had without the struggle." Her ankle swelled alarmingly and became discolored. She had it taped, tested its strength a few times, and got ready to run. For a girl who had been told she would never walk, a sprained ankle hardly qualified as a distraction.

The first thing you noticed when Wilma ran was how she exploded from the block, furiously pumping her arms to build up her astonishing speed. But her quick release and furious energy were not the most noticeable things about her running. People who saw her run never forgot her long, graceful strides after her initial burst of speed. She looked elegant and relaxed in a way that seemed to obscure the tremendous energy she was expending. She had grown very tall, six feet. It was her legs, taut and ropy and long, and her aristocratic bearing that reminded the spectators at Rome's Olympic Stadium of a gazelle, a particularly graceful, elegant, and fast gazelle. She had an easy smile and had become quite a beautiful young woman, as well as an athlete for whom the usual superlatives did inadequate justice.

As the sprinters stretched and paced around the infield in the minutes before the 100 meters, Ed Temple became alarmed when he didn't see Wilma among them. He sent a teammate to the locker room to look for her. She found her lying on the trainer's table. She had fallen asleep while being massaged. She had done all she could to prepare herself for the biggest race of her life to date. And as always, she had betrayed no anxiety before the event. Nothing seemed to make her anxious anymore. And she liked to catch a nap whenever the opportunity presented itself. She was calm, confident, and determined, and when her teammate woke her up, she was ready.

At the shot, she exploded. In less than a second she had blown by Jutta Heine, who would finish third, and Dorothy Hyman of Great Britain, who won the silver. She never looked back. When she crossed the finish line eleven seconds later, she had set a world record, but because the wind at her back blew over six miles an hour, a mile and a half over the allowable limit, the record was denied her. No one had ever seen a woman run as fast or as elegantly.

In the qualifying heats for the 200 meters the next day, she set another record, 23.2 seconds. She fought threw a stiff headwind to finish the final in twenty-four seconds, well ahead of her closest competitor. Again the crowd was awed by her speed, grace, and beauty, and by her long, flowing stride that made her speed seem effortless.

On the day of the 400-relay, the stadium filled beyond capacity, the crowd began first to chant and then roar, "Wilma. Wilma. Wilma," as the runners took their place. The Americans got off to a good start, fighting for the lead. The second Tigerbell took it, and Lucinda Williams, the third runner, had kept it as Wilma ran to take the baton from her and complete the race. Intent on her acceleration in the next moment, she took her eye off her immediate task, grasping the baton. She fumbled it. Had she dropped it the Americans would have been disqualified. She managed just to hold on to it but in the split second she had nearly lost it, two runners had blown by her. Jutta Heine was one of them.

The excited crowd gave an audible gasp when she fumbled the baton and groaned as Heine passed their Gazelle. Then they dropped their jaws in utter, disbelieving astonishment as Wilma pumped her arms like pistons and flew down the track with a blinding speed that caused her fans to joke later, "You would have missed it had you blinked." In seventy-five yards, she had retaken the lead, and seconds later crossed the finish line a little ahead of Jutta Heine.

It seemed quite a while before the crowd quieted down enough for the medal ceremony to begin. "The Star-Spangled Banner" could be heard as Wilma and her teammates bowed their heads to accept their gold medals. She was the first American woman to win three gold medals. And she was, beyond dispute, the fastest woman on earth.

The girl had beaten polio, poverty, and racism to become the greatest female athlete of her time, and one of the most beloved people in the world. She never raced in another Olympics. She would have surely done well, but she had already done her best. She had achieved excellence, and knew it couldn't be exceeded. So she turned her life to other worthy tasks.

The mayor of Clarksville, who had campaigned as an avowed defender of segregation, wanted to hold a parade to welcome Wilma home. In the strange customs of bigots, though, the affair would be restricted to whites. Wilma refused to participate until the mayor relented and allowed all the people of Clarksville to attend her parade. She insisted blacks be allowed to attend an awards banquet that night as well. They were the first integrated public events of that kind in the town's history. Sometimes, Wilma seemed more proud of that accomplishment than she was of her gold medals.

She might even have enjoyed it as much as she did another parade, a few days later. She rode in a pink Cadillac convertible through a black neighborhood in Louisville, with the brash and irrepressible Cassius Clay. The young boxer shouted to the crowd over and over again, "I am the greatest!" before he pointed at his beautiful, more modest, and broadly smiling companion, and declared, "This is Wilma Rudolph. She is the greatest!"

PART SEVEN

Love

A peace above all earthly dignities,
A still and quiet conscience
—HENRY VIII

SELFLESSNESS AND CONTENTMENT

Mother Teresa

She chose to live amid squalor and sickness and desperation,
endured hardship and endless toil, and might have
been the happiest person on earth.

IMAGINE A PLACE AS FAR REMOVED AS POSSIBLE FROM THE MATERIAL comforts that all but the least fortunate Americans enjoy. The image your mind conjures, however miserable, is unlikely to look as wretched and—we might be forgiven for assuming—as godforsaken as Moti Jihl in 1949, the Calcutta slum where human misery had sunk to its most extreme condition. But the little Albanian nun in her white and blue sari did not consider the place she had made her home to be lost to God's love. On the contrary, she believed the unfortunate souls who suffered there, though they had been abandoned by family and government and much of mankind, were no less loved by God than she was. Both she and they were vessels of His love.

One day, she happened upon a dying woman whose extremities had been partially devoured by rats, abandoned by her family and left on the filthy streets to endure the last days of her pitiful life in torment and despair. As she bent down to lift the unfortunate woman from the street and carry her to the nearest hospital, she smiled upon the face of Christ. For Mother Teresa, the multitudes of suffering outcasts who lived and died amid the squalor of Moti Jihl were not, as our own mental picture might suggest, the faces of the damned, but a portrait of Jesus "in distressing disguise." Jesus, who cried from the cross, "I thirst," existed in the person of these "poorest of the poor," and asks for our love by summoning our compassion for the least of His children. Mother Teresa, His most devoted servant, listened and followed.

I am obviously not the first admirer of Mother Teresa to offer a testament to her piety and profound compassion. But I could hardly claim to have represented in the lives of those I have chosen to include in this book a complete portrait of good character without sharing a brief appreciation for the life and works of this good woman, this saint of our times, whose mercy and sublime love for God and all His children touched the lives of millions, including mine. Few of us will ever live so perfectly in harmony with our conscience as she did. But few contemporary figures provide us with a better example of how to live a good life, to love as we were meant to love.

She was born in 1910, the youngest of three children in a prosperous family in what was then the Albanian province of the Ottoman Empire and is today Macedonia. Agnes Gonxha Bojaxhiu was raised in the Catholic Church although the vast majority of Albanians were Muslim. Her father, Nikola, and mother, Drana, were devout Catholics, generous to those less fortunate than they were, and affectionate but strict parents. Her father owned a construction company and an import business. Among Agnes's earliest memories of her father were his admonitions always to share their prosperity with the poor. He made certain to be an example of charity to his children, providing food, clothing, and shelter to those who needed it most. He was also an Albanian patriot. When the Balkan states rebelled against Turkish rule, he played an active role in the declaration of an independent Albanian state. It might have cost him his life. In 1919, while attending a dinner with other Albanian leaders, he fell mortally ill. Serbian partisans with designs on Albanian territory were suspected of poisoning him. He was only forty-five years old at his death. His youngest daughter was only nine.

Her mother was an even greater influence on Agnes. In their severely reduced circumstances following Nikola's death, Drana struggled to provide for her children by working as a seamstress. Yet despite their poverty, Drana was an admirably charitable woman who often cared for her less fortunate neighbors. Agnes's older brother, Lazar, remembered their mother always teaching them the virtue of charity, counseling them to do good "as if you were casting a stone into the depth of the sea." She was a pious woman, prayerful and selfless, who made certain her children were carefully raised in the teachings of their faith, and constantly involved in the activities of their church. Years later, long after mother and daughter were parted forever in this life, Drana counseled Agnes in a letter to remember why she had accepted the life of a Catholic missionary: "Dearest daughter, do not forget that you went out there to help the poor."

Agnes appears to have been most affected by her mother's piety and evident decency. She was a serious little girl, intent on living up to the moral example set by her parents. She wasn't severe or humorless or incapable of enjoying the warmth of her family's love, and was always a smiling, happy presence in their lives. But her siblings remembered that at an early age she seemed sensitive to some higher purpose than the typical mischief and play of children. When she was twelve she experienced her first call to a life of service to God.

A recently arrived parish priest, a Croatian Jesuit, Father Franjo Jambrenkovic, shared with his new parishioners the stories of Catholic missionaries who had devoted their lives to serving the desperate poor of India, and who had experienced great joy in return for their sacrifice. Agnes met several returning missionaries, and was greatly moved by their example of selfless love. When Father Jambrenkovic organized a youth lay association to promote the spirit of Christian benevolence, the Sodality of the Blessed Virgin Mary, she was its most active member. She soon felt pulled to follow the example of the missionaries whose lives had strengthened her commitment to her faith. When she asked Father Jambrenkovic how she could be certain that she had such a vocation, he answered that she would know the call was authentic if the prospect of it filled her with joy. Not long after, on an annual religious pilgrimage, Agnes prayerfully contemplated her vocation and the separation from her family and other sacrifices it would entail, and listened intently for God's response. The joy she experienced convinced her that God had spoken to her, and called her to Him. With her "heart about to burst," she decided, "I want to belong to God."

She was only eighteen when she bid her family farewell and left to join the Sisters of Loreto, an Irish order with missions in India. She would never see her mother and sister, Aga, again, and though their parting was tender and sad, she embarked on her new life having taken her mother's counsel to heart: "Put your hand in His hand and walk all the way with Him."

She spent several preparatory weeks in Ireland, and then boarded a ship bound for Calcutta, where the Sisters of Loreto had established a convent school. She arrived in January 1929, and was formally accepted as a novice in the order in May that year, and adopted the name Maria Teresa. She spent her first two years in Darjeeling, where novices were trained for the arduous life ahead in the cool environment of the Himalayan foothills. Shortly after she took her second vows in 1931, she was sent to work in a hospital in Calcutta where she had her first experience of serving the poorest of the poor. A terminally ill and blind child was given to her care, and she remembered how he became "the crowning joy of my weary day's work."

A few months later she entered the Loreto convent in Calcutta, which operated a large high school for relatively well-off Indian girls, and a smaller school, St. Mary's, which accepted children from poorer families. For the next nineteen years, Agnes, or, as she would soon be known, Mother Teresa, taught geography and history at St. Mary's. In 1937, she took her final vows, and soon after was appointed principal of both St. Mary's and the high school.

She loved her cloistered life in Calcutta. Though the convent was located near a notorious Calcutta slum, the Loreto Entally, as it was called, was housed in a comfortable and attractive compound. The company of her fellow nuns and their relationships with their pupils made for a warm and happy society that compensated the sisters for their separation from their families. She was a gifted educator, and was quite happy with her work and her life at the Entally. "I was," she remembered, "the happiest nun in Loreto."

In 1947, Mother Teresa became ill, and was believed to be suffering from the onset of tuberculosis. She traveled by train to Darjeeling to recuperate, or, as she recalled, "to participate in spiritual exercises." On the way, she heard quite clearly a command to leave the convent and devote herself completely to the care of the poor. She described the experience as "a call within a call," and she had no doubt Who's voice had commanded her. "I was sure this was the voice of God."

The Loreto sisters, as well as the archbishop of Calcutta, were not as certain as was Mother Teresa that it was in her or the Church's best interests to lose the services of such a capable educator. But she was sure. She had heard and she would follow. It was never any more complicated than that.

The archbishop instructed her to first write the Loreto's mother general for permission to work outside the convent. Mother Teresa, though she loved the Loreto order, knew that God expected her new life to be spent outside its security, in service to a new charitable order. The archbishop preferred that she remain within the Loreto even if she worked outside the cloister, and instructed her to seek Rome's permission to care for the poor as a Loreto sister. In 1949, two years after she first heard her call, Rome sent the permission to the archbishop, who instructed her priest, Father Celeste Van Exem, to inform Mother Teresa.

Father Van Exem asked to see Mother Teresa after Mass. He told her that she had received a response from Rome. She asked to be allowed a few moments of prayer before he shared the decision with her. When she returned, he told her that she was free to leave the Loreto sisters and begin a new mission of charity. She signed a few forms, looked at her smiling friend, and asked, "Can I go to the slums now?"

And so her life began anew. In those first months, she suffered from loneliness and anxiety. She had lived in the company of the Loreto sisters for half her life. She missed not only her work at the convent but the deeply satisfying companionship she had known in the cloister. But she never doubted her decision, for she believed it had not been hers to make or doubt. She chose the simple garment of India's poor, the sari, as her habit. She had two saris made of coarse white cotton with a blue border. To own only two was an example that a person needed just one change of clothes to remain clean. Then she departed for a hospital outside Calcutta for a few months' training as a practical nurse.

She returned on December 8, 1949, with no more than a dollar in her possession. She walked the streets of the Moti Jihl, and gathered the children of its desperately poor inhabitants around her in an outdoor school where she taught them. She was offered rooms in a nearby house, which would be her home for several years, as well as the home of novices to her charity, the young girls who had once been her students and now pledged their lives to God in service to the poor. Together they wandered the streets of Calcutta, ministering to its neediest, begging medicines from pharmacies, cleaning the filthy, educating the ignorant, loving the forgotten.

In 1950, the Church formally recognized their order as the Missionaries of Charity, and their numbers and duties increased. When Mother Teresa happened upon a dying woman in the streets, took her to the hospital, and refused to leave until the unfortunate sufferer was admitted, she recognized that the care of the dying was the purest expression of love. The streets of Calcutta in those days were crowded with the dying, who were considered by many Indians to be too vile to treat with respect or even pity. But they were nothing of the kind to the Missionaries of Charity, who lovingly spared them from dying "like an animal in the gutter." They lifted them from the gutter and carried them to a building the city had provided Mother Teresa. It was near the temple of a Hindu goddess, Kali, the goddess of death. The sisters named it Nirmal Hriday, a Bengali name: Pure Heart.

There the least of humankind achieved in the hour of their death through the loving ministrations of the sisters what they had never been allowed in life: dignity. For much of their lives they had been denied the comfort of another human being's touch. They had no mother to cool their fevered brow, no friend to hold their hand as they died. Now the smiling, gently encouraging women dressed in white and blue saris provided that comfort to them, and told them that to touch them was a privilege, because to touch them was to touch God.

At first many Indians treated the mission as sacrilegious, existing as it did approximate to a Hindu shrine, where those considered unclean, the destitute dying, were an offense to the goddess worshiped there. They threw rocks at the sisters and threatened them. Their anger subsided when the sisters took into their care a dying priest of Kali who had no one else to care for him.

People who have visited one of Mother Teresa's homes for the dying, even if for only an hour or two, are not likely to forget the experience. It isn't the memory of the horror of seeing people suffer the ravages of a painful disease or the torment of a life wasted in the most extreme poverty and isolation that they carry from there. Visitors recall the warm light that suffused the place, the tenderness and look of settled contentment that illuminated the sisters as they cleaned the wounds of and the dirt and human excrement from the bodies of their patients. The glow that seemed to arrive to the faces of those who had once been treated as nothing more than society's awful refuse in the moment before they would leave the suffering of this world forever. I have heard eyewitnesses recount these lovely mysteries too often to credit them to folklore. Love might not heal every wound or disease. But it heals the heart. Of that we need have no doubt.

In time, the Missionaries of Charity were joined by thousands of novices whom God had called to this great purpose, spread to the poorest corners of cities on every continent but uninhabited Antarctica, earned the admiration of countless thousands who supported their work, many of whom would donate a little of their time as well as their money to experience what Mother Teresa and her sisters experienced, contentment. As we hurry through our lives chasing our ambitions, contentment is seldom our reward. But it is all the reward the Missionaries of Charity have ever received in this world, and they know it to be a greater treasure by far than any other worldly possession.

The sisters had treated many lepers in their ministry to the poor. But these most reviled outcasts of Indian society needed a place where they could live free from the cruelty of people who took their affliction as a sign of God's contempt, and treated them as they would treat an animal with rabies. So Mother Teresa secured a land grant from the Indian government, and sought the funds to build a hospital, the first of eighty similar facilities, which the sisters called Shanti Nagar, or the City of Peace. There lepers could live with dignity, and know for the first time in their sad lives the blessing of mercy.

In 1955, the sisters opened the first of their children's homes for yet another class of forgotten Indians, the destitute and hopeless orphans of the poor. Many of the children had suffered a physical disability or serious illness at birth and were abandoned by their mothers in garbage heaps, back alleys, and doorsteps. The Missionaries of Charity welcomed them all. In her opposition to abortion, Mother Teresa beseeched young mothers to carry their unwanted babies to term. She would give them a home, and the love that their mothers denied them.

The children's homes have received many visits from curious patrons who wished to witness for themselves the healing power of love and mercy. Among them have been many Americans. Like those visitors who came away from the homes for the dying so moved by the experience, so, too, were visitors to the orphanages impressed with the ardor of the sisters' love for the children in their care. They were, in many instances, moved by the experience to make room in their own lives for the happiness they found there.

In 1993, my wife traveled with a medical team to Dacca, Bangladesh, where she visited one of Mother Teresa's children's homes. While there, she felt her heart drawn to the suffering of a three-month-old infant who had been born with a cleft palate, and was unable to take nourishment. The sisters worried that the child would starve to death despite their efforts to save her. A few days later, I stood at the Phoenix airport to welcome my wife home as she carried the daughter we would name Bridget. Now thirteen years old, Bridget has had several surgeries to correct her birth defect, and has endured them all with her usual grace and grit. She is a source of pride to her parents, and the vessel that has carried to our hearts, amid the distractions and commotion of our busy lives, the happiness derived from placing another's life before your own.

Mother Teresa became an international celebrity, a living saint to many, the most admired person in the world. But her celebrity hardly affected her humility or devotion to her causes. She knew, better than most, that the contentment and happiness she experienced in her life were not the advantages of celebrity but the rewards of sacrificing for and loving others. She used her celebrity to further her missions so that others might know the happiness that was hers.

A papal declaration in 1965 allowed her to expand her charities worldwide, establishing their first mission outside India, in Venezuela. Many other missions in dozens of countries soon followed. Her order grew to embrace thousands of sisters. Tens of thousands of volunteers serve in the order's homes for lepers, orphanages, hospices for AIDS patients, soup kitchens, schools, and homes for the dying. She became an inveterate world traveler, preaching her gospel of mercy and love to all who would listen, and seeking support for her many causes. She never begged for money; she said, "I have come to give you a chance to do something beautiful for God."

She received innumerable awards from admiring philanthropic organizations around the world. And in 1979, she received the Nobel Peace Prize. "With her message she is able to reach through to something innate in every human kind," the award committee recognized, "if for no other purpose than to create a potential, a seed for good. If this were not the case, the world would be deprived of hope, and work for peace would have little meaning." In her acceptance speech, she told the audience, "How can you love God whom you do not see, if you do not love your neighbor whom you see, whom you touch, with whom you live. . . . Love, to be true, has to hurt." She asked the committee to cancel the dinner they had proposed in her honor, and use the money it would have cost to "feed four hundred children for a year."

In Lebanon in 1982, she somehow managed to convince both the Palestinians and Israelis in the intense heat of a raging war to honor a cease-fire long enough for her to rescue the children of an orphanage trapped in the crossfire. Five years later, she won permission from Soviet authorities for her sisters to open homes in the city of Chernobyl to treat sufferers of the worst nuclear disaster in history, despite the radiation that still plagued the city.

As age and a chronically weak heart caused her physical decline, she kept the needs of others before her own. She considered retiring from the leadership of the Missionaries of Charity in 1989, but the sisters refused to let her. So she continued, through several heart attacks, to find and love her God where He lived "in distressing disguise." She left this world for her eternal reward in 1997. The whole world, with its many faiths, mourned her loss. Her funeral rites were conducted at an indoor stadium in Calcutta that held fifteen thousand people. Over half the mourners present were poor people, those whom she had loved and who had loved her best. Pope John Paul II, who revered Mother Teresa and knew her to be a saint, sent the Vatican's secretary of state to officiate.

She had critics. Some found fault with her relationships with supporters who possessed less than sterling character. Some disagreed with her opposition to abortion, though I don't know how we could have expected any less of a person who loved so deeply every child she ever encountered. Some accused her of mismanaging the finances of her charities. Some thought it hypocritical that Mother Teresa sought care for her own illness in modern medical facilities when the care her sisters provided the poor was less professional and advanced. Though I imagine that had the most expensive hospitals and clinics in the world admitted free of charge the destitute patients of the Missionaries of Charity, Mother Teresa and her sisters would have been only too willing to see them treated there. She gave her love, as much love as it is possible to give, to those who had been unloved for much if not all their lives. Even if all her sisters could provide was a comfortable and love-filled space to die in, a clean bed, and a few consoling words that God loved the least of His children, it was a great deal more than the rest of the world had done for them.

Although we are the only creatures on earth with reason, we do not always make the best use of that facility. We sometimes, out of intellectual vanity or an eccentric desire to differ from the consensus (a fault I have often been accused of, with merit, on occasion), dispute the obvious. In many instances we mean no harm. But to reject the deep morality, the godliness, of someone who has sacrificed virtually every day of her life to serve her God among the most scorned, reviled, tormented, and forsaken of His children, is, I think, an eccentricity that has descended into something less benign.

By political conviction we tolerate anyone's religious views or lack of them so long as they don't interfere with the practice of others. And so we must accept even views we find reprehensible so long as the rest of us are free to deny them. Liberty is an obligation to defend the rights of fools no less than the wise. But I cannot help but think that the critics of Mother Teresa, who never claimed perfection for herself but was closer to it than any of us will ever reach, have at a minimum lost a sense of the possibilities in the habits of the human heart. Perhaps some arrived at their unreasonable conclusions with motives that were better than their judgment. Some might just enjoy being the authors of controversy.

Some might deride her out of a conviction that we are all better off without believing in God because even those who have professed a religious belief have sometimes led humanity astray. Out of a dark fear, they are thus moved to denounce those who do good works in the name of God. But even atheists, I would think, who have enough wisdom to entertain the possibility that they are fallible, would be better off, happier even, by showing respect for the life of selfless love and unending toil that was so evidently Mother Teresa's. For to deny Mother Teresa is, in that instance at least, to deny even the possibility that there is a God, and that He loves us.

Those of us who are troubled by the few, excessive criticisms of Mother Teresa experience the fight rise in our heart when we hear them. That's a natural reaction, but it hardly does Mother Teresa any justice. Her mercy and her love earned her not only a reward in heaven but surpassing contentment, the contentment of an untroubled conscience. Her life was joyous amid the heartbreaking suffering and squalor whose victims she accepted as her duty to comfort. Whether others have devised systems to alleviate suffering more effectively or more inexpensively isn't really the point. No one ever did it with more love than Mother Teresa. But why should we fight about it? She never needed us to defend her honor, even when she was still among us. She loved and was loved, and her happiness was complete.

In the prison I lived in so far from here, and so very long ago, I served with men of extraordinary character, honorable men, strong, principled, wise, compassionate, and loving men. Better men than I, in more ways than I can number. As I mentioned earlier, we were often treated cruelly. For several years we were tortured by our captors. Some of us were beaten terribly, and worse. Some were killed. Sometimes we were tortured for information that could be used to help our enemy fight the war, and sometimes for information they could use against other prisoners. Most often, they tortured us to compel us to make statements criticizing our country and the cause we had been asked to serve. Many times, they would briefly suspend the torture and try to persuade us to make the statement by promising that no one would hear what we said or know we had sacrificed our integrity. Just say it, and we will spare you any more pain, they promised, and no one, no one will know. But the men I had the honor of serving with always had the same response. *I will know. I will know.*

That, dear reader, is good character. And I hope it is your destiny, your choice, your achievement, to hear the voice in your own heart, when you face hard decisions in your life, to hear it say to you, again and again, until it drowns out every other thought: *I will know. I will know. I will know.*

AFTERWORD

A WISER MAN THAN I ONCE EXPLAINED THAT TO LIVE A GOOD LIFE ALL YOU have to do is become less selfish on the way out than you were coming in. I used to think that sounded easy. But it's not. It takes many special habits of the heart and the mind to achieve. It's the hardest work of anyone's life. But it is the work that will make you the happiest. It takes strength, not physical strength, but moral strength, the strength to sacrifice for an ideal. It takes understanding and wisdom and a mind that questions beliefs and conventions that the heart suspects are false. And it takes love, love for something greater than yourself, love that is much more than desire or affection. It is a love that does not yield to disappointment or suffering, but recognizes and defends the good in this world, and in that purpose finds true happiness.

Selfishness is the enemy of these qualities and of happiness. The happiest people might not be the luckiest or the safest or the most comfortable or the most popular. But they are, I have observed, the least selfish. They are those people who are less selfish today than they were yesterday, and less selfish tomorrow than they are today. And on and on, day after day, until, many years later, they look back on their life and are happy to see that it was good, not perfect, not without mistakes, not without disappointment and hurt, maybe not all they once dreamed it would be, but good.

It is not my place to teach you these truths. But old men always seem to have more to say than the young care to hear. It's a bad habit, but we mean no harm. Perhaps it's because we have fewer choices of our own left to make, and fewer chances left to improve our character, that we cannot help but want to meddle with yours. So bear with me for one more reminiscence. It is a story of good character taught to me by men who had more of it than I have.

ACKNOWLEDGMENTS

MARK AND I ARE NOT PROFESSIONAL WRITERS. IF THAT IS NOT EVIDENT to the reader, honesty obliges us to give much of the credit to others. Jon Karp, our editor, has once again expertly guided us. He conceived the idea for the book; suggested the format; assured us we could do it; and, as always, edited the manuscript with intelligence, sensitivity, and passion for its subject. We owe him a debt we cannot hope to repay.

We are also blessed with a wonderful agent, Flip Brophy, our wise counselor, forceful advocate, and expert hand-holder. There never would have been a first book, much less a fourth, but for her encouragement, advice, and determination.

We are proud to write for the best publishing house in the business, Random House, and are very grateful to the many gifted people there who do so much to make our talents appear more credible than they are. In particular, we wish to thank our superb publisher, Gina Centrello; editor-in-chief Dan Menaker; deputy publishers Elizabeth McGuire and Anthony Ziccardi; associate copy chief Dennis Ambrose; copyeditor Karen Richardson; designer Barbara Bachman; publicity directors Carol Schneider and Tom Perry; and publicist Jynne Martin. It has always been a great reassurance to us to be in such capable hands. We want to give a special word of thanks to three people: Cathie Bleck, the illustrator whose very fine work in this book has improved its quality significantly; and Jonathan Jao and Jillian Quint at Random House, two people who stepped in during a certain transition period and helped calm the writers' nerves. Thank you very much.

Lastly, we remain in perpetual indebtedness to our wives, Cindy and Diane, and our children. If we don't always have their approval, we've been blessed with their forbearance and their love, which has made everything possible.

SOURCES

B OTH AUTHORS SAW THE LAST OF YOUTH QUITE A WHILE AGO, WHICH MEANS we are capable of marveling at today's conveniences. It seems so little time has passed since legal pads, typewriters, periodical guides, and card catalogs were the tools of research and writing. Now we live in the accelerated age of laptops, Google, and Wikipedia, placing a Worldwide Web of information at our fingertips and economizing for even the most leisurely writer the thing we prize the most and possess the least of, time. The sources of information cited below on which the authors relied include, as you will see, a great many Web sites. We readily recommend them to readers who are interested in learning more about the lives we have briefly profiled. Of course, we recommend the books we cite as well, for we know you will enjoy them as much as we did. Happily, reading books remains among the most satisfying of experiences. As a means of transporting us into other lives and times, they still have no equal, even if we are fast approaching the time when our home libraries will, like so much else, reside in microchips.

Honor

HONESTY

Ackroyd, Peter. *Thomas More.* Nan A. Talese/Doubleday, 1998.

Farrow, John. *The Story of Thomas More.* Collins, 1956.

Thomas More at *www.en.wikipedia.org/wiki/Thomas_More.*

RESPECT

The Complete Site for Mohandas Gandhi at *www.mkgandhi.org.*

The Man—the Mahatma at *www.library.thinkquest.org.*

McGeary, Johanna. "Person of the Century Runner Up: Mohandas Gandhi." *Time,* January 1, 2000.

M. K. Gandhi Institute for Nonviolence at *www.gandhiinstitute.org.*

AUTHENTICITY

Catholic Encyclopedia on Joan of Arc at *www.newadvent.org/cathen.*

Joan of Arc: Letter to the King of England, 1429 at the *Medieval Sourcebook www.fordham.edu/ halsall/source/joanofarc.html.*

Joan of Arc Online Archive at *www.joan-of-arc.org.*

Rempel, Gerhard. "Joan of Arc" at *www.mars.acnet.wnec.edu/~grempel/courses/wc1/lectures/28joan/ html.*

Russell, Christopher. "The Creativity of Joan of Arc" at *www.therussells.net/papers/joan.*

LOYALTY

Alexander, Caroline. *The Endurance: Shackleton's Legendary Antarctic Expedition.* Knopf, 1998.

Antarctic Explorers: Ernest H. Shackleton at *www.south-pole.com.*

Lansing, Alfred. *Endurance: Shackleton's Incredible Voyage.* Carroll & Graf, 1999.

Shackleton's Voyage of Endurance. *Nova Online* at *www.pbs.org/wgbh/nova/shackleton.*

DIGNITY

Boeree, C. George. "Viktor Frankl." Shippensburg University at *www.ship.edu/~cgboeree/frankl .html.*

"Dr. Viktor E. Frankl, Psychiatrist of the Search for Meaning, Dies at 92." *New York Times,* September 4, 1997.

Frankl, Viktor. *Man's Search for Meaning.* Pocket, Revised and Updated Version, 1997.

"Psychiatrist and Author Viktor Frankl Dies." *Washington Post,* September 4, 1997.

Scully, Matthew. "Viktor Frankl at Ninety: An Interview." *First Things,* April 1995.

Purpose

IDEALISM

Gage, Frances. "Reminiscences of Sojourner Truth" at *www.womenshistory.about.com.*

Sojourner Truth Institute at *www.sojournertruth.org.*

Truth, Sojourner, and Olive Gilbert. *The Narrative of Sojourner Truth.* Dover Publications, 1997.

RIGHTEOUSNESS

Dallaire, Romeo, and Brent Beardsly. *Shake Hands with the Devil: The Failure of Humanity in Rwanda.* Carroll & Graf, 2004.

Geyser, Georgie Anne. "A little fax and a big problem: A United Nations that can't stop genocide is a failure." *Charleston Daily Mail,* May 11, 1998.

Gourevitch, Philip. *We Wish to Inform You that Tomorrow We Will Be Killed with Our Families.* Farrar, Straus and Giroux, 1998.

Power, Samantha. *"A Problem from Hell": America and the Age of Genocide.* Basic Books, 2002.

Romeo Dallaire Interview. *Fresh Air with Terry Gross,* January 21, 2005.

"A hero for all reasons." *Toronto Star,* January 7, 2005.

CITIZENSHIP

Barnidge, Tom. "Tillman follows beat of a different drum." *NFL Insider* at *www.nfl.com/insider.*

Dufresne, Chris. "Special Teamer." *Los Angeles Times,* April 25, 2004.

Fainaru, Steve, and Blaine Harden. "Even in Death, Brothers in Arms." *Washington Post,* April 25, 2004.

Jenkins, Sally. "Life Is No Life to Him That Dares Not Die." *Washington Post,* April 24, 2004.

Johnson, Dirk, and Andrew Muir. "A Heroic Life." *Newsweek,* May 3, 2004.

Lacayo, Richard. "One for the Team." *Time,* May 3, 2004.

Prager, Dennis. "One of the 36." *Investors Business Daily,* April 27, 2004.

"Remembering Pat Tillman." *Sports Illustrated* at *www.SI.com.*

"Tillman killed while serving as Army Ranger." *Associated Press,* April 30, 2004.

DILIGENCE

The Churchill Centre at *www.winstonchurchill.org.*

Gilbert, Martin. *Churchill: A Life.* Henry Holt, 1991.

Manchester, William. *The Last Lion: Winston Spencer Churchill: Alone, 1932–1940.* Little Brown, 1988.

Manchester, William. *The Last Lion: Winston Spencer Churchill, Visions of Glory.* Little Brown, 1983.

RESPONSIBILITY

Herman, Arthur. *To Rule the Waves: How the British Navy Shaped the Modern World.* HarperCollins, 2004.

Keegan, John. *The Price of Admiralty: The Evolution of Naval Warfare.* Penguin, 1990.

Lord Nelson in the Age of Sail at *www.wargamer.com/aos/nelsonweb.asp.*
The Nelson Society at *www.nelson-society.org.uk.*

COOPERATION

Basketball Hall of Fame profile of John Wooden at *www.hoophall.com.*
Bill Walton on John Wooden at *www.billwalton.com.*
Coach Wooden Home Page at *www.coachwooden.com.*
Horowitz, Mitch. "From the Socks Up: The Extraordinary Life of John Wooden." *Science of Mind,* November 2004.
Interview with John Wooden. *Page 2* at *www.ESPN.com.*
John Wooden biography and interview, Academy of Achievement Museum of Living History at *www.achievement.org.*
Medal of Freedom profile of John Wooden at *www.medaloffreedom.com.*
Official Site of Coach John Wooden at *www.coachjohnwooden.com.*
Wooden, John. *They Call Me Coach.* McGraw Hill, 2003.
Wooden, John. *Wooden.* McGraw Hill, 1997.

Strength

COURAGE

Clowes, Peter. "Nurse Edith Cavell." *Military History Magazine,* August 1996.
de Leval, Maitre G., H. Stirling Gahan, Hugh Gibson, Arthur Zimmermann. Accounts of the last days of Edith Cavell at *www.firstworldwar.com/source/cavell.*
"Edith Cavell—A Norfolk Heroine 1865–1915" at *www.edithcavell.org.uk.*
Unger, Abraham. "Edith Cavell: No Hatred or Bitterness for Anyone." *British Heritage,* May 1997.

SELF-CONTROL

Brookhiser, Richard. *Founding Father: Rediscovering George Washington.* Free Press, 1996.
Chernow, Ron. *Alexander Hamilton.* Penguin Press, 2004.
Ellis, Joseph. *His Excellency: George Washington.* Knopf, 2004.
Henriques, Peter, Don Higginbotham, Dorothy Twohig. "George Washington and the Legacy of Character." Columbia University seminar at *www.fathom.com.*
Sayen, William Guthrie. "George Washington's Unmannerly Behavior: The Clash Between Honor and Civility." *Virginia Magazine of History and Biography,* Winter 1999.

CONFIDENCE

Erikson, Carolly. *The First Elizabeth*. Summit Books, 1983.

Elizabeth I. at *www.elizabethi.org*.

Queen Elizabeth I at *www.englishhistory.net/tudor/monarchs/eliz1.html*.

Queen Elizabeth I of England. *Selected Writing and Speeches*. Modern History Sourcebook at *www.fordham.edu/halsall/mod/elizabeth1.html*.

Tudor History at *www.tudorhistory.org*.

RESILIENCE

Abraham Lincoln Online at *www.showcase.netins.net/web/creative/lincoln.html*.

Basler, Roy P., editor. *Abraham Lincoln: His Speeches and Writings*. The Franklin Library, 1979.

Burlingame, Michael, and John R. Turner Ettlinger, editors. *Inside Lincoln's White House: The Complete Civil War Diary of John Hay*. Southern Illinois University Press, 1999.

Donald, David Herbert. *Lincoln*. Simon & Schuster, 1995.

Wilson, Douglas L. *Honor's Voice: The Transformation of Abraham Lincoln*. Knopf, 1998.

INDUSTRY

Bethell, Tom. "The Longshoreman Philosopher." *Hoover Digest*, Winter 2003.

The Eric Hoffer Resource at *www.erichoffer.net*.

Hoffer, Eric. *The True Believer: Thoughts on the Nature of Mass Movements*. Harper & Row, 1951.

Tompkins, Calvin. *Eric Hoffer: An American Odyssey*. E. P. Dutton, 1968.

HOPEFULNESS

Morgan, Edmund S. *The Puritan Dilemma: The Story of John Winthrop*. Library of American Biography, Talman Co., 1996.

Winthrop Society at *www.winthropsociety.org*.

Understanding

FAITH

McCain, John, with Mark Salter. *Faith of My Fathers: A Family Memoir*. Random House, 1999.

COMPASSION

Kolbe, the Saint from Auschwitz at *www.auschwitz.dk/Kolbe.htm*.

Kolbenet Catholic Networking at *www.kolbenet.com*.

Maximilian Kolbe. Catholic Community Forum at *www.catholic-forum.com/saints/saintm01.htm*.

Militia of the Immaculata National Center at *www.consecration.com/How%20the%20MIARCH .html.*

Neumann, John. "Maximilian Kolbe." St. Benedict Center at *www.catholicism.org/pages/kolbe.htm.*

Resources for Catholic Educators at *www.silk.net/RelEd/index.htm.*

Sicari, Antonion, editor, Jaca Book, translator. *Ritratti Di Santi* at the Vita dei santi Web site at *www.users.libero.it/luigi.scrosoppi/santi/kolbeing.htm.*

MERCY

Garrison, Jessica. "Daughter of Beverly Hills Found a New Life in Tijuana Prison." *Los Angeles Times,* December 25, 2002.

Jordan, Mary. "Tijuana's Live-In Prison Angel." *Washington Post,* April 10, 2002.

Jordan, Mary, and Kevin Sullivan. *The Prison Angel: Mother Antonia's Journey from Beverly Hills to a Life of Service in a Mexican Jail.* Penguin Press HC, 2005.

TOLERANCE

The Four Chaplains at *www.thefourchaplains.com.*

The Immortal Chaplains Foundation at *www.immortalchaplains.org.*

Kurzman, Dan. *No Greater Glory: The Four Immortal Chaplains and the Sinking of the Dorchester in World War II.* Random House, 2004.

FORGIVENESS

Gregory, James. *Goodbye Bafana: Nelson Madela, My Prisoner, My Friend.* Headline, 1995.

Mandela, Nelson. *Long Walk to Freedom: The Autobiography of Nelson Mandela.* Back Bay Books, 1995.

GENEROSITY

Bragg, Rick. "All She Has, $150,000, Is Going to a University." *New York Times,* August 13, 1995.

Oral History of Oseola McCarty. Center for Oral History and Cultural Heritage at the University of Southern Mississippi at *www.lib.usm.edu/~spcol/coh/cohmccartyob.html.*

Oseola McCarty Home Page. University of Southern Mississippi at *www.usm.edu/pr/oolamain .htm.*

Judgment

FAIRNESS

Branch, Taylor. *Parting the Waters.* Simon & Schuster, 1988.

King, Martin Luther, with Clayborne Carson. *The Autobiography of Martin Luther King, Jr.* Warner Books, 1998.

The King Center at *www.thekingcenter.org.*

"Martin Luther King Jr.: Never Again What He Was." *Time,* January 3, 1964.

Martin Luther King's "Letter from Birmingham Jail" at *www.nobelprizes.com.*

HUMILITY

Ambrose, Stephen. *Eisenhower.* Simon & Schuster Touchstone Edition, 1991.

D'Este, Carlos. *Eisenhower: A Soldier's Life.* Henry Holt & Company, 2002.

Eisenhower, Dwight D., Mamie Doud Eisenhower, John S. D. Eisenhower. *Letters to Mamie.* Doubleday, 1978.

Museum of World War II, Natick, MA, at *www.museumofworldwarii.com.*

GRATITUDE

Bent, Devin. "Tecumseh: A Brief Biography." James Madison University Madison Center at *www.jmu.edu/madison/center.*

Edmunds, David. *Tecumseh and the Quest for Indian Leadership.* Library of American Biography, Longman, 1997.

Hafley, T. J. "Fort Meigs: Unsung Sentinel in the War of 1812." *Military History Magazine* at *www.historynet.com.*

Sultzman, Lee. "Shawnee History" at *www.tolatsga.org/shaw.html.*

HUMOR

Kaplan, Fred. *The Singular Mark Twain: A Biography.* Doubleday, 2003.

Kaplan, Justin. *Mr. Clemens and Mark Twain: A Biography.* Simon & Schuster, 1991.

Ward, Geoffrey C., Ken Burns, Dayton Duncan. *Mark Twain: An Illustrated Biography.* Knopf, 2001.

COURTESY

Daw Aung San Suu Kyi at *www.dassk.org.*

McCain, John, with Mark Salter. *Why Courage Matters: The Way to a Braver Life.* Random House, 2004.

Creativity

ASPIRATION

Bergreen, Laurence. *Over the Edge of the World: Magellan's Terrifying Circumnavigation of the Globe.* William Morrow & Company, 2003.

Winchester, Simon. "After dire straits, an agonizing haul across the Pacific." *Smithsonian,* April 1991.

DISCERNMENT

BookRags. "Biography of Leonardo da Vinci" at *www.bookrags.com/biography/leonardo-da-vinci.*

Catholic Encyclopedia on Leonardo at *www.newadvent.org/cathen.*

Hughes, Robert. "Beyond the Skin's Frontier." *Time,* February 27, 1984.

"The Last Supper" at *www.schoolnet.gov.mt/da_vinci_lastsupper.*

"A Man of Infinite Possibilities." *Time,* June 20, 1969.

Museum of Science, Boston, at *www.mos.org/leonardo.*

Richter, Jean Paul, editor. *Notebooks of Leonardo da Vinci.* Dover Publications, 1970.

Web Gallery of Art at *www.wga.hu.*

WebMuseum of Paris at *www.ibiblio.org/wm/paint/auth/vinci.*

CURIOSITY

Charles Darwin at *www.AboutDarwin.com.*

Darwin, Charles. *On the Origin of the Species by Means of Natural Selection.* Bantam Classics, 1999.

Darwin, Charles. Nora Barlow, editor. *The Autobiography of Charles Darwin.* W. W. Norton & Company, Reissue edition, 1993.

ENTHUSIASM

Brands, H. W. *TR: The Last Romantic.* Basic Books, 1998.

McCain, John, with Mark Salter. *Worth the Fighting For: A Memoir.* Random House, 2002.

Morris, Edmund. *The Rise of Theodore Roosevelt.* Putnam Publications Group, 1979.

Morris, Edmund. *Theodore Rex.* Random House, 2001.

Roosevelt, Theodore. *The Strenuous Life.* Applewood Books, 1991.

Theodore Roosevelt at *www.theodore-roosevelt.com.*

Theodore Roosevelt at *www.theodoreroosevelt.org.*

EXCELLENCE

"Against All Odds: Wilma Rudolph" at *www.frankmarrero.com/AncientLessons/Wilma.html.*

"Fast Train from Clarksville." *Sports Illustrated,* November 21, 1994.

Krull, Kathleen. *Wilma Unlimited: How Wilma Rudolph Became the World's Fastest Woman.* Harcourt, 1996.

Miller, Dick. "Rudolph had bumpy path to greatness as Olympic sprinter." *Washington Times,* September 25, 2000.

Obituary, Wilma Rudolph, *St. Louis Post-Dispatch,* November 18, 1994.

Roberts, Mary Beth. "Rudolph ran and the world went wild" at *www.ESPN.com*.
"Wilma Rudolph, 1960 Olympic track star, dies at 54." *Michigan Citizen,* December 3, 1994.

Love

SELFLESSNESS AND CONTENTMENT
Aikman, David. *Six Who Changed a Century.* Lexington Books, 2003.
Eternal Word Television Network, Global Catholic Network at *www.ewtn.com/motherteresa/life.htm*.
Mother Teresa's Home Page at *www.drini.com/motherteresa*.

ABOUT THE AUTHORS

After a career in the U.S. Navy and two terms as a U.S. representative, JOHN McCAIN was elected to the U.S. Senate in 1986 and reelected in 1992, 1998, and 2004. He and his wife, Cindy, reside in Phoenix, Arizona.

MARK SALTER has worked on Senator McCain's staff for fourteen years and is the co-author with McCain of *Why Courage Matters, Faith of My Fathers,* and *Worth the Fighting For.* He lives in Alexandria, Virginia, with his wife, Diane, and their two daughters.